HISTORY
of the
WESTERN INSURRECTION
In Western Pennsylvania
commonly called the
WHISKEY INSURRECTION

H. M. Brackenridge

HERITAGE BOOKS
2008

HERITAGE BOOKS
AN IMPRINT OF HERITAGE BOOKS, INC.

Books, CDs, and more—Worldwide

For our listing of thousands of titles see our website
at
www.HeritageBooks.com

Published 2008 by
HERITAGE BOOKS, INC.
Publishing Division
100 Railroad Ave. #104
Westminster, Maryland 21157

Copyright © 1859 H. M. Brackenridge

Entered according to Act of Congress, in the year 1859, by
H. M. Brackenridge, In the Clerk's Office of the District Court of the United States for Western District of the State of Pennsylvania

All rights reserved. No part of this book may be reproduced or transmitted in any form or by any means, electronic or mechanical, including photocopying, recording or by any information storage and retrieval system without written permission from the author, except for the inclusion of brief quotations in a review.

International Standard Book Numbers
Paperbound: 978-1-55613-139-4
Clothbound: 978-0-7884-7132-2

CONTENTS.

INTRODUCTION.
Letter to Alexander Brackenridge, Esq., ... Page 5

CHAPTER I.
Western Pennsylvania — Population — Excise Law — Public Meetings — Acts of Violence, ... 15

CHAPTER II.
Popular Outbreak — Attack on the Marshal — Destruction of Neville's House — Alarm in Pittsburgh — Escape of the Marshal and Inspector, . . 39

CHAPTER III.
The Mingo Creek Meeting — Violence of Bradford — Speech of Brackenridge — Causes of the Outbreak — Case of Miller, ... 57

CHAPTER IV.
The Robbery of the Mail — The self-appointed Convention, and Circular to the Militia Officers, directing a Rendezvous at Braddock's Field — The Town Meeting at Pittsburgh, ... 79

CHAPTER V.
The Assemblage at Braddock's Field — Difficulty of Saving the Town, . 99

CHAPTER VI.
Acts of Violence following the Assemblage at Braddock's Field — Tom the Tinker — Delegates to Parkinson's Ferry, ... 127

CHAPTER VII.
The Meeting of the Delegates at Parkinson's Ferry — The Resolutions adopted there — Appointment of a Committee of Conference, . . . 152

CHAPTER VIII.
The Measures of the Government — Arrival of the Commissioners — The Conference, ... 190

CONTENTS.

CHAPTER IX.

Report of the Committee of Conference laid before the Standing Committee — Difficulties encountered — Vote by Ballot — Majority for Peace, but not satisfactory to the Commissioners, ... 218

CHAPTER X.

Reluctance of the People to sign the Submission — Meeting of the Congress of Delegates, and a general Submission, ... 246

CHAPTER XI.

Calling out the Military to suppress the Insurrection — The Delegation to the President from the West, ... 263

CHAPTER XII.

The Army enters the West — Its ferocious temper — The Attempt to Assassinate Mr. Brackenridge — The Military Inquests — Examination of Mr. Brackenridge, and Acquittal, ... 288

CHAPTER XIII.

The Military Arrests, and atrocious Treatment of the People — The Dreadful Night — Withdrawal of the Army — The End of the Insurrection, . 312

TO ALEXANDER BRACKENRIDGE, ESQ.

MANY years ago, we conversed together on the subject of republishing our father's work, entitled "Incidents of the Western Insurrection," which had been long out of print—although remarkable for the truthful and graphic account it gave of one of the most important occurrences of American history. But, after reflecting on the subject, we concluded, that however interesting as a piece of contemporary history, and however much it might conduce to his fame, there were considerations of delicacy and feeling which stood in the way of such republication. These were principally, the strictures on the acts of persons who had passed from the stage of life, but whose descendants might be pained by the exhibition of their forefathers in an unfavorable light. Instead of pursuing the course which at first suggested itself, I adopted the plan of writing a biographical notice, giving a brief outline of the incidents of the Insurrection, saying enough to do justice to our father, but carefully avoiding everything that could possibly wound the sensibility of any survivor, or descendant, of those with whom he came in conflict during those trying times. This was published in the "Southern Messenger," Richmond, Virginia, and afterward as an introduction to "Modern Chivalry."

This delicacy was not met in a corresponding spirit. A work, under the title of "History of Pittsburgh," was published by Neville B. Craig, the representative of the "Neville connection," in which there is a most perverted and false representation of the conduct of the people of Western Pennsylvania, and of the town of Pittsburgh, and, at the same time, the grossest misrepresentation of the actions and motives of individuals who were most active in restraining the excesses of the people, who considered themselves aggrieved by the excise laws. Our father, especially, who had been at variance with some of the Neville connection previous to the insurrection, in consequence of professional acts, which he thought honorable—was the object of the most indecent abuse by the scurrilous writer just mentioned. Charges and insinuations, which had been met and annihilated sixty years before, were revived, and where proof was wanting to sustain them, their place supplied by mere vulgar billingsgate epithets. It was not in my power to be silent; a newspaper controversy ensued, and the detractor was treated by me with unavoidable severity, as well as others whom I would willingly have spared. But I found that in the narrow bounds of a newspaper it was impossible to do justice to the subject; I, therefore, set about a more full and complete narrative, of historical acts, with the details of a connected memoir. This was due to my countrymen of Western Pennsylvania, and to my townsmen of Pittsburgh, so scandalously libeled by Neville B. Craig, in his pretended "History of Pittsburgh."

Our father was first drawn into the vortex of the popular movement, at the earnest solicitation of Col. Neville, the son of the collector of the excise, with the avowed object of preventing the excesses of the disaffected. Although opposed to the oppressive excise laws, as was every man west of the mountains, with the exception of those engaged in the collection of the revenue, he never for a moment encouraged any illegal opposition. Col. Neville was a gentleman of education, and the only one of the "connection" on friendly terms with him, and it is to be regretted that he failed to fulfill the engagement to which he was bound in honor, and which will be more fully explained in this narrative. Our father, thus placed between the people and the government, as negotiator and peacemaker, was peculiarly exposed to the dangers of misconception. In telling the truth to the people in the hearing of the government, and to the government in the hearing of the people; he suffered a temporary loss of popularity with the one, and incurred the suspicion of the other. This was only rectified by time and events, after exposing him to imminent danger from both parties. His efforts were directed to two objects: the first, to arrest the progress of opposition to the government; the second, to obtain an amnesty, or act of oblivion, for the imprudent acts of violence which had been rashly committed; in other words, to prevent riots from assuming the formidable front of insurrection. In this he succeeded, and for which, instead of being rewarded by the civic crown, he was exposed to the danger of assassination, of government prosecution, and popular obloquy. Those who had the government ear, succeeded in producing the impression that he was behind the screen, the instigator of every illegal movement; while the very same persons, with the usual disregard of consistency attendant on falsehood, insinuated to the people that he had sold them to the government for a consideration! The narrative now presented to the public, will exhibit one of the most extraordinary cases on record, of great services remaining not merely unrewarded and unacknowledged, but of the grossest injustice long continued, and not entirely corrected to this day; for we still occasionally hear of "the insurgent Brackenridge." In appealing to the unbiassed and impartial judgment of the American people, and especially of those of Western Pennsylvania, I will boldly put in issue the assertion, *that he saved the western country from the horrors of civil war, the town of Pittsburgh from destruction, and the Federal Union from the greatest danger it has ever encountered.*

Such was the sinister influence of these misrepresentations, by persons who had joined the army on its march to put down an insurrection which never existed, and even after mob violence had ceased, that even Alexander Hamilton, who was the head and front of the expedition, appears to have conceived the most unfounded prejudice against the people, and against individuals. A letter written by him from Bedford, which has been preserved, and very improperly published in his posthumous works, by those who did not know what they were about, contains the following language: "It appears that Brackenridge did not subscribe [the amnesty] until after the day, and it is proved that he is the worst of all scoundrels." Thus the author of the amnesty was to be denied its benefits, because being engaged through the day in riding through the rural districts, persuading the people to sign, he did not reach home until after midnight. And yet, nine days after, when Hamilton was enabled to judge for himself on the spot, and after hearing the "chief insurgent," and receiving the statements of reliable persons, he expresses himself as follows: "Mr. Brackenridge, my impressions were unfavorable to you; you may have observed it; I now think it my duty to inform you that not a single one remains; had we listened to some people, I know not what we might have done; your conduct has been horribly misrepresented, owing to misconception; I will announce you in this point of you to Gen. Lee, who represents the Executive; you are in no personal danger, and will not be troubled even with a simple inquisition by the judge—what may be due to yourself with the public, is another question."

On this hint our father prepared his account of the insurrection, published a year afterward, and containing the above passage, which was never contradicted, although Hamilton lived many years after the publication. Craig admits the fact of the "acquittal," as he calls it, but questions the language ascribed to Hamilton. On what grounds? On the principles of historical evidence? No—on the narrow technical rules of a court of justice. But when asked by me, was not this published at the time, and as it were in the presence of the Neville connection, who were implicated, and could they not have appealed to Hamilton? his only reply is an absurd equivocation, very little complimentary to the high aristocratic association or cabal, of which he is the representative: "Presley Neville was too indolent to undertake the task, and the others had not the ability." Alas! poor Yorick!

The suggestion of Hamilton was adopted, and produced a rare example of the value of contemporary history. There is not only the conscientious evidence of an honest witness, but also under the restraints of the thousand other witnesses, ready to challenge any material deviation from truth. No man having a regard for his reputation, would, under such circumstances, run the risk of contradiction. There is scarcely an instance in which the author relies on his own naked assertions, without reference to persons who were present, and who had it in their power to confute or confirm. Besides this, a case was regularly made before the great tribunal of public opinion, and a challenge formally given to all to appear before it, if they chose to call the author's veracity in question. They were silent, and this silence must be taken for an admission of the truth of his statements. It is, besides, in almost every material point, sustained by statements of unimpeachable witnesses, many of them under the solemnity of an oath. Among these statements are those of the most distinguished public men then in Western Pennsylvania. Short extracts were made from some of these, and added to the biography published in the "Literary Messenger." Neville Craig objects to these extracts, because they do not contain the whole, and falsely insinuates that, if the whole of the papers were published, there would appear certain qualifications which would change their character; secondly, that the persons who gave their testimony in his favor were actuated by charitable motives in disguising the truth. To meet the first objection, the documents are now published in full; as to the second, the only answer is silence—anything else would be an insult to the reader.

These few extracts, considering the standing and distinguished character of the persons from whom they were drawn, are sufficient, without any thing further, to satisfy any man of decent understanding—any man of candor—any man who pretends to have the feelings of a gentleman. James Ross was the Senator in Congress, and one of the Commissioners appointed by the government to treat with the supposed insurgents, and with whom our father was almost in daily conference during that period; his statement covers every ground which could possibly be occupied. General John Wilkins, who also acted with him—Judge Addison—John

Hoge, State Senator—Henry Purviance, Prosecuting Attorney—would alone carry with them an irresistible weight of authority.*

The "History of the Western Insurrection," by William Findley, was published the year after the "Incidents." These two contemporary publications are the sources whence the work now offered to the public was mainly drawn. I was but a boy at the time of the events related, yet from precocious training, and being constantly in the society of my father, I was accustomed to take an interest in public affairs far beyond my years; I heard all the circumstances related by eye witnesses, and heard it universally admitted, that by his address and activity, the town was saved from destruction by the mob which marched in from Braddock's Field.

In the face of the testimony of persons of the highest standing in the West, Neville Craig, in his book, insinuates that our father was the secret instigator of every unlawful act done by the mob! He also declares that his only motive was an insane ambition to be elected to Congress, for which he was then a candidate, without regarding the fact, that in the course pursued by him, he had entirely sacrificed his popularity! He tells us, also, that he was bought by the government; and again, that he only saved his life by agreeing to turn "State's evidence" against his instruments, affording a curious instance of a principal saving himself by denouncing his obscure accomplices. When these false and absurd assertions were nailed to the counter in our newspaper controversy, he endeav-

---

* In a recent publication of the Treasurer of the Pennsylvania Historical Society, a letter by John Wilkins, Esq., Sr., is given in mistake as from Gen. Wilkins, his son. The meagre memoirs of James Gallatin is scarcely deserving of notice. The extracts above referred to are as follows:

"I saw many alarmed for the safety of the country, and for the establishment of the government; I thought none of them more sincerely so than yourself." JAMES ROSS.

"My opinion of your conduct throughout the whole of the insurrection in this country, I will give without reserve. It appears to have two objects, *to arrest the progress of the present violence, and to procure an amnesty for that already committed*, and thus prevent the flame from spreading beyond the country in which it had originated." HENRY PURVIANCE.

"I had daily opportunity of observing your conduct, and conversing with you; I never had a doubt but that you were actuated by the purest motives, and anxious for the restoration of the laws."
 JOHN WILKINS.

"I know you have enemies, and believe they are my friends; I respect them and regard you; the belief that you directly or indirectly was concerned in the late insurrection, can only be entertained by those who, from their distance from the scene of action, have been imposed upon by misrepresentation, and have, therefore, formed conclusions upon illfounded premises, or by your enemies, have prevented inquiry." JOHN HOGE.

"It is impossible for me, without erasing all my impressions of your character and conduct, to suppose you ever advised any illegal opposition to the excise laws." ALEXANDER ADDISON.

ored to shelter himself behind Hildreth, from whose History of the United States he had extracted some of the offensive passages which he had adopted as his own. The character of Hildreth, as a mere partisan bigot, is well known: the disparaging manner in which he has spoken of Jefferson and Madison, and his idolatry of Alexander Hamilton, who had doubtless great qualities, but was not a god, have fixed a low estimate on his political works. It was reserved for Neville Craig to use such expressions as these—"Brackenridge was a cold-blooded, calculating villain"— he was the "worst of scoundrels"—which could not fail to rouse and justify the most indignant feelings on the part of his descendants and relatives. If Craig has been handled with severity, it is only the consequence of his own malignity.

There is one passage in his book which I cannot refrain from quoting, as a curiosity. It is a striking instance of that perverted view of persons and things, which characterizes his peculiar mind. Here it is: "Of the leading actors in this insurrection, Brackenridge, Gallatin, Findley, Smiley, *all foreigners by birth,* all subsequently partook largely of popular favor; and Bradford alone, a *native born,* the bravest and best among them, fled to Louisiana, then a Spanish province." Can any one point out the meaning of this stupid paragraph? What inference is to be drawn from the fact, of the four being foreigners by birth; although in America long before the Revolutionary war, having fought through it, and in the case of our father, having come in childhood? Before the Declaration of Independence, all were subjects of Great Britain, and all then living, according to this, must be regarded as foreigners! But the most singular part of this curious intellectual obliquity, is the saying, that Bradford, "the *bravest* and *best* among them, fled to Louisiana, then a Spanish territory." Is this the evidence of his being the "best and the bravest" among those who defeated his wicked and foolish attempt to excite an insurrection and civil war? It would be an idle waste of words to pursue such nonsense any further—such perverted notions of patriotism and moral worth, are deserving only of a verdict of lunacy.

But is there not a key to this *strange laudation* of the traitor Bradford, "the bravest and the best, of them all?" We shall see.

Neville Craig declared in his controversy with me, that from his earliest childhood he had conceived a deadly hatred to "the insurgent Brackenridge," and a firm conviction of his criminality—and of course imbibed from his elders of the "Neville connection." I will always except Col. Presley Neville, who might have cherished different feelings, under different circumstances. This deadly hatred is easily explained by the circumstance of "the insurgent Brackenridge" having on a certain occasion compelled one of the connection to bring back, and restore to freedom, a free colored woman, who had been run off to Kentucky. This led to a deadly feud, and fierce personal rencontre, and suits were depending in court at the time of the breaking out of the insurrection. Besides this, the lawyer, although no abolition fanatic, (as Neville Craig is at present,) was yet friendly to the scheme of gradual extinction of slavery, while the "connection," originally from Virginia, and holding lands under Virginia grants, were the only large slaveholders in the country.

A few days after the destruction of the house of the elder Neville by the rioters, a numerous meeting was convened at the Mingo creek meeting-house, a large majority of which was composed of persons who had been engaged in the outrage. At the solicitation of Neville the younger, (Presley Neville,) the "insurgent Brackenridge" attended. Bradford appeared, and in an inflammatory speech insisted on a vote to "sustain the *brave fellows* who had been engaged in burning Neville's house." This was defeated by the "insurgent Brackenridge," and which caused the meeting to break up. Is this a key to the subsequent conduct of Major Craig? Surely, that gentleman could not approve, *or ever after* consimilate with the man who could applaud the treason and the destruction of his father-in-law's property? This is not to be supposed. When Bradford, a few days after this, employed a half-witted desperado to stop the post rider, and steal the mail, and deliver it to him—this, certainly, did not meet the approbation of the Neville connection! When, again, the same individual, a few days later, of his own authority, issued circulars to the commanders of militia regiments, to assemble at the places of annual rendezvous, where important secrets were to be revealed to them, deeply affecting their interests and their safety—this, certainly, is no proof that Bradford was the "bravest and the best." When at that meeting the intercepted letters of the Neville connection were produced, and read by Bradford, and the intention was avowed to march into town, destroy the houses of the so-called public enemies—this project was again defeated by the address and management of the "insurgent Brackenridge." A *pretended* banishment of the obnoxious persons, by the town, had been enacted—a mere tub to the whale—the only thing which could have saved the lives and property of the proscribed persons, and consequently the town itself from destruction. Now, is there anything in this to approve in the conduct of Bradford? No, certainly. When, afterward, at the Parkinson's Ferry meeting of the delegates, Bradford brought forward his treasonable plans for levying war against the government, in which he was again baffled by the odious "insurgent Brackenridge," I would ask, whether such attempt was approved by the "connection," or their representative, Neville Craig? Surely no. Yet, according to this historian, Bradford was the "bravest and the best." When, after the conference of the commitcee of twelve with the United States Commissioners, they had agreed to submit to the government, on the condition of amnesty, and the "insurgent Brackenridge" repaired, with the report he had drawn up, to obtain the sanction of the standing committee of sixty, at Brownsville, Bradford was the only one of the twelve who opposed its adoption, and again brought forward his treasonable propositions, in which he was again defeated by the insurgent, who, in the boldest and most unqualified terms, denounced the conduct of the rioters, insurgents and traitors, or whatever else they may be called,—at the same time offering up the last shred of his popularity on the altar of patriotism. What says the representative of the "Neville connection" on this head? Bradford was the "bravest and the best," and "Brackenridge, a cold-blooded, calculating villain"— "a deceitful, unprincipled demagogue."

When the army and the government officials reached the scene of the recent outrages, their minds had been poisoned by the so-called exiles, and those who returned with the army; their rage was directed against those who had exerted themselves in the most meritorious manner on the side of the government, during the continuance of the disturbance, and against none of them more relentlessly than against the "insurgent Brackenridge." An inquisition was instituted, and evidence against him sought from every quarter, the Nevilles acting as prosecutors on this star-chamber tribunal. It was not long, however, before Hamilton and his associates began to open their eyes, and to see into the true motives and the falsity of the pretended accusation. A trivial circumstance served to cause the ungenerous persecution to explode like a rotten egg. A fragment of a letter had been picked up, addressed to Bradford, with the signature of H. H. Brackenridge appended. It alluded in a *mysterious* manner to some papers that were wanting before proceeding in the matter. According to the *conjecture* of the author of the "Incidents," this was done by Major Craig, in his capacity of notary public—for this was *one* of his offices—but he gives it only as *conjecture*, which he never substitutes for fact. When the investigation was nearly brought to a close, this ominous paper was produced by Hamilton, and turning to James Ross, he observed: "Mr. Ross, you have pledged yourself that there was no correspondence between Brackenridge and Bradford—what do you say to this—is not this the handwriting of Brackenridge?" "It is his handwriting," said Ross, "but there is only this small difference in the case—this letter is addressed to William Bradford, (Attorney General, and one of the Commissioners,) and not to David Bradford." A profound silence ensued, as if a rock had fallen—that silence was first broken by Hamilton. "Gentlemen," said he, "we are going too fast—we must stop here." It was but a day or two after this that the personal conference took place between him and the intended victim of the "connection."

Now, if the mere circumstance of addressing a letter to Bradford by the "insurgent Brackenridge," was a ground of suspicion, what shall we say of the friendly letter addressed to that person by Major Craig, shortly before Bradford's flight, as a self-convicted traitor, with all the wrongs done or intended to the "Neville connection" on his head? Could any one of the connection correspond with such a man, under any circumstances, without a disregard of all delicacy or propriety? There can be no excuse or apology for such an act; the only clue to it is the deep and deadly feeling of hatred to the "insurgent Brackenridge." The *ostensible* motive for this revolting act, was to learn from Bradford whether the "insurgent Brackenridge" had manifested hostile feelings to Craig, personally, especially at Braddock's Field, in the committee of officers, and had spoken of him in a disrespectful manner. Was there no other person but the traitor Bradford to whom such inquiry could be addressed? The truth is too palpable—and sustains the *conjecture* of the "Incidents"—that the *real* design was to make a witness of Bradford against the supposed insurgent; and knowing his reckless disregard of truth, it was supposed he would say anything to save himself, through the powerful influence of the "Neville connection." In this they were disappointed; for, although Bradford, in his reply to Craig, said enough to gratify hate, yet the main and real object, if the conjecture be correct, was not attained. Bradford dared not venture on the monstrous and self-evident falsehood, of implicating the hated enemy of the Nevilles, either as principal or accessory, in his treasonable designs! Besides, he began to fear that his case was so peculiar in its atrocity, that he could not count with certainty, even with the aid of the most powerful influence, on being included in the amnesty, which he had opposed, and then signed "on the day." His case was beyond the power of "mandragon or hellebore." He, therefore, "fled to Louisiana, then a Spanish province," where he "shared largely" of royal favor, in grants of land! I hope I have now done forever with the "Neville connection" and their representative.

Our father was ever morbidly sensitive to any imputation on his integrity or honor; knowing this, it becomes especially incumbent on us to suffer no stain to rest on his memory. He was ever doing benevolent acts, and repenting of them when he felt the sting of ingratitude—and yet repeating them whenever an appeal was made to his philanthropy. Smarting under a sense of this injustice, on some occasion during the insurrection, he uses this language: "I acted on the law of Solon—the *wise* and *just* being obliged to take some side, as well as the *envious* and *wicked*, matters were more easily accommodated. But if I were to go through these scenes again, I would not follow the law of Solon, but leave the government and the insurgents to settle their difficulties as best they could." It is very questionable whether he would have been able to resist his natural propensity, and remain selfishly neutral, and join—

>Aquel cattivo coro
>Degli angeli, que non furon rebelli,
>Ne fur fideli a dio, ma por se furon.—

>That caitiff crowd
>Of the angels, which neither rebelled,
>Nor faithful stood—from love of self alone.—

Your affectionate brother,

H. M. BRACKENRIDGE.

WESTERN INSURRECTION.

CHAPTER I.

WESTERN PENNSYLVANIA — POPULATION — EXCISE LAW — PUBLIC MEETINGS — ACTS OF VIOLENCE.

THE western part of Pennsylvania, lying around the head of the Ohio, in a radius of more than a hundred miles, and separated on the east by the Allegheny mountains, and extending to Lake Erie on the north, is one of the most beautiful portions of America—perhaps of the whole world. Eighty years ago, its finely wooded hills, fertile to their summits—its rich and delightful valleys, clothed with primeval forests, formed a hunter's paradise. At this day, instead of being an uninhabited wilderness, enlivened by the howl of the wolf or the gleam of the Indian tomahawk, it teems with an industrious, intelligent and Christian population, whose cattle feed on a thousand hills, and whose well watered, cultivated fields, gladden the eye; while cheerful dwellings on every slope are seen glistening in the warm light of its azure skies. It is now filled with cities, towns and villages, and is not surpassed by any portion of equal extent in the Union for its mineral, manufacturing and agricultural wealth. It is as lovely a land as ever opened its bosom to the genial sun. In its picturesque beauties, the lover of nature, the painter, and the poet, might revel in unsated delight.

Before the Revolutionary war, the possession of this country was often the subject of bloody contest between England and France—a struggle of incalculable importance, as it decided the ownership of the vast and majestic regions of the West. It was here the fame of Washington first dawned upon his country.* But it was not until the final expulsion of the French, about the year 1758–9, that any settlement could be attempt-

---

* "History of Braddock's Expedition," by Winthrop Sargent.

ed; and not until 1766, after the peace, or rather truce, made with the Indians, by Col. Boquet, that any white man ventured to make it his place of permanent abode. The first settlement was on Redstone creek, which empties into the Monongahela, forty miles above Pittsburgh; but under the too well grounded fear of the Indian tomahawk and scalping knife, which continued almost to the very period of the Insurrection, while war was still raging on the banks of the Ohio. There was a difficulty in their way, on account of the disputed boundary between Virginia and Pennsylvania; the former claiming the country in the neighborhoed of the Monongahela, which rendered the title to land uncertain, although it had been usual for both governments, for the purpose of encouraging settlements on the frontier, the outposts of civilization, to recognize preëmption rights in favor of the settlers, previous to issuing warrants, the first step toward legal title.

In the year 1768, the Proprietory (the Penn family,) had purchased the country from the Indians as far west as the Ohio and Allegheny rivers. The country north of the latter river was, and long continued to be known as the "Indian country," while the portion adjacent to the Monongahela continued to be the subject of contention between the two provinces, until finally settled after the Revolution, by a friendly commission. The office of the Proprietory for the sale of lands was opened in April, 1769, although the settlements had already commenced. The settlers (of Scottish descent,) were chiefly from the Pennsylvania counties, on the other side of the mountains, who by degrees extended the frontier, exposed to the same savage warfare which they and their fathers, on the eastern side of the Alleghenies, had already experienced, and perhaps too often provoked. Every man was accustomed to the use of the rifle, and seldom went abroad without that formidable weapon. They were, in fact, a warlike race; besides their Indian wars, they had sent two regiments to aid in the cause of independence. The facility for obtaining land, was no doubt a great inducement; but it is certain that the nucleus of these settlements was composed of an enterprising and intelligent population, and who, far from being a lawless people, as we have seen it the case in some of our new territories, held the law and constituted authorities in respect with an almost religious feeling.

The number of very superior men brought on the stage by the Western Insurrection, cannot fail to excite surprise. The rapid increase of population, toward the close of the Revolutionary war, somewhat alloyed the original character, by the accession of numbers, among whom there was a proportion of desperate characters; and although the farmers were orderly and respectable, many of them possessing considerable landed wealth, yet there were others, little better than mere squatters, ready to engage in lawless enterprises at the instigation of a popular leader. The four western counties, at the time of the Western Insurrection, or riots, (Westmoreland, Fayette, Washington and Allegheny,) contained about seventy thousand inhabitants, scattered over an extent of country nearly as great as that of Scotland or Ireland. Except Pittsburgh, which contained about twelve hundred souls, there were no towns except the few places appointed for holding the courts of justice in each county. There were scarcely any roads, the population had to find their way as they could through paths or woods, while the mountains formed a barrier which could only be passed on foot or on horseback. The only trade with the East, was by packhorses; while the navigation of the Ohio was closed by Indian wars, even if a market could have been found by descending its current.

The farmers, having no market for their produce, were from necessity compelled to reduce its bulk by converting their grain into whiskey; a horse could carry two kegs of eight gallons each, worth about fifty cents per gallon on this, and one dollar on the other side of the mountains, while he returned with a little iron and salt, worth at Pittsburgh, the former fifteen to twenty cents per pound, the latter five dollars per bushel. The still was therefore the necessary appendage of every farm,* where the farmer was able to procure it; if not, he was compelled to carry his grain to the more wealthy to be distilled. In fact, some of these distilleries on a large scale, were friendly to the excise laws, as it rendered the poorer farmers dependent on them.

Such excise laws had always been unpopular among the small farmers in Great Britain; they excited hatred, which they brought with them to this country, and which may be regarded as hereditary. Scarcely any of the causes of complaint which led to the revolution, had so strong a hold on the people of Pennsylvania as the stamp act, an excise regarded as an oppressive tax on colonial industry. Every attempt of the Colony, or State, to enforce the excise on home distilled spirits had failed; and so fully were the authorities convinced that they could not be enforced, that the last law on the subject, after remaining a dead letter on the statute book, was repealed just before the attempt to introduce it under the Federal

---

* "For these reasons we have found it absolutely necessary to introduce a number of small distilleries into our settlements, and in every circle of twenty or thirty neighbors one of these are generally erected, merely for the accommodation of such neighborhood, and without any commercial views whatever."—Petition of inhabitants of Westmoreland county, 1790. Pa. Arch., XI. 671.

financial system, by the Secretary of the Treasury, Alexander Hamilton. The inequality of the duty between the farmers on the west and on the east side of the mountains, could not fail to strike the most common mind; for the rate per gallon on both sides was the same, yet the article on the west was worth but half of that on the other side. There were, moreover, circumstances necessarily attending the collection of the tax revolting to the minds of a free people. Instead of a general assessment, a license system confined to a few dealers on a large scale, or an indirect tax on foreign imports, while in the hands of the importers or retailers; this tax created a numerous host of petty officers, scattered over the country as spies on the industry of the people, and practically authorized at almost any moment toi nflict domiciliary visits on them, to make arbitrary seizures, and commit other vexatious acts; the tax was thus brought to bear on almost each individual cultivator of the soil. Laws which cannot be enforced but by such means, no matter what may be their object or moral nature, will always be revolting to the spirit of our people, and be executed with difficulty, or often evaded, laying the foundation of distrust in the government, and want of mutual confidence between it and the people, which no fancied or real good can ever compensate. Nothing but the stern mandate of constitutional obligation can reconcile them to such laws. In this case, it is an act of duty; in the others, merely an experiment of expediency, which ought to be abandoned, when found to be in opposition to the wishes and feelings of the country—or even of a large portion of its citizens, no matter how plausible the reasons which sustain them. It is not the intention of the writer to discuss the intrinsic merits of the excise laws, nor to weigh the justice of all the complaints made by the people of the West against them. Secretary Hamilton, in his Treasury Report of 1792, has said everything in their favor necessary to form a sound judgment; and while much of his reasoning is satisfactory, there is also much, especially in what relates to the western counties, which is far from being so.

The first Pennsylvania excise law was passed in 1756,* then under the province or government of the Penns. A second act was passed in 1772; the object of these was to redeem certain bills for debts incurred by the government. An exception was made in favor of spirits distilled from the products of the province, for the use of the owner. During the revolution, 1777, the law was extended, and some new provisions made to render the collection more effectual. Collectors were appointed for the western counties, but no attempt was made to collect the duties. It was regarded

* There is mention of excise long before this date, but it appears to mean license or tax on sale; except, perhaps, that in Colonial Records, vol. 111-12: 248-9-50.

as an ignominious service, chiefly owing to the traditional prejudices of the Scotch-Irish, as already mentioned, who formed the great body of the population. The domiciliary visits, the arbitrary seizures, and other despotic acts, practically authorized,* as already observed, rendered them practically odious. The violation of the domicil was regarded by the common people with horror; they were always ready to treat with contempt, if not to assail with actual violence, those who, for the sake of a little money, would accept such disreputable employment. About the year 1783, the Council of State became satisfied, from the prevailing odium in the western country, that no person could be got to accept the office, or if appointed, would offend their neighbors by an inquiry on the subject of the duties, or by searching their premises for that purpose. A certain Graham, a man of broken fortune, who had kept a public house in Philadelphia, was found willing to accept the appointment of Collector General for the West; but when he undertook to exercise his office he was treated with every possible contumely. Being unable to execute the law, he occasionally compounded for small sums, which he appropriated to his own use. The people occasionally amused themselves at his expense, by singing his wig, or putting coals into his boots.

In the year 1784, at the court in Westmoreland, he was besieged in his room, and kept there all night, alarmed by uncouth noises and terrible threats. He endeavored to prosecute those who had been outside of the house; but on the trial, the persons sworn to by him, proved an alibi, and the prosecution failed. In the same year an advertisement was posted up, offering a reward for his scalp! These vulgar pranks were disapproved by the respectable part of the people, but it was not in their power to prevent them. He was obliged to fly to Washington county, but was openly attacked, in the neighborhood of Cross creek, by a number of persons in disguise. After shaving his head, they put him over the Monongahela, into Westmoreland county, and threatened him with death if he returned. Twelve of those concerned in the outrage were indicted, convicted and fined. A justice of the peace, of the name of Craig, accepted the office after this, and attempted to execute it, with no result, however, but that of becoming infamous with the populace. It does not appear that the law was executed in a single instance. Another attempt was made by a person of the name of Hunter, who made seizures in Pittsburgh in 1790, and instituted seventy suits against delinquent distillers; in these cases, the suits were set aside for irregularity. Hunter soon after left the country and resigned his commission.

* Blackstone says these powers are *necessary!*

Such was the state of the public mind when the United States excise law was enacted in March, 1791. While the bill was before Congress, the subject was taken up by the State Legislature, then in session, and resolutions were passed in strong terms against the law, and requesting the senators and representatives, by a majority of thirty-six to eleven, to oppose its passage; the minority voting on the principle that it was improper to interfere with the actions of the Federal government, and not from approval of the law. They objected, also, to the inconsistency of approving a United States excise law while the State law was still unrepealed. This had become absolute, but when attention was called to it, it was at once expunged from the statute book.*

Findley, of Westmoreland, and Smiley, of Fayette, being elected to Congress, took an active part against the law, and rendered themselves very odious to the Secretary of the Treasury, who was the father of it, as a part of his favorite financial system. The individuals before named, on their return to their constituents, contributed to increase, if anything could increase, the popular antipathy (not to use a stronger term,) to the law. "But," observes Mr. Brackenridge in his "Incidents,"—"if these persons had been quiescent, the prejudice among the people was of itself irresistible. Had they attempted to reconcile them to the law, they would have instantly lost their popularity. In fact, that popularity depended on their being with the people, and consulting their prejudices. The moment they opposed the prevailing feelings of the multitude, they would

---

* The following are the resolutions passed the State Legislature:

"HOUSE OF REPRESENTATIVES, June 22d, 1791.

"The Legislature of this commonwealth, ever attentive to the rights of their constituents, and conceiving it a duty incumbent on them to express their sentiments on such matters of a public nature as in their opinion have a tendency to destroy their rights, have agreed to the following resolutions:

"*Resolved*, That any proceeding on the part of the United States, tending to the collection of revenue by means of excise, established on principles subversive of peace, liberty and the rights of the citizens, ought to attract the attention of this house.

"*Resolved*, That no public urgency, within the knowledge or contemplation of this house, can, in their opinion, warrant the adoption of any species of taxation which shall violate those rights which are the basis of our government, and which would exhibit the singular spectacle of a nation resolutely oppressing the oppressed of others in order to enslave itself.

"*Resolved*, That these sentiments be communicated to the senators representing the State of Pennsylvania in the Senate of the United States, with a hope that they will oppose every part of the excise bill now before the Congress, which shall militate against the rights and liberties of the people."

be politically dead. And it was not enough for them to remain silent; they were charged in the newspaper with the unpardonable neglect of suffering, while members of the State Legislature, an excise law to remain unrepealed on the statute book! To atone for it, they were obliged to redouble their diligence against all excise laws."

Such was the state of things when Gen. Neville accepted the office of Inspector under the Federal government, for the survey comprehending the four counties west of the mountains, with Bedford on the east. This gentleman had been popular, perhaps in part, from falling in with the common opinions and prejudices as respects the excise laws; certainly not on account of sustaining them. He was in the State Legislature when the law was passed. The claim for disinterested patriotism, in taking the office under the circumstances, was not universally admitted; on the contrary, some said that in accepting, he was influenced by its emoluments, which would not have been the case if he had pursued the course of declining, and then recommending some one of equal respectability and capacity, and at the same time exerting his influence as a citizen to aid him in the execution of its duties. As it was, the course pursued by him tended greatly to increase the unpopularity of the excise. The people were indignant at the idea of his having sought their favors, and then deserting them for the sake, as they believed, of the emolument of an office, under the law which they detested! In fact, this is mentioned by Governor Mifflin as one of the causes of the insurrection.

The Secretary of the Treasury, in tracing these causes, laid great stress on the meetings held, and resolutions adopted by the people, against the law, but avoiding a reference to those passed by the State Legislature. Unfortunately he made no discrimination between the peaceful remonstrance and the passage of certain resolutions which he styled "intemperate." To his mind, they appeared equally factious, and even treasonable. According to this view, all right of remonstrance, or petition, or legal resistance to oppression, would be taken from the people. It was assuming the right to think for them, whether they were oppressed or not; as if those who feel the oppression are not the best judges of its extent and severity! Much of this, on the part of the Secretary, is to be ascribed to the imperfect ideas of the rights of the citizens at that day, compared with the more enlightened and liberal views which now prevail; among which is the unquestioned right freely to censure the conduct of government agents. It will be proper in this place to pass briefly in review the public meetings and the resolutions passed, so highly censured, in order that the reader may be enabled to judge for himself as to the soundness of the Secretary's report, drawn as it is, with great ability, and therefore requiring the more careful scrutiny. The writer does not approve of "violent and intemperate" resolutions, although they be but *words*.

The first meeting was at Redstone Old Fort, (Brownsville,) on the 27th July, 1791, at which Findley, Smiley, Marshall, and a number of the inhabitants were present. Col. Cook was chairman, and Albert Gallatin, secretary. It was resolved at this meeting, that it be recommended to the several counties to appoint delegates, at least three for each elective district, to meet at the seat of justice, and having collected the sense of the people in each county, from each of these delegates choose three to form a committee. These were to meet at Pittsburgh, on the first Tuesday of September, and there draw up and pass resolutions expressing the sense of their constituents respecting the excise law.*

The meeting at Redstone, it will be perceived, was only preliminary to that to convene at Pittsburgh. No resolutions were passed relative to the excise law, and according to Findley, many who attended it were desirous of reconciling the people to submission. He expresses his surprise that the Secretary should refer to it as one of the causes of the insurrection.

At the preparatory meeting for the county of Washington, some resolutions of a violent character were adopted by way of instructions for the delegates who were to attend at Pittsburgh. They were modeled after those passed before the Revolutionary war in relation to the stamp act and other excises. The *language* in which they were couched must be ascribed to the individuals who composed the meetings; it would be unfair to consider them as emanating from the majority of the people, who were but partially represented. At the meeting convened at Pittsburgh soon after, it was resolved to petition for a repeal of the law, but no resolution was passed which could be considered reprehensible, yet that meeting was particularly charged with having occasioned all the excesses which followed. Mr. Gallatin was not present, being at that time in Philadelphia.

A second meeting was held in Pittsburgh eleven months after the first, and may be noted as the last of these meetings which preceded the riots, which took place *two years after*, on the occasion of the service of process on delinquent distillers, compelling them to appear in Philadelphia. The meeting of 1792 was composed of delegates from Washington, Fayette and Allegheny counties, but was very far from being a full and complete

---

* See note to the resolutions passed at this meeting; also the exceptionable Washington resolutions.

representation; they prepared and published a petition for the repeal of the excise laws, and also adopted resolutions similar to those of Washington county the year before. Such language is highly censurable; it is undoubtedly an abuse of the right of remonstrance, even if attended with no *practical effect*, as was the case on the present occasion, that is, exciting to no act corresponding to the spirit of the resolutions. It could not create public opinion—it was the extravagant expression of the excited state of feeling already existing, and cannot be fairly enumerated among the causes of the insurrection arising out of that state of feeling. Col. Neville, the son of the Inspector, when examined as a witness on the trials, being asked whether the enmity to the excise law was increased by those resolutions passed at Pittsburgh, answered: "I do not know that the opposition was more general afterward than before, but immediately after that meeting, revenue officers were treated with disrespect; before that time some had been disrespectfully and injuriously treated; my father before was always treated with respect." Perhaps the word "disrespect" would have required explanation. It is more rational so refer any diminution of respect for the Inspector, among the people, to his loss of popularity consequent on his acceptance of the office.

The reader will probably conclude with the writer, that the meetings on the subject of the excise laws, and the resolutions passed in them, were not among the primary causes which led to the insurrection, as set forth by Secretary Hamilton, but the effect of the unpopular excise laws. The resolutions were nothing more than the strong expression of the popular sentiment, instead of the discontent being the work of "demagogues by speeches and public meetings." There is a reluctance in the rulers or public agent to admit that the discontent rises spontaneously among the people, instead of being manufactured for them—because the contrary would naturally raise a presumption against the former. There is no doubt that Mr. Gallatin took an active part in some of the meetings convened to remonstrate against the excise laws, and to petition for their repeal, and that he thereby incurred the displeasure of the Secretary of the Treasury and the Federal party. But he had a right to do what he did in the exercise of his privilege as a citizen, without incurring the responsibility of actual violation of law afterward committed by others. Who would dare to remonstrate against an odious law, if the remonstrance might possibly be followed by unlawful acts of others, who should transcend the bounds of that remonstrance? In this case, there would be nothing left to the people but silent submission and passive obedience! Instead of being masters of the government, the government would be their master. It is only a matter of astonishment to the writer, that he finds himself compelled to assert this unquestionable right, in opposition to the manifest tendency of the doctrine put forth by the Secretary of the Treasury, and the Federal party of that day. Findley's remarks on this subject may be quoted with propriety: "On the ground of discretion," says he, "these resolutions were censurable, and were in fact heartily disapproved by many who disliked the excise laws. That they were not contrary to law, is acknowledged by the Secretary himself, who informs us of procuring testimony, in order to prosecute the persons who composed the committees, but he adds, that the Attorney General did not think it actionable! There is no doubt that it is morally wrong in many cases, to refuse charity or assistance to any of our fellow-men, when their necessities require it; but these duties being of imperfect obligation, we are only responsible to our own conscience for the proper discharge of them. There are no doubt persons in society, whose manners are so disagreeable as to justify us in refusing all fellowship with them; and where the excise law is almost universally believed to be unjust and oppressive, men of this description will be found pretty readily among the excise officers. Indeed, this observation need not be restricted to persons so situated; it corresponds with the sentiments of the people generally, where excises have been long established. Their resolutions were, however, censurable on the ground of policy. They disgusted those members of Congress that would otherwise have been disposed to have eased, if not fully relieved them, from their grounds of complaint; and they offended the citizens at large, who had sympathized with them. In short, they undoubtedly caused less respect to be paid to their petitions." We may also record in this place, the observations of Mr. Gallatin in his speech on the Western Insurrection: "For by attempting to render office contemptible, they tended to diminish that respect for the execution of the laws which is essential to the maintainance of a free government; but whilst I feel regret at the remembrance, though no hesitation in the open confession of that *my only political sin*, [sustaining the resolutions of the Pittsburgh meeting of 1792,] let me add that the blame ought to fall where it is deserved."

On the other hand, the unqualified censure on the part of the Secretary cannot be sustained. "These meetings," says he, "composed of very influential persons, and conducted without moderation or prudence, *are justly chargeable with the excesses which have from time to time been committed*, serving to give consistency to an opposition which has at length matured to a point that *threatens the foundation of the government and the Union*, unless speedily and effectually subdued." The tendency of the Secretary's doctrine, we repeat, is to prohibit all remonstrance of any kind against any law or public measure, under the penalty of being regarded as responsible for every partial act of violence that may be committed by individuals smarting under a sense of oppression, while the real cause may be found in the unwise and unjust acts of the government itself. To condemn the remonstrance because made without " prudence and moderation," is to set up a right on the part of the public agents to judge of that prudence and moderation; and it is not improbable that remonstrance of any kind would be regarded by them as wanting in these desirable qualities! The holding responsible the " influential men" who attended the meetings, goes on the idea that the masses take no part in them, but as they are acted upon by a few individuals; a very great mistake, but very natural in those who hold the people in a low estimate, and doubt their capacity for self-government. This was the great error, or rather " political sin," of the Federal party. Whatever may be the fact in other countries, we are not willing to admit our incapacity for self-government. But we must allow for political progress; had Secretary Hamilton lived to this day, he would not have maintained such doctrines.

The legitimate effect of these remonstrances and petitions, notwithstanding the condemnation of the Secretary, was to produce *various salutary amendments of the excise laws*, and which were recommended to Congress by the Secretary himself; an admission that the complaints, if intemperate, were not groundless. The last of the public meetings, as already seen, was in August, 1792, and from that time until the riots of 1794, there was a discontinuance of them, while in fact the law, notwithstanding occasional acts of violence, appeared to be gaining ground in the favor of the people. The larger distillers, as we have stated, were disposed to favor it, as it gave them a kind of monopoly of the business, compelling the smaller distillers—the farmers—to bring their grain to the larger distilleries. There was another reason why the more reflecting and influential citizens were disposed to discourage such meetings; this was in consequence of the wild revolutionary spirit which began to show itself in a certain class, who began to entertain a thousand visionary and impracticable expectations. Not content with redress of real grievances, they thought of wild reforms tending to anarchy, such as rendered the Republicans of France unfit for any government but that of despotism. These visionaries inveighed against courts of justice, salaries, and in fact, were at war with all restraints of government whatever. These follies are the subject of the keen, yet philosophical satire, of Mr. Brackenridge, in his work styled " Modern Chivalry," published about this period. A sort of society, or club, had been established a year or two before the insurrection, which met at the Mingo Creek meeting-house, where political subjects were discussed, and these disorganizing doctrines asserted by some. Although the excise laws were not directly assailed in the club, yet it had the bad effect of lessening the respect for the government and the laws generally. A Democratic club had been established in the town of Washington a few months before the insurrection, but it had no effect in producing that event, notwithstanding the assertion of Hildreth, whose prejudices, and bigoted relation of these occurences, should be utterly disregarded.*

Notwithstanding the cessation, during the two years, of those meetings deemed treasonable by the Secretary of the Treasury, it is to be lamented that there were five or six unconnected riots, or assaults on collectors, in different parts of the western country, on account of the excise. Although of little importance separately, yet when brought together, and spread on the same page by the Secretary, they assume a formidable appearance; and this is ingeniously done to aggravate the case of the insurgents. The object is to prove a connected and concerted action, and a combination of the whole people to resist, and even overturn the government, thus doing them great injustice. So far from these outbreaks being ascribable to the previous meetings, those meetings had the tendency of repressing all violent and irregular acts of opposition, by resorting to the legal modes of redress by remonstrance and petition. It is the opinion of Findley, and we incline to the same way of thinking, but without attaching any blame to the Federal administration—"that if the government had shown a very small portion of that power and energy which afterward became necessary, the law could have been enforced by the judiciary, sustained by the influential citizens, and the majority of the people would have acquiesced." A circuit court of the United States should have gone into the country, on the first resistance to any officer of the revenue; or power should have been given to the State courts, which the people would have respected, although from fixed prejudice and habit disposed to hate the officers of the excise. The force of the State, or of the Union, should have been called out to repress in its infancy the spirit of illegal resistance. But above all, the real and most crying grievance should have been avoided—that of carrying persons from their districts or counties, to be taken across

---

*Hildreth says that a similar society, of which Mr Brackenridge was a member, was also established in Pittsburgh! No such society was established there, and Mr. Brackenridge never was a member of such a *society* anywhere.

the mountains, to answer suits or prosecutions for disregard of the excise law in not entering these stills, or not paying the excise duties, suits necessarily followed by ruin on account of the expense. A law, such as we have indicated, had been enacted, to go into operation in the month of June, 1794, only one month before the outbreak; but while this law was under discussion, and only a few days before it was signed, process as usual was issued returnable to Philadelphia; and it will appear that the service of this process was the *immediate cause of the riots*, which, to use the words of the Secretary, "threatened the foundations of the government and the Union."*

Findley ventures the assertion, that it was by design on the part of Secretary Hamilton that the disaffection of the western people was permitted to ripen into open rebellion, in order that he might have an opportunity of practicing on his favorite maxim, that the Federal government could not be considered as finally established until it proves that it could maintain itself by physical force! That he should avail himself of the unfortunate occurrence for that purpose, is very probable, but the idea of his creating it with that view is incredible. The assertion simply betrays the feelings of Findley toward Hamilton. This great man was the leader of the high-toned section of the Federal party, in opposition to the Democratic, or Republican party, and to the more moderate Federalists under John Adams. Hamilton and his party wre in favor of a degree of energy, in the form and action of the government, incompatible with the habits and genius of the Americans, which caused the downfall of the Federal party hastened by the unfortunate sedition and alien laws. It is the Hamilton party, those who idolize his name, who have incessantly labored to cover the opposers of the excise law in the West with lasting infamy, and are in the habit of denouncing them as brigands, rebels, banditti and robbers! Of this class of historians are Judge Wilkinson, Neville. B. Craig and

---

* The first ill treatment given to an excise officer under the Federal excise law, was in Chester county, but the rioters were prosecuted for the riot, convicted and punished severely by the State courts. On that occasion, the foreman told the Attorney General that *he was as much, or more, opposed to the excise law than the rioters,* but would not suffer violations of the laws to go unpunished. Findley, Hist. p. 40. In 1792, Findley, then in Congress, wrote to the President, at the instance of Gov. Mifflin, and again at that of the Attorney General of the United States and of the Attorney for the district of Pennsylvania, in relation to the case of Beer and Kerr; and in these letters gave the opinion, that if special sessions of the court were held in the counties, the courts would be protected, and competent juries found. Findley, p. 273.

Hildreth, the latter especially—which renders them as authorities on this subject unsafe.

We will now proceed to detail the cases of illegal opposition to the excise law, just alluded to. The first was that of Robert Johnston, collector for Washington and Allegheny counties. After cutting his hair, and tarring and feathering him, he was compelled to go home on foot. This occurred at an out-of-the-way place on Pigeon creek, and was the work of a small number of persons of the lowest class, while there is no proof that it was countenanced or approved by any reputable person in the neighborhood. This was the time for the Federal government to have taken active measures, and by a vigorous pursuit of the offenders in the State courts, to crush that bad spirit in its birth. Instead of this, an agent was dispatched to ascertain who were the leading individuals at certain meetings for the lawful purpose of petition and remonstrance.

The next case is that of Wilson, in another part of the county; a person somewhat disordered in intellect, who pretended to be an exciseman, was shamefully abused in consequence. Not long after, one Roseburg was tarred and feathered by some disorderly persons for speaking in favor of the law. In August, 1792, a Captain Faulkner, in whose house an office for the collection of excise had been opened, was attacked on the road by a ruffian, and threatened with having his house burnt if he did not cause the office to be removed; he accordingly gave public notice that it was no longer kept there. It would be unfair to consider these unconnected occurrences as proofs of the general disposition of the people, although ingeniously marshaled and magnified for the purpose.

In April, 1793, an armed party attacked the house of Wells, in Fayette county, but did not find him at home. The attack was repeated in November, and the assailants compelled him to give up his commission and books, requiring him to publish his resignation in two weeks or have his house burnt. According to Findley, a much more serious design was conceived by a number of persons in disguise, to seize the Inspector himself, in the town of Washington, where he was expected to be. He had been apprised of their coming, and did not attend at the office.*

James Kiddo and William Cochran, who had entered their stills, were first threatened, and then attacked. The still of the latter was destroyed, his valuable mills materially injured, if not entirely ruined, and he was obliged to publish in the Pittsburgh *Gazette*, an account of what had happened, as a warning to others. An armed party broke into the house of John Lynn, where an office was kept; after prevailing upon him to

* Findley, p. 50.

come down stairs, they tied and threatened to hang him; cut off his hair, tarred and feathered, and swore him not to disclose the names of his assailants, or permit an excise office to be kept in his house.

In June, 1794, several attacks were made on the office of Wells, who had opened at the house of Philip Regan, in Westmoreland county, but they were repulsed by the inmates.

These were doubtless revolting outrages, which cannot be condemned in language too strong, and ought to have been vigorously prosecuted; but it would be unfair to hold the whole population responsible for acts which were disapproved by the great majority. Occurring in distant localities, in a thinly inhabited country, it was impossible for the well disposed, if so inclined, to have united to prevent their perpetration. Even in cities, where there is a strong police force constantly on foot, we see how difficult it is to prevent the acts of lawless mobs. We might as well hold every peaceable citizen of the towns responsible for the burglaries and murders perpetrated within their limits. To say that the general hostility to the law was the cause of these outrages, is to deny all right of complaint, or discontent, or even the expression of conscientious opinion, as respects any law, however oppressive. The fault is in the Legislature passing laws revolting to the minds of the people, or in the executive branch in not seeing them executed at every hazard, suppressing at once the first indications of violent resistance. It is not the intention of the writer to defend, or even to make an apology for such acts, under any circumstances; and especially at this more enlightened period, when the principles of our representative government are so much better understood. In holding the scales of justice, it is necessary to poise them evenly and fairly. Although the constituent reserves to himself the right of remonstrance, it cannot be too often repeated, that he is bound in conscience, as well as on legal principle, to obey the law, and not oppose its execution. We go further, and hold, that he is not at liberty even to remain passive, if he means to do his duty as a good citizen, and has it in his power to aid in supporting the government.

The apology made by Mr. Brackenridge in his "Incidents," would be inadmissible at the *present day*, and goes as far in favor of the Western people, *fifty years ago*, as the most liberal view of the case will admit. "It will be conceded," said he, "that it was difficult for the common mind of this country to distinguish an attack upon the officer appointed to carry a law odious to them into execution, from that opposition under the stamp act of Great Britain, at a more early period. They could see no difference in the case of John Nevill and Zachariah Hood, the Stamp-Master General. The law was said to be grievous in both cases; and that was all they knew about it. In the case of the tea duty, also, an opposition by force took place, which is celebrated to this day as amongst the first acts of patriotism. Could you expect an accurate conception of the distinction which exists? These acts being against laws that were void because they were unconstitutional, and those being against a law, which, though unequal, is constitutional? It astonishes them to this day, that the authors of our revolution from Great Britain, should be celebrated, and yet talk of hanging those who were doing nothing more than opposing what was wrong among themselves! I know, to use the expression of one of them, 'they thought in taking up arms to oppose the excise laws, they were "doing God a service.'' The language of humanity then would be, ' forgive them, for they know not what they do." It is a hard case to punish when the mind is not criminal. The gradual improvement of education by public schools may inform the mass of the people, and correct a mistake of principle."

The reader will find that the Western riots, improperly called an insurrection, were not instigated by hostility to the government of the United States, nor did they originate merely on account of the excise on whiskey, but in a more excusable motive the service of process on delinquent distillers, who would in consequence be compelled to attend in Philadelphia, at the sacrifice of their farms and the ruin of their families. As the farmers were also the distillers, it was the only mode in which they could carry the produce of their fields to market. The taking persons "beyond seas for trial," is one of the grievances complained of in the Declaration of Independence, and the idea of trial by the vicinage, is one of the instincts of Saxon and American liberty. Out of about forty precepts, but one remained to be served. The last was unfortunately served during the harvest, the reapers in the field, under the free indulgence of whiskey, common at that season. The sudden outbreak, as will be seen, was almost exclusively confined to the rural population of the vicinage, although like other conflagrations, there was danger of embracing within it everything combustible; that it did not do this, was due to the wisdom and moderation of Washington, and to the patriotic exertions of influential individuals, who remained among the disaffected until the disturbance was quelled—*not by external or military force, but by their own sense of duty.* Never was there greater injustice done to any people, than by the assertion that the so-called insurrection was put down by an army. Surely that people must command our respect in a much higher degree, who possess within themselves the moral energy to restrain their own passions, than those who have been reduced to obedience by the outward pressure of a military force!

NOTES TO CHAPTER I.

"*The Neville Connection.*"—This expression is used by N. B. Craig, a grandson of Gen. Neville, in a work entitled "History of Pittsburgh," but chiefly laudatory of that "connection." This consisted of four wealthy families, monopolizing public offices, and closely united in interest and relationship. The reflecting mind will readily perceive the powerful influence that such a combination must possess, *in advancing their own fortunes*, or in crushing any single individual who might be so unfortunate as to incur their enmity. It would be felt even in a large community, and much more in a small village of twelve or fifteen hundred inhabitants. The public spirited lawyer who should brave this enmity, in the defense of the rights of the citizen, would run no small risk, especially at that more aristocratic period of our Republic, half a century ago. At present, it is the democracy which predominates; then, it was the aristocracy which ruled. We proceed to extract from the work of N. B. Craig his account of the heads of these families, accompanying it with such remarks as may be deemed necessary:

"Presley Neville, the only son of John Neville, (the Inspector,) married the daughter of Gen. Morgan, and Isaac Craig married the only sister of Presley. John Neville, as Judge Wilkinson states, was a man of great wealth for those days. He was the descendant of a lad who at a very early day was kidnapped in England and brought to Virginia, and who subsequently accumulated a good property there. John Neville was a man of good English education, of plain blunt manners, a pleasant companion, and the writer well recollects how eagerly he listened to his well-related anecdotes, and how by his manner he could give interest to trifling incidents. He was born on the head waters of the Ocoquan river, Virginia, on the direct road from Washington's paternal estate to Winchester and Cumberland, and the residence of his father is laid down in Spark's map illustrative of the 'operations in Virginia' during the war of 1754. From this circumstance, probably, it was that he became an early acquaintance of Washington, both of whom were about the same age, and thus with the ardor of a young man he engaged in Braddock's expedition. He subsequently settled near Winchester, in Frederick county, where for some time he held the office of sheriff. Prior to 1774 he had made large entries and purchases of lands on Chartiers creek, then supposed to be in Virginia, and was about to remove here when the troubles began. He was elected in that year a delegate from Augusta county, that is, from Pittsburgh, to the Provincial Convention of Virginia, which appointed George Washington, Peyton Randolph, and others to the first Continental Congress, but was prevented by sickness from attending. Subsequent to the Revolution, he was a member of the Supreme Executive Council of Pennsylvania. Presley Neville, his son, was an accomplished gentleman, having received the best education the country could afford; was a good classical and French scholar; had served throughout the Revolution, part of the time as aid to Lafayette. He and his father had together a princely estate on Chartiers creek, besides large possessions elsewhere in Virginia, Ohio and Kentucky. He had also large expectations from his father-in-law. But unfortunately for the comfort of his latter days, his heart was tenfold larger than his estate and all his expectations. In recently looking over some old letters from him, written *while he was yet in exile,* and while the ashes of his father's destroyed mansions, and barns, and stables, and negro huts, were yet warm, I was struck with the following kind-hearted expression: 'The prisoners arrived yesterday, 'and were, by the ostentation of Gen. 'White, paraded through the different 'parts of the city (Philadelphia). They 'had pieces of paper in their hats to 'distinguish them, and wore the appear-'ance of wretchedness. I could not 'help being sorry for them, although so 'well acquainted with their conduct.' "

"Major Abraham Kirkpatrick, a Marylander by birth, a soldier of the Revolution, as brave a man as drew his sword in the struggle for independence, of but ordinary English education, but of strong native intellect, kind and chivalric, though rather by fits and starts; shrewd in argument, and so fond of it that he would rather change sides than let the discussion cease." This is the *favorable* side of his character, as given by his kinsman; others spoke of him in very *different terms;* but a regard for the feelings of survivors forbids saying anything further.

"Isaac Craig, [the father of N. B. Craig,] an Irishman, born near Hillsborough, in the county Dover, of reputable Protestant parents, as certified in a paper in my possession, emigrated to Philadelphia in 1767, where he carried on his trade of housejoiner until the commencement of the Revolutionary war. He was then appointed, by the authorities of Pennsylvania, a Captain of Marines, and as such in the sloop-of-war *Andrew Doria,* Capt. Nicholas Biddle, sailed in Commodore Hopkins' squadron, along with Paul Jones, Barney and others, to the Isle of New Providence, in the West Indies, where they seized, and brought safely home, a large amount of arms and munitions of war, then much needed. Soon after his return he received an appointment as captain in Proctor's regiment of artillery, just in time to be present at the capture of the Hessians at Trenton. Subsequently he was in the battle of Princeton, Brandywine and Germantown, and about the time of Broadhead's expedition up the Allegheny, accompanied Gen. Sullivan's expedition up the Susquehanna against the hostile tribes of the Six Nations. He was then ordered to Pittsburgh, which after the war he made his home. He was but of common school education, but having a good mind for mechanics and mathematics, had in these branches added largely to his school acquirements, and was at an early day *a member of the American Philosophical Society.*"

So far, Mr. Craig; it is now my turn to make some remarks on the foregoing. First, as to Major Craig, his son might as well have omitted the circumstance of his being a member of the Philosophical Society, to which he had so little claim that it has been incorrectly supposed that the author of "Modern Chivalry" had his case in view in that work. As an individual he bore a respectable character, although clannish, and far from liberal in his opinions.

As to the letter of Col. Presley Neville, on the subject of the prisoners marched through the streets of Philadelphia with papers in their hats with the word "Insurgent," this would have been bad enough after *conviction,* but in the case of *innocent men,* as those proved to be, it was a shocking outrage, which can scarcely be conceived at the present day. Neville B. Craig is a great stickler for *dates* and *facts*, when they suit his purpose, and equally reckless of them, when they do not. In the newspaper controversy between him and the author, he announced in the most triumphant manner that he had detected him in an important error of fact. It was in reference to a contribution of whiskey on some occasion, which the author mentioned as of *five* barrels, which Craig after minute research discovered was only of *four*. But here, in respect to Col. Neville's letter, he has been guilty of a gross misrepresentation, which *he could not but have known to be such*. Why did he not give the *date* of the letter which he states he found among the letters of Col. Neville? The reason is, it would have shown the fact, that *he was not* in what Craig denominates *exile*, at the time of writing that letter. He had been restored to his home in triumph, by his father-in-law, and he was then in Philadelphia as a member of the Legislature, and *as a witness against the insurgents*. Col. Neville, who was a gentleman, and possessed of humane feeling, does not say in that letter that the prisoners had a hand in the acts of violence committed, but merely: "I could not help being sorry for them, *although so well acquainted with their conduct*." What conduct? It is impossible to extend this allusion further than to their opposition to the excise law, for two obvious reasons: first, when brought to trial, there appeared to be nothing against them; and secondly, when Col. Neville was called upon as a witness, he could allege nothing against their conduct which was illegal! It was reserved for his *unscrupulous nephew* to say, that they had been concerned in destroying the mansion of General Neville, his stables, negro huts, &c. Craig is pleased to say, that "Brackenridge and Findley have both written *apologies* for their own conduct, which have been looked upon as histories." What apology can be made for their treatment of the injured prisoners, marched on foot over the mountains, at an inclement season, driven ignominiously through the streets, confined in prison many months, and found at last to be not only innocent, but meritorious? Who were the parties chiefly concerned in this outrage? A rigid inquiry might possibly implicate a portion of the powerful "Neville connection."

If it requires an apology for having labored to induce the people to submit to the government, and having exerted themselves as *mediators and peacemakers* between them, the histories referred to are very effectual and unanswerable vindications. In doing this, they were necessarily compelled to implicate others, who would gladly apologize for their acts, if the truth of history would permit.

Col. Presley Neville possessed many estimable qualities. He was incapable of any mean act, but from the cabalistic influence of the "Neville connection," sometimes witheld his disapprobation of acts which his better nature condemned. He had much of the cavalier about him, and not a little of the false pride attending it; at the same time, he possessed the lofty feelings which characterize the Virginia gentleman. It is unfortunate that in his habits he was indolent, was a mere man of pleasure, having no occupation, yet by no means addicted to any vice. He wanted what the French express by the word *charactere*. In his early life he undertook to study law, under my father, but after six months abandoned it, and gave as his reason, that the profession of the law was not an occupation *fit for a gentleman!* His mode of living was expensive, never undertaking anything to render his fine landed estate more productive, or to effect any improvement; the consequence was, that he was eaten out of house and home by servants and retainers, and persons to whom he extended his hospitality, too often misplaced. The writer knew him when in his highest prosperity, and saw him in his old age, when greatly reduced in his circumstances, and thought him in the latter condition a wiser and better man than he had ever been in his most prosperous state. It was, perhaps, his misfortune that he was the inheritor of wealth. The contrast between him and the other members of the "connection," was very great. Every one esteemed and admired him, while toward the others a different feeling prevailed.

His father, although possessed of some good qualities, such as hospitality, &c., was a very different character. He was cunning, vindictive and selfish. His grandson has made some eulogistic extracts from a pamphlet published by a Judge Wilkinson, which we will insert in this place. Who was this Judge Wilkinson? Craig endeavors to leave the impression that he was some *grave judicial functionary*, who had lived his neighbor, and who, therefore, spoke from a personal knowledge! He was a boy of five or six years old when he lived near Neville—he removed to New York—there grew up, became a *justice of the peace*, was called Judge, and wrote his pamphlet about the Western Insurrection! That he was very imperfectly acquainted with the "Neville connection," will appear from the following extract from Craig's book: "His kind heart had not changed in the half century which had elapsed between the destruction of the property and the writing his account of it; but his memory, or his information of the family relations, was not so faithful as the kindness of his heart. John Neville was not the brother-in-law of Gen. Morgan, nor the father-in-law of Major Kirkpatrick. John Neville and Abraham Kirkpatrick married sisters of the name of Oldham, of as sound and true Whig family as any in the country." It is highly probable that Judge Wilkinson was no better informed on the other topics on which he writes. Mr. Craig introduces several extracts from the work. Here is one of them: "John Neville a man "of deserved popularity, was appointed "collector for Western Pennsylvania; he "was one of the few men of great wealth "who had put his all at hazard in the "cause of independence. Besides his "claims as a soldier and a patriot, he "had contributed greatly to the relief of "*the suffering soldiers*. [How?] If any "man could have executed this *odious* "*law*, Gen. Neville was the man. He "was the brother-in-law of the dis- "tinguished Gen. Morgan, and father- "in-law to Majors Craig and Kirk- "patrick, officers highly respected in "the western country." It would certainly not be consistent with truth to place Gen. Neville on a footing with Carroll or Hancock, with respect to the risk of fortune; for Neville's fortune, consisting of recently appropriated lands, worth at the commencement of the Revolution a few cents an acre, in all probability he ran less risk of injury than he had chance of pecuniary advantages by the Revolution. Wilkinson says in another place: "He accepted the "appointment (of Inspector) *from a sense* "*of duty to his country*. Besides Gen. "Neville's claims as a soldier and a "patriot, he had contributed greatly to "relieve the sufferings of the settlers in "his vicinity. *He divided his last loaf* "*with the needy;* and in a season of more "than ordinary scarcity, as soon as his "wheat was sufficiently matured to be "converted into food, *he opened his fields* "*to those who were suffering with hunger.*"

This reads very strangely! What season of scarcity does Wilkinson allude to? The neighbors of Neville were all cultivators of the soil, where land could be got for a trifle, and if their crops failed the General's would have failed also. The misfortune was, that they had a *surplus for which they had no market*, hence the cause of the excise riots! But in truth, there never was such a thing as an entire failure of crops in the fruitful region round the head of the Ohio; it was a thinly inhabited, glorious woody park, stocked with game of every description; deer and turkeys could be had merely for the trouble of shooting them. As to the *patriotism* of accepting a lucrative office, it is absurd to suppose that Neville was more patriotic in accepting than any other, unless it be shown that it involved a sacrifice which no other competent person was willing to make. We have seen in the text that his acceptance was a positive injury to the cause of the excise, for the reason that it involved a dereliction of the cause of the people, who had confided in him as their representative; and for the further reason, that he had been opposed to excise laws, as well as his neighbors, who very naturally concluded that he was actuated in his desertion solely by the prospect of personal emolument. Wilkinson's eulogistic notice must be taken as a rhetorical flourish, very agreeable to the Nevilles, but not exactly in conformity with rigid historic truth. Let all just praise be given, avoiding exaggeration. As to General Neville *sharing his last loaf*, it may be asked on what occasion was the wealthy Neville reduced to *his last loaf?* The writer of this was born in the neighborhood of the Nevilles, had much better opportunities of personal acquaintance with this subject than Judge Wilkinson, and never heard of these marvelous acts. In these traits of benevolence, the Nevilles were quite as good, but not superior, to many of their neighbors, who were equally humane and public spirited, but whose descendants have not thought necessary to emblazon their charitable acts.

But the Nevilles were regarded in a different point of view by others, and here some extracts will be made from the "Incidents of the Western Insurrection," leaving the reader to take them for what they are worth. The author of the Incidents relates a conversation between him and one Miller, a farmer and distiller, in whose field during the harvest the first outbreak took place, a narrative so characteristic that it carries conviction with it, and throws much light on the causes of the insurrection. "The Federal sheriff, said he, [the Marshal,] was reading the writ, and General Neville on horseback in the lane, where he called to the sheriff to make haste. I looked up and saw a party of men running across the field, as it were to head the sheriff. He set off with General Neville, and when they got to the head of the lane the people fired upon them. That night it was concluded we should go on to Neville's and take him and the marshal. I felt myself mad with passion. I thought two hundred and fifty dollars would ruin me; and to have to go to the Federal court in Philadelphia would keep me from going to Kentucky this fall and I was getting ready. I felt my blood boil at seeing General Neville along to pilot the sheriff to my very door. He had been against the excise law as much as any body. When old Graham, the excise man, was catched and had his hair cut off, I heard General Neville himself say they ought to have cut off the ears of the old rascal; and when the distillers were sued some years ago for fines, he talked as much against it as anybody. But he wanted to keep in the

Assembly then. But whenever he got an offer of the office himself, he took it. I am a relation of Kirkpatrick, his mother and my mother were sisters; I was always for General Neville in his elections, and it put me mad to see him coming to ruin me."

The same writer relates, that in a conversation with Col. Presley Neville, he said to him: "It is known that before your father accepted the office you were consulted, and advised the acceptance. It is known that application has been made to you to advise your father to resign; you have said no; *would any of them resign an office of such value?*" It would be superfluous to say any thing further respecting the preposterous claim of exalted pretensions in accepting the office. Such a claim might as well be made in favor of the others of the "connection," on account of the appointments held by them. Major Craig was United States Quarter-Master, a lucrative post, which gave him influence and the command of money—Major Kirkpatrick was Commissary, and Col. Neville, Brigade Inspector, and member of the Assembly.

Intemperate Resolutions.—The first of those resolutions against the United States excise laws, and which resolutions were characterized by the Secretary of the Treasury as *intemperate,* is as follows:

"At Pittsburgh, the 7th of September, 1791, the following gentlemen appeared from the counties of Westmoreland, Fayette and Allegheny, to take into consideration an Act of Congress, laying duties upon spirits distilled within the United States, passed the 3d of March, 1791.

"For Westmoreland county, Nehemiah Stokely and John Young, Esquires; for Washington county, Col. James Marshall, Rev. David Phillips and David Bradford, Esquires; for Fayette county, Edward Cook, Nathaniel Bradly and John Oliphant, Esquires; for Allegheny county, Col. Thomas Morton, John Woods, Esq. and William Plumer.

"Edward Cook, Esquire, was voted in the chair, and John Young appointed Secretary.

"*Resolved,* That having considered the laws of the late Congress, it is our opinion that in a very short time hasty strides have been made to all that is unjust and oppressive. We note particularly the exorbitant salaries of officers, the unreasonable interest of the public debt, and the making no discrimination between the original holders of public securities and the tranferrees, contrary to the ideas of natural justice in sanctioning an advantage which was not in the contemplation of the party himself to receive, and contrary to the municipal law of most nations and ours particularly, the carrying into effect an unconscionable bargain, where an undue advantage has been taken of the ignorance or necessities of another; and also contrary to the interest and happines of these States, being subversive of industry by common means, where men seem to make fortunes by the fortuitous concurrence of circumstances, rather than by economic, virtuous and useful employment. What is an evil still greater, the constituting a capital of nearly eighty millions of dollars in the hands of a few persons who may influence those occasionally in power to evade the Constitution. As an instance of this, already taken place, we note the act establishing a National Bank on the doctrine of implication, but more especially, we bear testimony to what is a base offspring of the funding system, the excise law of Congress, entitled, 'An Act laying duties upon distilled spirits within the United States, passed the 3d of March, 1791.'

"*Resolved,* That the said law is deservedly obnoxious to the feelings and interests of the people in general, as being attended with infringements on liberty, partial in its operations, attended with great expense in the collection, and liable to much abuse. It operates on a domestic manufacture, a manufacture not equal through the States. It is insulting to the feelings of the people to have their vessels marked, houses painted and ransacked, to be subject to informers gaining by the occasional delinquency of others. It is a bad precedent, tending to introduce the excise laws of Great Britain, and of countries where the liberty, property, and even the morals of the people are sported with, to gratify particular men in their ambitious and interested measures.

"*Resolved*, That in the opinion of this committee the duties imposed by the said act on spirits distilled from the produce of the soil of the United States, will eventually discourage agriculture, and a manufacture highly beneficial in the present state of the country. That those duties which fall heavy, especially upon the western parts of the United States, which are, for the most part, newly settled, and where the aggregate of the citizens is of the laborious and poorer class, who have not the means of procuring the wines, spirituous liquors, &c., imported from foreign countries.

"*Resolved*, That there appears to be no substantial difference between a duty on what is manufactured from the produce of a country and the produce in its natural state, except, perhaps, that in the first instance the article is more deserving of the encouragement of wise legislation, as promotive of industry, the population and strength of the country at large. The excise on home-made spirituous liquors, affects particularly the raising of grain, especially rye, and there can be no solid reason for taxing it more than any other article of the growth of the United States.

"*Resolved*, That the foregoing representations be presented to the Legislature of the United States.

"*Resolved*, That the following remonstrance be presented to the Legislature of Pennsylvania.

"*Resolved*, That the following address, together with the whole proceedings of this committee, which were unanimously adopted, be printed in the Pittsburgh *Gazette*."

Signed by order of the committee.
EDWARD COOK, *Chairman*.

In August, 1792, another meeting was held at Pittsburgh, and the following resolutions were adopted:

"That whereas, some men may be found amongst us, so far lost to every sense of virtue, and feelings for the distresses of their country, as to accept the office of collector of the duty.

"*Resolved*, Therefore, that in future we will consider such persons as unworthy of our friendship, have no intercourse or dealings with them, withdraw from them every assistance, withhold all the comforts of life which depend upon those duties that as men and fellow citizens we owe to each other, and upon all occasions treat them with that contempt they deserve; and that it be, and it is hereby most earnestly recommended to the people at large, to follow the same line of conduct toward them."

These resolutions, with those adopted on former occasions, are enumerated by Secretary Hamilton among the causes of the insurrection. This was attaching too much importance to them, and as was stated by Col. Neville, the opposition to the excise law did not seem greater after their passage than before it. The first resolutions, although badly worded, give a fair expression of the popular feeling, and certainly do not exceed the limits of lawful remonstrance. The second, two years before the insurrection, are intemperate, and rather calculated to do harm to the authors, than to injure the government.

Lynn's Case.—The different manner in which the same occurrence may be related by different persons, may be seen by contrasting the account of this affair, as given by Secretary Hamilton, in his report of August, 1794, and that of D. Carnahan, afterward President of Princeton College, who writes from personal knowledge. The following is the statement of the Secretary:

"About midnight on the 6th of June, a number of persons, armed and painted black, broke into the house of John Lynn, where the office was kept. By promises of safety to himself and his house, they treacherously got him into their power, when they seized and tied him, threatening to hang him. They carried him to a retired part of the neighboring woods, and there after cutting off his hair, and tarring and feathering him, they compelled him to swear that he would never allow his house to be used again as an office, never again to have any agency in the excise and never to disclose their names. After this they bound him naked to a tree and left him in that situation till the morning, when he succeeded in extricating himself. Not content with this, the rioters came again, pulled down part of his house, and compelled him to become an exile from his own home."

The other account differs from the above, as the reader will see. "The first acts of violence were done to the deputy inspectors, men generally of low character, who had very little sensibility, and who were willing, for the paltry emolument of the office, to incur the censure and contempt of their fellow citizens. These sub-excise men were seized by thoughtless young men, and received a coat of tar and feathers, more through sport than from deliberate design to oppose the law. Of several cases of this kind which occurred, I shall mention one, which in part fell under my notice. About the last of June or first of July, 1794, John Lynn, a deputy inspector, residing in Canonsburg, Washington county, was taken from his bed, carried into the woods and received a coat of tar and feathers, and he was left tied to a tree, but so loosely that he could easily extricate himself. He returned to his house, and after undergoing an ablution with grease and soap, and sand and water, he exhibited himself to the boys in the academy and others, and laughed and made sport of the whole matter."—Carnahan, p. 120.

CHAPTER II.

POPULAR OUTBREAK — ATTACK ON THE MARSHAL — DESTRUCTION OF NEVILLE'S HOUSE — ALARM IN PITTSBURGH — ESCAPE OF THE MARSHAL AND INSPECTOR.

HITHERTO the opposition to the excise only manifested itself in the general dissatisfaction with the law, and occasionally in unconnected acts of resistance and violence by individuals, but within the control of the ordinary administration of justice. We now enter upon the relation of those more extensive and serious riots which have been dignified with the name of "insurrection." After the most careful investigation, and the lapse of half a century, there has been no evidence adduced that a single individual had any settled design to make war against the government, for the purpose of overturning it; or that the great body of the people had any other aim in their unpremeditated violence, than to cause a repeal of what they regarded as an oppressive and unequal law! It does not even appear that their ordinary civil magistrates had been prevented from exercising their functions, or that the judges, justices of the peace and executive officers throughout the four western counties, had been absolutely superseded, even in the case of the excise law, although for a time the laws appeared to be silent. No people, we repeat, were ever more habitually, and even religiously, obedient to the law and magistrates than the people of Western Pennsylvania; and yet they did not consider it *immoral*, or treasonable, to resist in every way a particular law by "intemperate resolutions," and even by direct acts of violence. They had before them the example of their British ancestors, in Hampden, Cromwell and Pym, and more recently in the patriots of the Revolution, who encountered the stamp excise by "intemperate resolutions," and other odious measures of the British government, by violence, both open and disguised. During two years, they carried on a bloody war with the British sovereign, before taking the revolutionary step of their Declaration of Independence. It is true, the cry of treason had been raised against them; but were they traitors? No; and their enemies were compelled to refrain from treating them as such. It is also true that the case of those whose history I am about to relate, was different from that to which I have alluded; they were living under a government of their own choice, under a constitution which they had sanctioned, and under laws made by their own representatives. But let it be remembered that these establishments were recent; that old habits and opinions do not change suddenly, and although the educated and intelligent part of the community understood the difference, the great body of the people had not yet been trained to the new system and to the new ideas. It is also certain that those in authority had likewise something to learn and correct in their views of government—especially in their ideas on the subject of treason and sedition, which they retained as a part of the dross of monarchy, not yet purged away by the purer workings of republican institutions. The law of treason, as laid down by Chief Justice Marshall, on the trial of Aaron Burr, has completely banished the constructive or implied offense; there can be no treason except that which is exactly defined by the constitution and the laws; the attempt to overthrow the government itself, and not the mere opposition to particular laws or public agents, although accompanied by mob violence. Notwithstanding one or two convictions for treason, growing out of the Western riots, yet, according to the present well established doctrine, there was not a single overt act of treason committed or proved; and were the same cases to be tried now, the more enlightened tribunals of to-day—more enlightened, at least, on this subject—would not hesitate to declare the prosecutions for treason unwarranted. It does not follow, because it is the duty of the historian thus to discriminate, that he must approve the illegal acts; but they may be reduced in degree from treason to high misdemeanor: at the same time that the motive, or intention, may be weighed by him in estimating the moral turpitude of the offense. The law constitutionally enacted, until it be constitutionally repealed, must be obeyed; to suppose any higher law, or moral obligation, capable of sanctioning disobedience, is nothing short of anarchy.

Major Lenox, the Marshal, (the Federal sheriff, as the officer was generally called,) arrived in Pittsburgh about the 14th of July, 1794, after having served all but one of the forty writs against delinquent distillers, and without having met the slightest insult or opposition. The last was against a person of the name of Miller, whose house he passed, when he might have served the writ if he had thought proper; but unfortunately, before doing this he proceeded to Pittsburgh, probably to make his report to the Inspector, Gen. Neville. The next day he returned to Miller's in company with this gentleman, but after serving the writ, they were followed by a party of armed men, and one gun was fired;

but without effect. It is probable that it was not the intention of the assailants to injure them; every one at that time was a marksman, and seldom went from home without his rifle, with which he could strike off the head of a squirrel or pheasant at pleasure. This occurrence took place in the midst of the harvest, which usually brought a number of persons together in every neighborhood. The time was regarded as a kind of Saturnalia, when liquor was freely drunk by those who assembled to assist each other in taking off the grain with the sickle, no speedier method being then in use. With the blood already heated, it is not surprising that the additional circumstance just related heightened the exasperation. July may almost be designated the revolutionary month. It is possible that if the Marshal had gone alone, such was the habitual deference to the civil authority, that no opposition would have been made; but it was a different matter when accompanied by the excise officer, their own neighbor, against whom the country people had become incensed. Neville was regarded in a different light from the "Federal sheriff." There was a great contrast between his former professions and his thus piloting the officer to their forest homes, for the purpose of serving writs which would lead to the certain ruin of the delinquents. His acceptance of an odious office, merely for the sake of the emolument, as it was believed, when he was already the wealthiest man in the West, had not only deprived him of his former popularity, but rendered him an object of hatred. To this feeling of the people against the Inspector personally, has been ascribed in some degree the violence against the law in his neighborhood, where the insurrection, if it may be so termed, first broke out, and to which it was chiefly confined.

After the occurrence just related, the Marshal returned to Pittsburgh, and the Inspector to his house in the country, about seven miles from town. There had been on the same day at the Mingo Creek regimental rendezvous, not far from the scene of the assault, an assembly of the regiment, in order to form a select corps of militia, as their quota of the eighty thousand men required by the act of Congress.* In the evening, when about to separate, they heard of the service of the writ on Miller by the Marshal, in company with the Inspector, and of his having been fired upon. A party was made up, (it does not appear whether it was with the knowledge of any but those who composed it,) headed by one Holcroft,† (a person

---

* This is no proof of any premeditated design to overturn the government, certainly! See Findley.

† Holcroft was the supposed author of certain pasquinades, under the name of "Tom the Tinker;" they were in the nature of warnings to those who entered

of little note,) consisting of thirty-six others, who went early next morning, July 16th, with arms to the house of General Neville. It seems that being apprehensive of an attack he had been prepared, having armed his negroes. The assailing party, on being hailed, answering in a suspicious manner, were fired on from the house, and at the same time from the negro quarters; the party fired in return, but being thus unexpectedly attacked from the quarters, they retreated, having six wounded, one mortally.*

Whatever might be the causes which produced the popular state of mind, the Inspector was justifiable in defending his house when attacked; but it is questioned whether he was not blamable in being the first to fire, without being made acquainted with the intentions of the party, and using every precaution to avoid this lamentable necessity. They were not Indians, or plunderers, or robbers. Perhaps bloodshed might have been avoided. But blood being once shed, it was not in the nature of things for the matter to rest here. Blood had been spilled, and the populace, without stopping to reason, would be excited to renewed violence. It is to be remarked, that the mobs formed by the country population differ from those of towns, where there is always more or less of the materials of which genuine mobs are composed; a large proportion of such having no motive but the love of mischief. On this occasion they were composed of the rural population, actuated by a sense of real or fancied injuries, and mixed up with a smaller proportion of the dregs of society. We may take it for granted, that whatever may be the case with town mobs, the rising of the country people, especially so thinly scattered as it was in this quarter, furnishes a strong presumption of an honest, even if it be a mistaken, sense of injury and oppression. Those who are the primary cause of such movements, prefer tracing them to the instigation of a few

their stills under the law, that the Tinker would pay them a visit to mend, that, is to destroy them. The soubriquette became conspicuous, but Holcroft himself was of no importance during the " Whiskey Insurrection."

---

* "I desired him to give me the particulars of the attack on Neville's house the first day. He did so; he said they had about thirty-six men with fifteen guns, six only in order. They found the General just got up; after some words, he fired first. It was from the windows. A horn was blowing in the house the time of the firing. 'Was the door open?' said I. 'It was,' said he. 'Why then did you not rush into the entry?' 'We were afraid,' said he, 'that he had a swivel or a big gun there.' 'The negroes,' continued Miller, 'by this time fired out of their cabins upon our backs, and shot several; and we got off as well as we could.'"
—Incidents, I. 122, Miller's statement to Mr. Brackenridge.

ASSEMBLAGE AT COUCHE'S FORT.

designing demagogues, imposing on the simplicity of the people, instead of ascribing them to their own unwise and unjust measures.

The "intemperate resolutions," to which so much evil was ascribed, as already remarked, were not the causes of the popular excitement, but the effect. That excitement existed before, and the expression of it might even serve as a safety valve, to lessen its intensity. If no serious discontent existed, the mere passage of the resolutions would be insufficient to produce it, although no doubt they would help to fan the flame.

It is stated by Mr. Brackenridge,* that toward the middle of the next day, the Inspector, Col. Presley Neville, who resided in the town, had received a letter from his father, in the country, informing him that a large number were said to be collecting at a place known by the name of Couche's Fort, about four miles distant from his house. The son expressed to him his apprehensions for the situation of his father, and on asking Col. Neville what he supposed to be the object of their assemblage, he answered that it was to require his father to deliver his commission. "Deliver it, then," said Mr. Brackenridge; but this was answered by a peremptory negative. The reason given for this advice was "to put by the storm for the present, until the civil authority could interpose, and bring to account individually those who had disturbed the peace. If the mob who had burned the house of Lord Mansfield, in the riot in London, could have been put off by a delivery of his commission, it is presumed that he would have delivered up the parchment, as another could have been prepared." In a community almost purely democratic, where there was no military force to compel obedience, the people themselves, who constituted the mob, being the only force to apply to, it was useless for the few and unarmed to resist. It is possible that a sufficient number of the friends of the Inspector, and those disposed to encounter the risk, might have been collected to attempt a defense, which would have cost many lives: but from the overwhelming numbers opposed to them with increased exasperation, they would ultimately be subdued. By thus giving way to them, the attempt might afterward be made to bring them to justice by means of constables, sheriffs and judges. At least, this temporary yielding to the storm could not make it any worse, and might have been successful, which the other could not be; and when left to themselves, the people, many by their own reflections, would come to see the impropriety of their conduct. In arbitrary, despotic governments, the favorite, and almost only method pursued, is that of

* Incidents, p. 6.

dragooning people into submission,* and at the same time of considering every popular expression of dissatisfaction with their rulers as treasonable, or at least seditious. Mr. Brackenridge, afterward so conspicuous in these unfortunate transactions, had hitherto taken no active part for or against the excise laws, although entertaining the common opinion, and which had been held by the Neville's themselves previous to their taking office. He had not attended the meeting, which two years before had passed the "intemperate resolutions," which according to the Secretary of the Treasury, had sown the seeds of the insurrection. He had, however, appeared professionally for some of the defendants in court, and was naturally supposed to be identified in feeling with the people, and erroneously expected to go to all lengths. He was also popular, at the head of the Western Bar, and at this time, a candidate for Congress. These circumstances rendered his actions liable to misconception, and afforded an opportunity to his enemies, to misrepresent it. Col. Presley Neville, (son of the Inspector,) with but little energy of character, although possessing many fine qualities, appears to have had a large share of that cavalier pride, which does not know how to yield until it is too late. This was the misfortune of greater men, on more important occasions.

In the afternoon of the same day, the 17th, Gen. Wilkins, Brigadier General of the militia, called on Mr. Brackenridge, and informed him that a demand had been made by Col. Neville, in the name of his father, on Major General Gibson and himself, to call out the militia, to suppress the threatened riot, and requesting his opinion as a lawyer as to the power under the law to comply with his request. Mr. Brackenridge thought the power to call out the military rested in the Governor, by construction of the clause in the constitution, which makes it his duty "to see that the laws are faithfully executed." Gen. Wilkins shortly after returned, and stated that Col. Neville had applied to him and General Gibson, as judges of the court, to raise the *posse comitatus*, and again

*While this is very true of the arbitrary and despotic ruler, it is equally true of the mob; as the following anecdote related by Mr. Brackenridge will show. "I knew a man nearly related to me, (his brother, John Brackenridge,) on Brushy run, in Washington county, who, having no gun, sat two nights in his cabin, with his axe in his hand, to defend himself against his captain, of the name of Sharp, who had threatened his life for not going to the burning of Neville's house, agreeable to summons. He yielded on the order to go to Braddock's Field, and appeared there with a crooked horn by his side, but had no powder in it. He saw, as he went along, the tomahawk drawn over the heads of men, at their breakfast or dinner, and obliged to march."—Incidents, II. p. 64.

requested legal information.* He was told by Mr. Brackenridge that this was a power which belonged to the sheriff, and he suggested that he should be called upon. The sheriff and judges, shortly after, met at a public house, and sent a request to the lawyer to attend them for the purpose of consulting as to the law, the sheriff having doubted his authority. The power of the sheriff was fully explained; but although convinced that he possessed the power, he was of the opinion, that in the situation of the country it was impracticable. The mob itself was the posse, at least out of the town, and even if every man capable of bearing arms, in town, could be assembled, it would be greatly outnumbered; and besides, the fear of bringing the country upon them, would prevent them from going; and it was possible that some of them being connected in the country, sympathized with the rioters. It was then admitted on all hands, that neither the militia nor the posse were available. The United States soldiers at the garrison were not thought of; for besides their being too few in numbers, they could not be legally called out to aid the civil authority, at the pleasure of the commanding officer. Mr. Brackenridge, seeing these difficulties, proposed that the judges and sheriff, himself accompanying them, should go to the assemblage of the people, and try the effect of persuasion, as force in opposition to them was now evidently out of the question.

Having hastily mounted their horses, they proceeded to cross the river, on their way. At the ferry they fell in with Col. Neville, Marshal Lenox, and a young man of the name of Ormsby. Mr. Brackenridge relates that these three persons were armed, which he considered imprudent, and addressing himself to the young man, with whose family he was on terms of friendship, said: "What! armed!" "Yes," said he. "You will not ride with us armed." "You may go as you please," said Ormsby, "we will go armed." Col. Neville, who was mounted on a gay horse, with pistols in holsters, spoke: "We are not all born orators; we are going to fight, you to speak." "I thought him a better chevalier than a judge of the occasion," observes Mr. Brackenridge. The sequel proved this observation to be correct. The parties took different roads and separated— Neville's party taking the direct course to his father's house, the other pursuing the less frequented road to Couche's Fort, where they expected to find the persons who had collected with the intention of attacking the house of the Inspector. On their way they found the harvest fields deserted by

* In Pennsylvania, the district or presiding judge, is assisted by two associates, who are not required to be lawyers by profession—usually some private citizen of standing and character.

the men, and only women were to be seen. On coming within half a mile of the place they received information that the main body had marched for Neville's house. They set out with haste to overtake them, but when within a mile and a half of Neville's they learned that all was over; that the house had been burned, and that the people were returning, in a great rage at the loss of their leader, M'Farlane. It was thought not advisable to go further in the present state of things, nor safe to remain, lest their coming might be misconstrued; it was then agreed by all to return to Pittsburgh. Mr. Brackenridge had proposed to proceed alone to the house, but the proposition was not well received; it was thought that all should go or none.*

With respect to Neville's party, they had arrived at the outguard, (for it seems that a guard had been posted on the road in military style,) about the time the firing on the house commenced. Neville, on his first advance to the guard, cried out, "If there is a gentleman amongst you, let him come out and speak to me." This quixotic speech might have been fatal to him, as it was an offense to all, and several raised their pieces to fire, when, with some presence of mind and changing the tone of his voice, he cried out that he was not armed, which he might say, as he had not yet drawn his pistols from the holsters. He and his companions were made prisoners, and put under guard. Neville insisted much on being permitted to go forward, and would engage that any demand short of life should be complied with. In a short time he was compelled to witness the agonizing spectacle of the house in flames, uncertain of the fate of his father and family, or whether they were in the house or not. When the rioters were about to disperse, Neville and the Marshal were in great personal danger; some of the rioters having by this time become intoxicated. Young Ormsby, being known to many of them, was treated with some indignity and rudeness. The Marshal also, after some time, having stipulated to serve no more process west of the mountains, and to surrender himself when demanded, Neville becoming his sponsor—they were both permitted to go. They had demanded of the Marshal that he would engage not to return the process already served; this with a firmness which commanded respect, he refused to accede to, alleging that in complying with it he would violate his oath of office. The Marshal, after leaving the main body, was again taken by an out-party, many of them intoxicated, and

---

* He has been censured for not going to the house; but no reason is given why it was more incumbent on him to go than on the others whom he accompanied! It was less so, because he had no official duty to require his going. If he had gone he would probably have been accused of having an understanding with the rioters.

carried toward Couche's Fort, to which they were returning. His life was in danger. For some time he was in charge of James M'Alister, who had rescued him from great peril, but had given his word to the more violent, not to suffer him to escape. After some time M'Alister surrendered him to Col. David Phillips, who advanced some distance before the crowd, and was entreated by the Marshal to suffer him to escape. Phillips told him that his own life would answer for it. He was at last, just as they approached the main body with the corpse of M'Farlane, prevailed upon to show him a road in a certain direction, and suffer him to escape. He got in the main road toward Pittsburgh, and about two o'clock in the morning came to town.

We will now return to the assemblage at Couche's Fort on the 17th of July, and give some account of the proceedings. The habit of the Anglo-Saxon, especially of the American branch, of acting where numbers are engaged, under some kind of organization, civil or military, was displayed on this occasion. The assemblage was a part of Hamilton's regiment, and they came under the command of their officers, none of whom, except the Colonel, dared to refuse to lead their companies, however much against their inclination; and many probably shared in the inflamed state of the public mind, while others accompanied their men in the hope of being able to restrain them from acts of violence. The greater number of the privates were farmers and their sons; although there were others, such as are always to be found on such occasions, of a less scrupulous character. A venerable and aged clergyman, Mr. Clark, who attended the meeting, addressed them and used, to no purpose, every argument to dissuade them from their designs. Those whom he addressed were, with few exceptions, emigrants or their descendants from the North of Ireland, from the military colonies established after the natives had been expelled. They constituted also a large proportion of the population of the midland counties of the State, especially of Franklin and Cumberland; they are a religious, as well as a warlike race, qualities inherited from their ancestors, as well as their dislike to excises and excise officers. The names of the M'Farlanes, the Crawfords, the Hamiltons, the Bradys, the Butlers and the Calhouns, show their origin. Although strict Presbyterians, and usually obedient to their clergy, they neither considered it immoral nor unpatriotic, to oppose the execution of a bad law. The earnest admonitions of the venerable clergyman were disregarded. They thought him in his dotage; or as having skill in spiritual affairs, but not in the temporal interests of the country. It is barely possible that if the party of Mr. Brackenridge had arrived in time, the advice of a lawyer in whom they placed confidence, representing the unlawfulness of what they were about, and the probable consequences, and this backed by the friendly representations of the judges and sheriff, might have had better success. Many among the leaders would no doubt have been glad of an excuse to drop the undertaking; but this, although deserving an experiment, is uncertain. It is most likely that their passions had been too much inflamed to think of a retreat; and those in favor of it, especially after having contributed to the excitement, would be afraid to propose such a thing. There was also a hope among the more reasonable that Neville, seeing the formidable force before his house, and the utter uselessness of resistance, would have given up the papers which they had come to demand, and the destruction of property and loss of life might thus be prevented. But for the imprudence of those left in defense of the house, this would have been the case. The number is supposed to have been about five hundred, mostly armed. The first act was to appoint a committee like those of the National Commissioners of the French. This committee offered the command to Benjamin Parkinson, who excused himself as not having military knowledge. James M'Farlane was then nominated, and he agreed to accept. He was a major of militia, and had served with reputation as a lieutenant in the war with Great Britain, from the beginning to the end of it; was a man of good private character, and had acquired a very handsome property in trade after the close of the war.

The body having marched and approached the house, the horses were left under a guard, and arrangements made for an attack, should it be necessary. It seems that, in the mean time, those in the house were prepared. Early in the morning, having marched before day, Major Kirkpatrick had arrived with eleven soldiers, obtained from the commandant of the United States garrison, a circumstance unknown to the assailants as well as to the civil officers before mentioned; in fact, to all but the Nevilles and the commanding officer of the garrison. A flag was sent from the committee to demand the delivery of the Inspector's commission and official papers, a practice for which there were precedents previous to the Revolutionary war in the case of the stamp excise. From the withdrawal of the Inspector, it would appear that he did not count on being able to defend the house against the overwhelming force coming against him. It is asked, why not give orders not to attempt a defense? It has been conjectured that he did; but his brother-in-law, Kirkpatrick, being a mere soldier, judged less prudently, and determined to make the attempt. On the return of the flag, it being communicated that the Inspector had left the house, a second flag was sent, and a demand made that six persons should be permitted to search for his papers, and take them. This was refused; and notice was then given by a third flag for the wife of the Inspector and any other female of the family to withdraw;* they accordingly did, and the attack commenced. About fifteen minutes after the commencement, a flag was presented from the house, upon which M'Farland, stepping from a tree behind which he had stood, and commanding a cessation of firing, received a ball near the groin, and almost instantly expired.† The firing then continued, and a message was sent to the committee, who were sitting at some distance, to know whether the house should be stormed; but in the meanwhile fire had been set to a barn and to other buildings adjoining the mansion house, and in a short time the intenseness of the heat and the evident communicability of the flame to the house compelled those within to call for quarter; on which the firing ceased, and they were desired to come out and surrender themselves. The soldiers, three of whom were said to be wounded, were suffered to pass by, and go where they pleased. Major Kirkpatrick had nearly passed, when he was distinguished from the soldiers, and ordered to deliver his musket, which he refused; when one presenting a gun to his breast, he dropped on his knee and asked for quarter.

The buildings were all consumed, excepting a small out-house, over which a guard was placed on being informed by the negroes that it contained their bacon. When the house was in flames the cellar was broken open, the liquors rolled out and drank. Kirkpatrick, after being carried some distance under guard, was taken by David Hamilton behind him on horseback; when, thinking himself protected, he began to answer those who came up occasionally with indignant language, when Hamilton said to him, "You see I am endeavoring to save you at the risk of my own safety, and yet you are making it still more dangerous for me." On this, he was silent; and being carried some distance further by Hamilton, he was advised to make his escape, which he did.

* The author has heard it related as a common rumor, that the ladies had withdrawn, and that, after this notification, the Inspector, who was still in the house, escaped in female attire on a horse with a side-saddle, brought to the door!

† The following epitaph was lately copied from the tombstone in the Mingo Creek graveyard:

"Here lies the body of Captain James M'Farlane, of Washington county, Pa., who departed this life the 17th of July, 1794, aged 43 years.

"He served during the war with undaunted courage in defense of American independence, against the lawless and despotic encroachments of Great Britain. He fell at last by the hands of an unprincipled villain, in the support of what he supposed to be the rights of his country, much lamented by a numerous and respectable circle of acquaintance."

Notwithstanding the rolling out the liquors and drinking them, there is not to be found in the history of riots an instance of greater forbearance and less of savage ferocity. So much the historian owes to truth, while he condemns the folly and madness and the guilt of the outrage. It has no parallel with the revolutionary measures practiced about the same period by the savage peasantry of France, or more brutal mob of Paris. Although enraged by the fall of their favorite leader, whom they believed to have been a victim to treachery, they showed no disposition for cruel or vindictive retaliation. It is deemed of sufficient importance by Findley to contradict the assertion of the Secretary of the Treasury, who states that when the committee demanded the Inspector's papers, they were answered that they might send persons to search the house, and take away whatever papers they might find pertaining to his office. But not satisfied with this, they insisted unconditionally that the armed men who were in the house for its defense, should march out and ground their arms, which Major Kirkpatrick peremptorily refused; and that this put an end to the parley. Findley asserts, and correctly, that this is unsupported by the testimony taken on oath in the Circuit Court, and is entirely without foundation. It is certainly at variance with the fact that the assailants had no knowledge that Kirkpatrick was in the house with the United States soldiers; and it is also at variance with the account of Mr. Brackenridge. Allowance is to be made for the statement of the Secretary, who was endeavoring to make out a case of open rebellion, in the attack on a regular garrison of the United States; otherwise, it could be considered nothing more than a riot on the part of the assailants. The illegal employment of soldiers would not be so lightly passed over at the present day; perhaps the coloring attempted to be given to the affair was intended as an excuse for employing them.

This unfortunate occurrence took place only three days after the first assault on the Inspector and the Marshal, when serving the writ on Miller, which was succeeded by the abortive attempt on the house. It may be regarded as another scene of the same act—a continuation of the same offense, confined to a small portion of the western country, and to the immediate neighbors of Gen. Neville; for it does not appear that a single person residing in Pittsburgh was accused of taking part in it. If Col. Neville had been so fortunate as to have reached the house in time, there is a probability that the papers would have been given up, and the mob would have dispersed; but the matter was left to a soldier who knew nothing but to fight. If those papers had been surrendered, the insurrection would probably have extended no further, and would have ended where it first broke out, as there would have been no destruction of property or loss of life to incite to further and more violent measures of desperation.

The loss of private property was considerable, but afterward made good, it is believed, by an act of Congress.* An advertisement was about this time inserted in the newspapers by Presley Neville, calculated to give much offense. It related to some government certificates of funded debt, which were said to be *stolen*, and warned the public against any forged transfers, &c. These certificates being registered, were neither lost to the owners, nor could they be available to any one else. Those who had been engaged in the destruction of the house were not thieves or robbers, although violaters of the law. It was regarded as an unnecessary display of contempt for the people, and tended to increase the unpopularity of the Neville connection, which consisted of four influential and wealthy families, all enjoying offices and the favor of the government, and hitherto the favor of the people, who were thus unnecessarily provoked. The Nevilles had been injured, it is true, but they had in some measure brought it on themselves by their own acts. They had lost property, at least for the present, but they were regarded as the cause of shedding the blood of their fellow citizens, whether blamably or not, is a question about which there may be a difference of opinion.†

The day after the destruction of the house of the Inspector, David Hamilton, a justice of the peace, and accompanied by John Black, came to Pittsburgh, with an authority from the committee to demand of the Marshal the surrender of the writs which had been served, agreeably to his engagement, as they said, and for which Col. Neville had become sponsor. A conference took place, and it was denied on the part of the Marshal and Neville, that there had been any engagement, except not to make any service. It was understood otherwise on the part of Hamilton, who thought it of little importance to make no further service, as it could be of no use to those on whom the process had been already served. This led to the question, whether the Marshal was bound to return, and what would be the effect of the return? Whether judgment could be taken

---

*Act 5th February, 1795, 6th vol. U. S. at large, p. 20—"entitled an act to provide some present relief for the officers of government, and other citizens, who have suffered in their property by the insurgents of Western Pennsylvania."

† They certainly possessed the right of self-defense, but their previous conduct as respects the excise, and their relation to the people, must be taken into view before we pronounce them entirely blameless. If, according to Alexander Hamilton, the mere *opposition to the law* led to the insurrection, then the Nevilles must share the censure with their neighbors, for they had been equally opposed to it before their appointment to office.

which would bind the lands here so that they could be sold in Philadelphia?

The Marshal conceived it to be only an initiatory process, on which final order could not be taken; and that there must be another writ, and service of it, before judgment. Mr. Brackenridge was again consulted, and gave an opinion at the instance of the Marshal and Neville, which was to the effect that the process was similar to the subpœna in chancery, which must be first served before issuing the attachment; and that no judgment could be entered without another writ, the present process being merely a summons to show cause. Copies of this opinion were given to Hamilton, who thought that this would not satisfy the committee; that if the people had known that the Marshal was bound to return the writs, he doubted much if he ever would have got off the ground! The officer, on being informed of this, was convinced of the danger of his situation; it was impossible for him to satisfy the people, and extremely difficult to leave the country, the public roads, it was supposed, being completely guarded. In leaving the country, under these circumstances, Neville would be exposed to their vengeance, as he had become responsible for him. Mr. Brackenridge, from a willingness to serve Neville, proposed to proceed in person to the committee, and endeavor to convince them that there was nothing to fear from the return of the writs, and at the same time offer his services to go to Philadelphia for them. It was understood that the committee was sitting at Shockan's tavern, four miles from Pittsburgh, and the idea had been held out by Hamilton and Black, that there was a large body of men in that vicinity. This was done for their own safety, as they were not without apprehensions of being arrested in town. This circumstance shows the state of feeling between it and the country. Mr. Brackenridge, however, required that he should be accompanied by one or two more persons, feeling the delicacy of communicating with the rioters, unless in the presence of witnesses. Several offered to accompany him, who afterward made their excuses; but a person of the name of Johnston, who had been a deputy collector, and was a tenant of Neville, declaring his willingness to go, they set out in company. On their way Hamilton informed Mr. Brackenridge that he had, agreeably to the orders given him, demanded of the Inspector a resignation of his commission; that the two Nevilles had agreed to the resignation, and had written something to that effect, but it appearing to be merely conditional, it was rejected by him. He was apprehensive that the consequence would be bad; that there would be no restraining the people from coming to Pittsburgh to take him; that he was apprehensive, also, that they would demand the Marshal, or, at least, detain him a prisoner, to prevent his returning the writs. Such was the strange inconsistency of setting the government at defiance, and yet fearing the return of the legal process! Hamilton declared that it was to prevent mischief that he had proposed coming to Pittsburgh; that the people assembled at the interment of M'Farlane were in a violent rage, and proposed marching to the town to take the Marshal and Inspector. He declared, with respect to the former, that it was better that one man should die than so many persons, with their families, should lose their plantations. He further expressed the opinion, that on that day there would not be an excise office standing in the survey.

It is important to note the language of desperation, to show the state of mind to which the people had been wrought up, in consequence of their supposed grievances, and the recent acts of violence. It was the spontaneous working of their feelings, not the effect of the traitorous arts of demagogues, for the purpose of gratifying their wicked designs against the government, as has been so frequently represented by the Secretary of the Treasury and the supporters of the administration. Those who most unqualifiedly denounced the insurgents could not admit this fact without, at the same time, admitting that there was cause for complaint, although manifested in this short-sighted and unlawful mode.

It was ascertained by the party on the way that there was no committee in session nearer than the place of interment of M'Farlane. They proceeded to the house of the deputy Johnston, who made out and delivered in writing to Hamilton, his resignation as deputy collector, and which was afterward published in the Pittsburgh *Gazette*.* The next day the party, accompanied by the deputy, went to look for the body of a person who, it was supposed, had been killed at the time of the attack by the party under Holcroft, but it was not found until some days afterward, by the negroes, by whom it was buried. Hamilton and Black solicited Mr. Brackenridge to accompany them to the committee, but he excused himself. In fact, it was necessary for him to use the utmost caution in being seen among the rioters, without having some one with him to testify to his conduct.

During the same afternoon, while a violent storm of wind prevailed on the river, the Marshal and the Inspector took their departure in a boat to descend the Ohio, intending to effect their escape through the western

---

* " Finding the opposition to the revenue law more violent than I expected; regretting the mischief that has been done, and may, from the continuance of measures; seeing the opposition changed from a disguised rabble to a respectable party, I think it my duty, and do resign my commission. ROBERT JOHNSTON."

part of Virginia, and which they accomplished. There had been a rumor the day before that a large party was on its way to pull down the Inspector's office in Pittsburgh, and it was feared they would proceed to other enormities. It was the cry of the inhabitants, that rather than provoke the country, and bring an infuriated people upon them, it would be best to pull down the office themselves! The evening of the arrival of Hamilton and Black, the account of two having come was swelled to two hundred, and it was said there were a thousand on the hill on the other side of the river. The people were gazing everywhere; every one thought he saw some, and of course dressed in hunting shirts, the usual garb of riflemen. Application was made to the two men, stating particularly that the females of the Neville family were uneasy, and requesting one of them to cross the river and ascertain the truth. Black went over, and returned with the information that there were none there, or that they had dispersed. Major Craig, the son-in-law of the Inspector, after the departure of the Marshal, took down the paper on the Inspector's office, and called a gentleman to witness (Mr. Lang, of Brownsville), that it was down. He also offered the fragments to that gentleman, to bear to the country to convince them of the fact!

NOTES TO CHAPTER II.

The author of the "Incidents" says: "From the town the people could not have been commanded. Many of them had connections in the country, and would not submit to an order to take up arms against them. Besides, they had themselves a good deal of the same spirit of opposition to the laws; not so much from any consideration of the law, or its effects, but because it was patriotic and fashionable language. Others, as is natural, wished for something new; and would rather have joined them than fought against them. It is a fact, that some influential men and commanders in the militia, were heard to say that day, that if they were ordered out, and were to fight at all, it would be with the people. Thus the cause of the people and that of the government, were thought to be different things."

Notwithstanding the feelings above described, which would induce a large proportion to be passive, or even to give their sympathies to the country people, the majority were silently in favor of "law and order." The author continues:

"But even with the best disposition in the town of Pittsburgh, a concern for their general interest, as mechanics and shopkeepers, would render them reluctant to enter into a contest with the country, whence a great part of their custom came; and a concern for their immediate safety would prevent them altogether. They would reflect, the most ignorant of them, that the militia of the town, about 250 men, were they unanimous and spirited in support of government, would be nothing to the country; which would, in the next instance, after an attack on the excise officer, turn itself against the town. It could starve them out, and the garrison with them, by an interdict of provisions; or, as was threatened afterward, it could plunder, and burn. It would have been extreme cruelty to force the inhabitants to this danger. It would have been extreme impolicy; and would have answered no other end than to show the rioters the strength even they had in the town. The situation of the town became much more critical after the burning of Neville's house; there being none of the town's people in the riot, and it being known that the Inspector had many friends there, the whole town was regarded as in opposition to the county, and hence the inhabitants were regarded with distrust and even with enmity. It was safest to let the matter rest unknown. Persuasion for the moment, and the steady and accustomed step of civil authority, by the known officers afterward, were the only means that were eligible. The raising the posse of the county, as a legal act, was a thing unknown to the people, and would not be understood. It would be considered as the party of the excise officer, disposed to try their strength with the friends of liberty. It would have been a most rash act. I will trace what would have been the consequence. The posse could have been raised, or it could not. If it could not have been raised, the weakness of the government and the strength of the rioters was discovered by the experiment. If it could have been raised, and brought forward, a contest would have taken place, and lives been lost. The victory must have been on the side of the rioters, for the strength of the country was with them. The plundering and destruction of the town would have ensued. The garrison would have been stormed and taken; for there was not at that time more than a day's provision in it. The whole country would have been involved instantly. Desperation would have led to prompt and decisive measures. These would be, to cross the mountains, and receive an accession of force, and procure the means, and occupy the ground of war in the midland county."

The author thus speaks of the Neville family or "connection:"

"The Neville family is numerous and wealthy. The Inspector himself, with the advantage of an officer, which though it brings general odium, secures particular dependence; his son, (Col. Neville,) a member of the assembly, brigade inspector, and surveyor of the county; his son-in-law, Major Craig, deputy quarter master, with the care of the military stores, and the employment of mechanics. His brother-in-law, Major Kirkpatrick, commissary, with money and means."

Affidavit of David Hamilton.

Was at Pittsburgh at the request of a committee, in order to converse with Marshal Lenox on the subject of the agreements entered by him with the people after the burning of Neville's house; recollect no private conversation with Mr. Brackenridge, nor any conversation, but on the question which had been put to him respecting the return of the writs, which question was put to him by the consent of Mr. Lenox.

Same day after my return home, I wrote a note to Mr. Brackenridge, informing him of a meeting to be at Mingo Creek, wishing him to come up; it was our concern to mend what was done, and get advice from him as from others, to make what was bad, better; for we had a sense that everything was not right; received no answer, but Mr. Brackenridge came; did not understand Mr. Brackenridge as approving of what was done; in giving his opinion in the case of the writs, it appeared to be his wish to compromise the matter between the Marshal and the people.

City of Philadelphia, ss.

Personally appeared David Hamilton, of Washington county, in the Commonwealth of Pennsylvania, who being sworn, deposeth, that to the best of his knowledge, recollection and belief, the contents of the foregoing writing are just and true.

DAVID HAMILTON.

Sworn 19th day of May, 1795, before me, HILARY BAKER,
one of the Aldermen of Philadelphia.
—Incidents, III. 78, 79.

Affidavit of John Black.

Being about to go to Pittsburgh, fell in with a body of people collecting for the burying of Captain John M'Farlane, who had fallen at burning General Neville's house; David Hamilton had been deputed by a committee of these people to go to Pittsburgh, to return the pistols taken from the Marshal, and to have a fulfillment from him of what had been agreed upon, on his part. Understood from Hamilton, that he had consented to go, in order to prevent the people from coming in themselves, and doing mischief; for there was danger of their going in at that time. Went with Hamilton to Pittsburgh, and met the Marshal and Col. Neville. Hamilton explained his business, returning the pistols, and required a fulfillment of what was agreed upon, viz. that he would serve no further writs, and not return those that were served. The Marshal said he had not agreed not to return the writs. A query was then in the mind of Hamilton, what effect the returns would have. At his request, I went to Mr. Brackenridge, to ask his opinion as a lawyer. He said it was a delicate point, and he would talk to the Marshal. On this he went out, and came in with the Marshal and Col. Neville. Upon that I went out, and after some time returned; and Mr. Brackenridge said he was not much acquainted with the practice of the Federal courts, but would consult, and give his opinion in the morning. He gave his opinion in writing; which Hamilton thought would not be satisfactory to the committee. It was understood that the committee would be sitting till he returned. It was proposed to return by Neville's house; and it was our wish that some of the gentlemen of Pittsburgh should go with us; we wished to see whether a man that was missing, and from what had happened, did not wish to go ourselves. General Gibson, Doctor Bedford, Mr. Brackenridge, and others, had consented to go. The day looking for rain, or for other cause, some declined going. Mr. Brackenridge came; I understood him to be about to go forward to the committee, to see if he could not satisfy the people in respect to the Marshal. In my conversation with Mr. Brackenridge with respect to the burning of General Neville's house, he said it was an unhappy affair, and was afraid it would turn out a civil war, that government would call out the militia, and we were the militia ourselves, and have to be at with one another. He did not say a word to approve what was done, as to the burning of the house, or any act of violence.

Pennsylvania, ss.

Before me, William Meetkirk, in and for the county of Washington, came John Black, and made oath according to law, and saith, that the foregoing statement, to the best of his knowledge and recollections, is just and true.

JOHN BLACK.

Sworn and subscribed before me, May, 1795. WILLIAM MEETKIRK.

CHAPTER III.

THE MINGO CREEK MEETING — VIOLENCE OF BRADFORD — SPEECH OF BRACKENRIDGE — CAUSES OF THE OUTBREAK — CASE OF MILLER.

On Monday, the 21st of July, four days after the burning of the Inspector's house, and the second after the departure of the Marshal, a young man called in the afternoon at the office of Mr. Brackenridge, and delivered him a note from David Hamilton, informing him that the committee was to sit at the Mingo meeting-house the Wednesday following, and expressing a wish that he would be present. Mr. Brackenridge conceived that it was for the object he understood him to have in view on a former occasion, that is, to explain to the people the effect of returning the writs, and inducing them to be satisfied, and refrain from seizing the Marshal, or Col. Neville in his stead. He felt, notwithstanding, some uneasiness at the idea of holding a correspondence with one involved in the guilt of treason, as he then regarded the act of the rioters. He tore up the note and threw it among useless papers in the bottom of a closet, meaning never to make further mention of the matter.

The next day Col. Neville called and asked him "if he had not received a note from David Hamilton?" "I have," said he, "but how came you to the knowledge of it?" said Brackenridge, taking the pieces from the closet and putting them together. Col. Neville was a man of education, and thus assimilating, an apparent friendship had existed between them up to this period, although there was a different feeling on the part of some of the connection with Mr. Brackenridge. The Colonel inquired whether he intended to go, to which the other replied, "Certainly not; their conduct is high treason, and in that offense there are no accessories, all are principals. I have reflected on the subject, and do not consider it safe to go." "I wish you would go," said Neville, "it might answer a good end." Mr. Brackenridge, connecting in his mind the engagement of Neville for the Marshal, which had placed him in a delicate predicament, understood him that he wished him to go to reconcile the people to the circumstance, and perhaps dissuade them from any violent act in future. He was still, however, anxious to decline, even as a personal favor to Neville, but being earnestly solicited, he at length consented, but on condition that Col. Neville would vouch with what sentiments he went, and also provided some person should accompany him, to testify to what he might say or do on the occasion, and which was the same condition as that on which he had agreed to visit the committee two days before. Neville, with this understanding, made personal application to several persons, while some declined, and all appeared reluctant. Mr. Brackenridge also spoke to several. At length the following persons consented to accompany him: George Robinson, the chief burgess; Col. William Semple, Peter Audrain, Josiah Tannehill and William H. Beaumont, all persons of the most respectable standing in the town. We give in the foregoing the statement of Mr. Brackenridge, published the year after in his "Incidents," and which was not contradicted by those interested in doing so. It was, moreover, sufficiently corroborated by the affidavits of the persons chosen to go with him.* It is proper to remark, although in anticipation of the subsequent events, that the pledge thus stated by Mr. Brackenridge was not redeemed, when afterward the mere circumstance of attending the meeting was brought forward against him and others, as evidence of their complicity. This was seriously charged upon Col. Neville by the author of the "Incidents," and no denial attempted. His speech was shamefully misrepresented, but fortunately this misrepresentation is corrected by the affidavits of the persons who accompanied him. A generous acknowledgment of the fact by Neville would have been more consistent with his character, and his silence can be only accounted for from the influence over him possessed by the other members of the connection. This act of simple justice was the more called for, as the circumstance of attending that meeting, without regard to the motive, was afterward considered an act of treason.

These gentlemen set out, and arriving, found, to their surprise, not a committee of persons, but a large assemblage, or mass meeting; some from a distance, but the majority consisting of those who had been engaged in the riot and outrage at the house of the Inspector. If the party had known this, they could not have been induced, under any circumstances, to have left the town. It was thought, however, as there was a number of persons from a distance, and not implicated, that the object of these would be to counsel moderation, and stopping the further progress of violence; besides, if possible, to devise the means of repairing the mischief which had been done. The first act in organizing the meeting seemed to encourage this hope, by the choice of Col. Cook as chairman, and Craig

* See Notes to this chapter.

Ritchie as secretary, two men of high standing, and known to be friends of order and good government. There was, notwithstanding, the appearance of gloom and distrust in the countenances of all, especially of those who had taken an active part in the recent riots. The fury of the moment had passed off, but time had not yet been given for cool reflection; those who were committed began to have some vague idea of being involved in treasonable acts. The gloom of these was not that of sorrow or repentance; the unextinguished fire of rage still glowed in their bosoms, and required but little to fan it into fierceness. No one knew how far to trust his next neighbor; and however much he might be opposed to violence himself, was afraid that the first person he addressed might be one of the *enragé*, and himself suspected of *incivism*, for a vague and undefined apprehension hung over all, rendering life itself insecure.

Dr. Moore, in his admirable work, "Journal of a Residence in France," during the murderous reign of terror, says that "every shop-keeper distrusted his next door neighbor, and did not know but that he might be one of the *enragé*." Hence a mob composed of the very dregs of society, resembling a savage horde rather than a civilized people, were permitted to give vent to their fierce passions without control. But here there had not been, as in France, long ages of oppression by privileged classes; no system of laws fettering the people, and placing them at the mercy and in the power of the few, nor such continuance of this as to debase the masses and debauch the rulers, opposing thus the imbecility of the few to the ignorant and brute force of the many. Among a people who practiced and enforced obedience to authority, it seems impossible that the excise alone, (which appears, by their demands, the Western people knew might be repealed,) could have led to the state of feeling described by the author of the "Incidents," as is evinced in the following extracts:

"Every countenance discovered a strong sense of the solemnity of the occasion, those who had been involved not more than those who were afraid to be involved. It will be asked, how came any one there who was afraid to be involved? I have accounted for my being there; but how came David Bradford, James Marshall, Edward Cook and Craig Ritchie there? I select these instances; as to Marshall and Bradford, I am at a loss to say anything by way of opinion or deduction. I can only state what I have understood from others, or what is within my own knowledge. Not having had the least communication with Marshall or Bradford prior to that day, or on that day, on the subject, I have nothing of my own knowledge. I have understood from others, that after the first attack on the house of the Inspector, when the adjacent country was about to be roused to a second attack, persons went to the town of Washington and called on Marshall and Bradford to come forward on that occasion, which they declined. The expression of Bradford, reported to me, is, 'I cannot act; you may do as you think proper.' He alluded, or was supposed to allude, to his being prosecuting counsel for the Commonwealth, and in that case, not at liberty to do what others might."

"After the destruction of the house, persons went to Marshall and Bradford, demanding of them to come out and support what had been done, or they would burn their houses. They had a claim upon them, as having been conspicuous in the deliberative committees with regard to the excise law, and alleged that Bradford had encouraged them to do what they had done by his words, when he was urged to take part before the burning. 'I encourage?' said he, 'good God! I never thought of such a thing.' 'Yes, you did encourage,' said they, 'and if you do not come forward now and support us, you shall be treated in the same, or worse manner as the excise officer.' He found himself thus under the necessity of taking part, and that being the case, he would seem from that time to have adopted the most violent counsels. Marshall was also obliged to take part, and having done so, to pursue a violent course. I am of opinion that both of these men acted, in the first instance, under a subordination to popular influence. Be this as it may, it is not from a solicitude to make an apology for them that I state this, but from a wish to show the truth of the transaction. Edward Cook also came, probably, at the solicitation and under the fear of the people. Craig Ritchie, and many others, I know did. They had with great difficulty avoided going to the attack on the house of the Inspector, but could not avoid at least the appearance of being with the people now."

The first thing which took place after the opening of the meeting was the reading a letter, which was presented by Benjamin Parkinson, from Col. Neville, (and which had been brought by one of the Pittsburgh party,) stating that his father and the Marshal had left the county; that the Marshal had not considered himself bound by that part of his engagement, which was to surrender himself when demanded, and for which engagement he (Neville) had become sponsor, because, after the engagement made, and the Marshal dismissed upon it, he had been again arrested, and was indebted to himself for his escape. That with regard to what had been done by them, they had burned his father's house, and they might burn his, but he had enough beyond their reach. As men of honor, he conceived, they ought to approve the intrepidity of Kirkpatrick in defending the house of a friend. It is observed by Mr. Brackenridge, that this letter had a bad effect on those to whom it was addressed. Had better have been written in a different spirit, and better still not written at all. His praise of Kirkpatrick did not accord with public opinion, and his allusion to the particular case only excited indignation, as it was generally believed, perhaps erroneously, that M'Farlane had fallen by his hand, when, deceived by a flag of truce, he had stepped into the open space of the road, to command the assailants to cease firing. Besides, the defiant tone, and boast of wealth, tended to exasperate, instead of awakening within them a proper sense of the wrong they had committed. It added not a little to the embarrassment of the situation of those who now attended the meeting at his solicitation.

This and some other letters being read and remarked upon, Benjamin Parkinson addressed the chair. "You know," said he, "what has been done; we wish to know *whether what has been done is right or wrong*, and whether we are to be supported or left to ourselves?" These ominous words were followed by silence for some time. The Pittsburgh party was struck with astonishment, and Mr. Brackenridge declares that he felt in agony of mind for himself and his associates in that assemblage of persons who appeared to be excited to desperation, and feeling themselves thus placed in a situation to vote against a proposition perhaps at the peril of their lives, or to give a direct sanction to treason. They felt somewhat relieved when Marshall, who followed, observed that the question was not as to what had been done, but what was to be done in future? Bradford now rose, and in a most inflammatory speech sustained what had been done, and applauded the rioters, demanding that it be put to vote whether those present gave their approval, and would pledge themselves to support those who had attacked and destroyed the house of the Inspector. His violent declamation was of considerable length, "and yet," says Mr. Brackenridge, "from my knowledge of the man, I doubt whether he spoke according to his wish, or according to the humor of the people, and through fear of them!" There was again a dead silence for some time after he had concluded. Those who were implicated were no doubt eager and anxious for the vote, and the others, at least the more reflecting, were alarmed at this unexpected predicament in which they were placed. Marshall came to Mr. Brackenridge and requested him to speak. This gentleman had already settled in his mind some outline of an address, but called on so unexpectedly, and knowing that the popular current was strongly against him and his associates, he was much at a loss what to say; but the situation was too urgent to admit of much delay or reflection.

One of his associates, Mr. Audrain, in his statement, declared that he never felt himself in a situation so embarrassing in his life.

Mr. Brackenridge, observing the eyes of the audience turned upon him, advanced to the middle of the aisle, toward the chair, and began in a slow, deliberate, and even hesitating manner, encountering the angry scowls of the principal leaders, who were in favor of pushing the people to still greater acts of violence. He began by giving a narrative of what had taken place in Pittsburgh, the withdrawal from the country of the Marshal and the Inspector, and who were supposed to have descended the river. The inspection office which had been opened in town since the destruction of that in the country, had been closed, and the label which had been put on the door taken down. Here, in order to unbend his audience from their serious mood and conciliate them, he painted with a touch of humor the haste with which the paper was taken down by Major Craig, the son-in-law of the Inspector. Having thus partially succeeded in securing a favorable hearing, he ventured to enter more seriously on the grave question which had just been put by Parkinson, whether those concerned in the destruction of Neville's house were right or wrong in doing so? As a reason that he and his colleagues could give no vote on this question, he stated that they were not sent there to vote on any proposition, but simply to give an account of what had taken place in town, in order to satisfy the people, and to show that it was unnecessary for any force to come from the country to put down the excise office, as this had already been done. But he observed that although not authorized to vote, they were at liberty as fellow-citizens, identified with the welfare of the country, and would take upon them to give their advice. Then recurring to the question of Parkinson, and deferring somewhat to the received opinions of the people on the subject of the excise law, he said that the act *might* be morally right, but it was legally wrong—it was *treason*—it was a case for the President to call out the militia; in fact, it had become his duty to do so.* These ideas of the speaker, although thus cautiously

* The expression *might* be *morally* right, although hypothetically used, but not asserted as his opinion, was made a ground of accusation against Mr. Brackenridge, and an attempt to identify him with the rioters; and in order to accomplish this his language has been perverted by Hildreth and by N. B. Craig. He told them, say these writers, "that although *they were morally right*, they were legally wrong," and omitting altogether the words which followed, "it is treason." There is a difference obvious to every one between saying you *may* be morally right—that is, in your opinion—and saying you *are* morally right. One would suppose from them, that the few words thus falsified was the whole of his speech. This is a

unfolded, produced a startling sensation. A new view of the subject was suddenly presented to the guilty, and those not yet implicated found themselves standing on the brink of a precipice. Taking advantage of this, the speaker continued: But the President, said he, will reflect on the difficulty of getting the militia to march. They will be reluctant from the midland counties and the upper parts of Maryland and Virginia. It will probably be necessary to bring them from Jersey and the lower parts of the States. For these reasons, the President will be disposed to offer an amnesty. He then proceeded to state, as an example, the amnesty given in the State of Pennsylvania in the case of the riot in 1779, on Wilson's house in Philadelphia. But in order to obtain this amnesty, an application ought to be made to the Executive; that such application would come with a better grace and more support from those not involved than from those that were; that it was not the interest of the latter to involve others, but to let them remain as they were, in order to act as mediating men with the government! Here rage was plainly shown in the countenances of Parkinson and those who were implicated; a nod of approbation was given by the chairman, while many others plainly expressed approbation in their looks. It was evident that a line of separation had been drawn, of which many would be glad to avail themselves. But the displeasure of the violent portion was plainly discernible, although nothing was said. The speaker saw that they distrusted the certainty of an amnesty, or did not relish the idea of asking it, and resented the being placed in a different category from those not implicated; while the latter could with difficulty restrain the expression of their satisfaction at the turn which had been given to the affair by the speaker. It became necessary for him, on seeing this, out of regard for the feelings of the first, to exert himself to satisfy them of the probability of obtaining an amnesty;

species of falsification and misrepresentation of the most disgraceful kind. The idea that an act might be morally right, although legally wrong, was very prevalent, and is so still with many conscientious men. It is nothing more than the appeal to the *higher law*, which seems to have been revived within a few years. The reverse of the proposition may also be maintained, to wit: that a thing may be legally right, yet morally wrong. The feelings of the Irish and Scotch on the subject of the excise, and which was retained by them and their descendants in America, is not easy to be understood; they give a singular obliquity to their moral perceptions on the subject. There is an anecdote of an Irishman, who, in confessing to his priest a horrid mass of iniquities, was asked by him if he could remember no good act as a set-off to so much wickedness. He at first hesitated, then seeming to recollect, "Stay," said he, "*I once killed an exciseman.*"

he at the same time enlarged on the want of power on the part of the people to sustain what had been done — the narrow basis on which they had to stand — a small part of the country, not even the whole of the Western counties with them — unprepared with arms, munitions and resources of war, in opposition to a power comparatively vast and overwhelming! Returning to the subject of the amnesty, he stated minutely the repeated proofs given by Washington of his great anxiety to avoid war, especially civil war. That this benevolent policy had even been carried to an extent which had been blamed, or was blamable. The case of the countermand of the Presq' Isle establishment, at the instance or threats of the Indian chief Corn Planter, was referred to, and perceiving that his auditory was about to relapse into their serious mood, he indulged in some touches of pleasantry on the subject of Indian treaty negotiations, and introduced the Secretary at War and Corn Planter making speeches. Now, said he, if even an insignificant tribe of Indians can have treaties and negotiate with the government, why should the people of the four western counties despair? He then earnestly besought them, for their own sakes and the sake of their fellow-citizens, not to involve them in the same difficulties, when all would be equally guilty and none left to intercede! In conclusion, he used an argument against present action which would have great weight with his hearers from their republican habits; there was but a small portion of the people present, and who had no authority to speak for the whole western country; at the same time he advised the calling a larger meeting, co-extensive with the survey, before any important step should be taken. He advised the sending in the meanwhile a delegation to the Executive, on the subject of what *had been rashly and illegally done.* He proposed to undertake this mission himself, as one of such delegation, although greatly inconvenient to him, and disagreeable at that season to undertake the journey.

This impromptu effort, which has not been given, but only described, was attended with remarkable results. It was followed by a deep silence for some time, and no one rising to speak, the meeting spontaneously broke up; some went to the spring, as if to drink, others separated into knots, in close and grave consultation. In the meantime Mr. Brackenridge collected his companions and advised them to leave the ground without delay, to avoid the danger of being again called on by the meeting; but in order to avoid the appearance of retiring in haste, he returned to the ground to show himself for a few moments, and then joined his company and departed. After this the meeting again convened, but nothing further was done than to act on the suggestion of calling a meeting co-extensive with the survey, and passing a resolution to that effect, to be published in the Pittsburgh *Gazette*.*

It appears at a subsequent period that the speech of Mr. Brackenridge was unfavorably represented to the Executive by some *friend* or friends of the Inspector. It was stated that he had ridiculed the excise law, and had spoken disrespectfully of the President and Secretary at War.† It was fortunate for him that he was attended by persons who were ready and willing to vouch for his conduct. The affidavits of these persons, as will appear in the notes to this chapter, agree as to the general scope and the effect of the speech, although varying from each other on some unimportant particulars. The reader will see that it was one of these rare occasions, where a popular speech is a reality, not to amuse by a holiday exhibition, but to control the passions. The effect was to stop the ball of insurrection for the present, and to draw a line effectually between the guilty and those who feared to be drawn into treason against the government. The business was taken out of the hands of the mob led on by reckless men, and referred to a representation, a proceeding consonant to the habits and practice of the people; and as the natural consequence, every one would be disposed to await the action of this higher authority emanating from themselves; and here we see the great difference between the American republics and those revolutionary states whose peace is constantly at the mercy of some self-appointed chief or leader. Such delegations are so familiar to our democratic or republican habits, that we can scarcely appreciate their importance, without comparing them with the furious, unreasoning mobs of other countries. It is impossible to foresee the pernicious effect of the vote proposed by Parkinson, and supported by Bradford, in case it had been sanctioned. The probability is, that the flame would have extended at once over the whole western counties. But for the subsequent conduct of Bradford, and his misguided associates, in causing

---

* "By a respectable number of citizens who met on Wednesday, the 23d inst., at the meeting house on Mingo Creek, it is recommended to the townships of the four western counties of Pennsylvania, and the neighboring counties of Virginia, to meet and choose not more than five, nor less than two representatives, to meet at Parkinson's Ferry on the Monongahela, on Thursday, the 14th of August next, to take into consideration the condition of the western country." 17th July, 1794.

† It is probable that this proceeded from Major Craig, who could not brook the jest of tearing down the paper on the new excise office in hot haste! This, in his estimation, was a very serious offense against him, which he could not well afford to set-off against anything else.

the extraordinary assemblage of the people in arms at Braddock's Field, under a false pretext, and which may possibly have been projected before the meeting at Mingo Creek, the popular ebullition might have subsided, and the insurrectionary spirit died out of itself. In this case, the criminal act of the destruction of Neville's house would have been a partial and isolated affair—a serious and deplorable riot, instead of the commencement of an insurrection. The popular reflection of those at a distance from the scene, would have caused a reaction, and the local disturbance would have been extinguished for want of fuel to keep it up. The respectable and intelligent part of the community, although opposed to the excise law, had no other idea than to seek for its repeal by legal means; but it was impossible to ascertain in the first instance, what proportion of the people was in favor of resorting to violent means; and in this way many were swept along with the current which they could not resist.

The conduct of Bradford is best explained by the incidents related in the progress of this narrative. He was a vain, shallow man, with some talent for popular declamation, which in the present state of the public mind might be productive of mischief. Fortunately he had not the capacity to form any deep consistent plan, which looked beyond the present moment with a foresight of all consequences. It seemed to be his passion to ride on the popular wave, elated with popular applause, and at the same time fearful of popular displeasure.

The consequence to Mr. Brackenridge, besides the misrepresentation of his speech abroad, was a temporary loss of popularity, being at the time a candidate for a seat in Congress, with almost a certainty of election. The participators in the criminal acts were enraged against him, and those relieved from momentary embarrassment were not disposed to avow themselves in his favor. The practice of his profession had taught him the necessity of precaution, without which the most innocent may be involved in the appearance of guilt. An energetic and fearless lawyer cannot avoid making enemies in the discharge of his professional obligations. Mr. Brackenridge found such an enemy in one* of the Neville connection, which gave rise to a personal rencontre, and was probably the foundation of the difference between him and the powerful Neville connection. The intelligent and disinterested did him justice, and acknowledged the important services rendered by him to the country in this and other occasions in the course of the insurrection; but partial affidavits were procured, containing gross misrepresentations, and transmitted to the government;

* Major Kirkpatrick.

but these were never made public, and consequently could not be contradicted. It is certain that a most unfavorable impression was made against him in the minds of the President and some members of the Cabinet, afterward heightened and confirmed by those friends of the Nevilles who crossed the mountains; an impression which was not removed from the mind of Secretary Hamilton until his examination of that gentleman in person. For doing a laudable and patriotic act at the request Col. Neville, he was one time threatened with the loss of fortune, reputation and life. Nothing but his great abilities and moral courage could have extricated Mr. Brackenridge from the persecutions which afterward pursued him, and which were in preparation at the very moment he was hazarding everything in support of the government. It is not surprising that no means existed of contradicting these malignant machinations, when we consider that at that day the communication between the east and the west of the mountains was almost as difficult as at present between us and California. Why did not Col. Neville counteract these false impressions? Men of stronger minds and loftier principles have yielded to the influence of family and of party ties.

The reflections of the reader may induce him to think that the mere circumstance of being required to pay a duty on their stills, is not sufficient to account for the extraordinary degree of excitement and of passion which prevailed among these people. There was certainly a higher cause, already referred to, and one calculated to engender feelings which are entitled to much greater sympathy. The western people, with few exceptions, cultivated their own farms, and, as already stated, had no market for their produce until their grain was reduced in bulk by distillation into whiskey. Those farms were seldom worth more than from three hundred to one thousand dollars; thus, when delinquents, on account of the scarcity of money, were unable to pay their duties, they were exposed to suits in the Federal court at Philadelphia, which subjected them to an expense equal to the value of their homesteads. This will explain the earnestness on the subject of the return of the writs by the Marshal, and the expression of David Hamilton, "that it was better that one man should die, than so many men should lose their plantations." Their *homes*, the homes of their wives and children, were in jeopardy. Can we be surprised at this feeling, which we have seen and respected even among the Florida Indians, among the squatters of the West, and the settlers of Wyoming? A cause penetrated by these considerations, presented a very different character from that of mere opposition to an excise on whiskey; and it is beyond question, that the immediate cause of the outbreak was the service of process on Miller, the neighbor and relative of Neville. This cause of complaint, so uniformly overlooked by those who have written accounts of the Western Insurrection, was ever prominent in their minds. The outcry of taking men to a great distance from their vicinage, is of traditional aggravation with the Anglo-American, and is as old, at least, as Magna Charta. It forms a most prominent item in our Declaration of Independence, and while many of the grievances of the excise law had been redressed in consequence of remonstrances, this—the greatest of them all, and which should first have claimed attention—was disregarded, until the last moment. An act of Congress had at length been passed, as we have seen, authorizing the State courts to take cognizance of the matter, but for some unaccountable reason it was not carried into effect, but the proceedings against distillers commenced in Philadelphia, as usual.

NOTES TO CHAPER III.

AFFIDAVITS OF PERSONS WHO ACCOMPANIED MR. BRACKENRIDGE AT THE MINGO MEETING.

Allegheny County, ss.

Before me, Alexander Addison, Judge of the District Courts, personally appeared, &c. Adamson Tannehill, &c.

Extract, Appendix to "Incidents," p. 70, &c.

"That on the morning of the meeting of the Mingo Creek meeting-house, Hugh Henry Brackenridge, Esq. called on this deponent, and asked him if he would accompany him there, as he wished some person with him who might be an evidence of his conduct. The deponent declined, alleging that the *rioters* who had burnt General Neville's house might tender an oath, or something of the kind, to support them in what had been done; went away, returned a short time afterward to Mr. Brackenridge's house, and found him *and Col. Presley Neville in conversation on the same subject.* Was again solicited to go, and absolutely refused. Referred *them* to Josiah Tannehill, whom the deponent thought might go, provided he could get a horse. *Col. Neville replied, he should not want a horse, if that was all.* The deponent says that he understood at the time from the conversation that passed, that Col. Neville was apprised of that meeting, from the anxiety he appeared to have that some person should go with Mr. Brackenridge. It was at length agreed that Josiah Tannehill and George Robinson should go, who the deponent believes did."

Extract from the Affidavit of Peter Audrain.

"This deponent, the morning of the meeting at Mingo Creek, was requested by Mr. Brackenridge to accompany him to that meeting; hesitating very much, *but afterward seeing Col. Neville, was prevailed upon to go.*

"At that meeting, Mr. Brackenridge, at the beginning of a speech he made on that occasion, said that those concerned in burning of Gen. Neville's house were guilty of treason; he powerfully opposed and luckily defeated the resolution which was to support the brave fellows who had attended at the burning Gen. Neville's house; he advised to try by every possible means to make peace with the government, and get an act of oblivion, and offered to go himself to Philadelphia, if it was agreeable to the people. The turn he gave to the business, saved us from the most delicate situation that this deponent ever thought himself in; being apprehensive that if the question had been put, and we had voted against it, we would have been in personal danger, and voting for it would have involved us in a crime. After the speech of Mr. Brackenridge, there was *a long silence*, and most of the people went out. This deponent went out with the other persons of Pittsburgh; and shortly after, on the suggestion of Mr. Brackenridge that some other delicate questions might be brought forward, it was judged best to get off as speedily as possible. We went away, and Mr. Brackenridge with us, as unobservedly as we could. We came to the house, about half a mile, where we had left our horses, which had taken up an hour or more; it was suggested by some one present, that we had come off abruptly, and that a bad construction might be put upon it, that we had been there as spies, it would be well for Mr. Brackenridge, at least, just to go back, and take leave; which he did, and returned to us in as short a time as was necessary to go and come back. At that meeting, the deponent did not see Mr. Brackenridge having private conversation with Marshall or Bradford, nor does he think it probable that he could have any, from the shortness of the time we were there before the opening of the meeting."

Deposition of Josiah Tannehill.

"That this deponent accompanied Mr. Brackenridge to the meeting at Mingo Creek, at the request of Mr. Brackenridge, who was going, as this deponent understood, at the request of Col. P. Neville. Mr. Brackenridge, when he requested this deponent to go, said that he wished persons to go that were capable to take notice, and give information of what was said or done.

"Early in the morning, an inflammatory speech was delivered by Mr. Bradford to induce the people to pledge themselves to support what had been done at Gen. Neville's house, which Mr. Brackenridge *opposed by art and force of reasoning, and finally baffled the proposition.*

"This deponent can say on this occasion, and on every other within his knowledge, that Mr. Brackenridge, to the best of his judgment, acted a part favorable to the repressing the disorder of the time, and restoring order and good government."

Affidavit of Isaac Gregg.

"That about the 27th of July last, being at Mr. Brackenridge's house, this deponent heard him say (in conversation respecting the attack on Gen. Neville's house, which was a few days previous to that time,) that it was a very rash piece of business, and that he conceived the people to be mad, or words to that effect, and that it would be attended with serious consequences to them, as the government could not overlook it, but must take it up."

Extract of a letter from the Hon. James Ross, U. S. Senator, in answer to Mr. Brackenridge:

"I lived in Washington at the time Gen. Neville's house was destroyed, and during the time of the late disturbances. On the return of the Washington gentlemen from the Mingo Creek meeting, I understood from them that a proposal had been made in the meeting, that those guilty of the outrage should be supported by force against all attempts to punish them, and that this had been warmly advocated by some of our Washington people; but that you were of a different opinion, and had stated that in all probability the government would be induced to forgive it, and that a combination of this sort *would involve the whole country, and oblige government to take notice of those who had transgressed.* This meeting ended by a proposal to have a more general one, from the four counties west of the mountains in Pennsylvania, and as I understood, the western counties of Virginia."

Affidavit of John M'Donald.

"At the time of Marshal Lenox being at Pittsburgh, about the 13th or 14th of July last, being a few days before the attack on Gen. Neville's house, I was in the office of Mr. Brackenridge, on some business with him; was asked by him about the constitution of the Mingo Creek society, and laughing at some parts of it, he asked what could put it into the people's heads to form such a one; I said the people had all been running wild, and talked of taking Neville prisoner and burning Pittsburgh; and this forming the society was thought of by some persons to turn the people to remonstrating and petitioning, and giving them something to do that way to keep them quiet. Mr. Brackenridge asked what could put it in their heads to think of burning Pittsburgh? I said I did not know, but they have talked of it. I am of opinion that at the time of the march to Pittsburgh there was great danger. I was at the Mingo Creek meeting-house, and numbers of people were dissatisfied with Mr. Brackenridge's speech there, as it appeared he was unwilling to support what was done, *and supposed to be on the side of the government.*"

☞ Note on the above by Mr. Brackenridge: "After the burning of Neville's house, I had mentioned this information of M'Donald as a matter I thought nothing of at the time, but as a proof that the house was in danger. It has been the ground of a calumny, that I had a previous knowledge of the attack on the house."

Affidavit of George Robinson, (Chief Burgess.)

"That at the request of Mr. Brackenridge, he went to the meeting at Mingo Creek. Mr. Brackenridge informed him that it was at the request of Col. Presley Neville that he himself was going. Mr. Brackenridge said he wished this deponent to go, as being a public officer, the chief burgess of the town, as he wished to have some persons to bear testimony of his conduct, as *the situation might be delicate.* This deponent found the situation delicate enough, when a motion was brought forward to support what had been done at burning Gen. Neville's house, and which was warmly supported. This deponent being much alarmed at the time, lest the question should be put on this account, that by voting in the affirmative we should be drawn in as accomplices, and by voting against it we might be in personal danger. After an inflammatory speech by a certain person, there was a silence for some time. During this time the deponent was in great anxiety lest the question should be put, when Mr. Brackenridge addressed the meeting in a speech of some length, and as it appeared, with great anxiety of mind. The speech, in the opinion of this deponent, appeared to be calculated to parry the question. He informed them that we were not delegated by the town

MR. BRACKENRIDGE'S SPEECH.

to do any act for them, and therefore if we gave any vote, it could only be as individuals; that as an individual he would give his opinion. Here Mr. Brackenridge explained the nature and consequences of what had been done; he plainly told them that all concerned were guilty of treason, that it would be better not to draw any more in, as they could be of more use as mediators with the government than as accomplices; that the well known lenity of the President of the United States gave reason to suppose that an accommodation might be brought about before he would proceed to extremities; that the present meeting was but an inconsiderable part of the four counties; that a large meeting might be called by delegates regularly appointed, and that commissioners might be sent to the President in order to bring about an accommodation; that though it would not be convenient for him to go at that time, yet, if such a measure was adopted, he was willing to go and to render any service in his power. This deponent does not recollect particularly, but has some recollection of Mr. Brackenridge mentioning that the damage done must be repaired.

"After Mr. Brackenridge closed his speech, there appeared to be an adjournment without a motion made for that purpose. During the interval, Mr. Brackenridge urged us to get off as unobservedly as possible, lest we should be drawn further in. During the time that we were out there was a good deal of murmuring among the people, and this deponent sup poses this had gien Mr. Brackenridge apprehensions, and he has informed the deponent since that it was that which alarmed him. We went away on this, and Mr. Brackenridge slipped after us. As we crossed a small run a short distance from the meeting-house, we were called after by some persons to come back; but we hurried off as fast as possible to the house where we had left our horses. While there it was suggested by some of the company that as we had come off so abruptly, it might be well if Mr. Brackenridge or some one should return and make some excuse. Mr. Brackenridge took his horse, and said he would ride over and make some excuse. He rode over and came back in a very short time, so that we wondered he could have been there and come back, and said he had found them just breaking up. In our way home mentioning to Mr. Brackenridge the fortunate escape we had made, he made use of this expression, 'he had never been in so delicate a situation before in his life.' The deponent has been present at other meetings since in the town of Pittsburgh, and heard Mr. Brackenridge's sentiments on various occasions, and observed his conduct, and can say to the best of his knowledge, that with respect to the people that were expelled from the town, and every thing else that was done, he acted from no selfish motive of resentment, or disposition to hurt any man; but from motives of policy, to moderate matters and prevent mischief; and this deponent knows this to be the general sentiment of the people of Pittsburgh, and they consider themselves indebted to his policy in a great degree for the safety of the town in the affair of Braddock's Field, when we were led to apprehend plunder and destruction from the fury of the people that had met there."

Statement of Col. William Sample.

"SIR—At your request, I shall give you a short detail of the circumstances leading to, and of the principal traits of your conduct at Mingo meeting-house. I remember that it was the general opinion of the inhabitants of Pittsburgh, that it would be prudent that a number of persons should be sent from this place, to meet those who were collecting from various parts of the country. No instructions, to my knowledge, were given to those who went. But I understood the general purport of our going there was to hear and report. You asked me if I would make one of the number that would go. I hesitated for some time, and until I asked the opinion of Col. Presley Neville, which was, 'I see no harm in your going there if you choose to venture, and if you do, I will thank you to carry a letter for me to the chairman of the committee, contradicting some false aspersions which have been industriously circulated, respecting the Marshal and myself being released upon our words of honor to hold ourselves as prisoners on demand that night my father's house was burned.' I accepted the office and came back to you, and told you I would go. When we arrived at Jacob Friggley's house, near the meeting-house, in the course of various conversations, a tall man there, with red hair, frequently expressed a warmth of affection for Presley Neville; seemingly commiserated his situation, and took some credit to himself in rescuing him when he was made prisoner the night aforesaid; but at the same time was still making some sarcastic observations on his father. I found the temper of the people was wound up to a very high pitch, and I took this favorable opportunity of delivering Col. Neville's letter to him, after finding his name was Parkinson, and that he had considerable influence; telling him that the Colonel had desired me to deliver this letter to him in case I should find him, and requested he would deliver it to the chairman. He readily took it, and it was the first thing brought on the carpet at the meeting. The secretary read the letter, but no observations followed. After some silence a person stood up and made a motion, that the burning of Gen. Neville's house, and those concerned in it, should be justified and supported. I could observe the people of the meeting considerably agitated. Col. Marshall, of Washington, was the first who ventured to oppose this motion; and he appeared to do so both with *fear and trembling*. After this speech was over, David Bradford arose, and beckoned to Benjamin Parkinson, (as Capt. Josiah Tannehill informed, who had mixed with the crowd and happened to sit down on the forms close by him,) asked him if the relation Col. Neville had given in his letter was true. To which question Parkinson answered, putting his hand to his breast, it is true. Mr. Bradford then dropping the subject of the letter, began a most violent and inflammatory oration in support of the first motion. I observed Mr. Brackenridge in the course of this oration, who being seated at the west end of the church, and opposite to the principal part of the Pittsburghers, who had seated themselves at the east corner by themselves, in great agitation, often throwing his head down on his hand and in the attitude of study. At length Mr. Bradford's speech being ended, Mr. Brackenridge advanced nearly to the middle of the house, and opposite the chairman, and began his speech, slowly and irregularly; for the current of the people's prejudices seemed to be strongly against him. He first opened the reasons why the few persons from Pittsburgh came there; that they were not instructed; nor had they delegated powers to agree or to disagree on any proposition that might be made, that they came only to hear and report. He took various methods of diverting the audience from the speech that preceded his. Sometimes he would give a sarcastical stroke at the excise, and the inventors of it, and then tell

MR. BRACKENRIDGE'S SPEECH.

some droll story thereto relating; in order as I apprehend, to unbend the audience's minds from the serious tone to which they had been wrought up. He viewed the subject before him in various lights; and then entered warmly on his main argument, which was to dissuade the audience from the first proposition. He told them in direct words, 'that he hoped they would not involve the whole country in a crime which could not be called by less name than high treason; that this would certainly bring down the resentment of the general government, and there would be none left to intercede.'

"The audience seemed petrified, thunderstruck with such observations; and when he had done, not a person seemed desirous of renewing the arguments. Silence ensued for some time and then the company broke up, and some went to drink at the spring, and others in little knots or clubs were dispersed over the green. Those who came from Pittsburgh, finding that the audience was to be called to the church once more, took this opportunity to make the best of their way to Jacob Friggley's. The company met again, but I know not that they did any business of consequence; for Mr. Brackenridge was soon with us, and we took our horses and returned to Pittsburgh.

WILLIAM SEMPLE.

Pittsburgh, 20th Sept. 1795."

Extract from the Affidavit of William Beaumont.

"That the deponent was one of those who accompanied Mr. Brackenridge to the meeting at Mingo Creek; that it was at the request of Mr. Brackenridge that he went, in order to vouch for his conduct on that occasion, and bear testimony of what should be said or done by him, considering the situation as delicate.

"This deponent found the situation sufficiently delicate; and on a motion being brought forward early in the meeting and strongly supported, this deponent was greatly alarmed, being apprehensive of being brought to vote on a question of that nature, which was to pledge ourselves to support what had been done; which, as this deponent understood, was the violence and outrage that had just taken place. This deponent was alarmed, because to go away might expose to insult and personal danger, as he understood the people of Pittsburgh were considered in an unfavorable light by the people of the country; and to vote against the question would be equally dangerous, or more so; and to vote for it this deponent could not think of, as it would involve in criminality.

"In a speech of considerable length made by Mr. Brackenridge at this juncture, he appeared to have the same impressions; and with all the art and address that was in his power, wished to parry the question without rendering himself obnoxious to the multitude. The observations made by Mr. Brackenridge in the course of the speech, were, as nearly as this deponent recollected, to the following effect: those first made were of a nature to conciliate them (the persons present,) to the people of Pittsburgh, that they (the people of Pittsburgh,) were not abettors of the excise more than other people, nor did they undertake to support excise officers more than other people; they left these matters to the government. But at the same time it was a very different matter not to support, and to oppose; that be this as it might, we did not come as delegates from the town, but as individuals, and it would be no use for us to join in such a proposition, for it would not bind, as we represented nobody. That he, Mr. Brackenridge, had no objection to give his opinion on these matters; that what was done would be construed treason; it might be morally right, but it was legally wrong, and would subject those concerned to punishment, unless they had force enough to support an opposition to the laws; the matter must terminate in a revolution or a rebellion; if they had not strength to make it a revolution, it must be a rebellion: that that part of the country was but a small part to undertake such an object; that they had not even the four western counties, or neighboring counties of Pennsylvania, nor the three counties of Virginia, nor Kentucky, if that could be of any use; and that the undertaking afforded no rational prospect of success. That the case was not desperate; an accommodation might be brought about with the government, and that it would be much better for those not involved to remain so, as they would have more weight in their representations as advocates, than if involved themselves; and could with propriety come forward as a mediating party between the government and them. That there was reason to conceive that government would not be rash in taking vigorous measures; that the militia must be drafted; that there would be a reluctance in the militia of Pennsylvania to serve, and, perhaps, of the neighboring States; that the President would reflect on this and be disposed to an accommodation; that taking into view the disposition of the President, from what we had seen in the case of the British spoliations, it was a natural conclusion that he would not wish to involve the country in a war; and his conduct also in respect to the Indian tribes in treating with them to a degree that has been blamed where war has been thought better, gave reason to suppose that he would not be hasty in using vigorous measures in a case like the present; that the late instance of his lenity in the case of the Presq' Isle establishment, to which the letters of Cornplanter had put a stop, manifested the same thing. Here Mr. Brackenridge indulged some pleasantry on the apprehensions of government in this case, and created a laugh. In this and several parts of his speech, where Mr. Brackenridge indulged a vein of pleasantry and humor, this deponent saw through it, and thought it manifested a great degree of management and address, to play with the fancy of the people, and divert their attention from that intentness in having the proposition carried, which he was endeavoring to prevent. The result was, Mr. Brackenridge seemed to wish that all things should remain as they were, and be put in train of negotiation.

"Mr. Brackenridge's speech ended, a pause ensued; most of the members of the meeting left the meeting-house for a short period of time. On being desired to resume their seats, we thought it most prudent to retreat, Mr. Brackenridge telling us, 'we had better get off as soon as we can, or they will bring us into some other disagreeable predicament.' This deponent went with Mr. Brackenridge, came away with him, had an opportunity of seeing him through the whole of the time, *and did not observe him to have any private conversation with any person present.*"

The necessity for the *negative* evidence contained in the concluding part of the foregoing extract, and in some of the other affidavits, will create surprise in the reader, and may require some explanation. It was insisted on by the enemies of Mr. Brackenridge, especially of the Neville connection, that he had some secret and mysterious understanding with the rioters or insurgents. For instance, that he knew of the intended burning of Neville's house, and was the prime mover of all mischief, standing behind the scene and pulling the wires, while the apparent leaders were only puppets in his hand. Hence it became necessary for Mr. Brackenridge to guard against these continual misconstructions put upon his conduct, however absurd, even by those at whose instance he was induced by his benevolent and public spirited character to interest himself in their behalf. He subsequently expressed his regret that he had interfered in any manner, instead of leaving the people and the government to settle their differences in their own way. The publication of Craig's History of Pittsburgh led to a controversy on the subject of these shameful misrepresentations, groundless surmises, and falsifications, which were used for the purpose of gratifying a malignant feeling characteristic of the writer of that pretended history. These ungenerous, or rather dishonest surmises, are freely indulged in by Hildreth in his "History of the United States," published within a few years, and which are quoted in Craig's book. Hildreth is one of those narrow-minded, or rather narrow-hearted party bigots, who cannot do justice to any man in the opposite ranks of politics. Hence, like Craig, under the pretense of giving a rigid account of *facts*, he is continually perverting or discoloring the truth. Craig says that Mr. Brackenridge was such a rogue, that persons had to be sent with him to the Mingo meeting, as spies on his conduct! In point of fact, these men were required by him for his own safety, to guard against the misrepresentation of others. Craig was at first disposed to deny that he went at the instance of Neville—but when the affidavits, published in the "Incidents," were appealed to as establishing the fact, he with the astuteness of a pettifogger, referred to the narrow rules of evidence of courts of justice, designed, as it is said, for the purpose of excluding falsehood, but which much oftener *exclude the truth*. It is not by the narrow rule of judicial evidence that historical facts are established, or the credibility of testimony is determined. It is by the exercise of sound common sense and rational probability. The most liberal of the "connection," Presley Neville, was not free from this strange prepossession, although continually applying to Mr. Brackenridge for his advice, and which induced the latter to believe he was friendly to him. A curious instance of this prejudice on the part of Col. Neville, is given by Mr. Purviance, which will be inserted in another part of this work; in alluding to something in which he expressed his suspicion of Mr. Brackenridge, Mr. Purviance used a conclusive argument to show its utter fallacy, on which Neville replied, "Well, if he was not concerned in it, *he was pleased with it after it was done.*" How is it possible to contend with persons so unreasonable? It is nothing short of the moral of Æsop's fable of the wolf and the lamb. When, in reply to Craig, in the recent controversy, the conclusive argument was again and again repeated, to wit: that the "Incidents" were published under the very nose of the Neville connection, *and they were challenged to deny them, and yet never attempted it*,—the only answer of Craig, at last, when driven to the wall, was, that Col. Neville was too indolent to write and that the others were not possessed of the literary ability to do so. Yet his father could write letters to the Secretary at War, and was a member of the "Philosophical Society," as we are informed by his son. It was the belief of Mr. Brackenridge that it was by Major Craig, that the affidavits unfavorable to his conduct at the meeting were transmitted to the government. By whom were these made, what were their contents, and why were they not given to the public, like those of the persons who testified in favor of Mr. Brackenridge? These affidavits, no doubt omitting the *unimportant* facts of the defeat of the vote on Parkinson's proposition, and arresting the progress of violence, disclosed the allusions to the speeches of Cornplanter and the Secretary at War—but most heinous of all, the pleasantries of which the Major was the subject, and which in his opinion were of so serious a nature as to cause every thing else to be lost sight of! Having given a brief notice of the Nevilles, in a former chapter, it may interest the reader to have some account of Mr. Brackenridge in this place.

Mr. Brackenridge was born in Scotland, but came to this country with his parents at five years of age, about the year 1755. His father was a small Scotch farmer from the neighborhood of Campbelltown, in Cantyre, opposite the coast of Ireland, where the Kentucky branch of the family had settled previously to their emigration to Virginia. The family, consisting of H. H. Brackenridge and several brothers and sisters, settled in York county, near the Susquehanna, a very poor and thinly inhabited neighborhood. It is remarkable, however, for having produced several men of high distinction in American history; of these we may mention James Ross, John Rowan, and the Rev. John M'Millan. Under the greatest disadvantage, he not only succeeded in mastering the different branches of common school education, but before he was twelve years of age could read Horace, and had the rudiments of the Greek, from lessons at long intervals given him by the clergyman who officiated once every two weeks. Such was his passion for learning, that meeting with a young man who was much advanced in mathematics, he bartered his classics for some of that knowledge. At the age of fifteen, hearing of a vacancy in a free school in Maryland, he boldly presented himself as teacher, and was accepted. At the age of eighteen, with very insufficent means, but extraordinary acquirements for his opportunities, he presented himself to the President of Princeton College, Dr. Witherspoon, and agreed to teach two classes on condition of being permited to go through the college course. He did so, and graduated with honor in the same class with Mr. Madison, Luther Martin, Samuel Spring, and Philip Freneau, the poet. In his exercises he evinced extraordinary talents, and great versatility of mind. A poem, entitled "The rising glory of America," written by him jointly with Freneau, evinced a high poetic vein, but still more an enthusiastic feeling for the prosperity and glory of his country; for having had his mind formed in America, he cannot be considered as any thing else but an American. After graduating, he applied to the study of divinity, was licensed to preach, but never ordained, having determined to leave it for the study of the law. For some years before the Revolution he conducted a classical academy in Maryland, and applied himself to the law under Samuel Chase, afterward the celebrated Judge. The war breaking up his academy, he repaired to Philadelphia, and became conspicuous as a writer and speaker in the cause of Independence. During the campaign of 1778, he accompanied the army as the chaplain of a regiment, and published a pamphlet of six sermons, particularly addressed to the soldiers. He was a most enthusiastic patriot, as his fine oration on the 4th of July, 1779, delivered in Philadelphia, evinces.

About the year 1780, when the result

of the war was scarcely any longer doubtful, he crossed the mountains and established himself in his profession in the town of Pittsburgh, then in Westmoreland county. He soon rose to the head of the Bar in the western counties, and in 1786 was sent to the Legislature to obtain the establishment of the county of Allegheny. He took an active and zealous part in support of the Federal constitution, which was opposed by some of the prominent western politicians, such as Gallatin, Findley and Smiley, the leaders in the opposition to the excise law, and with whom he never was on friendly terms. He had laid the foundation of a moderate fortune, and had risen to eminence as a lawyer and speaker at the time of the outbreak, had been brought forward as a candidate for Congress, and but for those unhappy events would have been elected. He was ambitious, not for the mere possession of office or power, but for fame and superiority as a man of talents and learning. He was a philanthropist and a philosopher, and willingly sacrificed his popularity to the real welfare of his country. The history of the difficult and delicate part he was obliged to act during those trying times is detailed in this work. He declares that if he had foreseen the consequences he never would have involved himself in the thankless office of mediator between the people and the government; yet it could not but be very gratifying to him that he had been so eminently instrumental in preventing the horrors of civil war, and perhaps a fatal wound to the union of the States.

After the troubles of the insurrection had subsided, he rose higher than ever in public estimation, but except as a political partisan, never aspired to political life. He warmly espoused the Democratic cause with Jefferson and Madison and M'Kean. On the election of the latter to the government of Pennsylvania, he was appointed to the Supreme bench, which seat he occupied sixteen years until his death in 1816. He was a man of great acquirements on all subjects; rigidly honest and punctual in all his dealings. Possessing great opportunities of acquiring wealth, he rather shunned than sought to avail himself of them. He was honestly of opinion that good education was a better gift to his children than fortune, and no father ever devoted himself more anxiously to accomplish that object. So perfectly simple had he been in his worldly transactions, that he was enabled to arrange every thing in relation to them in six lines, dictated to the author of this note, leaving an ample provision for his family and the education of younger children; and as to debts, he had none. Various and most erroneous opinions have prevailed respecting him. It has generally been supposed that wit and humor were the predominating traits of his character, and that he was strangely and whimsically eccentric. On the contrary, he was a man of grave philosophical and moral turn of mind, an indefatigable student, and profound observer of men and things, as any one may see and judge for himself on reading his celebrated work, "Modern Chivalry," one of the most instructive this country has produced. The gift of wit and humor was rather added to him as an assistant to enable him to employ his other gifts to greater advantage. In fact, he rarely resorted to wit unless to effect some wise and or benevolent purpose, and not for its own sake. He loved to raise a laugh at times, and could do so when he pleased, but his object was always, if not to make others better, at least to afford an innocent pleasure. He possessed great sensibility, and the more impulsively he yielded to his benevolent feelings in serving others, the more keenly he felt the ungrateful requital. No candid and impartial man can read this history without the clear conviction, *that he saved the town of Pittsburgh from destruction, the western country from the horrors of civil war, and the Union from eminent peril.* As an orator he had few equals in this country, nature having bestowed on him every requisite of oratory, physical as well as mental; fine person, a powerful eye, a towering imagination, a mind highly cultivated, and a voice of uncommon excellence. Had he exhibited these powers on the larger stage of the National Councils, there is no doubt he would have placed many in the background who are ranked above him.

CHAPTER IV.

THE ROBBING OF THE MAIL — THE SELF-APPOINTED CONVENTION, AND CIRCULAR TO THE MILITIA OFFICERS DIRECTING A RENDEZVOUS AT BRADDOCK'S FIELD — THE TOWN MEETING AT PITTSBURGH.

BRADFORD, having joined the riotous party, which had committed the recent outrages, was resolved to be at its head. Although incompetent to organize any consistent plan of treasonable opposition, he could take advantage of circumstances as they arose; and hence the suggestion of a large meeting was adopted by him as the means of extending, or rather of giving the resistance to the law the character of insurrection, while those who originated the idea of the delegation considered it as the means of restoring order; at least, of arresting the progress of violence for the present. That he should have drawn in such a man as Marshall, and apparently against his will—a man of prudence and sound sense— would be difficult to account for, if we had not often witnessed instances of persons greatly superior being subject to the control of those of inferior understanding; probably from a false estimate of their abilities, or from some unaccountable influence. On the way to the Mingo meeting, it appears that the idea of stopping the mail between the town of Washington, where he resided, and Pittsburgh, had been suggested by Bradford to David Hamilton and John Baldwin, in order to find out what his townsmen might have written on the subject of the recent attack on Neville's house. This would seem to be a very childish motive for the commission of so heinous a crime, so far transcending any possible use to which it could be turned. The men to whom it was proposed declined taking any part in the reckless enterprise.

The relation between Brackenridge and Bradford was merely professional —the counsel who traveled the circuit were often engaged to assist in the argument of causes, by the resident members of the bar in each county, giving to the latter a certain patronage, which made it the interest of the former to cultivate a good understanding, and a kind of professional relation. The connection with Marshall, on the other hand, was more personal and political. They had taken part with Bradford, on the same side, in favor of the Federal constitution, when opposed to Gallatin, Findley and others. Some time before this, a project, warmly advocated by Bradford, for the establishment of a new State, to be composed of the western counties of Pennsylvania and parts of Virginia and Maryland, had been opposed and defeated through the exertions of Brackenridge and Marshall. It is very possible that dim visions of a new State still floated across the mind of Bradford, as an event which might grow out of a western insurrection. Whatever were the designs, if any, now concerted by Bradford, they were not communicated to Brackenridge, and probably not to Marshall. It was not pretended by Bradford, in his denunciation of the former, that there had ever been any understanding between them on the subject. Bradford and Marshall, notwithstanding the opposition at the Mingo meeting, perhaps entertained a hope of being able to draw Brackenridge in to take part with them, whilst he subsequently, at the Parkinson's Ferry meeting, or congress, resolved to avail himself of that disposition, to turn them aside from their treasonable plans and preserve the peace of the country. The idea of stopping the mail was not spoken of at the Mingo meeting, nor was it communicated to Col. Cook, or any of those who preferred to remain neuter.

On the failure of the first scheme of stopping the mail from Washington, Bradford determined to intercept that from Pittsburgh to Philadelphia, in order to find out what was written by persons in the former place to those at the head of the government. He sent his cousin, William Bradford, while David Hamilton sent an obscure, ignorant man, of the name of John Mitchel, who perpetrated the deed. The post was intercepted when about ten miles from Greensburg, on the 26th of July, three days after the Mingo meeting. The packets from Washington and Pittsburgh were taken out. They were carried by Benjamin Parkinson to Washington, and thence, accompanied by Bradford and Marshall, to Canonsburg, a small village seven miles distant. On the Washington packet being opened, no letters on the late affairs from any individuals of that place were found; but there were some from individuals of Pittsburgh, and as eavesdroppers seldom hear any good of themselves, these letters contained matters which gave great offense, especially to Bradford.

Various conjectures have been formed as to the ultimate design, if any, of that person; but there can be no doubt that his present intention was to involve as many, and spread the flames as widely, as possible; and this desperate act of intercepting the mail was one of the means resorted to

SELF-CONSTITUTED CONVENTION. 81

for that purpose. It was an act which seemed to indicate that the perpetrators were prepared to go all lengths. The opinion expressed by Findley, is not far from the truth. "Immediately after the Mingo Creek meeting, Bradford wrote to the principal persons in the neighboring counties of Virginia, pressing them in the most urgent manner to send delegates to the meeting which was appointed to be held at Parkinson's Ferry. His sending this letter, and the style in which it was written, indubitably proves the improvement he designed to make of the Parkinson congress. His robbing the mail, and directing the rendezvous at Braddock's Field, were calculated to inflame the minds of the people previously to that meeting, and increase the number of those who would be rendered desperate by their crimes. In this he was but too successful. The threatening letters to excite the people to attack Wells and Webster, though they have not been traced to Bradford, were, no doubt, part of the plan, and, by their means, the infatuation was vastly extended, and the number of offenses was increased after the meeting at Mingo Creek, and before that at Parkinson's Ferry. Even in Virginia, an excise officer had fled, and a riot was committed at the place of his residence."* Yet, it speaks much in favor of the excited population, that in spite of these pernicious measures, so few disorders occurred, so unlike an European "peasant war." This may be ascribed to the confidence reposed by the people in the representative meeting at Parkinson's Ferry. And, besides, there was no aristocratic class, distinct in interest from them, to make war upon. The French cry of "peace to the cottage, and war to the palace," could have no application where, out of the towns, log-cabins were the only dwellings to be seen.

It is a subject of curious reflection, that the first step toward connecting the partial riots and violations of law into a formidable insurrection, which if not crushed in embryro might have endangered this great confederacy of States, then in its infancy—was taken in a small country-tavern, by a self-constituted, secret convention of six men! Whether the idea was conceived before the Mingo Creek meeting, or not until after the robbery of the mail, it is impossible to know. Its origin was entirely unlike the resolution calling for a peaceful congress, or representation, publicly adopted at the Mingo meeting, and was also in direct conflict with that resolution; but whether owing to the expected congress, or to the fact that a mere military insurrection is at variance with the genius of our republics, certain it is, that this alarming gathering in arms at

* Findley, 109.

Braddock's Field, so imposing in appearance, was rendered by some management not only harmless, but even ludicrous, as we shall presently see. It is to be hoped, that if we should ever be so unfortunate as to experience an internal revolution, it will not assume a warlike appearance even of this description.*

The self-created convention having read over the letters thus feloniously obtained, proceeded to the consideration of measures to be adopted. The following circular, as the result of their deliberations, with a curious arrogance, was drawn up and signed by them, addressed to the colonels and other militia officers of the western counties, just as if signers had been invested with the supreme authority in the government of the State. They ordered out the militia, as if on a tour of military service, and this by men who held no public office, civil or military ! And what is strange, this impudent command, in several regiments, was promptly obeyed by officers and men. In others, the officers were obliged to lead the men from a regard to their own personal safety. We give the letter as drawn up, and despatched by messengers in all directions, by this self-created revolutionary junto :

"July 28th, 1794.

"Sir—Having had suspicions that the Pittsburgh post would carry with him the sentiments of some of the people in the country, respecting our present situation; and the letters by the post being now in our possession, *by which certain secrets are discovered*, hostile to our interests, it is, therefore, now come to that crisis, that every citizen must express his sentiments, not by his words, but by his actions. You are then called upon as a citizen of the western country, to render your personal service, with as many volunteers as you can raise, to rendezvous at your usual place of meeting,† on Wednesday next, and thence you will march to the usual place of rendezvous at Braddock's Field, on the Monongahela, on Friday, the first day of August next, to be there at two o'clock in the afternoon, with arms and accoutrements in good order. If any volunteers shall want arms and ammunition, bring them forward, and they shall be supplied as well as possible. Here, sir, is an expedition proposed, in which you will have an opportunity of displaying

---

* "John Canon and a Mr. Speer, a storekeeper in Canonsburg, were invited to the tavern, and the mail was opened. In the course of conversation at the tavern, it was asked what would be done with those known to be connected in the attack and burning of Neville's house ? Bradford replied, 'They would be hung,' and suggested, 'the only way to protect them was to involve the whole western country in the matter, and that the numbers concerned would prevent extreme measures on the part of the government.'"—Carnahan, p. 125.

† Braddock's Field was the place of the annual brigade muster, or review—each regiment previously assembled at its own rendezvous.

your military talents, and of rendering service to your country. Four days provisions will be wanted; let the men be thus supplied.

We are, (signed,)

J. CANON,   T. SPEARS,
B. PARKINSON,   L. LOCKNY,
D. BRADFORD,   J. MARSHALL.
A. FULTON,*

"To Col. —— ——"

It is difficult to know whether to laugh or be sad at this piece of mischief and folly! Our reflections would, perhaps, lead us to do injustice to the intelligence of our fellow-citizens of that period. Let us hope, that with our newspaper press and common-schools of the present day, it would be impossible to impose upon the people by such absurd usurpations of authority, "unknown to the constitution and the laws," although there may be some still ready to submit to usurpations without inquiry, where the idol happens to humor the popular prejudice or antipathies of the day.

At first, the avowed purpose of this military gathering was to attack the town of Pittsburgh, to seize the magazines of the garrison, and any military equipment that might be procured in the town. It was also contemplated to take the writers of the offensive letters, and imprison them in the jail of Washington. "These," says Mr. Brackenridge, "were the objects contemplated, according to the information given me." Whether it was resentment against the writers which gave rise to a "march to Pittsburgh, for the purpose of arresting these men, and that this drew with it the idea of taking the magazines, or whether the latter was the primary object, and the intended arrests the accidental, I am not sufficiently informed. It would seem probable that the march to Pittsburgh, and the seizure of the magazine, would have been at all events attempted, as a necessary act to furnish the means of defending what had been done, that is, the intercepting and robbing the mail. For it is to be presumed, if we suppose the actors in this affair to have had reflection, that they had made up their minds to set the government at defiance; in

---

* "Fulton was from Maryland; he was not only a Federalist, but an open advocate for the excise law, indeed the most openly so of any man I have met with in the western counties, and an avowed friend of the Inspector. He kept a large distillery, and expected by the operation of the excise law to have considerable advantage over the small distillers. He had also erected a brewery. I have never been able to account for the inconsistency of his conduct."—Findley, p. 96.

For notice of Bradford, Parkinson, Canon, Findley and Marshall, see Notes at the end of this chapter.

that case, it became them to arm themselves with the means of war. When an officer disapproved the circular letter, he did not dare to conceal from his battalion or company that he had received such a notice; and when communicated, it was the people commanding the officer, and not the officer the people. Call us out, or we will take vengeance on you as a traitor to your country! The whole country was one inflammable mass; it required but the least touch of fire to inflame it. I had seen the spirit which prevailed at the stamp act, and at the commencement of the revolution from the government of Great Britain, but it was by no means so general and so vigorous amongst the common people as the spirit which now existed in the country." *

As soon as this circular became known, strong remonstrances were made by persons to Bradford and Marshall, against it, with representations of its dangerous tendency; and this, with such effect, that they became alarmed, and wished to countermand their orders; but as only three days would elapse between their date and the time appointed for the assemblage, it was too late to put a stop to it, although in some quarters to which the countermand was sent it had its effect. The levity of the countermand was as ridiculous as the order was presumptuous; it was in these terms:

"DEAR SIR—Upon receiving some late intelligence from our runners, we have been informed that the ammunition we were about to seize was destined for Gen. Scott, who is just going out against the Indians. We, therefore, have concluded not to touch it; I give you this early notice, that your brave men of war need not turn out till further notice.

          Yours, &c.   DAVID BRADFORD.
"Col. DAVID WILLIAMSON."

No sooner was the news of this frivolous counter order rumored through the town of Washington—which being in the midst of a farming population, and entertaining feelings more in common with them than those of the town of Pittsburgh, where there was more trade and more government influence—than the people of Washington broke out into a furious rage, called a meeting at the court house, and those of the country hearing of it, came rushing in, under still greater excitement. James Ross, United States Senator, who then resided there, in a speech of great earnestness of two hours, endeavored to dissuade the populace. Thomas Scott, of the House of Representatives, Thomas Stokely, of the State Senate, David Reddick, Prothonotary (clerk of the court), Henry Purviance and others of the bar, exerted themselves to effect the same object.

* Incidents, p. 40, 41.

James Marshall was in earnest to retract, and spoke publicly. Bradford seeing the violence of the multitude, by which he was always swayed, was more inflammatory than he had ever been; denied that he had given his consent to the countermand, and asked with confidence who was the scoundrel who would say he had consented! There happened to be no one present who could contradict him, or was willing to do so. The countermand given above, was afterward procured by Col. Stokely in the handwriting of Bradford. It was now carried by a vote that the march to Braddock's Field should proceed. To show their displeasure with Marshall, the door of his house was tarred and feathered that night; threats of personal injury were thrown out, and he was compelled to declare his readiness to go. Others were threatened, for a revolutionary spirit, something like that which at that time raged in France, appears to have taken possession of the uninformed; they threw aside all respect for the laws, and talked familiarly of taking life and violating the rights of property—creating terror in the minds of the peaceful on the one hand, and licentiousness among the unprincipled on the other. Indisposition of pressing business was pretended to avoid going—many yielded to their fears, and thought it safest to comply. Others were induced to go with the patriotic motive of endeavoring to moderate the passions of the multitude, and prevent the commission of outrages. Of the last description, there were numbers of the principal officers of the militia, who came with battalions or companies, and who accompanied them not for the purpose of encouraging, but if possible of restraining the rank and file upon whom the Jacobin madness had seized.* The common language of the time in the country was, they were going to take Pittsburgh; some talked of plundering the town. It was an expression used, that as the old Sodom had been burned by fire from heaven, this second Sodom should be burnt by fire from earth! The shopkeepers were told at their counters by persons cheapening their goods, that they would get them at a less price in a few days. The very women coming in from the country would say—

* Col. John Hamilton, on receiving a circular, repaired immediately to Washington to countermand it, but arrived after the meeting had concluded; he was therefore compelled to accompany his regiment from the motive above mentioned, Col. Cook concealed the circular from his regiment—but went to Braddock's Field with the same intention.

"Great exertions," says Findley, "were made, however, in communicating the circular letters, and though many who probably wished to suppress them durst not, there were some who did keep their secret, and some clergymen, and others in the south of Washington county, were active and successful with their neighbors in dissuading them from going."—Findley, p. 97.

"That fine lady lives in a fine house, but her pride will be humbled by and by." Persons were coming to the blacksmiths with old guns that had lain by a long time, to be repaired. Others were buying up flints and powder from the stores; there were many who were supposed to be from distant parts, no one in the town knowing them. Some were supposed to be spies, to see the condition of the garrison or the town; without appearing to have anything to do, they were seen to be lounging about from place to place. If it excites surprise in the reader that there should be so many persons of this lawless stamp among a peaceful rural population, it must be recollected that at the close of the revolutionary war some of the dregs of the army would be emptied on the frontiers, and that these, with many desperate as well as enterprising characters, would seek the new settlements.

It was now understood that preparations were every where making throughout the survey, and especially on the south side of the Monongahela and in the neighborhood of that river, for the contemplated rendezvous at Braddock's Field. Major Butler had been industrious to improve the defenses of his garrison; Major Craig, the quarter-master, and company had removed into it with his family. Col. Neville had prepared to defend himself in his own house. Under these circumstances it was thought advisable by the citizens to call a town meeting, to consider what was to be done for their own safety, and that of the place thus threatened with destruction.

It is still a question what could have been the object of this alarming movement, now that the first idea, that of attacking the garrison, had been abandoned. After much reflection, it has appeared to the writer, that after making due allowance for the difficulty of stopping the ball once set in motion, as the measure originated immediately after the Mingo Creek meeting and the intercepting the mail, the design of both was to furnish a pretext for a military organization which would present at once a formidable front of insurrection. It would be raising a standard of rebellion in which the whole western country would be involved, and thus be the means of making easier terms with the government, or making it the commencement of treasonable plans, if any such existed, and the people found willing to embark in them. It was expected that the officer in command of the garrison, the officers of justice, and some of the leading inhabitants, would make representations to the Executive, and call for a military force to march immediately for their protection; and this would make it necessary for the rioters to prepare for their defense, by taking the garrison and sacking and destroying the town. When nothing of the kind was discovered, and the plans of the leaders had changed in consequence, no other motive can be discerned than the silly one of making war upon a few individuals for some offensive expressions contained in their private letters. However this may be, those who set the ball in motion were no longer able to stop it, even if it had been their wish to do so, and the consequence of the disorderly assemblage and disorderly march might have been as serious as at first intended. A very large number of those who came to Braddock's Field were still undeceived as to that intention, while the mass had the most vague and uncertain notions of what they were to do, or for what purpose they were assembled. It was thought by many that some *great secret*, as the circular expressed it—some gunpowder plot against the people—had been discovered, and was there to be disclosed. Whether these conjectures are well or ill-founded, it was a most mischievous, as well as foolish act, in the projectors, and which required the greatest caution and prudence, on the part of the leading citizens, to avert the most lamentable consequences.

A town meeting was convened about dusk; the whole town was assembled, General Gibson in the chair, and Matthew Ernest secretary. It was announced that persons had arrived from the town of Washington with a message to the inhabitants of Pittsburgh, on which a committee of three, General Wilkins, George Wallace and H. H. Brackenridge, were appointed to meet the messengers. Those were, Messrs. Baird, Meetkirk, Purviance and Blakeney. These gentlemen had brought the mail which had been delivered to them by Bradford and Marshall, and which was to be restored to the post office, with the exception of the offensive letters, which they were to retain. The letters were, from Col. Neville to Gen. Morgan; Gen. Gibson to the Governor of Pennsylvania; James Brison, Prothonotary, to the Governor; Edward Day to the Secretary of the Treasury; Maj. Butler to the Secretary at War. The messengers stated that these letters had rendered the writers obnoxious, and that it was determined by the people, now on their march to Braddock's Field, to take vengeance on them; and such was their fury that they appeared ungovernable, although every possible means were used to control them. The messengers further stated that a number of the principal men in the country had thrown themselves among them, in order, as far as possible, to restrain them from acts of violence, for which they were but too well disposed, and that disposition likely to increase. The prevailing idea among them, was to seize the obnoxious individuals and burn the town of Pittsburgh; and great doubts were felt by the messengers, who now came to them as friends, of the possibility of preventing the calamity. It was with great difficulty they had made their way hither, having been stopped more than once, and it had required address to enable them to pass, it being the desire of the country people that those of the town should not be informed of their coming. In making their way to Pittsburgh, it was the hope of the gentlemen from Washington to be able to concert some measure to *save the town*, now threatened with destruction. They could see but two things that could be done, with any prospect of success in saving themselves; the first was, to compel or induce the obnoxious persons to absent themselves for a time, under the idea of banishment by the citizens; and the second, the march of the latter in a body, to meet the assemblage, as if to make common cause with them; that in this way, finding friends instead of enemies with the people of Pittsburgh, their violence might receive a direction which would render it harmless; and perhaps they might be persuaded to proceed no further than Braddock's Field. They thought it certain that if this were not done, or if the slightest resistance were made, the town would be laid in ashes. Brison and Day were particularly obnoxious; Kirkpatrick also was, from his being the supposed cause of M'Farlane's death; that these were the primary objects of the popular resentment, but others were so in a secondary degree. They advised that all those against whom this resentment was directed should leave the town, for the safety of those who remained, and as a means of saving their own property. It was evident that the attempt of any individual to defend his house would be worse than useless; if present, he would be certain to lose his life, and the burning of his house would terminate in a general conflagration, with the loss of many other lives.

The committee now reported the message from Washington, and the names of the proscribed were read. Day and Brison were present—Neville, and probably Kirkpatrick, were there, as it was supposed that every one in town who could attend had taken part in the meeting. It struck every one present that it would be advisable for these to absent themselves, or keep out of the way until the danger were past. There was no objection made; all seemed tacitly to acquiesce. It was a manœuvre which all seemed to comprehend, as the only policy which could be adopted under the circumstances for the safety of the proscribed as well as of the rest of the citizens. To attempt a defense against overwhelming numbers of men capable of being rendered infuriate, would be certain destruction; the town could not bring out more than two hundred and fifty men capable of bearing arms, and even some of these could not be relied on; so that the joining the insurgents would be a measure of safety, even as respected them. If they attempted to use the protection of their wooden houses, fire could be put to them, and the lives of their families would be exposed, without speaking of the certain destruction of their property. As to the garrison, it was but a picketed inclosure, at the distance of a mile, with an open common between it and the village; and at this time the troops in it, all numbered, did not exceed forty men. It might afford a temporary refuge against Indians, but not against several thousand riflemen, urged on by fury, and could have been taken by a siege of a week, as it had no supply of provisions. The state of alarm among the towns people may be readily conceived. It will not do at the distance of sixty years to denounce them as cowards and traitors—they acted on the principle of self-preservation, which was perfectly justifiable. If the proscribed were put to the inconvenience of retiring for a time, leaving their property and families under the protection of their fellow-citizens who remainded, they were recompensed by the prospect of security, in lieu of the almost certain destruction to which they were exposed. No disreputation attended the fictitious banishment; on the contrary, they would be regarded by the government with favor, as objects of persecution by the mob. It was not an exile from civilization to the wilderness, but from the wilderness to the seats of civilization, in which they would be sure to meet with a cordial reception from their fellow-citizens, and restored to their homes in triumph in the course of a few weeks, as soon as the government should put down the insurrection.

It was agreed that the proscribed should leave the town ostensibly as if banished, and that those who remained behind, some of whom would have been glad to be banished also, should put on a mask of being with the mob, called "the people," and the insurgents at Braddock's Field. It was proposed that a committee should be appointed to conduct and manage the part which the inhabitants of the town should act. This committee, consisting of the number of twenty-one, was chosen, with power to elect their chairman. They were composed of the most respectable and substantial citizens; it is proper to record their names, as their descendants still continue to form a large proportion of the respectable part of the population. They are as follows—George Robinson, (chief burgess,) H. H. Brackenridge, Peter Audrain, John Scull, (editor Pittsburgh *Gazette*,) John M'Masters, John Wilkins, (father of Gen. Wilkins and Hon. William Wilkins,) Andrew M'Intyre, George Wallace, John Irwin, (merchant,) Andrew Watson, George Adams, David Evans, Josiah Tannehill, Matthew Ernest, William Earl, Alexander M'Nickle, Col. John Irwin, James Clow, William Gormly and Nathaniel Irish. Although no chairman was elected, the chief direction was left by common consent to H. H. Brackenridge. It was intrusted to him to draw up a paper, to be struck off from the press, and sent forward to the people at Braddock's Field, informing them of what had been done, and of the determination of the town to join them.

After the meeting adjourned, it was agreed by the committee to appoint particular persons from among the most intimate friends of those who were the subjects of the fictitious banishment, to wait on them, and make any further explanations that might be deemed necessary, and among the rest, Kirkpatrick in particular. They reported that the latter was perfectly satisfied of the necessity of the measure, and would set out next morning. Brison and Day had already in the meeting declared themselves perfectly satisfied to go; the latter avowed that he was pleased it had fallen upon himself, as he had no family, and intended to take a ride over the mountains at any rate, and it would be no great inconvenience. And yet all these persons, forgetting every circumstance, and the dangers which they escaped, through this pretended banishment, afterward raised a great outcry against their fellow-townsmen, who had thus cruelly subjected them to a Siberian exile! They made a great merit of their sufferings and persecutions, while fêted and entertained by the citizens of Philadelphia! It was well understood by their friends and neighbors of the town, that this terrible exile would be attended with no injury or dishonor, but on the contrary, the means of insuring their present safety, and serve as a recommendation to the government. They never thought of asking themselves, what would have been their situation if they had remained? They would have been compelled to fly for their lives, at any rate with a certainty of the destruction of their property! They were the cause, albeit the innocent cause—still the cause—of the danger incurred by their fellow-townsmen—and it was on their account that the insurgents were now marching to the town with the intention of giving it to the flames.

Late at night, the committee having separated, Henry Purviance, Esq.* of Washington, came to Mr. Brackenridge and expressed concern that the gentlemen of his company from Washington had, as he conceived,

* Mr. Purviance was an eminent lawyer, and prosecutor for the State, a gentleman of high character. He was a Federalist and a friend of government, and exerted himself on all occasions to prevent the discontents of the people from breaking out into open violence. When it did, he was one of the most active in endeavoring to restore order and submission. The family removed to Butler, where they still remain among its most distinguished citizens.

from motives of delicacy, hesitated to express to Col. Neville and General Gibson * the full extent of the danger in which they were; that he could not conceive on what principle Col. Blakeney,† who had undertaken to explain the information in a more specific manner, had omitted to speak to those gentlemen; that they were certainly equally obnoxious with the others, and would be equally unsafe in the event of being found in town if the people should march in, and that it was cruelty, in effect, not to inform them of the real predicament in which they stood. Mr. Brackenridge agreed with Mr. Purviance, and thought it extraordinary that the distinction had been made, as the letter of Gen. Gibson was to the same effect as that of Brison, and that of Neville was more likely to offend those who had become the leaders of the insurrection, than any thing in the letters of the others; and this, coupled with his being the son of the Inspector, would place him first on the list of the proscribed by the mob. It was thought, after this, advisable to call the committee together and bring the subject before them, when Mr. Purviance undertook the task of making the explanation. It was determined that Col. Neville and Gen. Gibson should in the morning be made acquainted with their situation, and that they might then do as they thought proper. This was communicated to them by Mr. Purviance. The fact is conclusive, that so far as respected the towns people, the banishment of the proscribed was dictated by considerations of their safety from the impending danger.

General Gibson came to Mr. Brackenridge the same evening, and appeared to have a just sense of his situation, and requested a candid opinion as to his danger in going to Braddock's Field. Mr. Brackenridge gave his opinion that it was not safe, and expressed his surprise that Col. Neville had not a just sense of his danger, as he understood that he had even talked of going to the rendezvous. The idea was a strange one, for he certainly could not expect to restrain the mob; and as to going there under the pretense of being an insurgent, it would place him and his townsmen in a curious predicament. If he had done so and escaped with

* General Gibson was a merchant, and one of the oldest settlers in the West. His brother, Col. George Gibson, fell in St. Clair's defeat; his nephew, of the same name, is still in the United States service, as an officer of high rank. Judge Gibson, of Pennsylvania, was also his nephew.

† Col. Blakeney was a revolutionary officer of distinction, a Federalist, and an ardent supporter of the government and the laws. His opinions on this subject were so well known, that on the withdrawal of the army sent out to quell the insurrection, he was placed in special command of the corps of militia who were continued in service until order was entirely restored. He was a friend to the Nevilles.

life, it might have had the effect of preventing the "connection" from representing the town committee, and all those who went to Braddock's Field, as traitors! The Colonel was persuaded not to think of going; it is inexplicable how he could have seriously thought of it. His going would have defeated the plan adopted by the people of the town, on the advice of their fellow-citizens from Washington; for the insurgents would naturally ask, can you be in earnest, and yet bring these obnoxious persons along with you? It was even doubtful as to Gen. Wilkins, who had been the most popular man in the country; but that popularity, often so fickle, had left him on a sudden, in consequence of an advertisement in which he said he would, as Commissary of Supplies, purchase only *duty-paid* whiskey! This gentleman determined to risk the going, as he was the senior militia officer, and would be in command of the Pittsburgh troops.*

Here we see the workings of democracy on a small scale, an Athens or Sparta in miniature, or Rome in its infancy; and we see characters on the stage, deliberations and incidents, worthy the pen of Livy. They are not less instructive than the doings of great commonwealths, where the passions and interests of men are at work among a greater number. It is such workings which give interest to the histories of great communities as well as small ones, and it is the minuteness of detail which constitutes the charm of the narrative.

NOTES TO CHAPTER IV.

Judge Addison to Mr. Brackenridge on the subject of Robbing the Mail.

"JANUARY 18, 1795.

"SIR:—I have been pursuing the plan for robbing the mail, and can trace it no higher than Bradford. It was proposed by him to Marshall, on their way to Mingo meeting-house; Baldwin and David Hamilton were in company, and it was put on them to execute it. The object to be obtained, was to know the opinions of the people on the business carried on. The post to be robbed was the post from Washington to Pittsburgh; and it was only when Baldwin and Hamilton sent word that they could not perform their part, and when it was then too late to intercept the mail to Pittsburgh, that the plan was changed to what was really executed. Bradford sent his cousin Wil-

* Gen. Wilkins, son of John Wilkins, Esq. a Justice of the Peace of the town, was a Revolutionary officer, and one of the manliest of manly men. Yet even his going there, although his attachment to the administration of Washington and Hamilton was beyond all question, did not escape the insinuations of the "connection." His steady friendship to Mr. Brackenridge was the great cause of their displeasure.

liam, and David Hamilton, I believe, sent John Mitchel, who executed the business. My information is from a good source, and may be depended on. The matter, I believe, was not talked of at the Mingo Creek meeting-house, nor did Edward Cook know anything of it.

ALEXANDER ADDISON."

David Bradford to the inhabitants of Monongahela—Virginia.

"WASHINGTON, Aug. 6, 1794.

"GENTLEMEN:—I presume you have heard of the spirited opposition given to the excise law in this State. Matters have been so brought to pass here, that all are under the necessity of bringing their minds to a final conclusion. This has been the question amongst us some days: 'Shall we disapprove of the conduct of those engaged against Neville, the excise officer, or approve?' Or in other words, 'Shall we suffer them to fall a sacrifice to Federal prosecution, or shall we support them?' On the result of this business we have fully deliberated, and have determined with *head, heart, hand and voice*, that we will support the opposition to the excise law. The crisis is now come—*submission or opposition;* we are determined in the opposition—we are determined in future to act agreeably to system; to form arrangements, guided by *reason, prudence, fortitude and spirited conduct.* We have proposed a general meeting of the four counties of Pennsylvania, and have invited our brethren in the neighboring counties in Virginia to come forward and join us in council and deliberation on this important crisis, and conclude upon measures interesting to the western counties of Pennsylvania and Virginia. A notification of this kind may be seen in the Pittsburgh paper. Parkinson's Ferry is the place proposed, as most central, and the 14th of August, the time.

"We solicit you by all the ties that an union of interests can suggest, to come forward to join with us in our deliberations. The cause is common to us all; we invite you to come, even should you differ with us in opinion; we wish you to hear our reasons influencing our conduct.

Yours, with esteem,
DAVID BRADFORD."

Resolutions of the Town Meeting, 31st of July, 1794.

"At a meeting of the inhabitants of Pittsburgh, on Thursday evening, July 31st, 1794, to take into consideration the present situation of affairs, and declare their sentiments on this delicate crisis,

"A great majority, almost the whole of the inhabitants of the town, assembled. It being announced to the meeting that certain gentlemen from the town of Washington had arrived, and had signified that they were intrusted with a message to the inhabitants of the town relative to present affairs, a committee of three persons were appointed to confer with them, and report the message to the meeting. The persons appointed were George Wallace, H. H. Brackenridge and John Wilkins, Jr.; these gentlemen made a report to the meeting, to wit: that in consequence of certain letters sent by the last mail, certain persons were discovered as advocates of the excise law, and enemies to the interests of the country, and that a certain Edward Day, James Brison, and Abraham Kirkpatrick, were particularly obnoxious, and that it was expected by the country that they should be dismissed without delay; whereupon it was resolved it should be so done; and a committee of twenty-one were appointed to see this resolution carried into effect.

"Also, that whereas it is a part of the message from the gentlemen of Washington, that a great body of the people of the country will meet to-morrow at Braddock's Field, in order to carry into effect measures that may seem to them advisable with respect to the excise law, and the advocates of it,

"*Resolved*, That the above committee shall, at an early hour, wait upon the people on the ground, and assure the people that the above resolution, with respect to the proscribed persons, has been carried into effect.

"*Resolved*, also, That the inhabitants of the town shall march out and join the people on Braddock's Field, as brethren, to carry into effect with them any measure that may seem to them advisable for the common cause.

"*Resolved*, also, That we shall be watchful among ourselves of all characters that by word or act may be unfriendly to the common cause; and when discovered will not suffer them to live amongst us, but they shall instantly depart the town.

"*Resolved*, That the above committee shall exist as a committee of information, and correspondence, as an organ of our sentiments until our next town meeting.

"And that whereas, a general meeting of delegates from the townships of the country on the west of the mountains, will be held at Parkinson's Ferry on the Monongahela, on the 14th of August next,

"*Resolved*, That delegates shall be appointed to that meeting; and that the 9th of August next be appointed for a town meeting, to elect such delegates.

"*Resolved*, also, That a number of handbills be struck off at the expense of the committe, and distributed among the inhabitants of the town, that they may conduct themselves accordingly."

From Findley's History—p. 94.

"Col. Marshall had been an early settler in the western counties, and a useful citizen during the course of the late war with Britain, and the territorial controversy with Virginia. He was successively Register, High Sheriff, member of the ratifying convention, (of the Federal constitution), of the Legislature, County Lieutenant,* and again Register in Washington county; and was respectable for the discretion he discovered in the discharge of the duties of the respective offices he filled. In the ratifying convention, he voted in favor of amendments previous to ratification, but refused to sign the reasons of the minority. Moderation was thought to have been a leading trait in his character. He is an industrious man, and possesses property to a large amount. From these circumstances, the part he took in the insurrection was truly surprising. He had come from the north of Ireland in his youth."

"David Bradford had been deputy of the Attorney General of the State, from the time that Washington had been erected into a separate county. He was originally from Maryland, where he studied law, and had been a member of the Virginia Assembly before the settlement of boundary line of the State, and still practiced law in some of the courts of that State. He had favored the plan of forming a new State. At the time of the adoption of the Federal government he was one of its most zealous advocates in that country."

"Benjamin Parkinson, a Pennsylvanian by birth, has always resided in that State. He also was a Federalist, and had supported General Neville's interest formerly; was reputed a good citizen, a man of influence in his neighborhood;

---

* The office of County Lieutenant was one o dignity, but fell into disuse after the Revolution. It was established by Henry VIII. It was the duty of the king's lieutenant, to hold the military force of the county in array.—2 Blackstone, 411.

had been a justice of the peace before the revision of the constitution of the State, was President of the Mingo Creek Association, and one of the committee who superintended the operations in the attack on Neville's house."

"J. Canon was from Chester county, Pennsylvania, had long been a respectable citizen south of the Monongahela, lived in the town called by his name, had attached himself to the government of Virginia, and favored the idea of a new State. He was afterward a member of the Legislature, and was an early advocate for the Federal constitution, and a supporter of General Neville's interest in the country."

"Fulton was from Maryland; he was not only a Federalist, but an open advocate of the excise law, indeed the most openly so of any I have met with in the western counties, and was an avowed friend of the Inspector. He kept a large distillery, and expected by the operations of the excise to have considerable advantage over the small distillers. He had also erected a brewery. I have never been able to account for the inconsistency of his conduct."

William Findley was born in the north of Ireland, came to this country young, and served with credit during the Revolutionary War. He was one of the earliest settlers in the West as a farmer. Being a man of considerable intelligence, and reading, and having a turn for public speaking, he soon took part in politics, and was elected to the Legislature. Here he came in conflict with H. H. Brackenridge, who was elected for the purpose of getting the new county of Allegheny struck off from Westmoreland, which was represented by Findley. They came in collision on various occasions, especially on the subject of a loan office, for which the people of the West were clamorous—Findley supported and Brackenridge opposed the law. When the latter was urged to support what he regarded as of a very pernicious tendency, he was told that the people called for it, "D——n the people," said he, "what do they know about such things." This hasty speech was reported against him, and a handle made of it. A long paper war ensued between him and Findley, which laid the foundation of a personal as well as political enmity. They differed also on the subject of the Federal constitution, Findley taking sides with Gallatin. Findley was one of those who took part in the meetings two years before the outbreak. He attacks Hamilton with severity in his book. He was one of the earliest to oppose the Federal administration, but was deficient in firmness of purpose. When the vote on Jay's treaty was taken, he left the House of Representatives to avoid giving his vote, and was brought up by the sergeant-at-arms. As to his history of the insurrection, in the simple statement of facts, he would not knowingly deviate from truth, but his prejudices were strong, and his personal enmity biassed his judgment. His book was written the year after that of Mr. Brackenridge, of which he makes occasional use, while he endeavors in a *sneaking way* to undervalue the author and detract from his merits. Instances of this are given in the progress of this work.

Extract from the Affidavit of Adamson Tannehill.

"That on the evening preceding the meeting at Braddock's Field, the inhabitants of Pittsburgh generally assembled to consult on what measures were necessary to pursue on the occasion. That before the people had proceeded to take the matter up in any order, it was announced to them that three or four gentlemen had arrived from Washington county, with some alarming information respecting the meeting of the people on the next day at Braddock's Field. George Wallace, John Wilkins, Jr., and H. H. Brackenridge, Esq., were immediately named to wait on them. On the return of these gentlemen they informed the people there assembled, that in consequence of letters being intercepted in the mail which had been taken, that certain persons were proscribed as obnoxious to the people who were to assemble at Braddock's Field on the next day; viz. James Brison, Edward Day, and Abraham Kirkpatrick, and that nothing short of their expulsion would satisfy the people and save the town. The question was then put by the chairman, General Gibson, whether they should be expelled or not? which was declared in the affirmative. The mode of expulsion was the next consideration, which was to be done by a committee of twenty-one, the choice of whom was vested in the chairman, who named them generally; the chairman was named as one of the committee himself, (his name set down by the secretary, Matthew Ernest,) and he appeared to acquiesce in the appointment. The deponent understood at the time, that a private suggestion was made the chairman by Mr. Brackenridge, that he, the chairman, was also obnoxious; on which he supposed his name to be erased, Mr. Brackenridge not thinking it prudent that he should be of the committee in going to Braddock's Field, and might induce suspicion of our sincerity in having him of the committee. This the deponent understood from Mr. Brackenridge on the same evening.

"Two of the persons proscribed were at the meeting, viz. James Brison and Edward Day, who appeared to acquiesce in the expulsion, *considering it for their own safety as well as that of the town*, from the manner they expressed themselves; and further, that the particular friends of these gentlemen were pointed out to consult them on the expedience of their removal. The deponent believes that it was perfectly understood at the time, to be the most politic thing that could be done on the occasion, in order to take away any pretense from the rioters at Braddock's Field, of coming to the town to seize them, and do other injuries; and that the same policy and necessity led the people generally to Braddock's Field. The deponent was one of the committee to Braddock's Field, and on the route there Mr. Brackenridge expressed himself to the deponent to the following effect: that after all that had been done, he did not consider it as perfectly certain that we might not suffer violence from the fury of the people, on account of the prevailing odium against the town, knowing that however far we had carried the appearance of union in sentiment with the rioters, they would see through the mask, and treat us ill on the first approach. Under these impressions, Brackenridge proposed advancing with a flag; the deponent objected to it, and observed that it was best not to seem to distrust. Mr. Brackenridge then declined it.

"That during the whole of the insurrection, so far as the deponent had knowledge, Mr. Brackenridge conducted himself as a friend to the government, and showed great anxiety to have peace and good order restored to the country. That his apprehensions appeared natural and unaffected. The deponent has further heard the citizens of Pittsburgh generally speak of him in the most favorable manner, *for his activity and address in saving the town.*"

Extract from the Affidavit of William Meetkirk.

"We accordingly went to Pittsburgh. When we arrived there a number of people came to the house where we put up, to inquire of us if we knew what object the people had in view that were to assemble at Braddock's Field? We informed them that it was in consequence of letters that had been found in the mail, written by several persons in that place to government, misstating their conduct (as they termed it), and that the people conceived them to be very obnoxious characters, particularly Major Kirkpatrick, Mr. Brison and Mr. Day; and it was our opinion that if some of those who had written the letters did not leave the town, that it was in danger of being destroyed from the apparent rage of the people. The same evening there was a town meeting of the inhabitants of the place, as we understood, to take into consideration what was best to be done for their own safety. On hearing that we had come to town, they appointed a committee, consisting of Mr. Brackenridge, Gen. Wilkins and Judge Wallace, to confer with us, and to have our opinion on the subject. We produced to them the letters that had been taken out of the mail, viz. Major Butler to Gen. Knox; Gen. Gibson to Governor Mifflin; Mr. Brison to the same; Col. Neville to Gen. Morgan, and one without signature to the Secretary of the Treasury, in the handwriting of Edward Day; which were read in their presence. They asked us what we thought was the intentions of the people that were to assemble at Braddock's Field the next day? We gave it as our opinion, that the town was in imminent danger of being destroyed if some of the obnoxious characters were not sent away, for that we ourselves had been insulted on the road coming there by some people, when they understood we were going to Pittsburgh; for they said we were going there as spies to tell the people to get out of the way, and that we ought to be taken prisoners, and they actually raised a party to follow us for that purpose, as we were afterward informed. After which they returned to the meeting and gave the information from us, in consequence of which they entered into resolutions to expel certain persons, and which was afterward published in handbills."

Extract from the statement of Col. Blakeney.

"We produced the letters which were to be considered obnoxious; they were read, and the committee were told by us to make what use they might think proper of them until to-morrow, as we had to produce them at Braddock's Field. The names of the obnoxious characters were given by us, viz. Major Kirkpatrick, Mr. Brison and Mr. Day. I mentioned to the committee that we had no real business at that time but to save the town. And if you did not comply with what was related, by the Lord, your town, as I believed, would be laid in ashes, and those persons probably massacred. I remember one question put by the committee, 'What will you advise to do for the real safety of the place?' Answer—Send off these characters; take your arms in your hands and meet the people at Braddock's Field to-morrow.

"Col. Presley Neville was present the most of the time. I remember the conversation with Col. Neville; he asked us to give him a pass, or passport, so that he might leave the place and travel without being molested. I replied that we were not invested with any such powers, that we were not committee men, and that we came of our own accord to inform the people of Pittsburgh of the impending danger they were in; nevertheless, he repeated this desire to have a passport of us the next morning. True it is, had it been in my power, nothing would have given me greater pleasure, as I always considered him an old fast friend. Yet I felt hurt at his request, and more so on the repetition of it, after the answer I had given him."

The foregoing extracts, taken from affidavits published in the appendix to the "Incidents," sufficiently sustain the account given in the text. Those papers, together with the statements of James Ross, Mr. Purviance, and Mr. Reddick and others, to the same effect, will appear in full as notes to other chapters in the progress of this work. The foregoing is deemed sufficient for the present.

CHAPTER V.

THE ASSEMBLAGE AT BRADDOCK'S FIELD — DIFFICULTY OF SAVING THE TOWN.

The people of Pittsburgh, having come to the determination already related, set out early in the morning of the first of August, 1794, for the place of rendezvous — the committee of twenty-one, composed, as already mentioned, of the most respectable citizens, being on horseback, unarmed, and followed by the militia of the town, numbering two hundred and fifty, under the command of Gen. Wilkins. It was not without misgiving that they reflected on the hazard of the experiment of joining several thousand armed men, whose purpose, (if any they had,) at least of a large portion of them, was to burn and plunder their town. But the towns people believed that this fraternization and display of willingness to join in whatever project was on foot, would turn aside the mischief of this methodical mob from them and contribute to prevent injury to others. Many, at the same time, indulged a hope that the multitude (or *army* as it was called,) could be persuaded to proceed no further than they then were, as the idea of attacking the garrison had been abandoned, and the obnoxious characters, whose presence now formed the only pretext for the march, had left the town or were supposed to have done so. About six hundred of the Pittsburgh resolutions had been struck off, and being sent through the Washington committee and distributed among the people, were reported to have produced a favorable impression. Under these circumstances the Pittsburghers marched into the field.

"On approaching the scene," says Mr. Brackenridge, "my feelings were by no means pleasant. I was far from thinking myself secure from personal danger. I knew I had stood, in general, well with the country before this period; but I had given myself a stab as to popularity, by what I had said at the Mingo meeting-house. I had understood that a current of obliquy ran strong against me from that quarter."

Besides this, there were persons who entertained unfriendly feelings toward him from previous causes; two of them, M'Farlane, the brother of him that had been killed, and Benjamin Parkinson, he knew would be there as leaders. The prevailing idea among the people was, that all law for the time was dissolved, as on the extreme frontier when lynch law rules the hour. There was no notion, under the circumstances, that there could be anything wrong in bringing a man to speedy end by the limb of a tree and hanging him, if obnoxious to the people. Although he had been on friendly terms with Bradford before, he did not know his standing at present. He might be suspected of having related his treasonable speech at the Mingo Creek meeting, which had been communicated to government by the writers of the intercepted letters, and who had drawn upon them the resentment of Bradford. If he should make inquiries into this matter, on the ground, it might place him in an awkward predicament, as he had in fact given the information with the others who had accompanied him. It might not be easy to save themselves from the tyrant of the day. Under these apprehensions for himself and the committee, he thought of advancing with a white flag, and placed a white handkerchief on the end of a whip for the purpose, but a moment's reflection impelled him to take it down, as it would show distrust and mar the plan which had been adopted. These fears may appear unreasonable at this distance of time, but not to one who has seen a large and enraged multitude, under the command of one as mad as themselves, or under no command at all. In the first case, they will execute whatever the leader dictates; in the other, what any one may suggest. In the present instance, Bradford would have great power, but the people would have more, and there was reason to fear both. As to burning the town, possibly it was more talked of than intended; but the talking of it would lead to the act, contrary to the wishes of many of the talkers. Such is the history of the human mind, when men are in a state of anarchy.

The account of the assemblage will be given in the words of the author of the "Incidents," whose graphic descriptions have been in great part adopted by Hamilton in his report.

"The ground where Braddock fought,* is on the east side (right bank) of the Monongahela, and on the same side with the town of Pittsburgh. The militia from Washington had therefore to cross the river in order to come upon the ground. They had crossed in great numbers, at the same ford where Braddock did, and were now on the ground. They were dressed in what we call hunting shirts, many of them with handkerchiefs on their heads; it is in this dress they equip themselves against the Indians. They were amusing themselves with shooting with balls at marks, and firing in the air at random with powder only. There was a continual

* At the time of the assemblage it was the private property of Geo. Wallace, Esq. one of the committee.

discharge of guns, and constant smoke in the woods and along the bank of the river. There appeared great wantonness of mind, and a disposition to do anything extravagant. We had advanced within the camp, as it was called, when the committee halted and waited for Gen. Wilkins, at the head of the Pittsburgh militia, to approach. I saw him march by us, and discovered in his countenance a sufficient evidence of a sense of danger; though I knew him to be a man of great personal intrepidity, yet I did not wonder at his apprehensions. Nothing but his appearing at the head of the militia could have saved him. I was thinking of his danger, when I turned my head a moment, and was struck with the sight of the very man I was most afraid of, Andrew M'Farlane, just by me. He was dressed in a blue coat, with a dark visage, lowering countenance, and a rifle in his hand, looking at me. I eyed him in my turn, but did not venture to speak. I trusted to his fear of the people, as he did not know perfectly how I stood with them; after some time he turned about and went away.

"The next object that arrested my attention was Bradford,* walking before a number of battalions that had just crossed the river, and were ranged on the bank to be viewed by him. I was solicitous to know what my reception would be. I knew that from his going on to the intercepting the mail, and the procuring of this movement of the people without my knowledge, he had not expected my assistance, and his not communicating his intentions discovered a distrust of me. But I found our proceedings in Pittsburgh had satisfied him, for he advanced and spoke to me. The usual questions by him, and every one else, were, had we sent away those men? Was there no danger of their coming back? Our usual answer was, they are gone—they will not be suffered to come back. Epithets of indignity were sometimes used respecting them, to mask our sentiments the better. It was said by them that more must go. Every one from Pittsburgh that I heard speak at all, assented to every thing that was said; for it was a part of the system adopted, and we trusted to the arrangements that could be made to soften all matters and prevent injury to any one, in proportion as we ourselves could acquire confidence with the leaders or the multitude.

* "David Bradford assumed the office of Major General; mounted on a superb horse, in splendid trappings, arrayed in full martial uniform, with plumes floating in the air and sword drawn, he rode over the ground, gave orders to the military and harangued the multitude. Never was mortal man more flattered than was David Bradford on Braddock's Field. Every thing depended on his will. The insurgents adored him, paid him the most servile homage, in order to be able to control and manage him."—Carnahan, p. 127.

"Having been some time on the ground, I fell in with Benjamin Parkinson, the other person of whom I had been personally apprehensive. He was in a group of men whom I knew to be warm in the cause. I advanced with great appearance of confidence and frankness of manner, and saluted them. I was received with cordiality, and thought myself very fortunate. All, or most of them, had been at the conflagration of the house of the Inspector, and had heard me at the Mingo meetinghouse; but the Pittsburgh handbill, and my appearance on the ground now to join them, had effaced the unfavorable impression.

"They sat in a group on the ground, each with his rifle in his hand, or lying by him. I sat with them. The conversation turned upon the burning of the house; and they expressed great rage against Kirkpatrick, who had been the cause of burning it, and the death of James M'Farlane, by his refusing to let the house be searched for the Inspector's commission and his papers. They expressed resentment against Major Butler, for sending out soldiers to the house of the Inspector. They had inquired for Ormsby, who had accompanied Neville, the younger, and the Marshal from Pittsburgh. I said he was upon the ground, but was scarcely worth inquiring after. He was an inconsiderate young man, that would go any where. He had gone there and had come here, and it was little matter what he did. That we had heard in what manner they had treated him when they had him a prisoner; that they had taken his horse and pistol and hanger from him; and put him on the bare back of a colt to ride, as a steed congenial with his years and discretion. I had heard something of this, but whatever might have been the case, I was disposed to give them the impression that I was diverted with the circumstance, and therefore put them on the relation of the circumstances, and laughed immoderately; but concluded that he had been sufficiently punished by his apprehension on that occasion; and that he had gone there without the knowledge of his parents, and had come with their approbation here, it was not worth while to mind him; it was agreed that it was not. I did not know that, in the meantime, the young man had been on the point of assassination. Fifteen men had painted themselves black, as the Indian warriors do when they go to war. They had gone in search of Ormsby. Zedick Wright, of Peter's Creek, had discovered it, and having a good will for the family, or from motives of humanity, made haste to give him the intelligence of it, a few minutes, not a quarter of an hour, when they were seen to pass by openly in pursuit of him. He made his way to Pittsburgh in the course of the day, by devious routes, and lay concealed in the barracks of the old garrison until the whole cavalcade was over.

"I was greatly disconcerted on one occasion, in the course of the day, by James Ross,* of Washington. It was the first time I had seen him on the ground, when sitting with two or three others at the root of a tree; passing by, he said to me, within a smile, 'You have got a great deal of subtlety, but you will have occasion for it all.' I was alarmed, and looked about to see who must have heard him. There were none near but those just with me, whom I knew, and who were wearing the mask also. But I gave him to understand that he had alarmed me, for he could not know the character of those with me. He said he did, and considered that before he spoke. Talking of the arrangements made, he thought the business well managed on the part of the town; and that nothing else could have saved lives and property.

"People were coming in from every quarter all that day, generally armed; but some without arms. It was impossible to know the real sentiments of almost any one amongst the multitude—how far they were there from necessity, or of choice. Every man was afraid of the opinions of another. Sometimes a word dropped, which might be construed away if not well taken, would lead to a confidence. The great bulk of the people were certainly in earnest; and the revolutionary language and the ideas of the French people had become familiar. It was not tarring and feathering, as at the commencement of the revolution from Great Britain, but guillotining—that is, putting to death by any way that offered. I am persuaded that even if Bradford himself, that day, had ventured to check the violence of the people, in any way that was not agreeable to them, and had betrayed the least partiality for the excise law, or perhaps even of a remission of his zeal against it, he would have sunk in an instant from his power, and they would have hung him on the first tree! Yet, he was weak enough not to have foreseen this; it had been an argument used with him, in dissuading from a perseverance in the measure undertaken, that no man could calculate the consequences of putting the mass in motion with arms in their hands. His answer was, that he could say to them, 'hitherto shalt thou go, and no further.' Certain it is, that his influence was great. I saw a man wade into the river, lift cold water from the bottom of the channel and bring it in his hat to him to drink. Applications were made to him that day for commissions in the service.

"Nevertheless, whatever his idea might have been, he would have seen the extent of his power, if he had ventured to tell the people that they

* Mr. Ross, U. S. Senator, then resided in Washington, and had come, like many others, with a view of exerting himself to control the people. He was afterward one of the Commissioners to offer an amnesty to the insurgents.

should return without going on to Pittsburgh. It was the object of all men who were apprehensive of the consequences, to dissuade from this; but it appeared very doubtful, through the whole day, whether or not it was practicable. It was afterward found that it was not.

"I had seen Gen. Wilkins through the day; he had remained close with the Pittsburgh people, and ventured little through the multitude. On his first coming he had gone up to Bradford, apprehensive that he might denounce him, and addressed him, 'Sir, have you any thing against me?' 'No,' said he. This resolute behavior probably prevented him from having any thing to say.

"Toward the evening, there was a council of the Pittsburgh committee. It had been represented to them, and was the fact, that the people of the town, not expecting to detain that night, had brought no provisions with them; it was suggested that they might be suffered to return to town, and be at the place of rendezvous early in the morning. It was thought expedient, and orders were given accordingly. On its being known that the people of Pittsburgh were going home for the night, there was a great clamor in the camp. It was said they were about to desert the cause, and in fact never had been sincere in it. The fact is, there were persons among them shrewd enough to discover this. Some would say they were pleased with our address, but would rather have had us all in concert. 'You have acted well, but we understand you; we give you credit for your management.' It would be answered: 'What! do you doubt our sincerity?' They would say, 'We do not dispute your good policy.'

"Finding the effect of the departure of the Pittsburgh people, it was thought desirable to countermand the leave given. I rode after them in great haste and turned them to the field, with orders not to leave it, let their want of food be what it might, rather than produce a dissatisfaction with the people on the ground, and bring them irregularly and in bad humor to the town. It will be asked, whence had I this authority? And how was I obeyed so readily? I was of the committee to whom the power had been intrusted of conducting all the affairs on this occasion.

"On my return with the Pittsburgh people, I saw James Marshall, for the first time, on the ground. I saw he was greatly hurt in his mind, at the trouble he had brought upon us; and had great solicitude with regard to the event. I explained to him the dissatisfaction that had taken place at the departure of our people, and wished him to ride through the camp and give information that he saw us all returned. He mounted his horse, with his rifle in his hand, and set out to do it.

"In the course of the day, a great subject of conversation had been the taking of the garrison. It would seem to have been the original object of the movement, but had been laid aside. On what principle, I do not know; whether on the ground of the difficulty of accomplishing it, or the projectors of the enterprise hesitating to make war so directly on the United States. I should rather think it was the danger of the enterprise that operated on the mind of Bradford; for he would naturally reflect that he could not avoid taking a part in the attempt himself, and I have no idea that he was a man of courage under certain danger. The reason ostensibly assigned at the relinquishment of this object, was, that it was found the military stores in the garrison were intended for the campaign against the Indians, and it would be improper to derange the operations of that campaign by seizing them. This part of the enterprise had been abandoned by the projectors of it, but the rumor had gone abroad, and it was not generally known to the people that it was abandoned. The query every where was, were we to take the garrison? I answered always, that we were. The query then was, could we take it? It was answered, no doubt of it. But at a great loss? Not at all—not above a thousand killed and five hundred mortally wounded. This loss, to the more thinking part, appeared very serious. Various modes were proposed of taking it; some thought of providing stakes with sharpened points, and rushing up with these and putting them into the port-holes, obstruct the firing from them, while others were cutting away the pickets. In the meantime others, with their rifles, taking off the men at the guns in the blockhouses of the bastions, as the Indians took off the artillery men at St. Clair's expedition. I was asked what was my plan of taking it? I suggested the undermining and blowing up a bastion; but they would fire upon the diggers; besides, it wasted powder. To some complaining, that called out so hastily they were not well supplied with powder, I proposed starving out the garrison; but these were apprehensive they would starve out themselves. After night I had a great deal of conversation on this subject, in the bushes and at the sides of the fences—laying our heads together and whispering. I was for the most desperate measures, but admitted that much blood must be lost.

"About midnight, I rode through the camp where the people were lying at the fires in their blankets or without. I made a pretense of inquiring for the Pittsburgh battalion, and this with a view at the same time to let them know that the Pittsburgh people were still on the ground. My principal object was to ascertain the determination of the people with regard to their coming to Pittsburgh. I found the universal sentiment to be, that they would see the town. There was little sleep in the camp. The firing and shouting had ceased, but there was a continued conversation.

"Coming up to a fire, a person to whom I was known accosted me. 'Is Kirkpatrick gone?' said he. He is gone. 'And why the devil did you let him go?' said a person starting up behind him. The question came so suddenly upon me, that I was a little struck with it; but recovering, I replied that it was no fault of mine that he went away; I would rather have kept him here, and punished him by the law. This was the truth, for I was prosecuting at that very time for misdemeanor. The enragé or enraged man, as I may call him, made no reply; but the person who first spoke to me gave me a touch on the side and said, 'Come, take a dram, we will not detain you.' This I understood to be a hint to go away.

"I give this incident, because that having mentioned it afterward, it was used as a proof that I had endeavored to influence the people against Kirkpatrick by talking of punishing by law. It is true the man deserves my resentment, nevertheless I had too much regard for my own feelings and the opinion of the public to avail myself of that occasion to do him an injury. But my loose expression in the case mentioned was equivocal, and was understood by them as it was intended to be understood, viz. to the circumstance which was the ground of their resentment, the defending Neville's house; my insinuation was that it was punishable by law. The thought was new to the man, and it occupied his mind for the moment.

"Passing on to a range of fires, I found Hamilton's battalion. This had arrived late in the evening; it had been long expected, and was called the 'bloody battalion.' The greatest part of it had been at the burning of the Inspector's house. We expected desperate measures when these came. It was commanded by John Hamilton, a man very moderate and reasonable, and who was disposed to restrain the people from acts of violence, and with that view had come with them. Daniel Hamilton, his cousin, was the first that accosted me, and wishing to serve me the people, called out, 'This is a true whig. But what do you think of that d——d fellow, James Ross? He has been here and all through the camp, persuading the people not to go to Pittsburgh!' I saw now that it was in vain to oppose the going, and it was better to acquiesce and say they should go. In that case there would be more management of them than if they came in spite of opposition. I saw this, and took my part decidedly. 'D——n the fellow,' said I, 'what business has he with Pittsburgh? The people of Pittsburgh wish to see the army; and you must go through it, and let the d——d garrison see that we could take it if we would. It will convince the government that we are no mob, but a regular army, and can preserve discipline and pass through a town like the French and American armies in the course of the last war, without doing the least injury to persons or property?' There was a general acclamation, and all professed a determination to molest no one. Returning to a farm house, just by the camp, where some of our committee were, I communicated the result of my observations. Some of them had been through the camp in the same manner, and had the same impressions that I had, with regard to the impossibility of preventing the people from coming to town."

The foregoing is given in the words of the author of the "Incidents;" it is the minuteness of the details which gives it its greatest value. The reader is placed in the very midst of the scene which passes before his eyes; he shares the author's feelings, and profits by his profound reflections drawn from human nature. More than one topic is presented for the study of our peculiar institutions, and the genius of our American people. If they have improved since that day, it is simply from the increase in the proportionate number of enlightened individuals, and the greater spread of knowledge and education.

In the morning, a council consisting of the principal officers was convened in the camp, and it was agreed to form a committee, to be composed of three from each regiment, to deliberate on what was to be done. Gen. Wilkins, H. H. Brackenridge and John M'Masters were chosen for Pittsburgh. In order that the deliberations might be more free, it was proposed to retire to some distance, which they did, to a shady ground in the woods. Edward Cook was appointed chairman, but no secretary was chosen.* Bradford opened the meeting by stating the cause of their assemblage in arms, viz. in order to chastise certain persons who had avowed sentiments friendly to the excise laws; that their sentiments had come to light through the vigilance of some persons who had intercepted the mail, and found their letters; that these letters would speak for themselves. Here taking out the letters from his pocket, he read them: from Major Butler of the garrison, giving an account of the outrages committed, and his sense of their atrocity; from Neville the younger, alluding to the authors of the disturbance, and applying to them the epithet

---

*Hildreth says (see Craig's History, p. 252,) that Gallatin was appointed secretary. He was not there at all. Craig ought to have known better. The three or four pages he extracts from Hildreth, on the subject of the insurrection, contain almost as many errors as they contain lines. Craig and Hildreth are of that class of old Federalists, who, like the ancient nobility in France, never learn and never forget anything.

of *rascals;* from Edward Day, suggesting a project for carrying the excise law into operation; from Gen. Gibson, stating a motion of Bradford, at the Mingo Creek meeting, to support the outrages committed; from the prothonotary Brison, to the same effect. At the authors of these two last letters he appeared particularly enraged, as distinguishing him at the Mingo Creek meeting, and representing him as making such a motion. Addressing himself to Mr. Brackenridge—"Were not you there," said he; "did I make such a motion?" "I looked at the man with astonishment, (says Mr. Brackenridge in the "Incidents,") is it possible, thought I, that you did not know the scope of your harangue? You did not make the motion, but you supported it, and that is all the inaccuracy in the statement in the letter. But is it possible you would regard the being distinguished to the government as supporting violent counsels, when you have distinguished yourself so effectually in the very act of obtaining these letters? However, it was no time to explain; it would involve myself and put it out of my power to save others, to enter into an altercation with the Robespierre of the occasion, by stating, as the fact was, that if he did not make the motion, he supported it.* I therefore evaded it, by saying that the statement in the letter was not accurate, but that might be the fault of the information given the writers. It was answered, that it became them to be more cautious in giving credit to information; and at all events it evinced a disposition unfriendly to the people, to be communicating information to the government of what they were about. There was no answering this." The reader must reflect, that Mr. Brackenridge was placed in a situation where the least imprudence on his part would not merely involve himself, but many others, his fellow townsmen, whose fate was extremely critical.

Bradford having read the letters, and put them up again, said, there is another person who is an object of resentment with the people, Major Craig; he has had the insolence to say, that if the Inspector's office is shut up in the town of Pittsburgh, he will open it in his own house. Calling on the deputation from Pittsburgh, said he, "Have any of you heard this?" It was answered in the negative. Mr. Brackenridge said that he had neither heard it from him nor from others, but stated something respecting the Major's uneasiness and alarm—his taking down the notice on the door, and giving the fragments to Capt. Long! He caused a laugh at the expense of the Major; thinking to save him, as well as

*It is very possible that it may have been designed by Bradford to bring on a row, which would end in getting rid of the whole Pittsburgh delegation. A violent altercation would have led to fatal consequences.

the Pittsburgh people by substituting mirth in the place of the angry feelings which prevailed. He also admits that he had some little malice in this piece of merriment, on account of the Major having accused the towns people of cowardice in not going out to defend the Inspector's house in the country. Bradford said that the language of the Major had been the talk of the camp.

It was now the question, what should be done with these men? It was resolved that the question should be taken with respect to them singly. The case of Major Butler was considered first; his offense was twofold—the interfering with the civil authority of the people, by sending a military force to the house of the Inspector; and by his correspondence with the government. There was no one so rash as to defend these acts; but it was observed by Mr. Brackenridge, that being an officer of the United States, Major Butler was amenable to the Executive for everything unconstitutionally done; and that on a representation to the President, there could be no question but that he would remove him from the command in the district. It would be most advisable, therefore, to take no order in his case, but postpone it until the meeting at Parkinson's Ferry, and then remonstrate to the Executive, and procure his recall, which was agreed to. The amusing inconsistency of petitioning the President for the removal of a subordinate officer, by persons in arms against the government, does not appear to have struck any one, nor does it appear that so transparent a piece of management on the part of Brackenridge led to any suspicion of his design.

The case of Major Craig was next taken up. It was observed by Mr. Brackenridge, that it was true that there certainly was ground of suspicion that he had been over zealous in favor of the excise law; nevertheless it might be bad policy to order him of the country at this time, for in his capacity as Quarter-Master, he had the care of the military stores that were intended for the Indian campaign; that it might derange these operations, and give offense to the people of Kentucky, who were also against the excise law. But he was also an officer of the United States, appointed by Gen. Knox, the Secretary at War, and the same steps might be taken against him as against Major Butler. The only difficulty in this case, was to whom the representation should be made, to the Secretary at War or the President? James Ross, who happened to be near, was appealed to, and he gave it as his opinion, that the Secretary at War was the proper authority to be addressed. The effect of the appointment of a delegation to meet at Parkinson's Ferry, was seen in the two foregoing instances, in the disposition to refer to its decisions as the highest authority instituted by the people themselves, although existing only *in futuro*. It also furnished a good excuse for giving the go-by to subjects not otherwise manageable. It was wise to refer such questions to that higher authority, as it took away the disposition of the people to act hastily, or from sudden impulse.

The next cases were those of the two other writers, Neville and Gibson. Mr. Brackenridge spoke in their behalf also, but it was discovered that the people were growing impatient at this special pleading of the Pittsburgh lawyer. With regard to Gibson, he observed, that he was a man of an inoffensive disposition, and could do little harm go or stay; being engaged in trade, to be compelled to leave home might injure not only himself but others, and that banishment, in his case, could do no good. As to Neville, he had used harsh language, but under the influence of passion, and in a letter to a relation. Some ill humor was now manifested: there were speakers for and against; a man leaning on his knees, with his chin on the head of his staff and a slouched hat on his head, spoke softly but with great eagerness, for Neville — but at this moment a Capt. Murray, a young Irishman, not long in the country, with great liveliness of manner, came forward, dressed in a light sky-blue camblet coat, leather overalls, buff waistcoat, and a cutlass by his side. He had not been present until that moment. In fact, fresh battalions of militia were continually arriving, and as they arrived they chose deputies to the committee. Murray wishing to make up for lost time, was very active now, and understanding that the question was for the banishmennt of a certain individual, was very strenuous for the banishment. If it had been hanging, it would have been the same thing; for the man had no resentment personally or politically, but simply wished to distinguish himself, and engage in the revolution.

"I felt little or no concern," says Mr. Brackenridge, "in the case of Neville,* for I did not see it to be of any consequnence to him whether he was to go or stay. I rather thought it was his interest to be sent away, and I had understood that it was his wish to get out of the country. He actually expressed himself to that effect to the messengers from Washington,† who came with the intercepted mail, and applied to them for a passport, mistaking their authority. I had seen him the morning of

---

*He was a man of *leisure*, and passed much of his time in Philadelphia. At this time he was a member of the State Legislature, and was summoned there shortly after to attend a special session. Craig speaks most pathetically of his *exile*.

†See Col. Blakeney's statement, of whom he requested a passport! Yet he made a great outcry about his banishment.

our march to Braddock's Field, and with as much anxiety of countenance as a man could discover, who could conceive his life to be in danger—his expression was, 'The only thing I think of is to escape assassination.' Well—I thought of nothing but this, the saving of his life and property. For Gibson I *was* concerned; not that I thought it would ultimately be of any damage to him to be banished, but I supposed his feelings would be hurt for the present, and he might think it of consequence to be sent away.

"I was standing by Bradford at this time—turning to him, I observed with some warmth, 'The sending away these people is a farce; it will be the best recommendation they can have to the government; they will get into office and be great men by it; it is better to let them stay and be insignificant where they are; you could not have done a better thing to those that are gone than to have sent them off.' My language was candid, and his answer especially so. 'But,' said he, 'the people came out to do something, and something they must do.' I now saw, that whatever his theory might have been with regard to the extent of his power over the people, his feelings for his own safety corrected his vanity; and he saw the necessity of giving a tub to the whale. He had heard the declamation of Murray, viz. that we must be firm, and clear the country of disaffected persons, &c.; and conceiving that Murray, being just fresh from the camp, had brought its sensibilities with him, he was unwilling to relax in his disposition with regard to the expulsion — we ought to be firm, said he, and unanimous."

At the first withdrawing of the committee, and taking their station in the woods, they were followed by numbers of outsiders. The committee being opened, it was moved, and the chairman was directed to inform the people, that it was their wish to deliberate in private, and the chairman addressed them to this effect. Some went away, but others remained, and accessions were certainly made by new comers. In spite of all that could be done, there was a gallery of riflemen around them. About a dozen came up from the camp, and having listened a little, leaning with their rifles on a log, while the committee was still deliberating on the cases of Gibson and Neville — "Gentlemen," said one of them, "do something speedily, or we will go to execution ourselves." This, with the disposition discoverable in the committee, induced the Pittsburghers to think it not advisable to delay the determination in the cases just mentioned, lest the multitude should go on, and the committee, of course, break up without any determination at all; and in that case, no resolution having been passed and announced with regard to these persons, they would be left to the mercy of the mob. Under these impressions, the Pittsburgh members consulting aside, were of opinion that it was best to say at once that they would be sent away, and they themselves would engage to have it done; but requested eight days for them to be ready. Some one of the members proposed to refer the case to the Parkinson Ferry meeting, but that was rejected. This undertaking of the Pittsburghers to expel their fellow townsmen, was not well received; their wish to do so was distrusted, and led to the inquiry whether those who were said to have left the town, were actually gone or not? It was affirmed by the towns people that they were gone, and that they had crossed the Allegheny river the preceding evening. They were anxious to satisfy the doubt, which seemed to be growing serious, and might have terminated badly, when fortunately a young man who had just come from the camp, announced that one of the spies employed in the Indian war had just come in, and brought an account that they had seen Brison and Kirkpatrick ten miles on the Sandusky road. Though not true, it answered the purpose. It was now stipulated that they should not be permitted to come back. Mr. Brackenridge told the people that if they did come back they might seize him in their place; some one said, "Remember the pledge."

Bradford now moved that the troops should go on to Pittsburgh; "Yes," said Mr. Brackenridge, "by all means; and if with no other view, at least to give a proof that the strictest order can be preserved and no damage done. We will just march through, and making a turn come out on the Monongahela bank, and taking a little whiskey with the inhabitants of the town, the troops will embark and cross the river." These words thus carelessly spoken, became the order of the day, there being no other orders issued by any other officer or commander. James Ross at this moment stepping from another part of the committee, whispered to Mr. Brackenridge, "The veil is getting too thin, I fear it will be seen through." But the committee had risen and were going away. "It is well for you," said Benjamin Parkinson, "that the committee has broken up in such a hurry; you would have been taken notice of, you gentlemen of Pittsburgh. Give us whiskey! we don't want your whiskey." "I considered his umbrage at these words," says Mr. Brackenridge, "as no more than a pretense for a quarrel, and was alarmed, but made, in the softest manner, an explanation that I meant no more than that we should drink together, and not any offense whatever; and that it would affect me in the most sensible manner, if anything inadvertently said by me should intercept harmony and injure the cause. I got him to seem satisfied; but I rather suppose he had begun to suspect me of not being in earnest in the cause, and that this was the real ground of his resentment."

The situation was a delicate one for those who were obliged to seem what they were not. Parkinson was a bully, but like such had more show of desperate courage than reality. The safety of those who were thus compelled to act so difficult a part, lay in the shortness of time that the insurgents were assembled together—they did not yet know how far to confide in each other—or what support they could count upon, and how far others were supported. The same collection of persons remaining together only a few days, in all probability would have exhibited a different character.

The Pittsburgh committee, in the mean time, had sent messengers to Major Butler to inform him of the state of things, and that the garrison would not be disturbed.* Others were despatched to have boats ready for crossing the river, and refreshments on the ground where they would halt, so as to leave no pretext for leaving the ranks. Some of the towns people had gone home, alarmed at the idea of the march, in order to put out of the way some of their most valuable articles. Some buried their books and papers. Mr. Brackenridge had given orders the day before for his papers to be carried out of town. Officers in the mean time had been appointed: Colonels Cook and Bradford generals; Colonel Blakeney officer of the day; Mr. Brackenridge led the army as guide, from his perfect knowledge of the country and the roads. In this order this extemporized army entered the town by the Fourth Street Road, keeping out of sight of the garrison; marching down the main street to the Monongahela, the whole body then passing along the river, and about four o'clock halted on the plain to the east of the town, the property of Mr. Brackenridge. Here every possible provision had been made that the short space of time allowed. Many of the inhabitants besides, had placed refreshments on tables before their doors. As soon as the Pittsburgh militia, who marched in the rear, could be dismissed from the ranks, they were employed in carrying water to the plain. Members of the committee set the example by carrying water and whiskey to these "Whiskey Boys," as they have since been called. "I was employed with the rest," says the writer of the "Incidents," "very busily. I thought it better to be employed in extinguishing the fire of their throats than of my house; most other persons thought in the same manner." In spite of all that could be done,

* It afterward appeared that a message to the same effect had been transmitted by Bradford.

straggling companies left the ground, came into the town, and were extremely insulting and troublesome. The taverns, by order of the committee, had been closed, but the tavern-keepers were obliged to distribute gratis.* According to the best estimates, the number which entered the town was 4,500—about a fourth part had returned home from Braddock's Field—so that the whole number assembled there was about 7,000. It is probable, that all who marched were provided with arms and well acquainted with their use. Here was without doubt a formidable army, which it would have been the extreme of folly in the two hundred and fifty militia of the town to attempt to resist. And yet the historian of Pittsburgh, Neville B. Craig, and his father, Major Craig, hang over them the imputation of cowardice and treason for not making the attempt! The charge is not, indeed, made in direct terms, but the inference from their language, as well as from their silence, is irresistible.†

Great activity was used by well disposed persons to preserve order. General Bradford left all to his officers, giving himself little trouble. He had retired to an arbor to cool himself in the shade, and receive the homage of his flatterers, to whom he expatiated on his great achievement, the expulsion of the obnoxious characters! It was an object of moment for the safety of the town, to have the multitude thrown across the river as speedily as possible. There were but three or four boats that could be collected from the ferries, and it would take a long time to transport so great a number with these. But it was remembered that the horse, which was about a third of the number, could ford the river, and Mr. Brackenridge being acquainted with the ford, undertook to lead them across, which he did near the junction of the rivers. The foot, in the mean time, at least the greater part, had crossed in boats.‡

* "Incidents," p. 66. Mr. Brackenridge says it cost him four barrels of whiskey for his share.

† See notes at the end of this chapter.

‡ There is an anecdote related by Combe, in his phrenological tour, that is similar to the foregoing, although on a smaller scale. Before the late war between this country and England, a mob had gone on board a British vessel in the port of Philadelphia, taken off the rudder, and were dragging it along the street with the intention of repairing to the residence of the British consul and breaking his windows. A gentleman of address and some personal influence joined them, and affected to aid in dragging the rudder, but taking advantage of a pause to rest addressed them in the following manner: "Fellow citizens, let us prove to those insolent British that we are not a rabble of disorderly persons, as they represent us, but a calm, reflecting people. Instead of insulting them, let us give three cheers before the consul's house, and lock up this rascally piece of British timber in one of the rooms

Notwithstanding the greatest exertion, a hundred or two had remained in town; these were in concert with some of those who had crossed the river, and who were to burn some farm buildings belonging to Kirkpatrick, on Coal Hill, opposite the town, which was to be the signal for those in town to set his house on fire. It was also said, that the house of the company where Day was clerk, was to be fired. Gibson's house, Neville's, Brison's, and probably Major Craig's, were to be burnt. The burning of these would probably have caused the destruction of the whole town. A company, commanded by a Capt. Riddle, dressed in yellow hunting-shirts, were seen in the evening parading the town, as having something in view, and appeared to be bent on mischief. About nine o'clock at night the alarm was given that they were about to burn Kirkpatrick's house. Mr. Brackenridge had just returned from bringing over all the boats to the town side, when the river was lighted up by the flames from the hill. He met General Wilkins marching in haste at the head of the Pittsburgh militia, for the purpose of defending the house, and thus addressed them: "This will not do—it is contrary to the system we have hitherto pursued, and which has been successful. Return and lay down your arms. If a drop of blood is shed between the town and the country, it will never be forgiven. It will be known that there is a tumult in the town, between the inhabitants and the country people, and those that have crossed the river, many of them will return and we shall fall a sacrifice. If the houses are to be defended, it must be by the people of the country themselves."

In fact, a number of the country people were in arms to defend the house. Col. Cook, James Marshall, and a brother of Maj. M'Farlane who had fallen, had gone down. He had been called upon, on the principle that having the greatest cause of resentment against Kirkpatrick, if he should oppose the burning, others could not insist on it. General Wilkins and his militia advanced no further, and Mr. Brackenridge proceeded to those who were endeavoring to burn the house, and appealed to them in a manner which those of the worst feeling among them

of the State House, and then disperse." The suggestion was adopted and literally obeyed. At night the rudder was secretly conveyed back to the ship by order of the mayor. It would have been of no use to attempt direct opposition; and yet Mr. Brackenridge was assailed for not making a direct and useless opposition to the march to Pittsburgh! We are told by sage moralists that we are on no account to countenance wrong, no matter what may be the intention, or what mischief it may prevent. If we see a madman in pursuit of another with a drawn sword, we must not set him on a wrong direction, although to save life, for this would be a violation of truth!

could not resist. He showed them that it would be impossible to burn the house of Kirkpatrick without, at the same time, burning that of Col. O'Hara, which was close by, both built of wood. That they knew the Colonel was from home with General Wayne, fighting the Indians; to destroy his property under such circumstances, would be an act for which they would never forgive themselves. If the house must be destroyed, let it be pulled down, not burned. If it be pulled down, he would be the first to pull off a board. But why give themselves the trouble; the Pittsburgh people would pull it down and throw it into the river. It was perhaps mainly owing to the determined stand of Col. Cook, Marshall and M'Farlane, that the house was saved. The offer to throw the house into the river, was another of those circumstances brought up afterward against Mr. Brackenridge, entirely omitting the attending circumstances. There is no doubt that his interference had considerable effect at the crisis, and especially in arresting the onset of the Pittsburgh militia, which in all likelihood would have brought on a hostile conflict.

Col. O'Hara was Quarter-Master General. He was one of the earliest settlers in the West, and more identified with the growth and prosperity of Pittsburgh than any other individual. He was a man of strong natural mind, of equal enterprise and business talent. He left his descendants the largest estate in Pittsburgh, arising chiefly from the increase in value in real estate acquired at an early period. He was the first to establish some of those manufactures on which the wealth of Pittsburgh rests at this day. Both houses spoken of stood near the bank of the Monongahela, and separated from each other only by a paling, and it was impossible to burn the one and at the same time prevent the flames from being communicated to the other. They both stood fifty years after their escape from the danger of this threatened conflagration, and were only pulled down a few years ago, for the purpose of erecting other buildings. They were occupied by descendants of Kirkpatrick and O'Hara.

The representations made to the government by its agents being partial and incorrect, produced false impressions, and did injustice, especially by omitting all explanatory circumstances, by which means facts may be made to tell greater falsehoods than falsehood itself. The praise was almost universally given to Mr. Brackenridge, of having saved the town by his activity and address. He was, in fact, the life and soul of all the measures which were put in practice, and without which it would have been doomed to destruction. The writer of this, in his youth, has heard this repeated by the people of the town, a thousand and a thousand times; and yet by some of his malignant enemies, Mr. Brackenridge was held up as the chief insurgent, and at one moment narrowly escaped being sent to Philadelphia in irons, for his pains in saving the town and the West from the horrors of civil war!

By the next day the formidable host had almost entirely disappeared, and the inhabitants once more breathed freely after their escape from the imminent peril which threatened them.*

NOTES TO CHAPER V.

The author of the "Incidents" placed in an appendix to his book, numerous affidavits and statements, either as proof of facts, or in corroboration of his own personal narrative. The inconvenience of this plan is, that the reader after reading the text will seldom be induced to peruse the whole of the documents by themselves. The author of this history adopted a different mode of giving these papers, in the way of notes to each chapter, in which mode they would be more likely to secure attention. But instead of giving the whole of each paper at once, he has only extracted such portions as relate to the matter of that chapter. To have pursued a different course, it would have led to awkward repetition, and as it is, some repetition is unavoidable. He has made an exception in the cases of the statements of Messrs. James Ross, Judge Addison, John Hoge, and some others, which cover the whole ground of the insurrection. He repeats, that there is no instance of a mere historical work better sustained by what approaches to judicial evidence; for to historical truth the narrow rules of evidence do not apply—rules which were invented, as is alleged, to exclude falsehood, but which, we say again, more frequently exclude the truth. Evidence has been defined to be "that which makes clear"—which produces conviction and belief, and this from its probability, vraisemblance, and the character of the witness. The evidence in the present case is not *ex parte*, but given under very peculiar circumstances. The enemies of the author of the "Incidents," endeavored to fix certain imputations on him; he boldly challenged them to appear at the bar of public opinion, and there confront him. The proceeding was analogous to that of a court of equity, where one party makes his statements, which others are called upon to answer or contradict, if they can; when no contradiction or de-

---

*The following is preserved by Mr. Brackenridge, partly as a literary curiosity, and partly to show the confused ideas among the people, of the object of the assemblage at Braddock's Field:

ADVORTUSMENT.

Notis is hearby givin to the publig that thare was a par of portmantles lost last time I went with the revue from Braddicks ground to Pisburg betwen the nine mild run and the too mild run, with purvishins in them and hankenther in them. But I care for noting but the sadlebags every person that his fond them will send them to Elizabetown, or live them at Mr. Wadsins tavrin Pisburg so that the oner may get them shall have risnable charges paid for there truble.

SUPTEMBRER 2, 1794.

nial follows, the bill is taken *pro confesso.* There was every opportunity that could be desired, afforded to the other party, to contest the allegations, and he or they were challenged to contest them. But they were silent at the time, and it was not until sixty years after the publication of the book, that one of the descendants of the "Neville connection," Neville B. Craig, undertook to question the facts, on the narrow technical ground, that the statements were *ex parte.* This is no objection even in the highest judicial tribunal, a court of chancery—but there is no such rule applicable to historical evidence—the very idea is an absurdity, and only proves the ignorant and contracted mind of him who suggested it. The historian of Pittsburgh has nothing to urge but vulgar and unmeaning epithets, such as scoundrel, *black-hearted villain,* and other manifestations of malice, which only recoil upon himself; and which can have no effect on men possessing a proper sense of justice, honor, or gentlemanly manners, none of which properties are evinced by the self styled historian.

Letter of Major Craig to the Secretary at War.

Craig, in his book, page 253, gives a letter from his father to Gen. Knox, on the subject of the Braddock's Field occurrence, prefaced with the remark that, "it was no doubt a fortunate circumstance that Major Butler commanded at that time." Why so? As it was not the intention of the rioters to attack the fort, what difference did it make whether Major Butler, or any other officer, was in command? It is well it was not attacked—forty men in a wooden stockade, against five thousand riflemen! The letter is as follows—a sense of propriety and ordinary judgment would have forbidden its publication, by the historian at least:

"On the first inst. a numerous body of armed men assembled at Braddock's Field, continued there till yesterday, their number increasing, it is said, to four thousand five hundred, *being joined by a number of the inhabitants of Pittsburgh,* and commenced their march about nine o'clock, as it was confidently reported, with the design of attacking the fort. But some of the leaders being informed that every possible means had been taken for its defense, they prudently concluded to postpone the attack, and sent a flag to inform the commandant that they intended to march peaceably by the fort into Pittsburgh, cross the Monongahela, and return home. Major Butler intimated to the flag bearer, that their peaceable intentions would be best manifested by passing the fort at a proper distance; they therefore took another road into town."

The foregoing contains several important errors. First, as to the simple fact to the joining the insurgents by the Pittsburghers, it was true—but unexplained by giving the circumstances, and the *quo animo,* would be a falsehood; for it conveyed the idea that they were also insurgents, and such must have been the idea conveyed to General Knox. If Major Craig possessed ordinary intelligence, he would have known better, as he certainly did. He at least knew that Gen. Wilkins, who commanded, was no insurgent. Was James Ross an insurgent? For he too was there.

The second error is the statement that they desisted from the attack, on account of hearing that Major Butler had prepared for defense, when in fact, they had already relinquished the idea for other reasons. As to the silly braggadocio message ascribed to Major Butler, such a message might have been sent by a corporal or a sergeant, but not by a brave officer, and man of sense, "by passing the fort at a respectable distance." What was that distance? The public highway passed within *fifty yards* of the walls of the stockade, and they certainly had a right to pass there without the leave of the commander. We have here a sample of the accuracy of the representations made to the government. It may be asked where were Neville, Kirkpatrick, and the other proscribed persons, during the march? Major Craig and his family were in the fort, and it is to be presumed that the others were there also. Their houses in town were vacant, or only occupied by servants. If the citizens had not yielded to the storm, under the advice and direction of the insurgent Brackenridge, these houses would have been the first to be given to the flames.

The historian has given us another paper, much worse than this, and it is a felicitous instance of that strange obliquity of mind which distinguishes him. His mental and moral vision seem to present things to him in a strange distorted manner, like objects seen by the natural eye in looking through a broken pane of glass.

"So general was the combined influence of actual disaffection upon one portion of the community, and dread of the violence of the turbulent among the others, that the writer has often heard Major Craig say, that out of the family connection of General Neville, and out of the employees of the government, James Baird, a blacksmith, and James Robinson, the father of William Robinson, Jr. were the only persons in Pittsburgh on whom reliance could be placed under all circumstances."

James Baird, the blacksmith, and James Robinson, were the only persons out of the "*Neville connection*" that could be relied on under all circumstances! For cool effrontery, it would be difficult to match this. I am unwilling to believe that Major Craig would ever use such language, and rather ascribe it to the blundering stupidity of his son. The two individuals named were, no doubt, good citizens and worthy men, although of humble rank; but why exalt them at the expense of all the other inhabitants of the town? Their names are not among the committee of twenty-one, and we must suppose that they were not in the ranks under the command of Gen. Wilkins; but were they better citizens and more trustworthy than the two Wilkins, or than George Wallace, Matthew Ernest, Col. Irvine, and others? Was not the historian aware of this sweeping denunciation, as traitors, of the whole town? Was he not aware, that a different interpretation might present another idea, viz. that the Neville connection was held in little respect or consideration, by their townsmen, with the exception of the two persons named, and the government employees? But this would not be just. They were neither held in odium by their fellow citizens, nor did they, or Craig, hold them in such low estimation. The blunder must be attributed to N. B. Craig.

Extract from the Deposition of Adamson Tannehill.

"The deponent hath further heard the citizens generally speaking of him, H. H. Brackenridge, in the most favorable manner, *for his activity and address in saving the town.*"

From the Affidavit of Peter Audrain.

"In general, the deponent can say, that in the affair of Braddock's Field, Mr. Brackenridge acted, as far as this deponent knows, *with good policy to save the town*; and on other occasions, to get an amnesty for the people, and save them from a war with the government."

From the Affidavit of George Robinson.

"The deponent has been at other meetings since, in the town of Pittsburgh, and heard Mr. Brackenridge's sentiments on various occasions, and observed his conduct, and can say, to the best of his knowledge, that with respect to the people that were expelled from the town, and every thing else that was done, he acted from no selfish motive of resentment or disposition to hurt any man, but from motives of policy to moderate matters and prevent mischief; and this deponent knows this to be the general sentiment of the people of Pittsburgh, *and they consider themselves indebted to his policy in a great degree for the safety of the town,* in the affair of Braddock's Field, where we were led to apprehend plunder and destruction from the fury of the people that had met there."

Extract from the Affidavit of William Meetkirk.

"We went next morning to Braddock's Field, with a great number of people from Pittsburgh in company. When we came there, I discovered a great number of people much dissatisfied, on account that Col. Neville and Gen. Gibson were not also expelled. I was chosen one of the committee which did not meet until the next morning; when Mr. Bradford produced the letters that had been kept out of the mail, and read them before the committee himself. He appeared much dissatisfied that Col. Neville and Gen. Gibson were not sent away; for he said they were as obnoxious to the people as any of them that were gone, and that they ought not to be suffered to remain in the country; for they were enemies of the people and must be sent off. It was motioned for them to be suffered to remain until the meeting that was to be at Parkinson's Ferry on the 14th of August, and for them to come forward to the meeting, and endeavor to exculpate themselves from the charges that were against them, but it was overruled. Mr. Brackenridge spoke particularly against the expulsion of Gen. Gibson, by observing that he was a man advanced in years, and that he always had conceived him to be a man who could do little harm, and therefore thought he might be suffered to remain, as he was far from being a dangerous man, in his opinion. Mr. Brackenridge, in my opinion, seemed to have a strong desire that the expulsion of both Gen. Gibson and Col. Neville should be at least postponed until the meeting above alluded to, in order to give them an opportunity to acquit themselves of the charges that the people had advanced against them. It was all overruled, and I believe through the interposition of Mr. Bradford.

"Mr. Bradford then spoke concerning the expulsion of Major Craig; for he had been informed that Major Craig should have said, (immediately after the burning of Gen. Neville's house,) that he would let the d——d rascals see that the excise law should be enforced, for that he would open an office of inspection in his own house. Mr. Bradford was requested to give his author, he replied that he could not recollect, but that he heard it mentioned among the people. It was then referred to the gentlemen, the committee who represented the people of Pittsburgh, Mr. Wilkins, Mr. M'Masters and Mr. Brackenridge; it appeared that neither of them could give any information on the subject. It was then motioned by Mr. Brackenridge, or seconded by him, that if Major Craig was to be immediatly expelled, it would lead in all probability to defeat the measures of government in their operations against the Indians, for Major Craig having charge of the whole quarter-master's stores then at Pittsburgh, then if he was then sent away, and nobody there to supply his place, it might be attended with very bad consequences to the community. Mr. Brackenridge said it would be much better to suspend the expulsion of Major Craig at this time, and wait for an opportunity of applying to the President of the United States to have him removed from office, and some other person appointed in his place. No objection was made to that proposition by any member of the committee, and after some trifling business more the committee rose."

Extract from the Deposition of Matthew Ernest.

"The deponent was present when the committee of twenty-one drew up certain resolves to be sent to the people at Braddock's Field; it was perfectly understood that these resolves were not serious, but for the moment, and the using the expression 'common cause,' in one of the resolves, produced a general laugh. In general, this deponent can say that the whole business of Braddock's Field, as far as respects the town of Pittsburgh, was a mask, and the expelling certain persons, *was for their own sakes,* as well as for the safety of the town. This deponent was present at the meeting of the committee of twenty-one, who were called upon to furnish Gen. Gibson and Col. Neville with passports and a guard when they left the town of Pittsburgh. That double passports were made out for them, dictated by Mr. Brackenridge—a private and a public one; a public one for the sake of the country, through which they had to pass, and a private one for the people elsewhere, to show the real cause of their going away. In all this the deponent could discover nothing but good will, and a disposition to save those gentlemen."

Statement of Mr. Bron, a French gentleman of information, who had resided some time at Pittsburgh.

"Having been forced by some circumstances to remain in Pittsburgh during the time of the disturbances which have lately agitated that country, I was present at a town meeting which was convocated upon the news of a large party of country people assembled at a place called Braddock's Field, whose intention was to come to town the next day to lay their hands on several people of Pittsburgh, and destroy the place if they should meet with any resistance; and I heard the discourse held by Mr. Brackenridge on that instance, in which he contrived to persuade the interested to quit the town in the shortest time, to save themselves and the people from the danger which was presented to them; and he advised the citizens to join the other part of the people at the rendezvous, that they might be induced to believe them to be in their party; but particularly expressing, that far from wishing them to undertake any thing against the government, these measures were only tending to furnish time to concert with the government for means to recall the tranquility. I was the more struck by this insinuation, that, (from the little time I had been in the country, and the imperfect knowledge I had of that business,) I was supposing there existed a coalition, whose end was to obtain the redress of grievances, which I did hear every day to be complained of in that country against the government. I thought I discovered a defect of good faith in Mr. Brackenridge, in this respect, and that he was rather inclined to support the government than to assist the people; but the rest of the business having soon demonstrated that the people in that country were acting without any sense in their undertaking, I perceived that he was acting not against the people, but against the measures they did employ; *and I have often heard the inhabitants of Pittsburgh acknowledge that his skillful policy had saved the place from the greatest danger.* I have given the foregoing statements of opinons and facts, asserting them on my word of honor.

GEORGE BRON.
PHILADELPHIA, 24th Aug. 1794."

Although somewhat out of the order of the incidents of the Insurrection, it has been thought convenient to insert in this place the statements of Gen. Wilkins, and that of Mr. Henry Purviance.

General Wilkins' Statement.
PITTSBURGH, 7th April, 1795.

"SIR—You desire me to detail the circumstances which led to the expulsion of the citizens of Pittsburgh by the committee of battalions on Braddock's Field. As far as it came within my knowledge, I shall do it with pleasure. David Bradford, who seemed to have all the power and to exercise it in a very tyrannical manner, opened the business by relating the preceding conduct of the people, the robbing the mail, and read and commented on the more obnoxious letters. He charged the writers with having misstated the facts, and to have misrepresented his conduct and the conduct of the people to government. He was warmly supported by many present, who were calling out for liberty whilst they were violently disposed to exercise great tyranny against those who thought different from themselves.

"The writers of the letters had most of them mentioned Mr. Bradford's name in an unfavorable manner, which was the cause of his immediate resentment; and their banishment was the consequence. The popular fury was sure to be directed against any man who offended him during his reign. A motion was made to expel Colonel Neville and General Gibson, whose letters had been interrupted in the mail, against whom Bradford had previously declaimed with great vehemence. It was thought by many people present, friendly to those two gentlemen, that they might be saved by the question of their banishment being postponed until the meeting which was to be soon after at Parkinson's Ferry.

"To accomplish this object, a motion was made to refer the case of General Gibson to that place. This motion was supported by you; but opposed and overruled by Bradford and others. David Bradford moved in addition to these two, that Major Craig should be expelled, saying it was reported that he had offered his house for an office of inspection, should another not be found. Bradford called on the Pittsburgh members to know if this was true. You answered it was not true; and stated some circumstances tending to show the falsehood of the report. But notwithstanding, Bradford and others pressed for his banishment, which in order to obviate, you mentioned that it would be an injury to the expedition then carrying on against the Indians, as he had charge of the stores for the use of the troops; and proposed that the committee should address the Secretary at War to remove him, which I considered as management on your part to save Major Craig.

"It was determined that the people should march to Pittsburgh. Every person belonging to the town was under great anxiety for their families and property. The town had every thing to fear from a violent mob of armed men, led by a few inconsiderate fools. Previous to the rising of the committee, some of the most violent exclaimed, that Major Kirkpatrick, and Mr. Brison, and Mr. Day, had not gone away; or if they had, it was only for a day or two, and that they would return. The Pittsburgh members alarmed lest the suspicions might induce the mob, when they came to town, to search for these gentlemen, not knowing what the consequence of such a search might be, pledged themselves that they were gone and would not return.

"I never heard you express a wish for the banishment of any individual. I have often heard you say that the people had essentially served those that had been banished; that government would consider them as martyrs, and reward them.

"I remember it was arranged previous to the election of delegates for the meeting at Parkinson's Ferry, to chose those that were most friendly to government. You mentioned to me that you meant to propose at the meeting, the sending commissioners to the Executive, to consult means to compose the disturbances. You expressed a wish of being one of the commissioners yourself. You showed me an address you had drawn up, to be proposed at the meeting, to be sent to the President of the United States. You often declared to me that if the violence continued, you were determined to leave the county and go to Philadelphia. I had daily opportunities of observing your conduct, and conversing with you, and never had a doubt but that you were influenced by the purest motives, and was anxious for the restoration of order and the laws.

I am sir, &c.   JOHN WILKINS."

Henry Purviance to Hugh H. Brackenridge.*

"In answer to certain queries proposed to me by Hugh H. Brackenridge, Esq.

* Mr. Purviance, receiving his appointment after the Insurrection, was at the time of writing this communication, District Attorney for the county of Washington.

I can certify, and were it necessary at this time, could depose as follows:

"I resided at Washington during the disturbances which lately took place in the four western counties of Pennsylvania, but was occasionally at some of the public meetings which were held in different parts of the same, in consequence of those disturbances. I have had frequent opportunities of observing the conduct of those who were most conspicuous in exciting the commotion, but never had the least reason to suspect him of any privity or concert with those leaders. On the contrary, from the period of my first conversation with him on the subject, which was on the evening that the intercepted mail was carried from Washington to Pittsburgh, throughout the whole of the transaction, he expressed uniformly to me sentiments in opposition to the violence and outrages which were taking place. My communications with him were frequent, and I am persuaded with the most perfect confidence and sincerity on his part. Some were made in company with James Ross, Esq. and others without the presence of any third person; but in either situation, was that of a strong disapprobation of the madness and folly which had taken place.

"On the morning that the intercepted mail was brought to Washington, immediately on hearing of it I went to Mr. Bradford's house, and in a few words requested him to explain to me the meaning of what I had heard. His reply to we was, 'We have discovered that there are traitors and aristocrats, (this, I think, was the language, for it made a strong impression on me,) who are forming schemes to trample on the liberties of the people;' and other conversation to that effect immaterial to be related. I asked him who they were, and what had been discovered? He answered, that there was a certain Mr. Day, and a certain Mr. Brison, also a certain General Gibson, who did not stand very fair, and that Presley Neville had not behaved very well. I may err as to the precise words, but am pretty certain as to the substance, and to the persons above mentioned. The letters were not shown to me by Mr. Bradford, nor did he proceed to detail to me what the particulars of the discovery was. The letters were read the same day at a town meeting in Washington, and also the next day, and the writers of them denounced as aristocrats, and deserving punishment.

"When I went in company with those who carried the mail from Washington to Pittsburgh, which was the day previous to the assemblage of the people at Braddock's Field, I certainly apprehended great danger of mischief to the town, and also to the persons whose letters had occasioned the summoning of the people to Braddock's Field. My opinion was, that the best mode of averting this danger, was for those people themselves to retire. General Gibson and Col. Neville can perhaps remember my communicating to them my sentiments to this effect. Though I felt all its harshness with respect to the individuals themselves, who were thus obliged to relinquish their families and country, I compared it with what appeared to me the very probably dangerous consequences, which were to result to the persons, and property of those persons, and of the inhabitants of Pittsburgh, for their omitting to do so.

"I was present at the conference between the gentlemen who took the intercepted mail to Pittsburgh, and the delegates from the town meeting at that place then sitting. As well as I can recollect, Col. Neville was there, if not all the time, certainly a part of it, and while the business on which the former had come was explained, which was done in a few words, and the letters which have been mentioned were shown.

"The gentlemen from Washington, at this conference certainly omitted to mention the names of Gen. Gibson and Col. Neville, as persons obnoxious on account of their letters, as being in personal danger; or that their removal was necessary for the safety of the town. My reason for remembering this, is that I was astonished at the omission, and felt the greatest apprehensions for these two gentlemen, and considered them as in danger, if they should be kept ignorant of their real situation. I also was alarmed for the safety of the town, if the measures recommended by the gentlemen who carried the mail, and by myself also, viz. 'that those whose letters had rendered them obnoxious should retire,' was not adopted as to the whole of them.

"I refrained with some difficulty from mentioning it to Col. Neville, and was persuaded that a very dangerous delicacy toward him on account of his presence, and no other cause, had prevented the mention of his name. I also felt myself in a situation too delicate to interfere thus far in the business; as I had only gone to Pittsburgh accidentally, in company with those who had the custody of the mail, and was not considered as one to whom the business was in any degree committed. My uneasiness, however, increased so much during the evening, that I determined to interfere for what I conceived to be the safety of the town, as well as of Gen. Gibson and Col. Neville. I called upon Mr. Brackenridge, at near 12 o'clock that same night; told him of the omission, and my opinion of its consequences. He immediately proceeded to call together as many of the members of the town committee as could be found. This was done. They met at his house perhaps in an hour and a half, and I then communicated to them what I have above stated to have been omitted, and I think that I also mentioned Major Craig, as one in similar circumstances with the other two gentlemen, and told them my opinion of the consequences. It is my belief that it was solely in consequence of my interfering in this manner, that those gentlemen first came to know that they were considered as in danger, and that General Gibson and Col. Neville were informed of their being considered as obnoxious. What took place at Braddock's Field the next day in the committee, confirmed my opinion of the night before with respect to them.

"I certainly did not observe in Mr. Brackenridge at any time during the business, the least symptoms of ill will or malignant disposition toward those two gentlemen last mentioned. I remember shortly after the above transaction, something like the following to have taken place between Mr. Brackenridge and myself: I mentioned to him, (in consequence of my having frequently heard that he was on bad terms, if not with Col. Neville, with some of the connections of the family,) that it was probable the banishment of Col. Neville, and perhaps I might have mentioned the burning of General Neville's property, would by some be attributed to his means. He replied that he supposed it might be so, but that it would be a great mistake; for if he had meant to serve them, he could not do it more effectually than by such conduct; that it would make their fortunes, as the government would certainly pay them well for all loss or injury.

"My opinion of his conduct in public at the Red Stone meeting, where the terms of accommodation proposed by the commissioners were discussed, was that it was influenced by the sincerest desire to procure the accession of that committee to the terms proposed, and his speech on that occasion contained the most unequivocal declarations of his sense of the propriety and necessity of accepting them.

"In private I do not recollect to have had any communication with him at that time, or to have made any remarks upon his conduct or conversation out of the committee.

"At Braddock's Field, as at Redstone, I had little communication with Mr. Brackenridge. He was engaged as a member of the committee, and of course principally taken up with those who were most immediately concerned in the transactions of the day. I rode in company with him from Pittsburgh to Braddock's Field on the day that the inhabitants of the town went to meet the people there assembled, and had some conversation with him on the road, relative to the business, in which conversation his mind appeared to me strangly impressed with the alarming situation of this country, and his sentiments and intentions to be such as I wished to find them. My opinion of his conduct on that day, formed partly from my subsequent conversation with himself on the various transactions of it, and partly from conversation with James Ross, Esq. and others there present, respecting the same, is that it had for its object the averting danger from the town of Pittsburgh.

"My opinion of the whole of his conduct throughout the insurrection in this country, I shall give without reserve: It appeared to me to have two objects—to arrest the progress of the present violence, and to procure an amnesty for that already committed, and thus prevent the flame from spreading beyond that country in which it originated. Though in some instances during the transactions, my opinion differed from his with respect to the measures adopted for the accomplishment of particular points, I never entertained any doubt of the propriety of the principle which actuated him.

"Whatever may be the solidity or justness of this, or any other opinion, I have here given of Mr. Brackenridge's conduct and principles, in the disturbances of the western country, I can with safety vouch for the sincerity with which it is given; and he is at liberty to make any use, either public or private, of these sentiments in reply to his queries.

HENRY PURVIANCE."

CHAPTER VI.

ACTS OF VIOLENCE FOLLOWING THE ASSEMBLAGE AT BRADDOCK'S FIELD — TOM THE TINKER — DELEGATES TO PARKINSON'S FERRY.

FINDLEY expresses the opinion, that the assemblage at Braddock's Field, and the presence of so many persons of standing and reputation, apparently giving it countenance, was attended with very bad consequences. This is probably true; it was an evil, and if those who contrived it were aware of the effects which might have followed, they deserved the most exemplary punishment. It was an affair of a most reckless character. But with respect to those who attended it, from the laudable motive of preventing or lessening the evils likely to attend the lawless gathering, a more philosophical historian would draw a wide distinction. Findley himself was not there, and the remark may be regarded as an excuse for his absence, when, according to the celebrated law of Solon, it is the duty of every citizen to take part. Perhaps he was governed by abstract considerations of moral propriety. Such considerations are often pernicious in real life, where mixed questions of right and of expediency so often occur; and the course to be pursued must be determined by the inquiry, whether the evils attending the unyielding perseverance in what may be absolutely right in the abstract, are not vastly greater than those arising from a compromise with circumstances. Findley enumerates the bad effects, yet admits that it was necessary to temporize on the occasion. No one could pretend that it was in itself a good thing, but only a choice of evils, and it is every day's experience, that we are compelled at times to make that choice. Your uncompromising men are children or bigots in the affairs of the world.* Let any one imagine the effect of burning the town, and of the blood which would have been shed in its defense! If so much madness and desperation were occasioned by the destruction of Neville's house, how much greater fury would have followed the destruction of the town, not to speak of the misery and distress of the population, and the loss of many lives!

* A learned Judge, Addison, on the trial of Norris Morrison, and others, 1795, said: "When there was real danger, all the town went to Braddock's Field"— regarding this case as one of necessity for self-preservation.—Addison's Reports, p. 276.

Although the popular rage was thus deprived of the aliment requisite to feed its fury, yet its manifestations were sufficiently deplorable. Something of the French revolutionary epidemic had seized on a portion of the people, but this was entirely independent of any influence of the society of Mingo Creek, or that in the town of Washington.* They were both very circumscribed and limited in their influence; and the latter had no concern or part in the insurrection. The imputations of this kind are supported by no evidence whatever. As to the former, although it had no direct bearing on the disturbances, yet the tendency of the principles of the Mingo Creek Society no doubt had the effect to lessen the respect for law and government in its immediate neighborhood. The hot-bed of the insurrectionary violence was in the vicinity of the residence of the Inspector, and of the offices in the survey, and in a great measure accompanied with personal hostility to the officers. Parts of Westmoreland, Allegheny and Fayette counties, were comparatively peaceful. The opposition to the excise law was not everywhere equally violent, but it was everywhere prevalent. No one dared to defend it openly, and none ventured to condemn the excesses which had been committed. One of the first evidences of excitement was the erection of what was called "liberty poles," with flags and emblazonings. This was generally practiced in the revolutionary war, and was regarded as an indication of popular rising on some common cause. Whether derived from the ancient Druidical custom of erecting "May poles," or from some German or Swiss custom, it is impossible to say. They were then regarded as ominous indications of popular movement pointing toward insurrection, treason, or rebellion, while they pointed toward the heavens! At the present day, they are among the harmless means of giving vent to party differences, and it is to be hoped will ever be regarded as only peaceful emblems of that salutary diversity in opinion which is the life of our free institutions.

A few days only had elapsed after the affair of Braddock's Field, when a party proceeded to the residence of Wells, the collector for Fayette and Westmoreland counties, burned his house, in spite of the remonstrance of the more prudent of them, and compelled him to resign his commission; at the same time requiring him to take an oath not to hold the office in future. The party which committed this outrage appeared to be

*The Democratic Society of Washington was instituted in April, 1794. Hildreth says Mr. Brackenridge was a member. This is an error; he never was a member of any such societies. When the word error is used here, perhaps a much more emphatic word would be more appropriate. The Mingo Creek Society was instituted some time before. See the note at the end of this chapter.

of a much more savage and revolutionary character than that which perpetrated the destruction of the house of Neville; few or none of the better class joining with the intention of restraining or moderating their violence, being fearful of being present at the commission of acts now condemned by the moral sense of the community. Threatening letters were sent into the southern and central part of Westmoreland county, and a comparatively small party, some of them from Bedford, went against Webster, the collector of Bedford county. He made no resistance, but brought out his papers, tore them up and trod upon them. Some were disposed to tar and feather him, and others attempted to burn his stacks of grain; but by the interference of the more moderate, he was, after some indignity, finally suffered to go free. It is alleged that in his case there were circumstances besides his connection with the excise, which had exasperated the people. That he had abused his official station, and used it as the means of oppression, having seized without the authority of law the whiskey of poor men on the road, while on their way across the mountains to purchase their small supply of salt and iron.* The general impression seemed to be, that the execution of the excise laws was now suspended by the immediate act of the people; and yet, in other respects, there was no disregard of the authority of magistrates, although a general feeling of insecurity prevailed. Mr. Brackenridge says: "Liberty poles, with inscriptions and devices were raised everywhere; such as 'an equal tax, and no excise;' 'united we stand, divided we fall;' with a snake divided for a device. I met no man that seemed to have an idea that we were to separate from the government, or to overthrow it, but simply to oppose the excise law; and yet the people acted and spoke as if they were in a state of revolution! They threatened life and property familiarly. Addison, the Judge of the district, was then absent in Philadelphia, and a report having been spread that he had encouraged the Marshal to serve process, they threatened to prevent his return." The alarm was general, and there can be no doubt that all restraint of law would have been thrown off, but for the contemplated assemblage of an authority emanating directly from themselves, and which kept in check the prevailing tendency to anarchy.

About this time, the term of "Tom the Tinker," came into very general use. Pasquinades were put up on trees in the highways, or in other conspicuous places, over the signature of "Tom the Tinker," threatening individuals, or admonishing them on the subject of the excise law. These letters threatening to burn houses and barns, produced great alarm among the peacefully disposed, over the whole country. In the march from

* Findley, p. 107.

Braddock's Field, the acclaim was, "Huzza for 'Tom the Tinker!'" It was not now, are you whig or tory, but are you a Tom the Tinker's man? Every one was willing to be thought so; and some had afterward trouble to wipe off the imputation to the contrary. Advertisements sometimes appeared averring the falsehood of the charge of favoring the odious excise law.*

Although the danger which threatened the town of Pittsburgh seemed for the present, at least, to be past, yet the inhabitants were far from thinking themselves safe. They knew the temper of the country people, especially toward the proscribed persons, and that they might at any moment be excited to return in sufficient numbers to burn the town, and as likely at night as in the day time. The garrison shared in the common apprehension. The commander labored to improve its defenses, and laid in two months provisions in case of siege. The danger of the town arose from the supposed want of good faith on its part in the banishment of the proscribed; it was believed by many to be only a sham, and that the real intention was to protect them from harm until they could reappear with safety.† This was no doubt the truth, but their own safety made it a serious matter to conceal it. To the obnoxious persons, it was an act of injustice and injury, especially to those who had families to protect, and business to transact. But then if the measure had not been adopted, the necessity of which was at first clearly seen by the objects of it themselves, they would have fallen the victims — their property first doomed to destruction, and if unable to effect their escape, their lives would have paid the forfeit. It was principally on their account that danger still hung

---

* The following is a specimen of this writing of "Tom the Tinker:"

"In taking a survey of the troops under my command, in the late expedition against that insolent exciseman, John Neville, I find there were a great many delinquents now amongst those who carry on distilling. It will therefore be observed, that 'Tom the Tinker' will not suffer any certain class, or set of men, to be excluded the service of this my district, when notified to attend on any expedition in order to obstruct the execution of the law, and obtain a repeal thereof.

"And I do declare upon my solemn word, that if such delinquents do not come forth on the next alarm, in equipments, and give their assistance as in them lies, in opposing the execution, and obtaining a repeal of the excise laws, he, or they, will be deemed as enemies, and standing opposed to the virtuous principles of republican liberty, and shall receive punishment according to the nature of the offense, and that at least consumption of his distillery."

Notices like this were sometimes addressed to particular persons, accompanied with threats of burning their houses, barns, or bodily harm.

† The inhabitants were not too confident that there were not some among themselves too ready to join the "Whiskey Boys."

over the town; it was therefore a choice of evils in which there was no room to hesitate. Mr. Brackenridge, in his usual vein of wit, illustrates the predicament of the proscribed, by a fable of Pilpay, whether original with himself, or taken, as he asserts, from an Eastern collection called the Negaristan, it is not material.

"Two travelers passing by a pool on the side of the road, one of them missing a foot, fell in. The surface of the pool was some feet beneath the level of the bank, and of itself deep; laying hold of the bank, he struggled to get up, but it was steep and he could not. His companion extending himself on his breast, and reclining over the bank of the pool, and reaching down his hands, got hold of the hair of the other, and with some difficulty extricated him from the pool. But in dragging him against the bank, by some means an eye was injured, so as to lose the sight thereof. The rescued man conceived himself entitled to damages against his companion, who had thus without his request dragged him out. He claimed the sum of ten thousand dinars. The cause came before the cadi, who was puzzled, and took the opinion of a famous lawyer, Ala Joseph.

"The decision recommended by Ala Joseph was, that the injured man should have his selection of two things; either to go back to the pool, from which he had been rescued, and take his chance of getting out, or be satisfied with the act of his companion, and the consequence of it, even though no application for assistance had been made, and his consent to be dragged out formally obtained."*

Two days after the alarming march of the Whiskey Boys from Braddock's Field, it was rumored that Kirkpatrick had been seen in town. The rumor was traced to one of the inhabitants, on which the committee was called upon to inquire of that person, and to admonish him in case he had circulated a false report. As the committee was assembling, Major Craig and Col. Neville were met coming from the garrison, and on being interrogated, acknowledged that Kirkpatrick was then in the garrison, having returned to town. The fact caused indignation in the committee; they considered themselves ill used, after the exertions they had made to save Kirkpatrick, and the dangers to which they had been exposed on his account and that of his connections, and resolved that Craig and Neville should be seized in his stead. The former returned to the garrison; the

---

* It has been seen that great complaints were made against the towns people, by the proscribed, for their civil treatment of the proscribed, in their saving their lives and property.

latter came before the committee, but in contemptuous manner smoking his cigar; but seeing they were in earnest, he expressed himself with discretion, and stated that Kirkpatrick had returned for want of an escort, having been dogged by a party from whom his life was in danger. The committee undertook to furnish the escort, which was done; and he escaped by a circuitous way, until he reached the mountains, where he took the direct road to Philadelphia.

While this affair was before the committee, but before it was generally known, the people of the town hearing of the return of Kirkpatrick, talked of seizing, and some were of waylaying and shooting him. On being informed of this, the committee called a town meeting, in the evening, in order to impress upon the people the impropriety of entertaining such ideas. Mr. Brackenridge was requested to address them, which he did at considerable length, denouncing in strong terms the purposed intention in the case of Kirkpatrick, and enlarging upon the false impression among many persons that all law was at an end. "It is only the excise law," said John Wilkins, the elder (who was much of a humorist), "that is repealed by the people."

Edward Day had gone down the river; Brison was concealed a few days at the house of Robert Galbraith, Esq. the prosecuting attorney, who resided a few miles out of town. The country getting wind of it, collected in a mob, and surrounded the house at night, and insisted on searching, but in the meantime he had left the place. Gibson and Neville, at the instance of the Pittsburgh committee at Braddock's Field, had been allowed ten days to prepare for their departure, with passports for their security. This comedy of banishment resembled the barring out of the school master during the holidays; the banished were sure to return with the force that would come to put down the insurrection, and with the recommendation of having been martyrs for the sake of the government. In order to enhance this merit, it afterward appeared that they took pains to exaggerate their sufferings, denouncing the towns people, as well as the insurgents, as the cause, observing a profound silence with respect to the circumstances which rendered their course unavoidable, as well for the safety of the supposed martyrs as of their own. Mr. Brackenridge, as being one of the most conspicuous, and at the same time personally at variance with two of the Neville "connection," had to feel in a special manner the effects of that enmity, and was assailed with groundless charges and insinuations. There can be nothing more absurd than to suppose that any man of common sense would resort to such a mode of gratifying personal enmity, which put his enemies to a mere temporary inconvience, for which they might be expected to be repaid, and which, at the same time, was their best security from present danger.

About this time Mr. Brackenridge was informed by Henry Purviance, Esq. of Washington, who had taken so patriotic a part in the late events, that Col. Neville had expressed the opinion that he (Brackenridge) was in confidence with Bradford; and had been privy to the intercepting the mail, as a part of a plan he had laid for the expulsion of the persons denounced. Mr. Purviance could not but express his surprise at such an absurd and groundless suspicion, and did not hesitate to say that it was not only utterly improbable, but impossible; for he could not, at the same time with the plan of intercepting the mail, contrive that the few individuals whom it was supposed he wished to expel should write letters by that mail, and of such a nature as to be laid hold of by Bradford and others—having no invisible power over the minds of such persons! This could not be answered, but Neville said, "If he had not projected it, he was pleased with it now that it had taken place." "I was struck," observes Mr. Brackenridge, "for the first time, that Neville had not perfect confidence in me; but it did not make much impression on me, as I conceived him in a fever, and, like persons in that state, ready to complain of those that were taking the best care of them." Although the author of the "Incidents" was thus disposed to excuse Neville, the impartial reader will be less indulgent. The frivolous suspicion will be regarded as an evidence of weakness, as well as of injustice, which was more likely to originate in the confused brain of some other of the "connection." In the controversy which was carried on some time ago between the nephew of Col. Neville, Mr. Craig, and the writer of this work, it was said by Craig, that in looking over some papers of the family, it appeared that Neville never had any confidence in Mr. Brackenridge! This, it may be presumed, is the extent of his crimination. In reply to this, it may be retorted, that Mr. Brackenridge had, unfortunately, too much confidence in Col. Neville, or he would not have yielded to his solicitations to attend the Mingo meeting, where, from motives of benevolence, and with a view of serving Neville, he had first involved himself in the affairs of the Whiskey Insurrection. The incident may serve as a clue to the subsequent hostile conduct of the Neville connection, which ultimately forced upon him the task of vindicating his cause, and which it would have been well for the connection they had never provoked. If he had harbored the malicious design of injuring those persons, instead of being willing that they should leave the place, he would have preferred their staying and risking the fury of the mob; and this would have made short work with them. But such a course would have been at variance with his well known benevolent and philanthropic disposition, even to his enemies.

"As to myself," says Mr. Brackenridge, "I canvassed my situation fully, and began seriously to think of emigration; but in that case, I would have been considered in the light of a deserter, and my property become a sacrifice. I thought of being absent on some pretense that might be plausible, and it struck me to prevail upon the people of Pittsburgh to appoint me as an envoy to the Executive, to state the motives of their conduct."

On inquiry, he found that the people were unwilling that he should leave the place; there were many of them in the same predicament, and they did not like to lose company. He therefore resolved to remain, at least until after the meeting at Parkinson's Ferry.

At the time appointed for the election of delegates to this meeting, Mr. Brackenridge publicly announced his desire not to be chosen, being of opinion, from occurrences since the Braddock's Field affair, and the increased excitement throughout the country, that there was little prospect of their stopping short of open hostility. Bradford, on his return to Washington, had used the expression, "a glorious revolution affected without bloodshed." From this it might be inferred that he was resolved on supporting what had been done at all hazards. Marshall had inconsiderately involved himself, and would perhaps have been happy to get out of the situation; but the people would not permit him; he would not dare to talk of any thing but war, and such was his situation, from his acts, that it had become his policy, as much as any man's, to meditate defense. On that principle, Mr. Brackenridge thought that it would be more advisable to send to the meeting some persons who would not be under the necessity of taking a conspicuous part, by being called upon to speak, not being in the habit of it, as he was, professionally. To save appearances, it was necessary to send some persons; but, at the same time, such as had it in their power to remain obscure. On communicating these sentiments to James Ross and Gen. Wilkins, they were of a different opinion; and thought it advisable to use endeavors to send delegates from all parts of the country, opposed to violent measures. In consequence of their reasoning, he consented to go, if elected. The same reluctance is stated by Findley to have occurred in Westmoreland and Fayette counties; these, although at first inclined to doubt the policy of the meeting, at length decided to send delegates to it. Gen. Wilkins exerted himself in Pittsburgh, and James Ross repaired to Washington with the same object. The Pittsburgh election was conducted by John Wilkins, Sr. a justice of the peace, who indulged his propensity for fun by making it the test of the right to vote, that the voter should declare himself in favor of "Tom the Tinker." Some, not aware of the joke, at first appeared to be offended, and refused to answer. When Mr. Brackenridge came to vote, Wilkins observed, "We need not require the test of you, as you are 'Tom the Tinker' himself;" alluding to his appearance at Braddock's Field at the head of the committee. But this jesting occasioned, afterward, some uneasiness to Justice Wilkins, affidavits having been collected respecting it, and transmitted to the Executive by its over zealous friends. Mr. Brackenridge, George Wallace and Peter Audrain, were chosen delegates.

"General Gibson," says Mr. Brackenridge, "at this time, or before it, had left the country; Col. Neville was about to go, but had some reluctance. It struck me with surprise, as he had been thinking how to stay, and I of getting away."* "He came to me after the election of delegates," (says the author of the "Incidents,") "and expressed the idea that he had a right to expect of me and others delegated from the town, that at the meeting we should demand an examination of his case, and repeal the sentence of the committee at Braddock's Field; that he had a right to expect this, inasmuch as it was on account of the town that the sentence was to be carried into effect. I was hurt at his want of a just conception of his case, in supposing that it was on account of the town that he was to go away. It was on his account, and of others, that the town was in danger, and it was for his own sake, more than that of the town, that he was to go away.† I had considered him as consigning his case to my management, from what he had said to me the morning I went to Braddock's Field, and I never managed a case at the bar with more fidelity than I did his, on this occasion. I had thought the business well managed in diverting an infuriated mob from coming to seize him and the others; and this was accomplished by the policy of getting the mob to condense themselves into a committee, and managing that committee to adopt the mild resolution of leaving him in the hands of the committee of Pittsburgh, as guardians in fact of his safety, though nominally the executors of the sentence. I stated this candidly to Neville; and perhaps in a more pointed manner than I would otherwise have done, had

* His family and property, under the guardianship of the town, was in less danger than if he had remained. Neville could not comprehend that the act was that of the country, of his own constituents, who had voted him into office.

† His own property would have shared the fate of others.

not my feelings been hurt by his suspicions, which had been suggested to me. But I further observed to him, that supposing it demandable of the town to go forward and propose the recalling of him, was it practicable? Did he not know that he was considered by the people as the Inspector himself? It is known that before your father accepted the office, you were consulted, and advised the acceptance. It is known that application has been made to you, to advise your father to resign the office. You have said no. Would any of them resign an office of so much value? It is known that you are the author of that advertisement which appeared in the *Gazette,* alleging that certain certificates and bonds were plundered and carried off at the time your father's house was burnt. Although there was a proportion of those at the house capable of what was alleged, yet the bulk of the leaders, although guilty of a great offense, would have shrunk from the violation of moral truth or the commission of dishonesty. They resent the idea of being thought capable of theft or forgery. In your letter to the Mingo meeting, you gave offense. They thought your casuistry, prevarication; and Kirkpatrick's intrepidity, of which you spoke, they thought stupidity. From this, they join you with Kirkpatrick in their feelings; and more especially as it is known to be a trait in your family character to support any branch of it, however insupportable. Neville behaved mildly, and said little; but I suppose thought the more, and set this down as a further proof that I was an insurgent, and has mentioned it as such." *

Shortly before this conversation, Mr. Brackenridge had received a note from Neville, addressed to him as chairman of the committee, demanding a passport and an escort. Although not the chairman, (as no chairman had been appointed,) he resolved to overlook the incivility, and calling the committee together, double passports were made out for him and Gen. Gibson; one to the country, for their protection, the other to produce when safe, showing that there was no real cause for their expulsion, and explaining the circumstance. The first one only, as we have stated, was used when in safety, and disingenuously, as a proof of the persecution they had suffered from their fellow townsmen, and especially from the author of the passports.†

About the same period, a letter was addressed by Mr. Brackenridge

---

*It was a sort of family quarrel between the Nevilles and their constituents, for they had contributed as much as any others to render excise laws odious. They paid the price of popularity; the people did not distinguish the State excise laws from those of the Federal government.

†See notes, as to the danger of those passports.

to Tench Cox, Esq. at Philadelphia, who was then connected with the government, but which was misunderstood by the person to whom it was sent. It was chiefly prompted by a conversation he had with Col. Neville, the day after the affair at Braddock's Field. The conversation turning on the state of the country, Mr. Brackenridge observed, that it would not be an easy matter to put down the insurrection by force. Neville was of opinion that three thousand men would do it; the former thought that if it was attempted with less than fifteen thousand men, it would only add strength to the opposition, and perhaps give rise to a dangerous civil war. Thinking that Neville, going to the government with this erroneous view, would lead to the same mistake that was made by Amherst in England, or by the French refugees at Coblentz, he wished to convey more correct information. His letter was in reply to one from Mr. Cox, and was intended to be communicated to the government, if thought advisable by Cox. Taking a wrong view of the letter, and strangely enough, Cox regarded it as a proof that the writer was an insurgent, threatening the government. Some expressions in relation to the excise were purposely introduced, in case it should fall into the hands of insurgents by another robbery of the mail; but even without this explanation, the letter was patriotic, and contained valuable information for the government. As it was in the first instance a private letter, it could not have been intended to inflame the public mind; and if it tended to produce that effect, the fault was in those who made it public, and to whose discretion it was confided.* It was dated the 8th of August, and coincides in a singular manner with the communication of Edmond Randolph, Secretary of State, of the 5th, three days before. A second letter was addressed by Mr. Brackenridge to Mr. Cox, contradicting the misconception, but which was not published, as it ought to have been, in justice to the writer, although requested by him. The subsequent action of the government, as respects the formidable character of the insurrection, was in conformity to the foregoing suggestions; whether in consequence of them, or incidental, is not material. The plan of the writer was, first, conciliation and amnesty; and if these failed, then to send a force sufficient to crush the rebellion at once.

The writer of those letters spoke his mind freely, as it became a freeman to speak, on the subject of the funding system, the favorite measure of the Secretary; and as he had a right to speak, even suppose on this question of expediency he was in error. But the strongest terms of vitupera-

*See the affidavits of H. Beaumont and others, in notes to this chapter. Also, the letter, and the reply to Mr. Cox.

tion were applied to him by persons who seemed not to be aware that there is a difference between a subject writing to a monarch and a citizen of a democracy addressing a public servant or agent, and expressing an opinion of the propriety of his acts. The insolence (the term applied to him,) consists in the agent taking offense, and not in the citizen who has freely used his privilege of expressing his opinion. The first letter was no doubt of a character to be made a handle of by the proscribed persons on their reaching the seat of government, who seized the opportunity of directing the displeasure of the government against those toward whom they were personally unfriendly. The letter certainly exhibited an alarming state of things in the West, and if the danger had not been put aside in the manner we are about to relate, there would have been no exaggeration.

Reports were now in circulation, but much exaggerated, that the people of the eastern counties were as much excited as those on the west of the mountains. It was said that they had everywhere raised liberty poles, and had committed various outrages. "I saw before me," says the author of the "Incidents," "the anarchy of a period; a shock to the government, and possibly a revolution impregnated with the Jacobin principles of that of France, and which might become equally bloody to the the principal actors. It would be unavoidably bloody to them and destructive to the people. Let no man suppose that I coveted a revolution. I had seen the evils of one already, the American — and I had read the evils of another, the French. My imagination presented the evils of the last so strongly to my mind that I could scarcely cast my eyes over a paragraph of French news. It was not the excise law alone that was the object with the people; it was with many not the principal object. A man of some note, and whose family had been at the burning of Neville's house, was seen on horseback in Pittsburgh, the day of Braddock's Field, riding along with a tomahawk in his hand and raised over his head, saying—'This is not all that I want; it is not the excise law only that must go down; your district and associate judges must go down; your high offices and salaries—a great deal more must be done. I am but beginning yet.'"

The Mingo Creek Society proposed, after dispensing with judges and justices of the peace altogether, to draw causes to their own examination, and exercise judicial authority. Benjamin Parkinson was the president of this disorganizing association. An incidental circumstance independently of other causes, aided in giving a wrong direction to the people's thoughts. In a contest for the office of sheriff, a candidate in order to secure his election and obtain the votes of the ignorant, was clamorous against offices and salaries, unconscious of the contradiction that on these principles his office, if elected, would be attended with no emolument. Like some other politicians, he did not mean what he said in any practical sense, at least where his own interest came in question. "I had frequently heard it said," says Mr. Brackenridge, "by the people of the country since the introduction of the excise law, that it were better for them to be under the British; and at this time such language began to be common. But I cannot say that I ever heard any person of note breathe the idea. It was also said, that arms and ammunition could be obtained from the British!"

There is no doubt that a vague notion prevailed among the ignorant, that if the march to Braddock's Field, and the expulsion of the persons who had become obnoxious for their peculiar support of the excise law, had not the effect of repealing that law, still it had accomplished something toward it; although they could not clearly discern in what way, unless by the mere effect of showing their strength in arms. It was regarded as a precedent to prove that an unpopular law could be annulled by the people assembling in force and expelling those connected with its execution, or compelling them to give up their commissions and their papers.

In Fayette county, a disposition had been shown to submit to the law. At a meeting of distillers, shortly after the service of the writs by the Marshal, they agreed to employ counsel and make defense. But it appeared that the writs were made returnable to a term when no court was sitting, and were, in consequence, set aside. In the course of this meeting, the invitation to attend the congress of delegates at Parkinson's Ferry was rejected; but afterward they thought it more advisable to send them. In Westmoreland county, according to Findley, there was, at first, the same reluctance. This is explained by the fact that the flame would be more fierce where it first broke out, and would thence more rapidly spread, the assemblage at Braddock's Field having greatly contributed to produce that effect. Washington county, and part of Allegheny, contained the most inflammable portion of the population, although the same feeling prevailed, more or less, over the whole of the western counties, and with some on the east of the mountains, with much less cause for discontent.

The more reflecting and intelligent, however, settled down under the conviction that the assemblage of delegates at Parkinson's Ferry was the last hope, the best remedy against the progress of anarchy, and against the necessity of calling out the military power of the general government. Accordingly, the elections for these delegates was general, although, as might be expected, not as regular, or conducted with as much care in the choice of persons, as could be desired.

NOTES TO CHAPTER VI.

The Mingo Creek Society.

"This society was instituted in February, 1794. It was to consist of Hamilton's battalion, and to be governed by a president and council. The council to consist of members chosen every six months by the people of the several captains' districts; the electors of every such district to be from eighteen years and upward; a councilman to be of the age of twenty-five years, and not when elected to be an inhabitant of that district in which he shall be chosen. The members of council not to exceed one for every district; in the case of a vacancy, notice to issue of an election to fill such vacancy. The society to have a treasurer, secretary and other officers, and to choose deputies to confer occasionally with deputies from other societies of the like nature that might be formed; a majority of the society to constitute a quorum; but a minority to have the power to adjourn, and to compel the attendance of the absent members; two-thirds to have the power of expelling. The society to meet the first day of every month; to keep a journal of its proceedings; the secretary and deputies to be rewarded at the discretion of the society; the president, council and deputies, for any speech or debate in the society, not to be questioned in any other place. No person holding an office of trust or profit under the State or United States, to be president, &c. The societies to have the laws of the United States, minutes of Congress, acts of Assembly of Pennsylvania, necessary books, &c.; to have power to recommend capable persons to the several legislative bodies; to hear and determine all matters in variance and disputes between party and party; encourage teachers of schools; introduce the Bible and other religious books into schools; to encourage the industrious, and the man of merit. No money to be drawn from the society but in consequence of appropriations made by law; no district citizen to sue, or caused to be before a single justice of the peace or any court of justice, a citizen of the district, before applying to the society for redress, unless the business will not admit of delay; the president not to be under twenty-five years of age, and to be elected by ballot; in case of vacancy of the president, a temporary one to be appointed by the council. The president and councilmen to be removable from office on impeachment, and conviction of bribery and high crimes and misdemeanors. Nothing in this constitution to be so construed as to prejudice any claims of the State or of the United States. The constitution to be amendable by a convention for the purpose."—Incidents, p. 148-9.

"The place of convening was usually the meeting-house; they did not as a society project the first outrages, but these naturally sprung from that licentiousness of idea with regard to law and liberty, which the articles of their institutions held out, or were calculated to produce. The society was to have a cognizance of suits between the members, and they actually went on to determine in all cases."—Incidents.

Affidavit of John M'Donald, Secretary of Mingo Creek Society.

"At the time of Marshal Lenox being in Pittsburgh, about the 13th or 14th of July last, being a few days before the attack on General Neville's house, I was in the office of Mr. Brackenridge, on some business with him; was asked by him about the constitution of the Mingo Creek Society, and laughing at some parts of it, he asked what could put it into the people's heads to form such a one. I said the people had been all running wild, and talked of taking Neville prisoner and burning Pittsburgh; and this forming the society was thought of by moderate persons, to turn off to remonstrating and petitioning, and giving them something to do that way to keep them quiet. Mr. Brackenridge asked, what could put it in their heads to think of burning Pittsburgh? I said, I did not know; but they talked of it. I am of opinion that at the time of their march to Pittsburgh, there was great danger. I was at the Mingo Creek meeting-house at the time of the meeting there after the burning of Gen. Neville's house; and numbers of people were dissatisfied at Mr. Brackenridge's speech there, as it appeared he was unwilling to engage to support what was done, and was supposed to be on the side of government." Sworn and subscribed before William Meetkirk, &c.—See Incidents.

Extract from the Affidavit of James Clow.

"At a meeting of the committee [of twenty-one, of which Mr. Clow was a member,] some time after the day of Braddock's Field, it was explained to the committee by Mr. Brackenridge, that the two gentlemen, Gen. Gibson and Col. Neville, who were to leave the town by order of the committee of battalions of Braddock's Field, and which the committee of Braddock's Field had undertaken to see carried into effect (as this deponent understood), wished the committee to appoint persons to go with them on their way, as a guard, until they should be at such a dis____ as to think themselves safe, and_____ ish them with passports. At the opening of the meeting of the committee, John Wilkins, Esq. was first in the chair, but leaving it to attend to some business, this deponent was appointed to the chair, but had some hesitation, as not knowing but it might bring him into trouble. On which Mr. Brackenridge said, that it was at the request of the gentlemen themselves, that the committee met to give a guard and passports, and that it was for their service and not their injury, so there need be no apprehension of giving offense; and that if this deponent did not take the chair, and sign the passports, he himself was willing (if chosen) to do so.

"On this the deponent took the chair, and it was agreed that persons should be appointed, and that the gentlemen themselves, who were to go away, should choose who they would wish to go with them, and that any or all of the committee would go with them to any distance.

"Double passports were made out for each; the one of a few lines, the other of considerable length, dictated by Mr. Brackenridge to the clerk. The having double passports, was suggested by Mr. Brackenridge. The question being asked by some person, what was the use of the double passports, Mr. Brackenridge, to this effect, said the one would serve as a mask, and show to the people in the country that the committee had done what they had undertaken to do, and would serve as a safeguard to the persons sent away, as no one would molest persons supposed to be under guard; and the other would explain to the people below, how it was they were sent away, and for what cause, and that it was by the people of Braddock's Field, and not by the people of Pittsburgh; and that it was not for anything that could hinder them gaining a favorable reception where they went, it not affecting their characters.

"This deponent, in all the course of this business, did not discover the smallest design in all Mr. Brackenridge's actions but for the safety of those gentlemen."

Sworn, &c. February 10th, 1795.

Affidavit of Alexander M'Connel.

"After the meeting at Braddock's Field, the country was in a ferment, and every body was afraid of another to speak their minds. The people seemed to think that law was at an end, every one was ready to fall upon another, where there was a difference; it being supposed they could not be called to account for it. Guns were fired into a house near me. I came into Pittsburgh and talked over this with Mr. Brackenridge; and as to myself, not knowing what to do, said, many of the people talked, if matters got worse, of coming into town, if they could be safe. Mr. Brackenridge said the town was obnoxious enough already; that people taking refuge there would make it much worse, and the country would rise against it; that it was not our interests nor theirs, that any should come into town; that if we could stand it out a little while, matters might be got settled. I asked Mr. Brackenridge if an army could be got to come. He said it could, and he feared it would be necessary."

Statement of John Scull.

"I can certify, and am ready to make oath if required, that a day or two before Gen. Gibson left Pittsburgh, when he was ordered to quit the country by the committee at Braddock's Field, in conversation with Mr. Brackenridge on the subject, Mr. Brackenridge expressed concern that Gen. Gibson intended taking his family with him, as he considered that he would soon be enabled to return, and if not, that many more of ourselves would be obliged to follow; and it would then be time enough to remove his family. Mr. Brackenridge requested me to mention this to Gen. Gibson as his opinion. I called on Gen. Gibson that evening in company with Gen. Wilkins, but did not mention the conversation I had with Mr. Brackenridge, but advised him not to take his family for the same reasons. I never discovered any symptoms of satisfaction in Mr. Brackenridge, on the expulsion of any of the persons in any manner whatever."

Extract from the Affidavit of Jacob Ferree.

"I was a member of the meeting of battalions at Braddock's Field, and in case of expelling Gibson and Neville, saw that Mr. Brackenridge opposed it as long as it seemed to do any good. The danger seemed to be that the people would go into Pittsburgh and take them themselves; parties of riflemen were coming and going and about us, and lastly some of them said, we do not understand this way of mystery; the men will wait no longer; do something immediately or we will go and execute it ourselves. I was a member of the meeting at Parkinson's Ferry, and Mr. Brackenridge said something to humor the people (in my opinion), that might seem to favor them, but I saw that it was to manage the minds of the people to keep them from mischief; and I am of opinion, on the whole of what I have heard and saw, that Mr. Brackenridge being much in the minds of the people at that time, had it in his power, and did render great service in keeping them from going to war against the government."

Statement of Judge Addison, with respect to the letter to Mr. Cox.

"I was in your house on the 5th of September last (1794), when you received by post an answer from Mr. Tench Cox to your letter to him. You showed me a copy of your letter and his answer. You expressed surprise that he mistook the aim of your letter, (which you said you had calculated without exposing yourself to the raging prejudices of the people here, to convey to government an impression of the magnitude of the disturbances and the propriety of conciliatory previous to coercive measures,) and that he should have thought it necessary to convince you of the necessity of submission; and you observed that he reasoned with you as if you was an insurgent."

Extracts from Statement of William H. Beaumont.

"That Mr. Brackenridge usually dictated his letters of correspondence to deponent; [he was his clerk;] that during the whole of the insurrection but two letters were dictated by Mr. Brackenridge to this deponent that had the least reference to any political subject; nor does this deponent know of any written or sent by Mr. Brackenridge to any person on any political subject whatever, except these two letters which were to Tench Cox, Philadelphia, both dictated to this deponent, viz. one of the 8th of August, 1794, and the other of the 15th of September following.

"At the time of the writing and dictating the first, this deponent suggested to Mr. Brackenridge that it was necessary to be cautious how he expressed himself with regard to the country, at that moment, as it was probable the mail might again be robbed, and he might be rendered obnoxious to the people. His answer was, near as this deponent can recollect, in words to this effect, that he had taken care of that; that he meant to give government a real statement of the ferment the country was in, but at the same time had put in some things that would save him from the people, should the letter fall into their hands. This deponent understood at the time, that Mr. Brackenridge was apprehensive that the government might be misled by wrong information respecting the magnitude of the danger, and the extent of the insurrection, and it was his wish that the danger might be viewed in the light it appeared to himself, great and momentous, not trifling and insignificant; that measures might be taken accordingly. That this deponent had that impression at that time, as he expressed apprehension that a just statement would not be given by the proscribed persons who were sent away. That at the time Mr. Brackenridge dictated the second letter to this deponent, he expressed some warmth and irritation of mind that his first letter should have been misunderstood by the government, as he was informed it was; that he wrote this second letter to explain it. This deponent understood Mr. Brackenridge, that it would be natural for these persons (the expelled persons,) to wish a force sent at all events, and as it might alarm the government to be under the necessity of sending a large force, they would be disposed to represent it as repressible by a small one. Whereas, in Mr. Brackenridge's opinion, the policy should be an accommodation in the first place, and if that should fail, an efficient force."

Extract from the Statement of Judge Lucas with respect to the letter to Mr. Cox.

"The deponent says, that by the answer of Mr. Cox, in answer to one from Mr. Brackenridge, that gentleman did repeatedly say, that Mr. Cox had not understood him on many things he had expressed to Mr. Tench Cox, to secure himself in case his letter had been intercepted on this side the mountains."

Mr. Brackenridge to Tench Cox.

"PITTSBURGH, Aug. 8th, 1794.

"SIR—I have received no papers from you; your letter by the post is the first I have heard from you. I take the opportunity to give you in return, a summary of the present state of this country, with respect to the opposition that exists to the excise law. It has its origin not in any anti-Federal spirit, I assure you. It is chiefly the principles and operations of the law itself that renders it obnoxious. Be this as it may, the facts are these:

"The opposition which for some time showed itself in resolves of committees, in representations to government, in masked attacks on insignificant deputy excise officials—for only such would accept the appointment—did at length, on the appearance of the Marshal in this county to serve process, break out into an open and direct attack on the Inspector of the revenue himself, General Neville. These circumstances you will by this time have heard from the General himself, and from the Marshal, Major Lenox.

"Subsequent to their departure from the country, notice was given of a meeting on the Monongahela river, about eighteen miles from the town of Pittsburgh. Six delegates, of whom I was one, were sent from this town. Nothing material was done at this meeting, but the measure agreed upon of a more genaral meeting, on the 14th of August, near the same place, to take into view the present state of affairs of the country.

"Subsequent to this the mail was intercepted, characters in Pittsburgh became obnoxious by letters found, in which sentiments construed to evince a bias in favor of the excise law were discovered.

"In consequence of this, it was thought necessary to demand of the town that those persons should be delivered up, or expelled, or any other obnoxious character that might reside there; also, that the excise office, still kept in Pittsburgh, or said to be kept there, should be pulled down; the house of Abraham Kirkpatrick burned or pulled down; other houses also, that were the property of persons unfavorable to the cause. For this purpose, circular letters were sent to the battalions of the counties, detachments from which met on Braddock's Field, to the amount of at least five thousand men, on the second of the month. It was dreaded on the part of the town, that from the rage of the people involving the town in the general odium of abetting the excise law, it would be laid in ashes. And I aver that it would have been the case, had it not been for the prompt and decisive resolutions of the town, to march out and meet them as brethren, and comply with all demands. This had the effect, and the battalions marched into town on the 3d, and during their delay there, and cantonment in the neighborhood, with a trifling exception of a slight damage done to the property of Abraham Kirkpatrick, in the possession of his tenant, which was afterward compensated,* behaved with all the regularity and order of the French or American armies in their march through a town during the revolution with Great Britain.

"The town of Pittsburgh will send delegates to the meeting of the 14th instant. What the result will be, I know not. I flatter myself nothing more than to send commissioners to the President with an address proposing that he shall delay

* In this I was mistaken; it had been proposed to compensate, but had not been done. I have called it a slight damage, as I presume the value of the house and grain destroyed could not have been more than one hundred dollars; perhaps not so much. [An Act of Congress passed subsequently.]

any attempt to suppress this insurrection, as it will be styled, until the meeting of Congress. This will be the object, simply and alone, with all that labor to avert a civil war. On the part of the government, I would earnestly pray a delay, until such address and commissioners may come forward. This is my object in writing to you this letter, which I desire you to communicate either by the *Gazette*, or otherwise.

"It will be said, this insurrection can be easily suppressed—it is but that of a part of four counties. Be assured it is that of the greater part—and I am induced to believe, the three Virginia counties this side the mountain will fall in. The first measure, then, will be the re-organization of a new government, comprehending the three Virginia counties, and those of Pennsylvania to the westward, to what extent I know not. This event, which I contemplate with great pain, will be the result of the necessity of self-defense. For this reason, I earnestly and anxiously wish that delay on the part of the government may give time to bring about, if practicable, good order and subordination. By the time the Congress meets, there may be a favorable issue to the negotiation with regard to the navigation of the Mississippi, the western posts, &c. A suspension of the excise law during the Indian war, a measure I proposed in a publication three years ago, in Philadelphia, may perhaps suffice. Being then on an equal footing with other parts of the Union, if they submitted to the law, this country might also submit.

"I anticipate all that can be said with regard to example, &c. I may be mistaken, but I am decisive in opinion that the United States cannot effect the operation of the law in this country. It is universally odious in the neighboring parts of all the neighboring States, and the militia under the law in the hands of the President cannot be called out to reduce an opposition. The midland counties, I am persuaded, will not even suffer the militia of more distant parts of the Union to pass through them.

"But the excise law is a branch of the funding system, detested and abhorred by all the philosophic men, and the yeomanry of America, those that hold certificates excepted. There is a growling, lurking discontent at this system, that is ready to burst out and discover itself every where. I candidly and decidedly tell you, the chariot of government has been driven Jehu-like, as to the finances; like that of Phæton, it has descended from the middle path, and is like to burn up the American earth.

"Should an attempt be made to suppress these people, I am afraid the question will not be whether you will march to Pittsburgh, but whether they will march to Philadelphia, accumulating in their course, and swelling over the banks of the Susquehanna like a torrent—irresistible, and devouring in its progress. There can be no equality of contest between the rage of a forest and the abundance, indolence, and opulence of a city. If the President has evinced a prudent and approved delay in the case of the British spoliation, in the case of the Indian tribes, much more humane and politic will it be to consult the internal peace of the government, by avoiding force until every means of accommodation are found unavailing. I deplore my personal situation; I deplore the situation of this country, should a civil war ensue.

"An application to the British is spoken of, which may God avert. But what will not despair produce?

Your most obedient servant, &c.

HUGH H. BRACKENRIDGE.

TENCH COX, Esq."

Mr. Brackenridge to Tench Cox.*

"PITTSBURGH, Sept. 15th, 1794.

"SIR—Suppressing your name, I have just given your letter to the printer of the *Gazette* of this place, conceiving that it will be of service in composing the minds of the people of this country.

"It is an elegant and sensible essay; but would be entirely lost upon me, as inculcating sentiments with which I have no need to be more impressed than I am.

"In some expressions I had used in my letter, you have understood me as speaking of the excise law. Review it, and you will find it was of the funding system in general. Of that system I have been an adversary from the commencement, in all its principles and effects. At the same time, I have never charged the Secretary, who was said to be the author of it, with anything more than an error in judgment.

"A scale ought to have been applied to certificates in the market, and redeemed at that rate. The case of the Continental money was an example. I would refer you to a famous letter of John Adams to the Count De Vergennes, containing reasonings in the case of the Continental money, that would equally have applied in the case of certificates. But at all events, the assumption of the State debts was unnecessary and impolitic.

"Were it possible that we could be freed from this system by a revolution without greater mischief, it is possible I might be brought to think of it. But that is impossible. The remedy would be worse than the malady; honest creditors would suffer, and we should lose the advantages of a general union of the States. These advantages are immense, and far outweigh all other considerations.

"Though in a country of insurgency,

---

* From the original, furnished by Mr. Brinton Cox.

you see I write freely; because I am not the most distantly involved in the insurrection; but deserve the credit of contributing to disorganize and reduce it.

"From paragraphs in the papers I find it is otherwise understood with you; but time will explain all things.

"The arrival of commissioners from the government was announced to the delegates of the 14th at Parkinson's Ferry, when actually convened, and superseded what was contemplated, the sending commissioners from hence.

"You will have heard the result.

"By the measures taken, the spirit of the insurrection was broken. The government has now nothing to fear. The militia may advance, but will meet with nothing considerable to oppose them. But had it not been for the pacific measure on the part of the President, and the internal arrangements made by the friends of order here, which I cannot in a few words develope, affairs would have worn a different aspect, and the standard of the insurrection would have been by this time in the neighborhood of Carlisle. But I hope that this will always remain matter of opinion, and have no experiment in the like case to ascertain the event.

"My writing to you at first was owing to my having received a letter from you on an indifferent subject, and it struck me that through you government might receive information that might be useful, and if published, which was left to your discretion, it might operate as an apology for the government with the people, in adopting pacific measures, representing in strong terms the magnitude and extent of the danger; for it was not the force of this country that I had in view, but the communicability to other parts of the Union, the like inflammable causes of discontent existing elsewhere. I am told my letter has been considered as intending to intimidate the government, and gain time until the insurrection should gain strength.

"It might have been with that view; but that it was not so, will be proved by my conduct and sentiments here. No; from the tenor of my life, I expect and demand to be considered as the advocate of liberty, a greater injury to which could not be, than by the most distant means endangering the existence or infringing the structure of the noblest monument which it ever had, or ever will have in the world—the United States of America.

"You will do me the justice to communicate this letter to the same extent with the first.

"I have further to observe that I am in the meantime not without apprehension for the town of Pittsburgh. The moment of danger will be on the advance of the militia; if the insurgents should embody to meet them, they will, in the first instance, probably turn round and give a stroke here for the purpose of obtaining arms and ammunition; and, if resisted, and perhaps whether or not, will plunder the stores, and set on fire all or some of the buildings.

Yours, with respect,
H. H. BRACKENRIDGE.

"P. S. Since writing the within, which was two or three days ago, apprehension of danger, with ourselves, or opposition of force, considerably vanishes or diminishes.

"I have received your publications. They are ingenious and useful. At present, our papers are filled with our political affairs. In due time they will be inserted.

"As an instance of order gaining ground, I am just informed from the town of Washington that the liberty tree was cut down, and none came forward to erect another, or revenge the affront.
H. H. B."

Secretary of State to the President.

"PHILADELPHIA, Aug. 5th, 1794.

"SIR—The late events in the neighborhood of Pittsburgh appeared, on the first intelligence of them, to be extensive in their relations. But subsequent reflection and the conference with the Governor of Pennsylvania, have multiplied them in my mind ten-fold. Indeed, sir, the moment is big with a crisis which would convulse the oldest government, and if it should burst on ours, its extent and dominion can be but faintly conjectured.

"At our first consultation, in your presence, the indignation which we all felt, at the outrages committed, created a desire that the information received should be laid before an associate justice, or the district judge; to be considered under the act of May 2d, 1792. This step was urged by the necessity of understanding without delay all the means vested in the President for suppressing the progress of the mischief. A caution was prescribed to the Attorney General, who submitted the documents to the judge, not to express the most distant wish of the President that the certificate should be granted.

"The certificate has been granted, and although the testimony is not, in my judgment, yet in sufficient legal form to become the ground work of such an act, and a judge ought not, *a priori*, to decide that the Marshal is incompetent to suppress the combinations by the *posse comitatus;* yet the certificate, if it be minute enough, is conclusive, that, 'in the counties of Washington and Allegheny, in Pennsylvania, laws of the United States are opposed, and the execution thereof obstructed by combinations too powerful to be suppressed by the ordinary course of judicial proceedings, or by the powers vested in the Marshal of that district.'

"But the certificate specifies no particular law which has been opposed. This defect I remarked to Judge Wilson, from whom the certificate came, and observed, that the design of the law being that a judge should point out to the Executive where the judiciary stood in need of military aid, it was frustrated if military force should be applied to laws which the judge might not contemplate. He did not yield to my reasoning, and therefore I presume that the objection will not be received against the validity of the certificate.

"Upon the supposition of its being valid, a power arises to the President to call forth the militia of Pennsylvania, and eventually the militia of other States which may be convenient. But as the law does not compel the President to array the militia in consequence of the certificate, and renders it lawful only for him to do so, the grand inquiry is, *whether it be expedient to exercise this power at this time.*

"On many occasions have I contended that, whensoever military coercion is to be resorted to in support of law, the militia are the true, proper and only instruments which ought to be employed. But a calm survey of the situation of the United States has presented these dangers and these objections, and *banishes every idea of calling them into immediate action.*

"1. A radical and universal dissatisfaction with the excise pervades the four transmontane counties of Pennsylvania, having more than sixty-three thousand souls in the whole, and more than fifteen thousand white males above the age of sixteen. The counties on the eastern side of the mountains, and some other populous counties, are infected by similar prejudices, inferior in degree, and dormant, but not extinguished.

"2. Several counties in Virginia, having a strong militia, *participate in these feelings.*

"3. The insurgents, themselves numerous, are more closely united by like dangers with friends and kindred scattered abroad in different places, who will enter into all the apprehensions, and combine in all the precautions of safety adopted by them.

"4. As soon as any event of eclat shall occur, around which persons discontented on other principles, whether of aversion to the government or disgust with any measures of the administration, may rally, *they will make a common cause.*

"5. *The Governor of Pennsylvania* has declared his opinion to be, that the militia which can be drawn forth *will be unequal to the task.*

"6. If the militia of other States are called forth, *it is not a decided thing that many of them may not refuse.* And if they comply, is nothing to be apprehended from a strong cement growing between all the militia of Pennsylvania, when they perceive that another militia is to be introduced into the bosom of their country? *The experiment is at least untried.*

"7. *The expense of a military expedition will be very great;* and with a devouring Indian war, the commencement of a navy, the sum to be expended for obtaining a peace with Algiers, the destruction of our mercantile capital by British depredations, the uncertainty of war or peace with Great Britain, the impatience of the people under increased taxes, the punctual support of our credit; it behooves those who manage our fiscal matters to be sure of their pecuniary resources, when so great a field of new and unexpected expense is to be opened.

"8. Is there any appropriation of money which can be immediately devoted to this use. If not, how can money be drawn? It is said that appropriations are to the war department generally, but it may deserve inquiry whether they were not made upon particular statements of a kind of service *essentially distinct from the one proposed.*

"9. *If the intelligence of the overtures of the British to the western counties be true,* and the inhabitants should be *driven to accept their aid,* the supplies of the western army, the western army itself, may be destroyed; the reunion of that country to the United States will be impracticable; and we must be engaged in a British war. *If the intelligence be probable only,* how difficult will it be to reconcile the world to believe that we have been consistent in our conduct; when after running the hazard of mortally offending the French, by the punctilious observance of neutrality; after deprecating the wrath of the English, by every possible act of government; after the request of the suspension of the settlement of Presq' Isle, which has in some measure been founded on the possibility of Great Britain being roused to arms by it; we pursue measures which threaten collision with Great Britain and which are mixed with the blood of our fellow citizens!

"10. If miscarriage should befall the United States in the beginning, what may not be the consequence? And if this should not happen, is it possible to see what may be the effect of ten, twenty, or thirty thousand of our fellow citizens being drawn into the field against as many more? *There is another enemy in the heart of the Southern States, who would not sleep with such an opportunity of advantage.*

"11. It is a fact well known, that the parties in the United States are highly inflamed against each other; and that there is but one character which keeps both in awe. As soon as the sword shall be drawn, who shall be able to restrain them?

"On this subject the souls of some good men bleed. They have often asked themselves, why they are always so jealous of military power, whenever it has been proposed to be exercised under the form of a succor to the civil authority? How has it happened that with a temper not addicted to suspicion, nor unfriendly to those who propose military force, they do not court the shining reputation which is acquired by being always ready for strong measures? This is the reason: that they are confident that they know the ultimate sense of the people; that the will of the people must force its way in the government; that notwithstanding the indignation which may be raised against the insurgents, yet if measures unnecessarily harsh, disproportionably harsh, and without a previous trial of every thing which law or the spirit of conciliation can do, be executed, that indignation will give way, and the people will be estranged from the administration which made the experiment. There is a second reason: one motive assigned in argument for calling forth the militia, has been, *that a government can never be said to be established until some signal display has manifested its power of military coercion.** This maxim, if indulged, would heap curses upon the government. The strength of the government is the affection of the people; and while that is maintained, every invader, every insurgent, will as certainly count on the fear of its strength, as if

* Hamilton!

it had with one army of citizens mown down another.

"Let the parties in the United States be ever kindled into action, sentiments like these will produce a flame *which will not terminate in a common revolution.* Knowing, sir, as I do, the motives which govern you in office, I was certain that you would be anxious to mitigate as far as you thought it practicable, the military course which has been recommended. You have accordingly suspended the force of the preceding observations, by determining not to call forth the militia immediately to action, and to send commissioners who may explain and adjust, if possible, the present discontents.

"The next question then is, whether the militia shall be directed to hold themselves in readiness, or shall not be summoned at all?

"It has been supposed by some gentleman, that when reconciliation is offered with one hand, terror should be borne in the other, and that a full amnesty and oblivion shall not be granted unless the excise laws be complied with in the fullest manner.

"With a language such as this, the overtures of peace will be considered delusive by the insurgents, and the most of the world. It will be said and believed, that the design of sending commissioners was only to gloss over hostility, to endeavor to divide, to sound the strength of the insurgents, to discover the most culpable persons to be marked out for punishment, to temporize until Congress can be prevailed upon to order further force, or the western army may be at leisure from the savages, to be turned upon the insurgents, and many other suspicions will be entertained which cannot be here enumerated. When Congress talked of some high-handed steps against Great Britain, they were disapproved as counteracting Mr. Jay's mission—because it could not be expected she would be dragooned. Human nature will, to a certain point, show itself to be the same, even among the Allegheny mountains. The mission will, I fear, fail; though it would be to me the most grateful occurrence in life to find my prediction falsified. If it does fail, and in consequence of the disappointment the militia should be required to act, then will return that fatal train of events, which I have stated above to be suspended for the present.

"What would be the inconvenience of delay? The result of the mission would be known in four weeks, and the President would be master of his measures without any previous commitment. Four weeks could not render the insurgents more formidable; that space of time might render them less so, by affording room for reflection; and the government will have a sufficient season remaining to act on. Until every peaceable attempt shall be exhausted, it is not clear to me that as soon as the call is made, and the proclamation issued, the militia may not enter into some combination which will satisfy the insurgents that they need fear nothing from them, and spread those combinations among the militia.

"My opinion, therefore, is, that the commissioners will be furnished with enough on the score of terror, when they announce that the President is in possession of the certificate of the judge. It will confirm the humanity of the mission; and, notwithstanding, some men might pay encomiums on decision, vigor of nerves, &c. &c., if the militia were summoned to be held in readiness, the majority would conceive the merit of the mission incomplete if this were to be done.

"It will not, however, be supposed that I mean these outrages are to pass without animadversion. No, sir! That the authority of the government is to be maintained, is not less my position than that of others. But I prefer the accomplishment of this by every experiment of moderation, in the first instance. The steps, therefore, which I would recommend are:

"1. A serious proclamation, stating the mischief, declaring the power possessed by the Executive, announcing that it is withheld from motives of humanity and a wish for conciliation.

"2. Commissioners properly instructed to the same objects.

"3. If they fail in their mission, let the offenders be prosecuted according to law.

"4. If the judiciary authority is, after this, withstood, let the militia be called out.

"These appear to me to be the only means for producing unanimity in the people; and without their unanimity, the government may be mortified and defeated.

"If the President shall determine to operate with the militia, it will be necessary to submit some animadversions upon the interpretation of the law. For it ought closely to be considered, whether if the combinations should disperse, the execution of processes is not to be left to the Marshal and his *posse*. But these will be deferred until orders shall be discussed for the militia to march.

I have the honor, sir, to be,
With the highest respect,
And sincerest attachment,
Your most obedient servant,
EDMUND RANDOLPH."

CHAPTER VII.

MEETING OF THE DELEGATES AT PARKINSON'S FERRY—THE RESOLUTIONS ADOPTED THERE—APPOINTMENT OF A COMMITTEE OF CONFERENCE.

On the day appointed, the delegates elected from each township convened at Parkinson's Ferry, on the Monongahela, afterward Williamsport, now Monongahela City. The place was an open field on the banks of the river, with fallen timber and stumps, with a few shade trees, instead of buildings, for the accommodation of this important assembly, whose deliberations might be attended with the most serious consequences for good or evil. The number of members was two hundred and twenty-six; from Allegheny forty-three, from Washington ninety-three, from Bedford two, from Fayette thirty-three, from Westmoreland forty-nine, from Ohio in Virginia six. There was a still greater number of spectators, or outsiders.

The point of assemblage might have been better chosen, as it was too near the scene of the recent disturbances, and too convenient for the attendance of those who had been actually engaged in them. It cannot be supposed that the utmost fairness had prevailed at the elections. There was too large a proportion from the infected district, (if the expression may be used,) and sufficient pains had not been taken, every where, to send to the meeting only the well disposed, and the men of most weight and influence. Still it was superior to the promiscuous mob it was intended to supersede. It was impossible to ascertain, at a glance, what proportion was in favor of peaceful measures, or disposed to apply for an amnesty, or oblivion of the past, according to the suggestion of Mr. Brackenridge at the Mingo meeting-house, and where the idea of the present meeting, composed of delegates from the whole of the western counties, was adopted at his instance.* But no one entertained a doubt, that in spite of this first winnowing, there would still be a majority, in the present state of things, who would vote for any measure that might be proposed by Marshall or Bradford, the acknowledged leaders in opposition to the excise law.

* See the account of the meeting at the Mingo meeting-house, chap. III.

The proceedings of the assembly were happily controlled by Messrs. Brackenridge, Gallatin, Edgar and others, who succeeded in retarding, if not defeating for the present, the extreme and violent measures contemplated by the enemies of peace and order. Messrs. Brackenridge and Gallatin were chiefly looked to by the friends of order; the former at the head of the western bar, and occupying the highest rank in point of talents; the latter already distinguished, but with a reputation far short of what he afterward attained, when elected to Congress, and a career and opportunities of distinction were opened to him. They attended with the same motive, but under different circumstances, and with different views as to the mode of action. These two gentlemen had never before met, and had no interchange of sentiments, until after the business of the meeting was ended. They had taken opposite sides some years before, in the animated contest for the adoption of the Federal Constitution; Brackenridge on the Federal side, and Gallatin Findley, and Smiley, on the anti-Federal. These latter had also been engaged in those meetings against the excise law which the Secretary of the Treasury had stigmatized as bordering on treason, and alleged by him to have greatly contributed to bring about the present disorder. Gallatin had regretted the part he had taken at the meeting which had passed "intemperate resolutions," to which so much evil had been ascribed, and was desirous to make amends, by exerting himself at this meeting on the side of the government, in the most direct and decided manner. Indeed, it was asserted that he had made his peace with the government on this condition; but this surmise must be rejected as not supported by any tangible evidence, and he must be regarded as entitled to the merit of pure motives until the contrary appears. Gallatin was closely allied with Findley and Smiley in party politics, local as well as Federal, although not personally at enmity with Brackenridge, as was the case with the other two. He had no intimacy, or perhaps even acquaintance with Marshall and Bradford; and not much personal influence with the delegates, while a friendly understanding had existed between Brackenridge and Marshall and Bradford, and with many others of the assembly. The former regarded Marshall as a moderate sensible man, until he became involved in the recent difficulties. With Bradford he had been frequently associated professionally; and they had agreed in their support of the Federal constitution, and until the Mingo creek meeting had been on familiar terms. Marshall and Bradford had come prepared with resolutions, to be offered to the meeting, contemplating hostile opposition to the government. Having exhibited them to Gallatin, he without hesitation declared his objections, and made known his determination to oppose them. This at once deprived him of any influence he might have had with the assembly, and placed it out of his power to defeat any measure by direct attack, no matter what might be his power of persuasion, or force of reasoning, the two leaders having the control of the majority of the body. It will be seen, hereafter, how unavailing were the efforts of Gallatin, with the exception of some unimportant changes of words, or phrases, in the resolutions as at first presented. His influence would be still further impaired, by the circumstance of his having taken a conspicuous part against the excise law, while he was now taking a stand on the side of the government, in opposition to those with whom he had formerly acted. Such, at least, would be the light in which his course would be regarded. The situation of Mr. Brackenridge was entirely different from that of Mr. Gallatin; as was also the policy which he had determined to pursue. He had taken no part at the public meetings against the excise law, although understood to be, like every other person in the western counties, opposed to it, and this doubtless exaggerated by the circumstance of having occasionally been of counsel for persons under prosecution by the government. The popularity he had lost at the Mingo meeting, he had partially regained at Braddock's Field, and there now existed a desire on the part of the insurgents to enlist him in their cause. He had, therefore, ground to stand upon in a course dictated by policy, and he knew that from the position he occupied, something would be conceded to him, which could not be accomplished by direct attack. He determined to take advantage of these circumstances, and pursue a course different from that of Gallatin; that is, to effect, if possible, by indirect means, what he knew Gallatin would fail to accomplish by a different course. Affecting to act with the two leaders, at least to some extent, he determined to avail himself of legislative tactics, which like strategy in war, often gains victories without battles. With the generous design of preventing the horrors of civil war, and even of saving those leaders themselves from the ruinous course they were prepared to pursue, dissimulation was not only justifiable, but became a duty. In this course, the sequel will show he was so fortunate as to be successful, but in the peculiarly delicate situation in which he was placed, not without much difficulty. The impartial reader will see the absurdity of attempting to give to Gallatin the credit of results which his very position prevented him from effecting. But for the management and address of Mr. Brackenridge, the leaders would have been precipitated into the very measures from which they were to be diverted. He acted in pursuance of a plan he had carefully settled in his mind; the first step had already been taken—the withdrawal of power from the mob,

THE SIFTING OPERATION. 155

and placing it in a delegation; the next was at this meeting, by a set of resolutions, to continue the sifting operation, through a standing committee; and from this, again, choosing a smaller committee of conference; every remove from the mob increasing the chances of having men of good sense to deal with. The object at present, was to prevent any decisive measures. Mr. Gallatin, on the other hand, offered no resolutions, had no plan, and depended entirely on the effect of direct opposition to that which might be offered by Bradford and Marshall. In the plan of Mr. Brackenridge we recognize the principle that "power is ever stealing from the many to the few;" and in the present instance it was curiously exemplified.* The sub-committee of three, consisting of Messrs. Cook, Gallatin and Brackenridge, finally confided the business chiefly to the latter, and this was scarcely perceived or suspected, until the winding up of the negotiations. We are, however, anticipating the proceedings of the assembly, to which we return. "In the morning of the meeting at Parkinson's Ferry," says Mr. Brackenridge, "I saw James Marshall, and in order to reconcile him with his own feelings, and dispose him favorably toward me, I observed that the calling out of the people at Braddock's Field was a rash act, but it might have a good effect. It would impress the government with a fear of the extent of the opposition to the law. He seemed pleased with the apology made, and observed, 'that Bradford was hasty in undertaking things, and had not abilities afterward to manage them.' I considered this as an apology to me for the rashness of what had been done. But I found that he contemplated the going on to support by force of arms, those unlawful acts. He showed me a set of resolutions, which he had drawn up to lay before the meeting, one of which contemplated force against the government. He gave me to understand, that Bradford also had made a minute of some things he meant to move. Bradford here joined us, and I saw his schedule. It contained the heads of particulars that would be the subjects of consideration. A committee of safety, magazines, clothing, provisions, &c.

"There were two or three of the resolutions of Marshall, in substance, the same with those I had discussed in my mind, and I approved of them. I developed my plan of sending commissioners to the Executive, and showed the address I had drawn up to be presented to him. They approved of it.

* First, the standing committee of sixty—then the committee of conference of twelve—these chose a sub-committee of three, and thus the principal share of the negotiations was placed in the hands of Mr. Brackenridge, who was on that committee.

"In order to retain the management of Bradford, it was my policy, at that period, to conceal from him my total disapprobation of what had been done; nor did I venture to oppose him on the subject of making war; but to keep him from thinking, and coming to a close conversation, I amused him with pleasantry and kept him laughing."*

The meeting was organized by placing Edward Cook in the chair, as was usual at all meetings where he was, on account of his age and high respectability of character. Albert Gallatin was appointed secretary. Bradford now opened the business with some account of what had taken place—the appearance of the Marshal to serve writs, the attack on Neville's house—the flight of the Inspector—the expulsion of obnoxious characters, &c.—here he read the letters intercepted in the mail.

"Marshall, who followed Bradford, now brought forward his propositions.

"First—The taking citizens of the United States from their respective abodes or vicinage, to be tried for real or supposed offenses, is a violation of the rights of the citizen, is a forced and dangerous construction of the constitution, and ought not under any pretense whatever to be exercised by the judicial authority.

"It was alleged by Marshall that the language of this resolve, as of the others, might not be correct, or the idea well expressed; and wished the secretary to frame it as it might seem proper. I spoke on this occasion, and observed, that by the constitution the whole State was made the vicinage; and the judiciary had it in their power to make use of it to that extent. Nevertheless, it certainly was an abridgment of that advantage which the citizens had before the constitution existed, where the vicinage was the county; and that it was a hard construction of the constitution, to suppose that it contemplated such a judiciary system as would bring citizens from one end of the State to the other. For that reason, I approved of the substance of the resolution; but as probably it might be improved in expression, I proposed that we should go over the resolutions, and having agreed upon the substance, refer them to a committee of three or more, to digest the arrangement, and express the same in the best manner, and lay them before the meeting for their final consideration. It was agreed, and we passed on to the second resolution."

The foregoing, the reader will perceive, was a most important move. The object was to prevent a final vote being taken on any of the resolu-

*The course of Gallatin was the reverse—and what was gained by it? But for the address of Mr Brackenridge, everything would have been lost.

tions in their present form, by referring them to a small committee, where they would be calmly dicusssed, and the dangerous debates, which might ensue in the meeting of delegates, already much inflamed—surrounded by persons still more so—might be avoided. It was subsequently adopted as the means of escaping such debates, by a reference of the resolution under discussion to the committee suggested by Mr. Brackenridge; it was therefore vastly more important than the verbal alterations afterward suggested by Mr. Gallatin, in the committee of four.*

The second resolution—"That there shall be a standing committee to consist of —— members from each county, to be denominated a committe of public safety, whose duty it shall be to call forth the resources of the western country to repel any invasion that may be made against the rights of the citizens or of the body of the people."

"Comparing this resolution," observes Mr. Brackenridge, "with the first, I saw that Marshall had conceived that the act of the district officer, in serving writs in the country to answer at Philadelphia, was illegal and void, and that it might be constitutionally resisted; and also, that an attempt of the government to enforce such an act by pursuing those that had resisted, might be constitutionally opposed, on the same principle that the money tax, and the force of government in aid of it, was constitutionally opposed by Hampden, or the declaratory act, and the enforcing of it, was opposed by America against Great Britain.† Coupling, therefore, these resolutions, they would seem to contemplate the resisting the officer of the district, and protecting by arms those who resisted him. Taking the words by themselves, they were not exceptionable, for doubtless the people retain the right to repel hostile attempts against their rights; on the same principle that I may repel the officer who would seize me without process. But coupling the word with the preceding resolution, (that of 'taking persons from their abode, &c. is a violation of the rights of the citizens, is a forced and dangerous construction of the constitution,') with the acts perpetrated in the country,

---

* Findley and others erroneously confound the private disussions in the committee with the proceedings before the delegates in public. It was in the committee that the verbal alterations of Mr. Gallatin, to which Findley attaches so much importance, were made. The real difficulty was to prevent a declaration of war, which was defeated by Mr. Brackenridge seeming to coincide with Bradford.

† The power of the Supreme Court of the United States to decide on the constitutionality of an act of Congress at that time, was not even suggested—it is of a later growth.

and with the state of it, they appeared to be exceptionable. These were my reflections from the time I had read the resolutions in the morning until the present moment.

"The resolutions being read, secretary Gallatin now rose, 'What reason,' said he, 'have we to suppose that hostile attempts will be made against our rights? and why, therefore, prepare to resist them? Riots have taken place, which may be the subject of judiciary cognizance; but we are not to suppose a military force on the part of the government.'*

"If I am not accurate in stating this language or these words of the secretary, it ought to be attributed to defect of memory, not design. It was my impression at that time, either that it was the only pretense that occurred to him to use to evade the resolution, or that actually he did not know that the acts committed brought it within the power of the President to call out the militia."†

Not to suppose a military force on the part of the government! A case had occurred, and during the session of this assembly the proclamation of the President was actually received, producing a bad effect. It was the general belief that the military would be called out, and would march unless prevented by the submission of the people, or an amnesty obtained. The latter could only be attained in one or two modes; by a delegation from the meeting bearing a petition to the President, as was contemplated by Mr. Brackenridge, or by a voluntary offer on the part of the government—which actually took place. The design of the hostile resolution, was to meet the force expected; and those who desired to give it the go-by, placed their hopes on being able to induce the assembly to solicit an amnesty, which would render the march unnecessary. In whatever manner Mr. Gallatin would have been replied to by Bradford, the actual state of things would have been represented, and a question put, which might have committed the assembly in favor of defensive war. It was afterward admitted by Mr. Gallatin, in his evidence on the trials, "that it appeared to me, from the temper of those present, that if the question had been put it would have been carried." The merit, then, of having parried

---

*Wilkinson (American Pioneer, a work of more fancy than authority): "Gallatin presented the folly of past resistance, and the ruinous consequence to the country of a continuance of the insurrection. He urged that the government was bound to vindicate the law, and that it would surely send an overwhelming force against them." On what authority does Wilkinson make this assertion or venture to contradict Mr. Brackenridge? Was he there? He was but a child at the time, perhaps not yet born. If he ever made those remarks at all, it must have been *at a late period*, at the Brownsville meeting. Wilkinson is no authority.

†"Incidents."

the dangerous question is due to Mr. Brackenridge, and it was thus accomplished.

"I knew," continues the author of the "Incidents," "that this resolution was a favorite one with all those who had been involved in any of the outrages, and at the same time a popular one generally. I was alarmed, therefore, at the idea of any discussion of it; and instantly, before any one could have an opportunity of speaking, affected to oppose the secretary, and thought it might not be amiss to have the resolution, but it might be softened in terms, without altering the substance; it might be said, 'the committee shall have power to take such measures as the situation of affairs may require,' and that the committee of four should have the modeling of the terms. Marshall acquiesced, and there was no debate."

It is highly probable that the success of Mr. Brackenridge in fending off the debate, is in part to be attributed to the disposition of the leaders to indulge him, in the hope of securing him on their side, which he appeared to take on this occasion. Afterward, in the committee of four, (not in the assembly, as stated by Findley and others,) following up the above suggestion of a vague diplomatic generality, Mr. Gallatin introduced in the resolution the words, "and in case of any sudden emergency, to take such means as they may think necessary." The words in the original resolution were, "to repel any hostile attempts that may be made against the rights of the citizens or the body of the people." This mere verbal alteration was unimportant, compared to the main object in view—the preventing a direct vote in the assembly on the resolution as at first presented. Gallatin is lauded for the change of phrase, the merit of which, if any, does not belong to him. Such quibbling would not have been listened to by the assembly, or the bystanders, if brought to a serious discussion.

The third resolution—"That a committee of —— members be appointed to draft a remonstrance to Congress, praying a repeal of the excise law, and that a more equal and less odious tax may be laid, and at the same time giving assurance to the representatives of the people that such tax will be cheerfully paid by the people of these counties, and that the said remonstrance be signed by the chairman of this meeting, in behalf of the people we represent." This resolution was opposed on the ground that it was useless to remonstrate to Congress, that body having treated with contempt all former remonstrances on that subject; it was, however, carried—those who had opposed it acquiescing.

Fourth resolution—"Whereas, the motives by which the western people have been actuated, in the late unhappy disturbances at Neville's house, and in the great and general rendezvous of the people at Braddock's Field, and we are liable to be misconstrued as well by our fellow citizens throughout the United States as by their and our public servants, to whom is consigned the administration of the Federal government; *Resolved*, That a committee of ―― be appointed to make a fair and candid statement of the whole transaction to the President of the United States, and to the Governors of Pennsylvania and Virginia; and if it should become necessary, that the said committee do publish to the world a manifesto or declaration, whereby the motives and principles of the people in this country shall be fairly and fully stated."* This was committed to the committee of four without debate.

Fifth resolution—"That we will, with the rest of our fellow citizens, support the laws and governments of the respective States in which we live, and the laws and government of the United States, the excise laws and the taking away citizens out of their respective counties only excepted; and therefore we will aid and assist all civil officers in the execution of their respective functions, and endeavor by every proper means in our power to bring to justice all offenders in the premises."

On the consideration of this resolution, the state of the country, without law or safety to persons or property, was represented at some length by Mr. Brackenridge. Mr. Gallatin followed on the same side, supporting the resolution with a view to the establishment of law and the conservation of the peace. Though he did not venture to touch on the resistance to the Marshal, or the expulsion of the proscribed, yet he strongly arraigned the destruction of property; the burning of the barn of Kirkpatrick, for instance. "What!" exclaimed a fiery fellow in the meeting, "do you blame that?" Mr. Gallatin found himself embarrassed; he paused for a moment—"If you had burned him in it," said he, "it might have been something; but the barn had done no harm." "Aye, aye," said the member, "that's right enough." This shows how much easier it is to talk of an open and undisguised opposition to the measures and temper of such a meeting, than to practice it. The secretary was obliged to dissemble as well as Mr. Brackenridge, with whom he is so favorably contrasted. Perhaps his allusion to Kirkpatrick would not have passed unnoticed, if, like the former, he had been on unfriendly terms with the "Neville connection!"

A member who had seen the schedule of Bradford, relating to providing arms, &c. now moved that it be brought forward and laid on the table. Several persons spoke on the subject of forming magazines of arms and

* This is the only language from which a contemplated declaration of independence, and withdrawal from the Union, can be inferred.

ammunition, and seemed to desire that resolutions be introduced, carrying into practical detail the principle of Bradford's schedule. Gallatin labored in direct opposition to the principle itself, but apparently with no success; and there was danger of a question of some kind being put. Mr. Brackenridge had been out of the circle, but at this juncture returned. As before, he affected to oppose Gallatin; he began by making some remarks to conciliate those who were for providing the means of war; and then observed, "that it was well to talk of such things, to show that the people were in earnest. By holding out an idea of fighting, the necessity for it might be avoided; just as a general displays column, to avoid an engagement. The idea of a preparation for defense may quicken the disposition of the government to come to an accommodation, and grant the reasonable demands of the country. But enough has been said, let these things be left to the committee of four."

This apology saved the pride of the speakers, and satisfied the hopes of the violent, and there was nothing more said. Mr. Brackenridge was thought to be for war; he was applauded by the outside people; and it was said that he now had regained what he had lost at the Mingo Creek meeting.*

* Findley says Brackenridge "was *probably* actuated by the same motives as Gallatin, but supported the measure in a different manner. He often kept up the appearance, and sometimes the boasting language which was acceptable to Bradford's party, and opposed Gallatin; yet always contrived to bring the proceedings to the same issue." If Mr. Brackenridge always brought the proceedings to the same issue with Gallatin, it was not only *probable*, but pretty *certain*, that he was actuated by the same motives! And why not say, that the first effected by superior address what the other failed to accomplish by direct means? Mr. Brackenridge proved himself the abler man on this occasion. He could act with policy for wise and benevolent ends; but when it was necessary to go straight forward to his purpose, and there was a prospect of success in doing so, he could do it as boldly as any one; as was afterward proved at the Brownsville meeting, in reference to which the same writer, Findley, observes, "that his argument was of the more consequence, that it was decisive; as formerly he had temporized so as to induce the rioters to believe that he was friendly to their cause."

He had, at the Brownsville meeting, different minds to deal with from those at Parkinson's. If at Parkinson's he had pursued the same course with Gallatin, like him, he would have effected nothing. That gentleman, in his evidence on the trials, says, "I doubted his (Brackenridge's) real intentions. He explained to me his real meaning five or six days afterward, the first time we had a private conversation. He had disapproved the proceedings which had taken place as much as I did, but was attempting to do by art, what I had tried to do by direct means." He might have said, with more candor, Mr. Brackenridge had accomplished by address, what he, Gallatin, had failed to do by direct means. James Ross and

The assembly adjourned to the next day. The committee of four, who were to model the resolutions, were to meet early the next morning; they were Messrs. Gallatin, Bradford, Brackenridge and Herman Husbands.*

"I lay that night," says the author of the "Incidents," "at a farm house in the neighborhood, with a hundred or more of the gallery spectators and of the assembly, about me. The whole cry was war. From the manner in which they had understood me, I was greatly popular with them." 'Stand by us,' said they, 'and we will stand by you.'

"I felt my situation with extreme sensibility. I had an attachment to the people because they had an attachment to me; and I thought of the consequences. Suppose that in the prosecution of the plan I have in view, arrangements cannot be made to satisfy them, and that a war must come, what shall I do? I am under no obligation of honor to take part in supporting them, for I have no way contributed to produce the disturbance. And though on principles of conscience it may be excusable in them to make war—for they think they are right—yet it would not be so in me, for I think them wrong. But on the score of self-preservation and personal interest, what am I to do? It is a miserable thing to be an emigrant;† there is a secret contempt attached to it, even with those to whom he comes. They respect more the valor, though they dis-

General Wilkins were in Mr. Brackenridge's confidence at this time, and not Mr. Gallatin until after the assembly had adjourned.

*"I had heard of this extraordinary character (Husbands) many years ago, when a principal of the insurgents known by the name of Regulators, in North Carolina. I had seen him in the year 1778, when he was a member of the Legislature of Pennsylvania. I was present when a Quaker lady was introduced and preached before the House. Herman, who was a divine as well as a politician, thought her not orthodox, and wished to controvert; but the House, willing to avoid religious controversies, would not permit.

"I had visited him in the year 1780, in the glades of the Allegheny, on my return from Philadelphia to Pittsburgh. He had then just finished a Commentary on a part of the prophet Ezekiel; it was the vision of the temple, the walls, the gates, the sea of glass, &c. Loggerhead divines had heretofore interpreted it of the New Jerusalem, but he conceived it to apply to the western country; the walls were the mountains; the gates, the gaps in them by which the roads pass; and the sea of glass, the lakes on the west of us. I had no hesitation in saying that the Commentary was analogous to the vision. He was pleased, and said I was the only person, except his wife, that he ever got to believe it. Thought I, your church is composed, like many others, of the ignorant and dissembling."—Incidents, p. 95.

† He alludes to the French emigrants from political causes compelled to leave their country.

approve the principles, of those that stay at home. All I have in the world is in this country; it is not in money; I cannot carry it with me, and if I go abroad I go poor; and I am too far advanced in life to begin the world anew.

"But as to these people themselves, what chance have they? They may defend the passes of the mountains; they are warlike; accustomed to the use of arms; capable of hunger and fatigue, and can live in the rocks and woods, like badgers. They are enthusiastic to madness, and the effect of this is beyond calculation.

"The people to the east of the mountains are, many of them, dissatisfied, and will be little disposed to disturb the people here, if they should mean to defend themselves. It is true, the consequence of war, supposing the country independent of the United States, will be poverty and a miserable state of things for a long time; but still, those who stand by the country where they are, have the best chance and the most credit in the end. In either case, the election is fearful; the only thing that can suit me, considered merely as a matter of personal interest, is an accommodation without civil war. But is there a prospect of this? Will the Executive be disposed to act with mildness or severity? The excise is a branch of the funding system, which is a child of the Secretary of the Treasury, who is considered the Minister of the President. He will feel a personal antipathy against the opposers of it, and will be inclined to sanguinary counsels. The President himself will consider it a more dangerous case than the Indian war or the British spoliations, and will be disposed to apply more desperate remedies. He will see that here the vitals are attacked, whereas there the attack was on the extremities. Nevertheless, the extreme reluctance which he must have to shed the blood of the people, by whom he is personally beloved, will dispose him to overtures of amnesty. These were my reveries, as I lay with my head upon a saddle, on the floor of a cabin.

"In the morning, the committee of four having met, we proceeded to the arranging and amending the resolutions. Bradford was not satisfied with the indefinite power given to the standing committee, (to provide for defense, &c.) but wished to have it in plain terms; probably with a view to get something to pass the assembly that would involve all equally with himself in the treasons committed. I wished to evade it, and endeavored to divert his attention by keeping him laughing. I put Husbands on the explanation of his vision of Ezekiel, and endeavored to amuse Bradford with him, as a person would amuse a boy with a bear. But Bradford was too intent on getting the resolutions amended to an explicit declaration of war; he complained of the laughing, and wished him to be serious. Gallatin, not perceiving the drift, said, cynically, 'He laughs all by himself.' He let Bradford alone then, who puzzled the secretary enough, and obliged him to put in a sentence, to avoid a worse, 'and in case of any sudden emergency, to take such temporary measures as they may deem necessary,' instead of the expressions of the resolution of Bradford, 'whose duty it shall be to call forth the resources of the country, to repel any hostile attempt that may be made against the rights of the citizens or the body of the people.'"

It may be remarked that the aim of the friends of peace was to restrain the violence of the people, led by inconsiderate men; this was to be accomplished by keeping the assembly from taking any action whatever; but the mere substitution of an ambiguous phrase—this diplomatic fence of words—would do but little toward the accomplishing of that end. The secretary's amendment had somewhat the appearance of precaution against the use of treasonable words; and it may be recollected that a design had been entertained of instituting prosecutions on a former occasion, against the authors of the "intemperate resolutions." Nor were the other objectionable words of the resolution much improved by substituting the phrase, "to support the municipal laws, &c." in the place of the words, "the support of the laws and government, &c. *the excise law and the taking citizens from their vicinage excepted.*" There is little difference between not *supporting* the excise laws, and *opposing them;* and moreover, an unconstitutional law, that is to say a law that is void, may be opposed by legal means, through the courts, or by efforts to procure its repeal—or even by force at the peril of the person who resists the unconstitutional law. What was accomplished by Mr. Gallatin in the committee of four, amounted to nothing, although exalted by Findley above his associates. Gallatin is applauded by his partisan, for his direct and open opposition to the measures of Bradford, which opposition, it is admitted, was a failure; his diplomacy was no better; and yet he is favorably contrasted with the politic course pursued by Mr. Brackenridge, which proved effectual. It is not always that the motive sanctifies the act, but where it is to prevent bloodshed and civil war, the decision may be safely left to the judgment of upright and sensible men, whatever may be the opinions of mere casuists or fools.

The resolutions being perfected by the committee of four, were reported as soon as the assembly met in the morning. They were reduced to *three* in number, instead of the original five, several having been condensed into one.

First, *Resolved*, That taking the citizens of the United States from their respective abodes, or vicinage, to be tried for real or supposed offenses, is a violation of the rights of the citizens; is a forced and dangerous construction, and ought not, under any pretense whatsoever, to be exercised by the judicial authority.*

The foregoing resolution, which expressed a grievance that none could deny, was in fact the immediate cause of the insurrection. It constitutes one of the most serious of those complained of in our Declaration of Independence—"for carrying us beyond seas to be tried for imaginary offenses." What would we now say of taking persons from the remote parts of Texas or California to be tried at Washington City? The constitution limits the trial or venue to the State or district, leaving it to the discretion of Congress to designate the district. The common law principle of confining the trial to the county was familiar to the people. The government had become convinced of the injustice of making Philadelphia the place of trial for the people west of the mountains; a law to remedy it, as we have seen, had been passed, but had not gone into operation. If this act had been in practical operation before the service of the writs returnable to Philadelphia, it is highly probable that no riots or insurrection would have taken place.

The second resolution, that a standing committee of members from each county be appointed, for the purpose hereinafter mentioned, viz.:

To draft a remonstrance to Congress, praying a repeal of the excise law; and at the same time requesting that a more equal and less odious tax be laid; and giving assurances that such tax will be willingly paid by the people of these counties; to make and publish a statement of the transactions which have lately taken place in the country, relative to the excise law, and of the causes which gave rise thereto; and make a representation to the President on the subject; to have power to call together a meeting of the deputies, here convened, for the purpose of taking such further measures as the further situation of affairs may require; "and in case of any sudden emergency, to take such temporary measures as they may think necessary."†

Third. That we will exert ourselves, and that it be earnestly recommend-

---

* This unquestionable grievance, it will be seen, was foremost in the minds of the people.

† These words were introduced by Mr. Gallatin, according to the previous suggestion of Mr. Brackenridge.

to our fellow citizens to exert themselves in support of the municipal laws of the respective States; and especially in preventing any violence or outrage against the property and person of any individual.

The first resolution was read and adopted unanimously.

On reading the second, it was moved by Mr. Brackenridge, to fill the blank with the word two, and to change the word county for township. His argument was, that they might act as conservators of the peace in support of the civil magistrate. It was necessary that they should be distributed as much as possible over the four counties, so as to enable the committee to act more promptly, and at the same time to disseminate their ideas and resolutions among the people. The real object, although not avowed, was to prevent promptitude of action, and the violent measures which a concentrated, permanent body might be induced to adopt.

It was further moved by him to insert, instead of "to call together a meeting of the deputies," these words, viz. "a meeting either of a new representation of the people, or of the deputies here convened." His argument was, the democratic principle of a frequent change of representatives. His real object was to enable him to withdraw, in case he could not succeed in bringing about an accommodation. It was seconded with avidity by James Edgar, and probably with the same view, and was carried.

An adjournment now took place to choose the standing committee, which was done by each township for itself. Mr. Brackenridge was chosen as one for the township of Pittsburgh. This committee, although an improvement on the assembly, in temper and intelligence, was still far from being all that could be desired. It still contained too large a portion of the violent; but nearly an equal number were openly in favor of peace, another portion was also in favor of moderate measures, but obliged to conceal their real sentiments through fear. After electing the standing committee the deputies again assembled.

Mr. Brackenridge had drafted the following resolution: "That ——— commissioners be appointed to wait on the President of the United States, with the representation of the people, and report to the standing committee the answer they may receive."

But it having been announced in the course of the sitting, that commissioners from the Executive to the assembly of deputies had unexpectedly arrived in the country, he changed his resolution to the following: "That a committee of ——— members from each county be appointed to meet any commissioners that have been or may be appointed by the government, to report the result of this conference to the standing committee." It was carried, and the blank filled with the number three.*

There was considerable opposition to this resolution. It was said that as the commissioners were now in the country, and supposed to be but half a day's journey distant; the assembly would wait until their arrival, and hear their propositions and determine for themselves.†

This was extremely dangerous to the object now in view. James Ross, who was present, and had received his appointment as commissioner, but known only to a few of the leaders on the pacific side, was of opinion that in the present temper of the assembly, and the people around, no proposition which the commissioners had in their power to make would be accepted. It was, therefore, of the greatest moment to carry the resolution as it stood. In support of it, the inconvenience of staying at the place was alleged; there was no accommodation for the members, or the commissioners; it would take a long time to understand each other; the negotiation must consist of conference and correspondence; that there was not even the convenience for writing at the place. These, and many other reasons, were urged. It was not without great difficulty that the resolution to appoint a committee of conference was carried.

It was again moved, that the assembly of delegates should wait where they were until the committee of conference should report to them. This was considered equally dangerous. It was plain that the chances would be more favorable in reporting to the standing committee, both on account of the time gained and the larger proportion of the friends of peace on that committee. The length of time required for the conference, and the inconvenience of remaining on the ground, were urged, again and again; but the avidity of curiosity was such, that they were anxious to remain. Gallatin had exerted himself very much in these debates, and on the last especially; others had supported him, but seemed to fail. Gallatin was

* William Beaumont, in his affidavit, says that Mr. Brackenridge did not appear to be one of the principal speakers at this assembly. The reason is, that his mind was more intent on the moves of the game than in making speeches. Few persons are aware of the importance of these noiseless steps, and attribute all to the loud declaimers, who seem to make the day-light.

† It was about this time that William Findley made his appearance, having hitherto kept aloof *probably* from design! To make amends, he officiously brought the intelligence of the arrival of government commissioners; but who they were and where, was not yet known, although James Ross was on the spot conferring with the friends of order, especially Brackenridge and Gallatin. Findley's officiousness led to serious embarrassment among the friends of peace, when they attempted to effect an adjournment of the assembly.

now pursuing, by indirection, the design of defeating the insurgent leaders, after his open opposition had been unavailing.

Mr. Brackenridge was walking outside the circle, much disheartened, when Commissioner Ross came to him and wished him to make another effort. "I do not see that I can do anything," said he; "Gallatin and others have said every thing that is reasonable in the case, and yet have failed." "You can do it," said Ross. Determined to make another trial, and knowing that it was the impatience of curiosity which made them anxious to stay, he observed, that it was not probable that the commissioners had any thing of consequence to propose, the President not having the people's representations before they set out; and therefore, although on principles of common decency it was proper to hear them, yet it was not worth while for the committee to waste their time in waiting for them. This had its effect. Something is to be ascribed to the disposition of people, when wearied with discussion, to lay hold of some plausible reason to end it, especially coming from one who had not been so warmly engaged in the debate. It is also probable that Mr. Brackenridge had, by this time, established an influence with the members; even the more violent regarding him as having, in some measure, come over to their side. The resolution was then carried, as it stood.

Instruction movers now appeared; the committee of conference must be instructed by the assembly! This was parried by getting it to be observed and pressed, that instructions could not be given in regard to propositions when it could not be known what those propositions were.

It is stated by Findley, that the day after the announcement of the arrival of the commissioners, the President's proclamation and the orders to call out the militia, reached the place, and were made known. Its effect was unfavorable—it seemed only to displease the people, already too much excited, and increased the difficulty of bringing them to reason. It was but the day before that Gallatin expressed his surprise that any one should suppose that the military would be called out by the government!

It was now moved, that the time of meeting of the standing committee should be fixed. It was agreed that it should be fixed by themselves.

The *standing* committee met and appointed the second day of September, and the place Brownsville, on the Monongahela. *They* chose the committee of conference of twelve, three from each county, and these fixed the time of conference with the commissioners, the 20th of August, the place Pittsburgh.

The committee of *conference*, which had thus been double-distilled from the mob of deputies, contained, as had been expected by Mr. Brackenridge, a decided majority—almost an unanimity in favor of submission to the government. The whole power of the assembly being merged in the standing committee and committee of conference, the three resolutions adopted by the assembly were lost sight of, and were no longer regarded of any consequence; and it mattered little in what terms expressed, either in those of Marshall, or in the diplomatic phrase of Gallatin. They had served to let off the surplus steam, and that sufficed for the moment.

The committee of conference consisted of the following members, viz. Messrs. John Kirkpatrick, John Sneth and John Powers, for Westmoreland; David Bradford, James Marshall and James Edgar, for Washington; Edward Cook, Albert Gallatin and James Lang, for Fayette; Thos. Morton, John B. C. Lucas and H. H. Brackenridge, for Allegheny. Three other gentlemen from Ohio county, Virginia, united with the above named; they were, Messrs. Robert Stevenson, William M'Kinley and William Southerland. Col. Cook was chosen chairman of the committee.

"The point was now gained, to which I have always looked forward— the point where the foot was to be fixed in order to make an open stand against the insurrection." This was Mr. Brackenridge's language to Mr. Ross, as he stepped from the circle after carrying the committee of conference. "There is a basis now laid from which we can act: to this point I have always looked forward, not expecting commissioners from the government to commissioners on our part, holding out an amnesty, which I took to be the great secret of composing the disturbance. Until that appeared, the disposition of those involved would lead them to cut throats to support themselves; and the whole country, conscious that every man had in some degree contributed, by words or actions, to produce that mental opposition to the law which had terminated in actual force, could not reconcile it to their feelings to abandon those who had acted with precipitation in the late instances. But, an amnesty being given, these could say to their countrymen, You are now on the same ground with us—stop, we will go no farther! I considered the appointment of commissioners on the part of the government as a pledge of amnesty, though I had yet no information of their power. I, therefore, saw the way clear for the country to get out; and now the conduct ought no longer to be a concealment of the intentions, and half way acquiescence, but an explicit avowal of opinion.

"On this principle, I took the first opportunity I had with Marshall and Bradford, and it was in the presence of one of the committee, before any conference with the commissioners, to inform them of my real sentiments with regard to the violations of the law which had taken place, and particularly with regard *to those in which they had been implicated*—the intercepting the mail and the rendezvous at Braddock's Field. Bradford looked red and angry; Marshall, pale and affected."

These men, especially Bradford, could not forgive the being treated like children by the person they supposed they had half converted and enlisted in their designs, whatever they might be. The vanity of Bradford was offended, and the advice given him to cease opposition to the government and submit to its authority, was thrown away. With Marshall it was different, and from that moment he acted with the friends of the government with sincerity; but, such is human nature, cherished ever after in his heart an unkindly feeling, to use no stronger expression, toward his adviser. It has been asked, why did not Mr. Brackenridge address them in this manner at the opening of the assembly? If he had done so, he would have had no influence over them, and if they had listened to him, they would have lost all influence over the assembled deputies. He found it necessary to use them as the instruments for indirectly controlling that body, and effecting the transfer of power, first to the sixty, and then to the twelve. And it may be asked, what injury was done to those men beyond the mortification of vanity and pride? None—but a real, though no flattering benefit, was conferred by opening a door for them to escape; and at the same time the momentous object of a pacification of the country was accomplished. No confidence was violated, for none had been reposed in Mr. Brackenridge.

What would have been the consequence if the pernicious measures of Bradford had not been baffled, and a direct vote defeated on his proposition to prepare for war, collect arms, magazines, and organize a military force? There is no doubt an armed opposition would have been set on foot; and possibly an army of riflemen would have occupied the passes of the mountains, while the people of the counties of Bedford, Franklin and Cumberland, almost as much excited as those in the west, with much less cause, would have harrassed the rear of a force sent to subdue the insurgents, as soon as they entered the defiles of the Allegheny, where neither cavalry nor artillery could be employed to advantage. The war once begun against the excise law, who could tell where it would end? Kentucky and Western Virginia shared the same feeling, and at the time were bound by slender ties to the States of the Atlantic. There were men who had already conceived the idea of a western confederacy, embracing the magnificent region which now forms the body of the American empire. The hostile feeling of Great Britain and Spain would eagerly embrace the opportunity of dismembering the Union, of whose future, if preserved, they already entertained a just conception. The rise and progress of the young giant republic was regarded with extreme jealousy and dislike by those powers. Here is a subject for deep reflection; and when thus viewed, the Western Insurrection might have swelled into an importance equal to that of our war with Great Britian. It was regarded by Washington in that light. It is true, there was the army of Wayne on the frontier—but its supplies could have been cut off, and in case of domestic war, many of the soldiers would desert rather than fight against their countrymen. We should have, at least, witnessed those demoralizing dissensions and unhappy divisions, which have prevented all steady progress in the republics of South America. It is fortunate that no one possessed of abilities and daring held the position of Bradford at this crisis —some bold spirit, actuated by a criminal ambition, and regardless of consequences. It was well that Washington was so fully alive to the momentous dangers which threatened the Union, and called out a sufficient force "to crush to atoms," at once, every particle of rebellion; and it is still more fortunate, that there were men of patriotism and talents in the West, with so large a proportion of enlightened and virtuous citizens, who were enabled to arrest the growth of the insurrection, even before the march of that army, and which, joined to the wise and humane policy of Washington, had rendered it unnecessary.

A very incorrect account is given by Findley of the proceedings of the assembly. He either did not comprehend them, or was influenced by his prejudices against Mr. Brackenridge, and his desire to exalt Gallatin at his expense. Why did he not pursue the report of Mr. Brackenridge in the "Incidents," while it was before him, and which is minute, clear and consistent? He would thus have avoided the gross blunders, which any one may see by comparing his "History" with the detail which has been here faithfully given from the "Incidents."

Bradford complained that Mr. Brackenridge had not given him his confidence at an early period. On this, the latter exclaims,* " Heigh, indeed! Give my confidence to a man who had gone on to the commission of high crimes, and had a mob at his command! But did I not speak plainly at Brownsville? Surely he had my confidence there, for all the meeting had it; and yet, he answered me with all the pomp that his idea of superiority over me, in the possession of the public confidence, could inspire; and if he insulted me *after* our negotiations with the commissioners, what would he not have done at an earlier period, when he had those at his back, who, having no amnesty to which they could look for-

* Incidents, II. p. 47.

ward, would be disposed to take the most desperate resolutions in regard to all who differed from them? I did speak as soon as it was prudent to do it; that is, in the committee of conference at Pittsburgh."

The most disgusting epithets have been applied to Mr. Brackenridge by N. B. Craig, who avows his *hereditary prejudices* against him, and among other terms, applies that of "cold-blooded, calculating villain," in reference to his skillful course at Parkinson's Ferry. The writer of this, although viewing this impotent malignity with the indignation it is calculated to excite, can safely plead the vindication of his father on the *motive in view, and the object accomplished by him*, which must command the gratitude of every honest man, of every friend of humanity and of his country. He must go farther, and unhesitatingly declare that his case is one of the most extraordinary in history, of great services remaining not only unacknowledged, but even denounced as criminal by a few malignant individuals. But it so happens, that the most irresistable testimony is contained in the Appendix to the "Incidents," from men whose veracity and impartiality cannot be doubted for a moment, and which annihilates all the insinuations, slanders and vulgar epithets of his enemies, at whatever period. No one having the feelings of common honesty, or a single characteristic of the gentleman, can indorse such language, after reading the testimonials of Messrs. Ross, Wilkins, Addison, Purviance, Hoge, Reddick, Scott, and many others, who speak from intimate and personal knowledge. With Mr. Ross he was on terms of close confidence during the whole of the insurrection; his letter, which will be placed in the note to this chapter, completely covers the whole ground. It will be followed by those of Judge Addison, Senator Hoge, Mr. Scott and Judge Lucas—the others have been placed at the end of different chapters, as they seemed more particularly to relate to the subjects narrated in them.*

---

*The vindication of his father's memory, it is hoped, will not be regarded by the generous reader as incompatible with his obligations as a truthful and honest historian.

NOTES TO CHAPTER VII.

Letter addressed to James Ross, Esq., and Reply.

"SIR:—I take the liberty of making to you a few queries relative to myself, in the transactions of the late insurrection in this country, your answer to which will oblige me.

"1st. Were you not in the town of Washington at the time of the return of individuals to that place, who had been at the meeting at Mingo Creek; and what was the impression which seemed to have been made on their minds with respect to what was said by me at the meeting; was it that of having supported or evaded the proposition of Bradford, and the measures proposed by the more violent?

"2d. At what point of the business did you come forward, and was present in the committee of battalions at Braddock's Field; and what was the impression on your mind with respect to my conduct in the cases of Neville, Gibson and Craig; and what do you recollect, or was your impression with respect to our engagement, I mean those of the committee from Pittsburgh, with regard to Abraham Kirkpatrick and others that had been sent away; did we not pledge our persons for theirs, that they had gone and would not return; and did not this stipulation appear to you to be the result of necessity at that juncture to allay the rage of the people against the town on account of these persons?

"3d. Shortly after the day of Braddock's Field, do you recollect my stating to you the delicacy of my situation, and wish to extricate myself from it; that I had thought of procuring myself to be sent to the Executive, on behalf of the people of Pittsburgh, to represent their situation and the motives of their conduct; and having done this, not to return; and that with this view, I wished you to sound some principal persons, and see whether it would seem that I could be so appointed; and did you not give me information afterward, that you had sounded, and found an unwillingness that I should leave the town or the country, but rather remain, in order to assist in ways of our general safety?

"4th. Before the election of delegates for the town of Pittsburgh to the meeting at Parkinson's Ferry, did I not express to you my determination of not suffering my name to be mentioned as a delegate, recollecting with what difficulty I had extricated myself at the Mingo meeting-house; that it would be better, in order to save appearances on the part of the town, to let some person go forward who would not be expected to speak, or take any conspicuous part in the business; was it not rather your opinion, that it was a turning point in the business to get forward as many as possible of moderation, address, ability and influence, in order to parry the desperate measures that might be proposed; and did you not undertake to go to Washington, and accomplish as far as in your power, the procuring persons to be elected of that description; and was it not on this ground that I acquiesced and changed my determination?

"5th. At the meeting at Parkinson's Ferry, did I not explain to you the plan I had devised, which was that of sending commissioners to the Executive; and did not I then show you an address I had prepared to the President, such as I thought the people would be willing to send; that the commissioners sent would expose the real situation of the country, and devise measures for the pacification of it; and did I not suggest to you that the obtaining an amnesty for what was done, would be the means—those that were desperate, from a sense of the violation of the law, seeing then a prospect of safety, or a way of getting out; and did you not, with my consent, take this address to read over, and show to the commissioners, as it would give them the same information which was intended for the President?

"6th. At Parkinson's Ferry, toward the close of the business, at what was considered a delicate crisis, when it was agitated whether the commissioners who had been announced as having arrived, should come forward to the people there present, or a delegation to be made of persons to confer with them at a separate place; and was it not considered by us, that the coming forward there would be fatal, as whatever propositions were brought forward would at this instant be rejected by the multitude; and when several speakers of the moderate description seemed to have failed in advocating a separate conference, was I not called upon by you, and addressed in these words, 'This is the turning point; you must now speak.' I had a considerable time before that left the circle, and was walking at some distance from the crowd. Did I not inform you that I despaired of it, so many others having spoken in vain; you said I could do it. Did I not then come forward, and with great difficulty accomplish it, and returning to you from the crowd, say, 'The point is now gained; there is a ground whereon to establish peace?'

"7th. What, in general, is your impression of my zeal in accomplishing the point I had in view, of serving the people by saving them with the government; and at the same time serving the government with them.*

"You may, if you please, annex your answers to these queries, or answer the substance in a letter.

I am, your humble servant,
    HUGH H. BRACKENRIDGE.
11th April, 1795."

"PITTSBURGH, 11th April, 1795.

"SIR—Want of time before you leave this place, prevents me from answering your queries of this day so fully as I could wish, but I shall endeavor to state as concisely as possible, my recollection of the facts to which they are pointed.

"I lived at Washington at the time General Neville's house was destroyed, and during the time of the late disturbances. On the return of the Washington gentlemen from the Mingo Creek meeting, I understood from them that a proposal had been made in the meeting, that those guilty of the outrage should be supported by force against all attempts to punish them, and this had been warmly advocated by some of the Washington people; but that you were of a different opinion, and had stated that in all probability the government might be induced to forgive it, and that a combination of this sort would involve the whole country, and oblige government to take notice of those who had transgressed. This meeting ended by a proposal to have a more general one from the four counties west of the mountains, in Pennsylvania, and as I understood, the western counties of Virginia were to be notified to attend on the 14th of August, at Parkinson's Ferry. Before this day arrived the mail was robbed, several obnoxious letters were found in

* "To speak the truth to the king in the hearing of the people, and to the people in the hearing of the king."—*Junius.*

it; a project for taking the public arms, ammunition and stores at Pittsburgh was set on foot; this plan also embraced the seizing and punishing in an exemplary manner, the writers of those letters, who were called traitors to their country; and the militia were called to assemble at Braddock's Field, and to march from thence to Pittsburgh.

"The names of those publicly denounced in Washington in presence of the troops, (who were hesitating whether they would march or not,) were Thomas Butler, Abraham Kirkpatrick, John Gibson, James Brison and Edward Day. When the troops were assembled at Braddock's Field, a large committee was appointed to consider and settle what should be done. This committee sat for a long time, and the soldiers became clamorous for a march to Pittsburgh. At this time I came to the committee, who were at some distance from the main body. I then learned that the design of attacking the fort was abandoned; that the committee had resolved to petition the President for the removal of Col. Butler from the command of the fort; that they had ordered the banishment of Major Kirkpatrick, Mr. Brison and Mr. Day; and they were taking the question whether Col. Neville and General Gibson should not be banished. John Wilkins and you made a proposal to postpone their banishment until the meeting of the 14th of August; but this was negatived. I am not certain whether this proposal was confined to these last named gentlemen, or extended to all, but rather think Neville and Gibson only included. One of the committee then denounced Major Craig for having said he would keep an inspection office in his own house, rather than the excise law should be defeated. A good deal was said on this subject; his expulsion was at last prevented by a proposal of yours, that a petition should be sent to General Knox for his removal. It being very questionable whether Butler would not protect him in fort as belonging to the army; and at all events the public business would suffer from the want of a proper person to take care of the military stores. This was agreed to. The time within which the banished men must depart was fixed, and passports allowed them. The Pittsburgh committee now were called upon to pledge themselves for the full execution of the resolutions, which they did; but whether their own persons were pledged or not, I do not recollect. After this was settled, one of the Washington members rose and proposed that the troops should march home through Pittsburgh, and that they should all go in a body, professing his belief that they would do no harm, and stating that the news of the five thousand men having marched through that place, would strike terror into the minds of all below, who might dream of punishing any thing that had been done. From the first of the meeting at Braddock's Field until this time, it had been my opinion that we could prevail on the troops to go home from thence; but finding a majority of the committee for marching to town, I doubted of the practicability of preventing them, and it was evidently the best policy to carry the well disposed along with the violent in order to control them.

"This was the opinion of all the well disposed part of the persons assembled there, and accordingly the unarmed, as well as the armed, were put in the ranks and proceeded to Pittsburgh. These expulsions, and this march, was the result of the meeting at Braddock's Field; and nothing but the apparent concert of the Pittsburgh people to all these measures could have saved their property from utter destruction. Almost all the inhabitants of the town were at the Field, and expressed their despair of saving the town, provided the insurgents marched into it. You exerted yourself amongst others to the utmost in order to prevent this measure. But when it was resolved on, in my opinion, no person who wished the safety of the place, would either have opposed the march by force, or sent home the peaceable and well disposed part of the militia.

"The facts mentioned in your third, fourth, fifth and sixth queries, are, to the best of my recollection, correctly stated. I may forget words; but the impressions made on me, and sentiments expressed by you, are substantially as there stated; and it would be only a waste of time to repeat the several subjects there alluded to. I saw many alarmed and anxious for the safety of their country, for the re-establishment of the government, and who expressed an abhorrence of all that was doing. I thought none of them more seriously so than yourself; and when you came as a committee man to settle the terms of submission, I am persuaded there is none will deny that you exerted yourself to get every reasonable concession on the part of the government in favor of your constituents.

"Finally, sir, there is no impression on my mind, from any part of your conduct in the late disturbances, which I have seen, nor from anything I have heard you say, that attempted in any instance to inflame the minds of any of the people against an individual, or to turn the force of others against a private enemy.

I am, sir, yours, &c.

JAMES ROSS."*

* The ancestors of Mr. Ross settled in the same neighborhood with those of Mr. Brackenridge, in York county, Pennsylvania, and those of M'Millan and John Rowan. Mr. Brackenridge found him at

Letter of Mr. John Hoge.

"WASHINGTON, Feb. 16th, 1795.

"SIR—I received your letter of the 13th instant, and have no doubt but that you are entitled, at least, to a full statement by letter, of your expressions to me in Pittsburgh; but I much doubt the propriety of voluntarily going before a magistrate, and making a deposition on the subject. And as it is an extra-judicial business, I presume no magistrate will call on me by subpœna for the purpose.

"I know well you have enemies, and believe they are my friends. I respect them and regard you. It is not for me, therefore, on the one hand, by a voluntary act of mine, to lose my friends, or wound their feelings, even though they be your enemies; nor on the other hand, to retain their friendship, by withhold-

Canonsburg, teaching the first classical school opened in the West. He, at first, designed to enter the ministry; but afterward resolved to study law, and Mr. Brackenridge furnished him copies of Reeve's history, and of Blackstone, brought in his saddle-bags, on his way to Washington court. He afterward gave him letters to Philadelphia, where Ross completed his studies; after which he soon rose to distinction in the West; married a lady of fortune, and devoted himself chiefly to politics. He became one of the Federal leaders in the Senate of the United States. He was a splendid man; great as an orator, in the Senate and at the bar. He was a truly great man. Washington appointed him one of the commissioners to the insurgents; here he met Mr. Brackenridge, as negotiator for the people. Mr. Ross showed himself a true friend to Mr. Brackenridge, when the latter was exposed to false accusations, and but for him, would probably have been carried a prisoner to Philadelphia. There is the greater merit for this, when it is considered that his brother-in-law and bosom friend, General Woods, and Mr. Brackenridge were bitter enemies.

* Mr. Hoge was at this time in the Pennsylvania Senate, a particular friend of Col. Neville, and an ardent supporter of the Federal administration. He was a gentleman of fortune, of fine character, and splendid talents. He wrote with the elegance of a Junius. His character for manly independence was remarkable. The testimony of such a man is peculiarly important.

ing an act of justice from you. I have, therefore, determined to do no more on either side than strict justice, which will be effected by answering your letter. If any man doubts my words, I presume he would not respect my oath; and I flatter myself that all who know me, will doubt neither.

"I recollect perfectly, that on the day I think previous to conference being opened, between the commissioners on the part of the United States and the committee appointed by the deluded people, I entered without reserve into a short conversation with you, relative to the situation of the western country. Your sentiments, I recollect fully, co-incided with mine on that occasion. One sentiment of yours struck me as strongly characteristic of your opinion, which was, 'that if the designs of individuals, or the obstinacy of the multitude, should prevent submission to the government, you were determined to leave the country; that the consequent sacrifice of your property should not influence you; that the sacrifice would probably be but temporary; for that obedience would, and ought to be enforced; that government had the power, and, no doubt, would exert it on that occasion.' One of us mentioned the necessity of inducing Mr. Bradford to comply with the terms which might be proposed by the commissioners. I suggested the propriety of the use of your influence with him. You doubted whether you had any; and said, the only way you ever could manage him, was by pretending to anticipate his opinions, and thus persuade him to come into measures as his own, than which nothing could be more foreign to his thoughts; but that you would leave no means unessayed, to effect a change of his mind.

"It cannot be expected that I should now give the words of our conversation without occasion; but I am persuaded I have given the ideas. The belief that you were directly or indirectly concerned in the late insurrection, can only be entertained by those, who, from the distance from the scene of action, have been imposed upon by misrepresentations, and have therefore formed conclusions upon ill-founded premises; or by your enemies, whose prejudices have totally prevented inquiry.

"The dangerous and unpopular part I took in the late insurrection, and the detestation I entertain for all those defamatory societies, which have for their object the dissemination of jealousies against the government; and which, I have no doubt, contributed greatly (perhaps undesignedly,) to the late dishonorable insurrection, are, I hope, sufficient pledges of the truth of this statement, even when it is made in favor of you, who unfortunately by misrepresentation, or partial statements of facts, have incurred the displeasure, or at least the suspicion of government.

I am, sir, with respect,
Your obedient servant,
JOHN HOGE."

Letter of Judge Addison.

"SIR:—I have received your letter desiring me to state to you my knowledge of your sentiments and conduct respecting the adoption of the Federal constitution; and to state also whether I have discovered from you any idea of overthrowing it; or have any reason to believe that you advised or countenanced any illegal opposition to the excise law; or had any concern in exciting or supporting the late disturbances.

"In making this statement as sincerely and as candidly as I can, I shall speak from my observation of your conduct in an acquaintance of more than nine years, and in your company in social and familiar conversation at the courts of this circuit within almost the whole of that time; from my confidence that your conversation on political subjects is frank and sincere; and from my opportunity of learning the opinion entertained of you by the judges, my associates, and other respectable citizens in the respective counties of this circuit.

"Your approbation of the Federal constitution, from its publication, and your exertions to incline the minds of the people toward it, and promote its adoption, are notorious. Since its adoption, I believe that you have constantly retained your respect and attachment to it; and I know nothing to induce any suspicion of your conceiving any idea of overthrowing it.

"It is impossible for me, without erasing all my impressions of your character and conduct, to suppose that you ever advised or countenanced any illegal opposition to the excise law; I think your sense of civil duty strong and accurate, and believe you incapable of suggesting or approving any unlawful act.

"During the disturbances here, until the first conference with the commissioners at Pittsburgh, I was absent from this country. At the time of that conference, you there expressed to me the utmost disapprobation of the preceding acts of violence, and regret for their effects; your perfect satisfaction with the terms proposed by the commissioners, as the best that could be offered, and your resolution to exert every endeavor to induce the people to accept them; and if you should fail—to leave this country. I am persuaded that you spoke your mind; all your subsequent conduct, so far as I can understand, (and I knew much of it,) uniformly corresponded with those declarations; *and I believe you contributed greatly to the restoration of peace and civil submission in this country. It must be supposed, that the outrages which had been committed would be frequent subjects of conversation; but I have never heard from any man of understanding, information and impartiality, that you had any participation in the guilt of them.*

"The imputation of this to you was matter of surprise to me; and I am persuaded that it arose from ignorance and misconception of your motives, or from prejudice.

I am, sir, yours, &c.

ALEXANDER ADDISON."

After reading the foregoing letters, and those of General Wilkins, H. Purviance, Judge Lucas, and many others of the like import, or confined to particular instances, it must certainly excite astonishment in the reader, greater than the surprise of Judge Addison, that Mr. Brackenridge should have come under the suspicion of the government, or that a participation in the insurrection should even be imputed to him by any individual—that he should have been subjected to an examination by Secretary Hamilton, and compelled to vindicate his innocence by the publication of numerous documents, and a general narrative of the incidents of the insurrection! It is, if possible, still more astonishing, that at the distance of half a century, his descendants have been compelled to restate his case, and reproduce his evidence, to repel slanders, renewed in a form of ten-fold malignity, which it was supposed he had lived down; or at least, that it was rectified by time, the great corrector of error. But, it is an instance to show the wonderful vitality of slander and malignant misrepresentation. It seems almost immortal—crush it out a thousand times, and it will still come to life, while there is a human bosom in which malignity and falsehood hold their abode. It is even more astonishing, that one pretending to the high functions of a historian, like Hildreth, in a grave production, having the ambitious title of a "History of the United States," should attempt to revive these obsolete slanders, when he had before him the "Incidents of the Western Insurrection," containing the documents now re-published! That N. B. Craig, the descendant of the Nevilles and Craigs, should have availed himself of Hildreth's disreputable pages, as the foundation of his own vile insinuations and falsehoods, is not surprising. There was a settled enmity on the part of the "Neville connection" against Mr. Brackenridge; and although the fire was smothered down for a time, it broke out at length in the misnamed "History of Pittsburgh," after the lapse of two generations, and that fire has been attempted to be rendered immortal! That enmity had its origin in something besides the excise law. It is due to truth and justice that it should be exposed; it is necessary, although painful and unpleasant.

The character given by N. B. Craig of his relative Major Kirkpatrick, might prepare the reader for what the author of this work is about to relate. About two years before the insurrection, it became the professional duty of Mr. Brackenridge to institute proceedings against Kirkpatrick, to compel him to bring back a free colored woman, named Eve, whom he had sent off to Kentucky, and either sold into slavery or intended to sell. The cause was prosecuted with energy, and the defendant held so firmly in the grip of the law, that he was compelled to bring the woman back and restore her to freedom. Kirkpatrick was furious, and threatened assassination; and his brother-in-law, General Neville, and perhaps Major Craig, entered warmly into his feelings. It was a subject peculiarly calculated to excite the anger of the old Virginian, and his Maryland brother-in-law. The grandson of Gen. Neville is now one of the ultra abolitionists of the country, the very opposite of his ancestor! Kirkpatrick, armed with a bludgeon, came suddenly on Mr. Brackenridge, while sitting carelessly under the shade of some trees, on the bank of the river. The blow missed his head, but fell on his left shoulder, from which he never entirely recovered. They seized each other, and rolled down the bank, but were almost immediately separated. A prosecution was pending for this, during the insurrection; and it was in reference to it, that at Braddock's Field he said he would rather keep Kirkpatrick, in order to prosecute him according to law, and which was understood by the insurgents as referring to the attack on Neville's house. The writer of this, then only ten years old, was present at the trial in the old tavern court in Pittsburgh. He saw the round drops of sweat roll down Kirkpatrick's face, as his father lashed him with terrific severity. The writer had crawled just to the foot of the bench, where sat Judges Yates and Smith, and (according to the etiquette not then obsolete, of inviting old and respectable citizens to take a seat with the Judges,) where also sat General Neville; and he heard him say, in a whisper, to Yates, "In Virginia, in a case of this kind, we would impose a fine of five shillings." The Judges, no doubt, dined that day with one of the Neville connection, a practice continued long afterward, and which Mr. Brackenridge, when appointed to the bench, condemned in no measured terms. True to his profession, he never would accept an invitation to dine out while on the circuit, and which was, no doubt, set down as one of his *eccentricities*. Major Craig had also his particular cause of offense from being made the butt of ridicule by Mr. Brackenridge, on various occasions. It was even said, by some, but very erroneously, that he was intended to be represented in the character of Teague O'Regan, in his satirical production, "Modern Chivalry." The reader will now be at no loss for the key to the abiding and rancorous enmity of the Neville connection to the "insurgent" Brackenridge.

Affidavit of Judge Lucas.*

"That on the 13th or 14th of last July (1794), being lately returned home from a voyage which he had undertaken to the Illinois country, Hugh Henry Brackenridge, attorney-at-law, living in Pittsburgh, Allegheny county, State of Pennsylvania, came to his house, being one or two days before the first riot had taken place at General Neville's house, and as it was the first time this deponent had seen Mr. Brackenridge since his arrival, a miscellany of news, reciprocally given, soon became the whole topic of their conversation. This deponent perfectly remembers, that among other things, he mentioned to Mr. Brackenridge, that while he was passing through Kentucky, he had heard that numbers of people in that State were displeased at the conduct of the Federal government toward them; that several committees had been held there, and had already went to great lengths; that this said deponent had read a printed paper, pasted up in a public place in Kentucky, containing several resolves of a committee, and especially one by which the people of Kentucky were invited at large to meet and take in consideration the circumstances of the country; that some talked of a separation from the Union, others thought of other measures to be adopted. Upon which account so given Mr. Brackenridge by this deponent, he appeared to be highly displeased, and asking this deponent who might be the leader in this system of reform, this deponent says he answered him, that he, this said deponent, had been told that several lawyers were amongst the leaders; to which Mr. Brackenridge replied, that he supposed those lawyers must be trivial ones, probably shifting in that manner to obtain some notice from the public. This deponent further says, that he told Mr. Brackenridge he had heard of several lawyers, distinguished by their talents, who were at the head of these committees, and many other persons of good standing in Kentucky; which Mr. Brackenridge appeared to wonder at greatly, and seeming to sink into himself with great concern, in a deep reflection, for a little while, this deponent says, he soon expressed himself in the following manner: 'I cannot perceive what advantage the people of Kentucky could obtain by disturbing the Union. But should they separate, our situation in this part of the country would become very critical. On the one hand, the people of Kentucky would not fail to interrupt our trade on the Ohio, should we refuse to join with them; and should we join them, we would immediately lose the great advantages we derive from the Union.' This deponent further declares, that the first opportunity he had of perceiving the disposition of Mr. Brackenridge, in the late disturbance, was a few days after the committee held at the Mingo meeting-house, where Mr. Brackenridge said to this deponent, that on his going to meet with the committee

---

* This gentleman was a native of France, who came to this country after the revolution. He was of a noble French family, son of the Chief Justiciar of Normandy; but being a republican in principles, left his native country. He settled near Pittsburgh on a farm, was elected to Congress, and afterward appointed by Jefferson, Judge of the Superior court of Missouri, where some of his descendants still reside.

at Mingo meeting-house, he fairly expected he would be able to defeat any violent measures that could be proposed there; but to his astonishment he had met with a numerous assembly of men, respectable by their property, their abilities, and the popularity a great many of them enjoyed; that things seemed going to take a more serious turn than he expected; and added, only that the condition of an emigrant was but a sorry one, that for his part he did not like to emigrate. The deponent says, that the next opportunity he had after, of perceiving the disposition of Mr. Brackenridge in the late disturbances, was on the 14th of August last, at Parkinson's Ferry, where the said Mr. Brackenridge gave him to read, (a letter before the committee* was formed,) a piece of writing intended to be an address to the President of the United States, in behalf of the people of the western part of Pennsylvania; which writing, Mr. Brackenridge told to this deponent, he would present to the then committee, and would exert himself to make it be adopted. The deponent further says, that the object of that draft, was to solicit from the Executive to suspend its activity in putting the excise law in force, until the next session in Congress, upon the solemn promise from the people of the fourth survey to obey and to continue to keep in force among them, without interruption, all other laws, both of the Federal and State governments. This deponent says, that Mr. Brackenridge told him since, that he had not thought proper to present the said draft of address to the committee, upon his hearing during the time the committee was holding, that commissioners from the Executive were arrived on the spot. This deponent says also, that the third circumstance that drew his attention to the conduct of Mr. Brackenridge, took place on the 21st of August, when the committee of twelve went to confer at Pittsburgh with the commissioners in behalf of the Executive. The nine deputies from Westmoreland, Washington and Alleghany counties, met together, and while they were waiting for the three deputies from Fayette, who were not yet arrived, Mr. Brackenridge opened the conversation on the momentous subject of resistance or acquiescence in the laws of the United States; and this deponent, who was one of the three deputies from Alleghany county, says he witnessed Mr. Brackenridge saying openly, before any body had given his opinion, that he thought that submission was the best step to be taken; that for his part he was determined to submit to the laws. The deponent says, that amongst the many that were wishing secretly to see the people returning to obedience to the laws, *Mr. Brackenridge is the first man he did hear speak of submission, after the insurrection.* The deponent further says, that he went the best part of the was from Pittsburgh, to attend the committee of Redstone, held on the 28th and 29th days of last August; and as they were going along the deponent saw in Mr. Brackenridge all the tokens of distress at the appearance of so many liberty poles raised through the country, and so little corresponding with the pacific views, he (Mr. Brackenridge) was going with his other colleagues to propagate and support before, the standing committee of Redstone.

"This deponent says likewise, that after the report of the conference held on the 21st was made on the 28th to the standing committee, and the said committee having adjourned to meet on the morrow, 29th, Mr. Gallatin came to Mr.

---

* The meetings were sometimes called *committees;* which is at present understood of a smaller body taken from a larger one.

Brackenridge in the street, and in presence of this deponent, Mr. Gallatin proposed to Mr. Brackenridge to open the matter on the following day, which Mr. Brackenridge declined, devolving the task on Mr. Gallatin, with promise that he would support him with all his might. This deponent says, that he went that night to lodge at a neighboring farm with Mr. Brackenridge, that the said Brackenridge gave to him, the deponent, during the whole evening, the most persuasive tokens of anxiety and dissatisfaction, expressing repeatedly, how unwell the good of the country appeared to be understood by many members of the standing committee. This deponent says, that on the day following he attended this committee as a member of it, and heard Mr. Brackenridge echoing there in his own language, the cogent and powerful arguments first made use of by Mr. Gallatin, and adding new ones of his own; all to the purpose of disposing the committee to submit to the laws, and propagate that disposition among their constituents.

"This deponent recollects that not long after the beginning of the late disturbances, Mr. Brackenridge read to him a letter he had received from a gentleman of Philadelphia, in answer to another one he had written first to that gentleman, whose contents Mr. Brackenridge had mentioned in substance to this deponent, who remembers that, amongst other things. Mr. Brackenridge told him he had written to this said gentleman of Philadelphia, (which he told me since was of the name of Tench Cox,) to wit: that government had perhaps as much reason of being afraid of the western people, as the western people had of fearing government; that should a few hundred of the western insurgents attempt to pass over the mountains, thousands, greatly displeased at the funding system and its effects, would immediately flock with the former ones, and like a torrent would increase more and more in their rapid course toward the seat of government. This deponent declares, that this idea so suggested by Mr. Brackenridge, seemed to him rather grounded on exaggeration, at the early period Mr. Brackenridge mentioned to him the contents of this letter of Mr. Tench Cox; but having been informed since by the most undoubtful reports, the discontent that had prevailed through the minds of a considerable number of people, in the counties of Bedford, Cumberland, Franklin, Northumberland, and in some parts of Maryland, &c. this deponent is at present fully persuaded, had the leaders of the insurgents thought of such measures, and given execution to it, that what seemed to him an exaggeration at the first, might have been literally a fact, and considers that the hint Mr. Brackenridge had so justly given of the impending danger, to a gentleman near government, must have been of a great use to the Executive, if justly appreciated. The deponent says, that Mr. Tench Cox, by his answer to the one of Mr. Brackenridge, Mr. Brackenridge did repeatedly say to this deponent, that Mr. Tench Cox had not understood him upon many things he had expressed to Mr. Tench Cox, to secure himself in case his letter should be intercepted this side the mountains. Lastly, the deponent declares, that he knows Mr. Brackenridge since more than ten years; that during that period of time he has cultivated his acquaintance without interruption as a literary and a philosophic man. That although he spoke seldom with him on political subjects, nevertheless, from some conversations he had with him relating to politics, and from other circumstances, the said deponent has been and is strongly impressed with the idea, that Mr. Brackenridge is a warm and zealous supporter of the present Federal constitution, a real friend to the Union; and from some former instances, the deponent further says, that he thinks Mr. Brackenridge is even an admirer of the Federal constitution, or at least has been so perhaps in a greater degree than many other persons from this part of the country, who bear, very deservedly in the opinion of this deponent, the name of good citizens.

John B. Lucas."

Sworn before A. Addison.

" *Proclamation.*

"Whereas, Combinations to defeat the execution of the laws levying duties upon spirits distilled in the United States and upon the stills, have, from the time of the commencement of those laws, existed in some of the western parts of Pennsylvania. And whereas, the said combinations, proceeding in a manner subversive equally of the just authority of government and of the rights of individuals, have hitherto effected their dangerous and criminal purpose by the influence of certain irregular meetings, whose proceedings have tended to encourage and uphold the spirit of opposition; by misrepresentations of the laws calculated to render them obnoxious; by endeavors to deter those who might be so disposed from accepting offices under them, through fear of public resentment and injury to person and property, and to compel those who had accepted such offices, by actual violence, to surrender or forbear the execution of them; by circulating vindictive menaces against all those who should otherwise directly or indirectly aid in the execution of the said laws, or who, yielding to the dictates of conscience and to a sense of obligation, should themselves comply therewith, by actually injuring and destroying the property of persons who were understood to have so complied; by inflicting cruel and humiliating punishment upon private citizens for no other cause than that of appearing to be the friends of the laws; by intercepting the public officers on the highways, abusing, assaulting, or otherwise ill treating them; by going to their houses in the night, gaining admittance by force, taking away their papers, and committing other outrages; employing for their unwarrantable purposes the agency of armed banditti, disguised in such a manner as for the most part to escape discovery. And whereas, the endeavors of the Legislature to obviate objections to the said laws, by lowering the duties and by other alterations conducive to the convenience of those whom they immediately affect, (though they have given satisfaction in other quarters,) and the endeavors of the executive officers to conciliate a compliance with the laws, by explanations, by forbearance, and even by particular accommodations founded on the suggestion of local considerations, have been disappointed of their effect by the machinations of persons whose industry to excite resistance has increased with every appearance of a disposition among the people to relax in their opposition and to acquiesce in the laws: insomuch that many persons in the said western parts of Pennsylvania have at length been hardy enough to perpetrate acts which I am advised amount to treason, being overt acts of levying war against the United States; the said persons having, on the sixteenth and seventeenth of July last, proceeded in arms (on the second day amounting to several hundreds,) to the house of John Neville, Inspector of the Revenue for the fourth survey of the District of Pennsylvania, having repeatedly attacked the said house, with the persons therein, wounding some of them;

having seized David Lennox, Marshal of the District of Pennsylvania, who previous thereto had been fired upon, while in the execution of his duty, by a party of armed men, detaining him for some time prisoner, till, for the preservation of his life and the obtaining of his liberty, he found it necessary to enter into stipulations to forbear the execution of certain official duties, touching processes issuing out of a court of the United States, and having finally obliged the said Inspector of the Revenue and the said Marshal, from considerations of personal safety, to fly from that part of the country in order, by a circuitous route, to proceed to the seat of government; avowing as the motive of these outrageous proceedings an intention to prevent, by force of arms, the execution of the said laws, to oblige the said Inspector of the Revenue to renounce his said office, to withstand by open violence the lawful authority of the government of the United States, and to compel thereby an alteration of the measures of the Legislature and a repeal of the laws aforesaid.

"And whereas, by a law of the United States, entitled, 'An Act to provide for calling forth the militia to execute the laws of the Union, suppress insurrections and repel invasions,' it is enacted that whenever the laws of the United States shall be opposed, or the execution thereof obstructed in any State by combinations too powerful to be suppressed by the ordinary course of judicial proceedings, or by the powers vested in the Marshals by that act, the same being notified by an Associate Justice or the District Judge, it shall be lawful for the President of the United States to call forth the militia of such State to suppress such combinations, and to cause the laws to be duly executed.

"And if the militia of a State where such combinations may happen, shall refuse or be insufficient to suppress the same, it shall be lawful for the President, if the Legislature of the United States be not in session, to call forth and employ such numbers of the militia of any State or States most convenient thereto as may be necessary, and the use of the militia so to be called forth may be continued, if necessary, until the expiration of thirty days after the commencement of the ensuing session; Provided always, that whenever it may be necessary in the judgment of the President to use the military force hereby directed to be called forth, the President shall forthwith and previous thereto, by proclamation, command such insurgents 'to disperse and retire peaceably to their respective abodes within a limited time.'

"And whereas, James Wilson, an Associate Justice, on the fourth instant, by writing under his hand, did, from evidence which had been laid before him, notify to me, 'that in the counties of Washington and Allegheny, in Pennsylvania, laws of the United States are opposed, and the execution thereof obstructed by combinations too powerful to be suppressed by the ordinary course of judicial proceedings, or by the powers vested in the Marshal of that district.'

"And whereas, it is in my judgment necessary, under the circumstances of the case, to take measures for calling forth the militia in order to suppress the combinations aforesaid, and to cause the laws to be duly executed, and I have accordingly determined to do so, feeling the deepest regret for the occasion, but withal the most solemn conviction, that the essential interests of the Union demand it—that the very existence of government, and the fundamental principles of social order are materially involved in the issue; and that the patriotism and firmness of all good citizens are seriously called upon, as occasion may require, to aid in the effectual suppression of so fatal a spirit.

"Wherefore, and in pursuance of the proviso above recited, I, George Washington, President of the United States, do hereby command all persons being insurgents as aforesaid, and all others whom it may concern, on or before the first day of September next, to disperse and retire peaceably to their respective abodes. And I do moreover warn all persons whomsoever, against aiding, abetting, or comforting the perpetrators of the aforesaid treasonable acts. And I do require all officers and other citizens, according to their respective duties and the laws of the land, to exert their utmost endeavors to prevent and suppress such dangerous proceedings.

"In testimony whereof, I have caused the seal of the United States of America to be affixed to these presents, and signed the same with my hand.

"Done at the city of Philadelphia, the seventh day of August, one thousand seven hundred and ninety-four, and of the Independence of the United States of America the nineteenth.

By the President,
 GEO. WASHINGTON. [L. S.]
EDM. RANDOLPH."

"*By the President of the United States of America.*

A PROCLAMATION.

"Whereas, from a hope that the combinations against the constitution and laws of the United States in certain of the western counties of Pennsylvania would yield to time and reflection; I thought it sufficient in the first instance rather to take measures for the calling forth of the militia than immediately to embody them; but the moment has now come when the overtures of forgiveness with no other condition than a submission to law, have been only partially accepted; when every form of conciliation not inconsistent with the being of government has been adopted without effect; when the well disposed in those counties are unable by their influence and example to reclaim the wicked from their fury, and are compelled to associate in their own defense; when the proper lenity has been misinterpreted into an apprehension that the citizens will march with reluctance; when the opportunity of examining the serious consequences of a treasonable opposition has been employed in propagating principles of anarchy, endeavoring through emissaries to alienate the friends of order from its support, and inviting its enemies to perpetrate similar acts of insurrection; when it is manifest that violence would continue to be exercised upon every attempt to enforce the laws; when, therefore, government is set at defiance, the contest being whether a small portion of the United States shall dictate to the whole Union, and at the expense of those who desire peace, indulge a desperate ambition. Now, therefore, I, George Washington, President of the United States, in obedience to that high and irresistible duty consigned to me by the constitution, 'to take care that the laws be faithfully executed,' deploring that the American name should be sullied by the outrages of citizens on their own government; commiserating such as remain obstinate from delusion, but resolved in perfect reliance on that gracious Providence which so signally displays its goodness toward this country, to reduce the refractory to a due subordination to the law; do hereby declare and make known that with a satisfaction, which can be equaled only by the merits of the militia, summoned into service from the States of New Jersey, Pennsylvania, Maryland, and Virginia, I have received intelligence of their patriotic alacrity in obeying the call of the present, though painful, yet commanding necessity; that a force, which, according to every reasonable expectation is adequate to the exigency, is already in motion to the scene of disaffection; that those who have confided or shall confide in the protection of government, shall meet full succor under the standard and arms of the United States; that those who having offended against the law have since entitled themselves to idemnity, will be treated with the most liberal good faith, if they shall not have forfeited their claim by any subsequent conduct, and that instructions are given accordingly. And I do moreover expect all individuals and bodies of men, to contemplate with abhorrence the measures leading directly or indirectly to those crimes which produce this military coercion; to check in their respective spheres the effort of misguided or designing men to substitute their misrepresentations in the place of truth, and their discontents in the place of stable government, and so call to mind that as the people of the United States have been permitted under the Divine favor, in perfect freedom, after solemn deliberation, and in an enlightened age, to elect their own government; so will their gratitude for this inestimable blessing be best distinguished by firm exertions to maintain the constitution and laws. And lastly, I again warn all persons whomsoever, and wheresoever, not to abet, aid, or comfort the insurgents aforesaid, as they will answer the country at their peril; and I do also require all officers and other citizens according to their several duties as far as may be in their power, to bring under the cognizance of law all offenders in the premises. In witness whereof, I have caused the seal of the United States of America to be affixed to these presents, and signed the same with my hand. Done at the city of Philadelphia, the twenty-fifth day of September, one thousand seven hundred and ninety-four, and of the Independence of the United States of America the nineteenth.

GEO. WASHINGTON. [L. S.]

By the President,

EDM. RANDOLPH.

(True copy.) GEORGE TAYLOR."

Findley's account of the proceedings at Parkinson's Ferry

As a matter of curiosity we here extract from Findley's History of the proceedings related in the foregoing chapter. It has been generally followed by other writers to the disparagement of Mr. Brackenridge, and to the advantage of Gallatin. It is a striking instance of the errors which may be perpetrated by prejudiced, or ignorant and stupid chroniclers.

"The meeting at Parkinson's Ferry was pretty full, but not a true or equal representation. There were upward of two hundred delegates; three of them were from Ohio county in Virginia, and two from Bedford county in Pennsylvania, besides those from the four counties. The place of meeting was unfavorable, being in the neighborhood in which the resistance had originated, and within a mile of the dwelling house of M'Farlane, who had been killed, and there were probably a greater number of spectators than of delegates.

"The delegates convened on an eminence under the shade of trees; Col. Cook was appointed chairman and Albert Gallatin secretary. It was soon discovered that there were a number of inflammatory persons among the delegates; few of them, however, had talents. Bradford opened the meeting with a statement of the events that had taken place and concluded with reading the letters which had been taken from the intercepted mail, with some explanatory comments thereon."

[Thus far, Findley is tolerably correct.]

"At *this time* the arrival of commissioners from the President—with power for restoring order in the western country, if a corresponding disposition was met on the part of the people—was announced to the meeting."

[This is not true. The arrival of commissioners in the country, was first announced by Findley toward the close of the meeting, and after the report of the resolutions of the committee. Findley himself *was absent* until this time. The resolutions reported by the committee of four proposed sending commissioners to the President, with an address, but on hearing of the appointment of commissioners by him, this was changed at the instance of Mr. Brackenridge, and a committee appointed to confer with those of the government. Findley proceeds:]

"After a short pause, Col. Marshall rose and expressed some satisfaction at the information of the commissioners, but said that they should not on that account neglect the business of the meeting, *and read some resolutions which had been agreed on between him and Bradford.*"

[The resolutions were read on the *first day* of the meeting, not on the announcement of commissioners. The remarks of Bradford were made after the report of the resolutions by the committee, and then adopted by the meeting. It was at that time that the resolution to send commissioners was changed in consequence of the intelligence just received. Findley proceeds:]

"The first resolution being against taking the citizens out of the vicinity for trial, occasioned no contest; the second and most important resolution was in the following words:

"*Resolved*, That a standing committee to consist of —— members from each county, to be denominated a committee of public safety; whose duty it shall be to call forth the resources of the western country, to repel any hostile attempt that may be made against the citizens or the body of the people."

[This was one of the five resolutions presented by Bradford, on the first day of the meeting. It was directly opposed by Gallatin, on the ground that it was not necessary, as there was no reason to expect the resort to force on the part of the government. It would have led to a dangerous discussion, in which Gallatin would have been in a hopeless minority. But it was most adroitly parried by Mr. Brackenridge, who proposed a reference of this and the other resolutions to a committee of four to perfect them, and report. He at the same time suggested a modification of the terms so as to be less definite—as for instance, "to take such measures as the situation of affairs may require." The resolution was then passed over without vote or debate. We continue Findley's version:]

"This, compared with the subsequent resolutions, was preparing the proceedings of the meeting by a direct question whether the western counties would raise the standard of rebellion or not. This was certainly a bold attempt to form a combination hostile both to the government of the State and of the United States. If such a resolution had been offered before such a number of persons had become desperate by being involved in the preceding riots, it would not have been heard with patience, but now it required both patience and great address to parry it."

[And who parried it? Hear Findley:]

"Fortunately there was a man among the delegates; a man well qualified for that purpose, I mean Mr. Gallatin, the secretary. He rose, and began by *criticising* on the word hostility; asked what it meant, or from whence the hostilities were to come? He alleged if it was the exactions of the government that was to be opposed, the time was improper; the exactions of the government on the citizens in support of the laws, being coercive and not hostile. He encouraged them to expect no other means of coercion from the government but through the judiciary; and after a number of sensible observations, moved to refer the resolutions to a select committee. [This is false; the motion was made by Mr. Brackenridge.] But so great was the prevailing panic, that notwithstanding the number of well disposed persons that were in the meeting, he was not seconded; after some delay, however, Marshall himself offered to withdraw the resolution, that a committee of sixty should be appointed with power to call a new meeting of the people or their deputies. [What an absurd mixture of the different stages of the proceedings, as well as palpable falsehoods. We refer to Mr. Brackenridge's statement, Mr. Ross's letter, and the evidence of Gallatin himself.] This was instantly agreed to, and a new resolution was *studiously* modified so as to insure its adoption, and was agreed to by the meeting. [The resolution was modified in the committee of four, and reported the next day.] In it a determination was expressed to support the State laws and afford protection to the citizens; this was an important step toward the restoration of order, for at that time no man thought himself safe, in many places, in telling his real sentiments; threats were not only circulated in anonymous letters, but were contained in the mottoes of liberty poles; one was erected on the morning of the meeting, and within view of it; it was erected under the direction of those who signed the Braddock's Field orders. The motto was: LIBERTY AND NO EXCISE, AND NO ASYLUM FOR COWARDS. Every man was esteemed a coward or traitor by these disorganizers, who disapproved of their measures."

[Making every allowance for the blunders of an illiterate man, it still is a matter of wonder, that any man of common sense should exhibit so much confusion and absurdity in his attempt to play the historian, and record the proceedings of an important assembly. He appears to have been totally ignorant of the difference between the *five* resolutions, as read in the meeting on the first day, and the *three* reported by the committee on the day following. He mingles what passed in the committee with the speeches in the Assembly. He proceeds:]

"Mr. Gallatin had the fortitude to object to the exception against the excise law, originally contained in the resolution [before the committee] for the support of the municipal laws, and had it struck out; but durst not offer an affirmative resolution in favor of submitting to it. Indeed, the doing so at this time would have been imprudent, nor would success in such a resolution have been of use till the submission to the municipal laws had been restored.

"In short, the resolutions being *five* in number, [the resolutions read by Bradford; Findley ignores the resolutions reported by the committee, *three* in number, and adopted by the assembly,] were discussed, [the discussion was *prevented* by Mr. Brackenridge,] and referred to a committee, consisting of Bradford, Gallatin, Brackenridge, and Herman Husbands, who new-modeled them before the next day's meeting, at which they passed without much difficulty, [we refer the reader to Mr. Brackenridge's account, contained in the foregoing chapter—"without much difficulty"—these are Findley's words.] The committee of sixty, or one from each township, to meet at Redstone Fort, (Brownsville,) on the second of September, and a committee consisting of twelve, three from each of the four counties, was appointed to confer with the commissioners appointed by the President.

"The commissioners came to a house near the meeting before it adjourned. [Not true.] This rendered the situation of the friends to order more delicate. It was urged by some, that the meeting should not be dissolved till they would know, and decide on the terms proposed by the commissioners. [Mr. Ross was the only one present, but it was not known at that time that he was a commissioner.] With great address, however, they were prevailed upon to adjourn without day. [Who prevailed upon them to do this?] Men of discernment knew that nothing would bring the people to a proper sense of their duty without time for reflection, and for the present agitated state of the public mind to subside. They knew also, that if time could be procured to disseminate knowledge among the people, every thing that was necessary would be gained. Therefore to restore quietness, and gain time, was the great object of Mr. Gallatin. [The object of that gentleman was to oppose Bradford, and he failed in every thing he attempted. For of what importance was his petty *criticism* alluded to by Findley? The assembly did not care a straw for it. The thing was to keep them from taking any decisive step until the power could be taken out of their hands,* and this was accomplished by Brackenridge, and not by Gallatin.] "Brackenridge, *probably*, was actuated by the same motives as Gallatin, but supported the measures in a different manner; he often kept up the appearance, and sometimes the boasting language of Bradford's party, and opposed Gallatin, yet he always *contrived to bring the proceedings to the same issue.*" [What amusing simplicity and innocence, on the part of "Traddle the Weaver," the name under which Findley is alluded to in "Modern Chivalry." If it were possible for the weaver to be a devil, the cloven foot is here discoverable.]

The account of the meeting given by Wharton is an abridgment of Findley, with additional errors. Hildreth is no better. He represents Gallatin as being secretary to the meeting at Braddock's Field—he was not there at all. Pity it is that historians do not always inform themselves on the subjects of which they write!

* By means of sub-committees.

CHAPTER VIII.

THE MEASURES OF THE GOVERNMENT—ARRIVAL OF COMMISSIONERS—THE CONFERENCE.

As soon as information of the burning of the house of the Inspector, and the march from Braddock's Field, reached Philadelphia, then the seat of government of the State of Pennsylvania, and also of the Union—great alarm was occasioned. The President called a council of the heads of the departments, while the subject was also taken into consideration by the Governor,* with the Chief Justice,† and the Secretary of State.‡ A certificate was obtained by the Federal government from Judge Wilson, of the Supreme Court, to meet the requisition of the act of Congress for calling out the military, in consequence of opposition by armed combinations, too powerful to be controlled by the civil authorities. This certificate was given on mere rumor, or on private letters, and not on evidence on oath, and cannot be approved as a precedent, whatever justification it may find in the urgency of the occasion.

The President, in conformity with his benevolent character, was in favor of mild measures, and the offer of an amnesty to the country; provided forcible and unlawful opposition would cease. Some of the cabinet were for the most prompt and energetic course;‖ the Secretary of State§ was opposed to calling out the militia, before exhausting every means of pacification. The State authorities differed from the general government, appeared disposed to palliate the conduct of the rioters, and to throw the blame on the excise law, regarding it as a personal affair between the people and the collector of the western district or survey. The Chief Justice, M'Kean, at this juncture suggested the sending commissioners, both on the part of the State and of the Federal government, directly to the disturbed district, and endeavoring to bring about a peaceful submission to the laws. This mild and pacific course met the approbation of the President; and Messrs. Ross, Yeates and Bradford, (U. S. Attorney General,) were selected for the United States, and M'Kean and Irvine on

---

* Mifflin.   † M'Kean.   ‡ Dallas.   ‖ Hamilton.   § E. Randolph.

the part of the State. The President had previously issued his proclamation, dated the 7th of August, only six days after the assemblage at Braddock's Field; and at the same time a requisition was made on the adjoining States for a draft of militia to the number of fifteen thousand men, to be ready to take the field at a moment's notice.

These commissioners on the part of the State and Federal governments, hastened to the West; and as already related, reached the country about the time of the assemblage of the delegates or deputies at Parkinson's Ferry. Their instructions had been to communicate at once with this body;* but when near it, it was found not to be safe or judicious with the respect to the objects proposed, from the inflamed state of mind among the deputies and through the country. They repaired to Pittsburgh, to meet the committee of conference, at the time fixed by that committee.

On the first consultation held by the conferees among themselves, all, except Bradford, agreed that the interests of the country and the duty of the citizens rendered submission necessary and proper. It was opened by Mr. Brackenridge, who at once recommended submission, and declared his determination to do so, as respected himself. Every effort was made within, as well as out of the committee, to overcome the obstinacy of Bradford; persons having influence with him, were engaged to speak to him, especially General Irvine, for whom he professed particular respect; and it was thought he had been brought over, for at the next meeting of the committee he declared himself perfectly reconciled to submission. Marshall was sincerely so, and was pleased with the first opportunity of abandoning a cause so much at variance with his better judgment; and it is really surprising, that a man of his sense and high character should have ever seriously engaged in it. Neither of those men had led the people. It was the voice of the mass, which they obeyed and feared to offend; and if, in consequence of allowing time, and taking pains to enlighten those very people, they should happen to change, those who now seemed to be their leaders would change with them. Bradford, as the most obstinate, proved the most wanting in the moral courage necessary to encounter the popular displeasure. He was too short-sighted to see the more distant danger from the government, but was alarmed at that just before his eyes from the people. To be the idol of the populace

---

* If this assembly had not been convened, the commissioners would have found no organized body with which they could open a communication. This fact furnishes an argument in favor of such a delegation, although springing directly from the people, and revolutionary in its origin.

was the ruling passion of his nature, and this is the key to his whole conduct, for he does not appear to have been otherwise a bad or unprincipled man.

Mr. Brackenridge being personally acquainted with Judge Yeates and the Attorney General, Mr. Bradford, with whom he had a friendship of early years, called on the commissioners at the public house where they lodged. Here he found Major Craig, giving a tragical account of the treatment of Kirkpatrick, Neville and others, by the people of Pittsburgh in sending them away. Mr. Brackenridge was indignant, and said, "The representation is unjust—you are imposing upon these gentlemen—you are leading them to suppose that the people of Pittsburgh expelled those men; it was the country. We acted as their guardians in sending them away; the act was for them, more than for ourselves." He then related the circumstances which had evidently been misconceived, and of course not fairly represented by Major Craig; that the property, and perhaps the lives of the obnoxious persons would have been the first to be sacrificed, and then the destruction of the town would have followed. Craig soon withdrew. Mr. Brackenridge's feelings were much hurt by an inconsiderate remark of Mr. Bradford. In his observations, he had said, "I am not an insurgent, but engaged in negotiating for those that are, which does not imply the fact that I am one." Mr. Bradford replied, "That will be a subject of future consideration."

This remark was exceedingly wounding, especially from an old friend. It struck him with astonishment, after the stand in favor of submission which he had taken in the committee, which he supposed was well known. He knew that he had enemies among the violent of the people, but this was the first intimation that his loyalty to the government was suspected. It caused him to retire at once, and with the impression that the commissioners were already prepossessed against him. He did not attach so much importance to Craig's representations, but supposed them to indicate the sentiments with which Col. Neville had left the country, and which had thus found their way to the gentlemen delegated by the government. He thought it poor encouragement after the exertions he had made, and was making in behalf of the government, to be treated in this injurious and repulsive manner. He had not reflected sufficiently on the extent to which he was liable to be injured by misrepresentation, perhaps misconception. He relates, that his thoughts that night were very serious, and the temptations from the indignity just offered, and a sense of desperation which suddenly came over him. But they were only the thoughts of a night, and passed away after more cool and just reflections. These

INJUDICIOUS REMARK OF A COMMISSIONER. 193

thoughts he very ingenuously reveals. "I began to consider whether it would not be better to stand with the *sans culottes* of the country; but I could not reconcile it to myself, to disturb the Union; that would be a wickedness beyond all possibility of contemplation. But this country might secede from it! That is a right that is never given up in society. A part of a country, as well as an individual, may quit a government; and, no doubt, this country will quit the United States in due time. That may be by the consent of the Union, or without.* But at present, there would be no consent; the example would be dangerous to give. Common interest would not suffer it. We are bound to the Union for our portion of the public debt, contracted in the struggle for independence; demands against the Union must first be satisfied, before it can be dissolved. The United States have lands beyond us; they cannot be shut out from these, by an independent government between. But is it practicable to establish and support such a government? Perhaps it might claim those lands to the westward, and invite all the world to take possession of them; collect all the banditti of the frontier of the States to help us to fight for them—tell the Spaniards to come up to the mouth of the Ohio and give us free trade—let the British keep the posts and the southern shores of the lakes, and they will gladly furnish us with

---

* It must be recollected that these observations relate to a period when the Union was not yet consolidated under the Federal constitution, although the ideas are remarkable, coming from one who was almost an enthusiast in its favor. The idea of future distinct confederacies was then common. The vast extent of country, separated by natural boundaries, and great diversity of interests, opposed apparently hopeless obstacles to a permanent union. The day of steam had not yet risen; there were no canals, rail roads, or even turnpikes, scarcely any thing more than pack-horse paths. The lakes and the south belonged to foreign nations, and the wilderness was held by the savages. The idea of identity of interests was then new; that of separation, as necessity prompted, was still fresh from the recent separation from Great Britain. It was impossible to have foreseen the changes effected in the habits, history and attachments of the people during three generations. The immense increase in the facilities of communication could not have been conceived by the most poetic imagination. No one could have conceived that in half a century the country should have thus become consolidated, and for all practical purposes diminished in extent; unless he could also have foreseen the giant progress of invention and science. If Mr. Brackenridge had lived to this day, he would have opposed the separation under all circumstances, as creating ten thousand evils, when it might possibly escape one by that fatal resort. In the expression that the time would come when the West would fall off from the East, he spoke according to the prevailing opinion and the state of the country at the time, which no one could foresee would in so short a period be so marvelously altered, and fitted for a PERPETUAL UNION.

arms and means of war—get the Indians of the woods to assist us, which could be done by the British, in spirit still hostile and eager to embrace the opportunity for revenge, and willing to check the progress of this republic. We might wage war—formidable war—and might succeed. But what would be that success? A poor and dependent republic, instead of this great and rising confederacy. If selfish considerations should prevail, even this would be better than to be suspected by the government, while acting with fidelity to it, and at the same time incurring the contumely of the people for supposed infidelity to a cause which I condemn. But these were only the thoughts of a night. I saw Mr. Ross the next morning, and explained to him my chagrin of the preceding day, and my reflections in consequence of it; giving him to understand that I had half a mind to become an insurgent in earnest. He took it more seriously than I intended. His expression was, 'The force of genius is almighty—give them not the aid of yours.'* I told him that nothing but self-preservation would lead me to think of it." Mr. Brackenridge's mind was soothed by Mr. Ross, who assured him that no suspicion could possibly fall on him; that the commissioners, the preceding day, were perfectly satisfied with the explanations he had given in the presence of Craig; and that what the latter had said, had not left the least impression.

The expressions of commissioner Bradford, considering the critical situation of the country, were, to say the least, inconsiderate. The relations of the United States with Spain and Great Britain were such, that it must be admitted, that the reflections of Mr. Brackenridge were not altogether visionary. The consequence of spurning such a man with contumely, without first hearing him, might have been followed by serious consequences. He might have been placed at the head of the insurgents, if possessed of less exalted and patriotic feelings; in that case, he would soon have established relations with the two powers just named; organized a force to seize the passes of the mountains—procured money and arms, until a war would speedily have issued between those

---

*Mr. Brackenridge never professed to be a fighting man, but somehow or other was never found wanting when it was necessary for self-defense. He speaks very candidly of the *fears* he experienced on various occasions, and even with a touch of humor. Cowards do not jest about their fears. His courage was of the kind described by Abbé Barthelmy, "He knew his danger, feared it, yet met it." If he had taken hold of the insurrection, it would soon have worn a different aspect. Like Rienzi, his habits were literary, but his instincts those of the statesman and soldier.

powers, which, "if not victory, would have been at least revenge." But Mr. Brackenridge was an enthusiast in the "rising glory of America,"* and could not be, however wounded by the remarks of those who did not know his real sentiments and position, induced to swerve from the path of patriotic duty. As a speaker and a writer, he had taken a decided part in the revolution, and was a zealous supporter of the Federal constitution and that of the State. He was neither a demagogue nor an aristocrat, but gave his support both to the people and to the government. Still he had within him a fiery spirit, a keen sense of injustice, capable of being roused to desperation by insult and contumely.

An occurrence took place almost immediately after the arrival of the commissioners, calculated to produce a very unfavorable impression, and which disclosed the existence in town of a dangerous spirit among a small portion of the thoughtless and worthless. A riotous and disorderly assemblage raised a liberty-pole before the lodgings of the commissioners, and would have run up a flag with seven stars for the four western counties, and for Bedford and the two counties of Virginia, but this was prevented by the well disposed citizens, who prevailed on them to substitute the flag of the fifteen States. This was the first and only distinct manifestation among any class of a desire to separate from the Union, even if such an inference must be necessarily drawn from this act. The matter was afterward the subject of indictment as a disturbance of the peace, and the parties were convicted by a jury and fined by the court.†

The commissioners of the United States and on the part of the State, and the conferees on the part of the people, having met, the conference was opened on the part of the commissioners, by expressing the concern they felt for the events which had occasioned that meeting; but they declared their intention to avoid any unnecessary observations on them, said it was their business to endeavor to compose the disturbances which prevailed, and to restore the authority of the laws by measures wholly of a conciliatory nature.

It is important here to bear in mind that this was a formal recognition of the committee of conference, instead of being regarded as a mere off-

---

* When a student at Princeton College, he wrote, in conjunction with Freneau, a poem entitled the "Rising Glory of America," in the form of dialogue. It is printed in Freneau's works, and in a late edition the part appertaining to Mr. Brackenridge is left out. The poem foreshadowed in a remarkable manner the future greatness of America. It was composed some years before the American revolution.

† Addison's Reports, 274.

shoot of a treasonable assemblage. Although representing the people, they at once united with the government commissioners for the purpose of accomplishing the same object, the pacification of the country. This was equivalent to an act of oblivion as respected them, as to every previous act, provided their subsequent conduct continued in conformity with their present action; and yet, strange to say, even those who exerted themselves most to bring about the desired submission, and especially Mr. Brackenridge and Mr. Gallatin, were still regarded as traitors by the intemperate partisans and supporters of government!

It was further stated by the commissioners, that the forcible opposition which had been recently made to the laws of the United States, violated the great principles on which the republican government is founded; that every such government must at all hazards enforce obedience to the general will; and that so long as they admitted themselves to be a part of the nation, it was manifestly absurd to oppose the national authority.

The commissioners then proceeded to speak of the obligation on the part of the President of the United States to cause the laws to be executed; the measures he had taken for that purpose; his desire to avoid the necessity of coercion, and the general nature of the powers he had vested in them; and finally requested to know whether the conferees could give any assurance of a disposition in the people to submit, or would recommend such submission to them?

The commissioners on the part of the State of Pennsylvania, after this, addressed the conferees on the subject of the late disturbances in that country; forcibly represented the mischievous consequences of such conduct; explained the nature of their mission, and declared they were ready to promise in behalf of the Executive authority of the State, a full pardon and oblivion for all that was past, on condition of entire submission to the laws.

It is proper here to remind the reader that the conferees were intrusted with the cause of the people whom they represented, and it was their duty to represent it in the most favorable light as negotiators, and obtain for their constituents the best terms they could, although the conferees for themselves had unanimously agreed to submit to the government. They had appointed a sub-committee, consisting of Messrs. Cook, Gallatin and Brackenridge, which chose the latter to conduct the negotiations, both verbally and in writing, and who now made the following reply. He gave a narrative of the causes of discontent and uneasiness which very generally prevailed; these were stated not with a view of founding any demands, but for the purpose of explaining the existing disaffection. Many of the causes had long existed, and some from the first settlement of the country. Among other things, the people complained of the decisions of the State courts, which discountenanced improvement titles, and gave the preference to those existing only on paper. They complain of the war with the Indians, which has so long vexed the frontier; and of the inefficient manner in which it has been conducted by the government; they complain, that they have been continually harassed by military duty, in being called out to repel incursions; that the general government had been inattentive to the treaty of peace, respecting the western posts, which formed the rallying points of those Indians; they complain of the indifference of the government as to the securing the free navigation of the Mississippi, in consequence of which, together with the hostility of the Indians, the people of the West had no outlet by the natural channel for the produce of their farms, while the mountains shut them in on the East. That in consequence of these things, the tax on distilled spirits was particularly unequal and oppressive; and this, together with the ruinous practice of compelling them to appear in the Federal courts in Philadelphia, was particularly grievous, which last was the immediate cause of the late disturbances. That Congress had neglected their remonstrances and petitions; and that there was a great hardship in being summoned to answer for penalties in the courts of the United States, at such a distance from the vicinage. The suspension of the settlement at Presq' Isle—the engrossing large bodies of land as purchasers from the State, by individuals, was mentioned among the prevailing causes of discontent. Also the killing certain persons at General Neville's house, and the sending soldiers from the garrison without authority of law. To these was added the appointment of General Neville as Inspector of the survey, whose former popularity, and favors received from the people, had made his acceptance of that office particularly offensive. It was observed, in conclusion, that the persons who were the actors in the late disturbances, had not intended originally to proceed to such extremities, but were led to it from the acts of those who opposed them, which occasioned the shedding of blood; that the forcible opposition which had been made to the law, was produced by the pressure of grievances, and not by hostility to the government; but if there was any prospect of redress, no people would more readily show themselves good citizens, and cease their opposition to the obnoxious measures of the government.

The commissioners expressed their surprise at the extent of these complaints, and intimated that if all these matters were really causes of uneasiness and dissatisfaction in the minds of the people, it would be impossible for the government to satisfy them. But some of them were of a nature more serious than others. Though they would not speak officially, they stated what was generally understood as to the conduct, measures and expectations of government with respect to the Mississippi navigation, the treaty of peace, the suspension of the settlement at Presq' Isle, &c. That as to the acts of Congress which had been forcibly opposed, if it were proper that they should be repealed, Congress alone could repeal them; but while they were laws, they must be carried into execution. That the petitions of the western counties had not been neglected, nor their interest overlooked; that in fact, the local interests of these counties were better represented than those of any other part of the State; they having no less than three gentlemen in the House of Representatives, when it appeared by the census that their numbers would entitle them only to two. That the acts in question had been often under the consideration of Congress; that they had always been supported by a considerable majority, in which they would find the names of several gentlemen, considered in these counties as the firmest friends of the country. That although the laws relating to the general interests of the Union did not admit of a repeal, modifications had been made, and some favorable alterations in consequence of their representations; and that at the last session, the State courts had been vested with jurisdiction over offenses against those acts which would enable the President to remove one of their principal complaints. That the convenience of the people had been, and always would be consulted; and the conferees were desired to say, if there was any thing in the power of the Executive that yet remained to be done, to make the execution of the acts convenient and agreeable to the people, it would be granted.

One of the conferees then inquired, whether the President could not suspend the execution of the excise acts, until the meeting of Congress; but he was interrupted by others, who declared that they considered such a measure as impracticable. The commissioners expressed the same opinion, and the conversation then became more particular, respecting the powers the commissioners possessed; the propriety and necessity of the conferees expressing their views upon the proposal to be made, and of their calling the standing committee together before the first of September. But as it was agreed that the propositions and answers should be reduced to writing, these must be referred to for the result of the conference, of which the outline has just been given.

When men of sense, and honest intentions, come together, it does not require much discussion to arrive at a proper understanding. It had been represented on the part of the conferees, that they did not consider themselves authorized to do more than report to the standing committee, and these again to the deputies at Parkinson's Ferry. It was also said, that time was very desirable to reconcile the people to the result of the conference. But the commissioners gave the most cogent reasons against this, and among others, that much dissatisfaction was beginning to show itself on the other side of the mountains, and if any thing could be done to obtain the Executive clemency, it must be done at once. The conferees, in consequence of this representation, agreed to yield to the wishes of the commissioners. They had done their duty to their constituents in fully representing all their complaints, well or ill-founded; it now became them as lovers of peace, not to persist with obstinacy in unreasonable demands. The following correspondence now took place. A similar and separate conference was held by the conferees and the commissioners on the part of the State, Messrs. M'Kean and Irvine, and followed by a similar correspondence.

From the Commissioners on the part of the United States to the Committee of Conference Assembled at Pittsburgh.

"PITTSBURGH, August 21st, 1794.

"GENTLEMEN:— Having had a conference with you, on the important subject which calls us to this part of Pennsylvania, we shall now state to you in writing agreeably to your request, the nature and object of our mission hither. Considering this as a crisis infinitely interesting to our fellow citizens, who have authorized you to confer with us, we shall explain ourselves to you with that frankness and sincerity which the solemnity of the occasion demands.

"You well know that the President of the United States is charged with the execution of the laws. Obedience to the national will being indispensable in a republican government, the people of the United States have strictly enjoined it as his duty, 'to see that the laws are faithfully executed.' And when the ordinary authorities of the government are incompetent for that end, he is bound to exert those higher powers with which the nation has invested him for so extraordinary an occasion.

"It is but too evident that the insurrections which have lately prevailed in some of the western counties, have surpassed the usual exercise of the civil authority; and it has been formally notified to the President by one of the associate Judges, in the manner the law prescribes, 'that in the counties of Washington and Allegheny, in the State of Pennsylvania, laws of the United States are opposed, and the execution thereof obstructed, by combinations too powerful to be suppressed by the ordinary course of judicial proceedings or the powers vested in the Marshal of that district.' He, therefore, perceives with the deepest regret, the necessity to which he may be reduced, of calling forth the national force, in order to support the national authority, and to cause the laws to be executed; but he has determined previously to address himself to the patriotism and reason of the people of the western counties, and to try the moderation of government, in hopes that he may not be compelled to resort to its strength. But we must not conceal it from you, that it is also his fixed determination, if these hopes should be disappointed, to employ the force—and if it be necessary, the whole force of the Union, to secure the execution of the laws. He has, therefore, authorized us to repair hither, and by free conferences, and the powers vested in us, to endeavor to put an end to the present disturbances, and to the opposition to the execution of the laws, in a manner that may be finally satisfactory to all our fellow citizens.

"We hope that this moderation in the government will not be misconceived by the citizens to whom we are sent. The President, who feels a paternal solicitude for their welfare, wishes to prevent the calamities that are impending over them—to recall them to their duty, and prove to the whole world, that if military coercion must be employed, it is *their* choice, not *his*.

"The powers vested in us, will enable us so to arrange the execution of the acts for raising a revenue on distilled spirits and stills, that little inconvenience will arise therefrom to the people—to prevent, as far as is consistent with the public interests, the commencing prosecutions under those acts, at a distance from the places where the delinquents reside—to suspend prosecutions for the late offenses against the United States—and even to engage for a general pardon and oblivion of them.

"But, gentlemen, we explicitly declare to you, that the exercise of these powers must be preceded by full and satisfactory assurances of a sincere determination in the people to obey the laws of the United States; and their eventual operation must depend upon a corresponding acquiescence in the execution of the acts which have been opposed. We have not, and coming from the Executive, you well know that we cannot have any authority to suspend the laws, or to offer the most distant hopes, that the acts, the execution of which has been obstructed, will be repealed. On the contrary, we are free to declare to you our private opinions, that the national councils, while they consult the general interests of the republic, and endeavor to conciliate every part, by local accommodations to citizens who respect the laws, will sternly refuse every indulgence to men who accompany their requests with threats, and resist by force the public authority.

"Upon these principles, we are ready to enter with you into the details necessary for the exercise of our powers—to learn what local accommodations are, yet wanting to render the execution of the laws convenient to the people—to concert with you measures for restoring harmony and order, and for burying the past in oblivion, and to unite our endeavors with yours, to secure the peace and happiness of our common country.

"It is necessary to apprize you thus early, that at present we do not consider ourselves as authorized to enter into any conferences on this subject after the first of September ensuing. We therefore hope that the business will be so conducted, that some definite answer may be given to us before that day.

"We cannot believe, that in so great a crisis, any attempts to temporize and procrastinate will be made by those who sincerely love their country, and wish to secure its tranquility.

"We also declare to you, that no indulgence will be given to any future offense against the United States, and that they who shall hereafter, directly or indirectly, oppose the execution of the laws, must abide the consequences of their conduct.

JAMES ROSS,
J. YEATES,
WM. BRADFORD."

To the foregoing, the conferees made the following answer, signed by the chairman:

Answer of the Committee.

"PITTSBURGH, August 22d, 1794.

"GENTLEMEN:—Having in our conference, at considerable length, stated to you the grounds of that discontent which exists in the minds of the people of this country, and which has lately shown itself in acts of opposition to the excise law, you will consider us as waiving any question of the constitutional power of the President to call upon the force of the Union to suppress them.* It is our object, as it is yours, to compose the disturbance.

"We are satisfied, that in substance you have gone as far as we could expect the Executive to go. It only remains to ascertain your propositions more in detail, and to say what arrangement it may be in your power to make with regard to convenience in collecting the revenue under the excise laws; how far it may be consistent with the public interest, to prevent commencing prosecutions under those laws at a distance from places where the delinquents reside; on what conditions, or circumstances, prosecutions for the late violations shall be suspended; that is to say, whether on the individual keeping the peace, or on its being kept by the country in general—and also with regard to the general amnesty, whether the claiming the benefit of it, by an individual, shall depend on his own future conduct, or that of the whole community?

"We have already stated to you, in conference, that we are empowered to give you no definitive answer with regard to the sense of the people, on the great question of acceding to the law; but that in our opinion, it is the interest of the country to accede; and that we shall make this report to the committee, to whom we are to report, and state to them the reasons of our opinion; that so far as they have weight, they may be regarded by them. It will be our endeavor to conciliate, not only them, but the public mind in general, to our views on this subject. We hope to be assisted by you, in giving all that extent and precision, clearness and certainty, to your propositions, that may be necessary to satisfy the understandings, and engage the acquiescence of the people.

"It is to be understood, that in acceding to the law, no inference is to be drawn, or construction made, that we will relinquish a constitutional opposition; but that we will, undeviatingly, and constantly, pursue every legal means and measures for obtaining a repeal of the law in question.

---

* A doubt existed in the mind of the Secretary of State, Edmund Randolph, whether a case had been made out, by the certificate of Judge Wilson, to authorize the calling out of the militia. Whatever might be the legal question, the fact of the necessity was notorious.

"As we are disposed with you, to have the sense of the people taken on the subject of our conference as speedily as may be, with that view, we have resolved to call the committee to whom our report is to be made, at an earlier day than had been appointed, to wit: on Thursday, the 28th instant, but have not thought ourselves authorized in changing the place, at Redstone, Old Fort, on the Monongahela.

By order of the committee.

EDWARD COOK, *Chairman.*

"To the Commissioners on the part of the Union."

In compliance with the request for more specific details as to the conditions, &c. the commissioners communicated the following note:

"The commissioners appointed by the President of the United States to confer with the citizens in the western part of Pennsylvania, having been assured by the committee of conference of their determination to approve the proposals made, and to recommend to the committee appointed by the meeting at Parkinson's ferry, a submission to the acts of Congress, do now proceed to declare what assurances of submission will be deemed full and satisfactory, and to detail the engagements they are prepared to make.

"1. It is expected, and required by the said commissioners, that the citizens composing the said general committee, do on or before the 1st day of September, explicitly declare their determination to submit to the laws of the United States, and they will not directly or indirectly oppose the acts for raising a revenue on distilled spirits and stills.

"2. That they do explicitly recommend a perfect and entire acquiescence under the execution of said acts.

"3. That they do in like manner recommend that no violence, injuries or threats be offered to the person or property of any officer of the United States, or citizen complying with the laws, and to declare their determination to support (as far as the laws require) the civil authority in affording the protection due to all officers and citizens.

"4. That measures be taken by meetings in election districts, or otherwise, the determination of the citizens in the fourth survey of Pennsylvania to submit to the said laws, and that satisfactory assurances be given by the said commissioners that the people have so determined to submit, on or before the 14th of September next.

"The said commissioners, if a full and perfect compliance with the above requisition shall take place, have power to promise and engage in the manner following, to wit:

"1. No prosecution for any treason, or other indictable offense, against the United States, committed in the fourth survey of Pennsylvania, before this day, shall be proceeded on, or commenced, until the 10th day of July next.

"2. If there shall be a general and sincere acquiescence in the execution of the said laws, until the said 10th day of July next, a general pardon and oblivion of all such offenses shall be granted, excepting therefrom, nevertheless, every person who shall in the meantime willfully obstruct, or attempt to obstruct, the execution of any of the laws of the United States, or be in any wise aiding or abetting therein.

"3. Congress having by an act passed on the fifth day of June last, authorized the State courts to take cognizance of offenses against the said acts for raising revenue upon distilled spirits and stills, the President has determined that he will direct suits against such delinquents to be prosecuted therein; if upon experiment, it be found that local prejudices, or other causes, do not obstruct the faithful administration of justice. But it is to be understood, that of this he must be the judge, and that he does not mean by this determination to impair any power vested in the Executive of the United States.

"Certain beneficial arrangements for adjusting delinquencies and prosecutions for penalties, now depending, shall be made and communicated by the officers appointed to carry said acts into execution.

"Given under our hands at Pittsburgh, this 22d day of August, 1794.

JAMES ROSS,
J. YEATES,
WM. BRADFORD.

"To the Committee of Conference."

The following note was sent by the committee of conference:

"PITTSBURGH, August 23, 1794.

"GENTLEMEN:—We presume it has been understood by you that the conference on our part consists of members, not only from the counties west of the Allegheny mountains, but from Ohio county in Virginia, and your propositions made in general by your first letter, being addressed to this conference, the Ohio county was considered as included; yet in your propositions made in detail by your last, you confine them to the survey within Pennsylvania. We would request an explanation on this particular.

"We have only further to say, we shall make a faithful report of your propositions, which we approve, and will recommend them to the people; and however they may be received, we are persuaded nothing more could have been done by you, or us, to bring the business to an accommodation.

By order of the committee.

EDWARD COOK, *Chairman.*

"To the Commissioners on the part of the Union."

Reply of the Commissioners. *

"PITTSBURGH, August 23d, 1794.

"GENTLEMEN:—Having received your assurances of your approbation of the propositions made by us, and your determination to recommend them to the peo-

---

* This letter does not appear to be in the report made by the conferees to the committee. It says: "In consequence of the above, a conference took place with the gentlemen from Ohio, and some arrangements were made accordingly."

ple, we have nothing further to add, except to reply to that part of your letter which relates to the gentlemen from Ohio county.

"The whole tenor of our letter of the 21st inst. shows that we had come among you in consequence of the disturbances which had prevailed in the western parts of Pennsylvania; to prevent the actual employment of military coercion there, as contemplated by the President's proclamation; and that the late offenses referred to, were the insurrections which had prevailed in some of the western counties. We therefore cannot extend our propositions.

"In addition to this, we were well assured that the people of Ohio county have not generally authorized those gentlemen to represent them, and we cannot at present undertake to make any definite arrangements with them.

"We are, however, willing to converse with those gentlemen on the subject; and we have no doubt that on satisfactory proofs of their determination to support the laws of their country, and of an entire submission to them by those from whom they came being given, the President will, upon our recommendation, extend a similar pardon to any late offense committed against the United States, if any such have been committed. We are willing, on receiving such assurances from them, to recommend such application accordingly.

JAMES ROSS,
J. YEATES,
WM. BRADFORD.

"To the Committee of Conference."

While the commissioners prepared their report to the government of the United States of the result of the conference, the conferees committed to Mr. Brackenridge the task of preparing that to be laid before the standing committee at Brownsville. Mr. Gallatin in his speech in the Legislature, states that he differed from its author, in some particulars. He might have been right, but a mere difference does not of itself prove him to have been so. This report was submitted to a friendly examination by the commissioners, who made some suggestions which were adopted by the author.

The following letter was delivered to Mr. Brackenridge just before his departure from Brownsville, directed to Messrs. Kirkpatrick, Smith, Powers, Bradford, Marshall, Edgar, Cook, Gallatin, Lang, Martin, Lucas, and Brackenridge, late conferees:

"PITTSBURGH, August 27, 1794.

"GENTLEMEN:—Since your departure from Pittsburgh, we have transmitted information of our proceedings to the Secretary of State, and it being evident from them, that the satisfactory proof of a sincere submission cannot be obtained before the first of September, we may undertake to assure you, that the movement of the militia will be suspended until further information is received from us.

"We also authorize you to assure the friends of order, who may be disposed to exert themselves to restore the authority of the laws, that they may rely upon all the protection the government can give, and that every measure necessary to repress and punish the violence of ill-disposed individuals who may dissent from the general sentiment, (if there should be any such,) will be promptly taken in the manner the law directs.

We are, gentlemen, your most obedient servants,
JAMES ROSS,
J. YEATES,
WM. BRADFORD."

"In drafting the report," says Mr. Brackenridge, "I had introduced the general statement of grievances, with a view to show that we had made the most of our case.* But the commissioners thought it would rather encourage opposition than submission—it was therefore stricken out.

"I had stated, strongly, the sense of the commissioners of the outrages committed; the burning, the expulsion, the intercepting the mail, the march from Braddock's Field. It was with a view of placing these things in the strongest light before the people, in order that they might the better appreciate the value of the amnesty. I am disposed to believe that these gave offense to Bradford and Marshall. From this time they showed a marked coolness toward me. I cannot believe that Marshall was at all dissatisfied at being relieved from the extremely hazardous situation in which he had been placed.

"I added, in the conclusion, some reasons as grounds for conceding to the propositions of the commissioners. They were such as I thought would have weight with the people. Mr. Gallatin, in his speech in the Legislature of Pennsylvania, on the subject of the Insurrection, says, 'They were such, I suppose, as, in the judgment of the author, would make most impression upon the people; on that head, however, I think he was mistaken.' I think now (continues Mr. Brackenridge,) as I did then, that they were the most likely to produce the effect; but that is a mere matter of opinion, which I am not going to dispute. The true democratic principle on which I think it should be put, was, without doubt, that the will of the people should govern. The national will had made the law, and should be obeyed. It is an abstract argument that must satisfy the understanding, but cannot reconcile the heart. It is difficult to reconcile the idea that the majority made the law, however oppressive to us, yet the good of the whole, or of the greater number, requires us to submit. My argument, therefore, chiefly contemplated the want of

---

* It is to this Mr. Ross alludes, in his letter to Mr. Brackenridge, when he says: "And when you came as a committee-man to settle the terms of submission, I am persuaded there is none will deny that you exerted yourself to get every reasonable concession on the part of the government, in favor of your constituents."

power. I also introduced the idea of postponement, and submitting under present circumstances, and thus acquiescing in a present evil, in the hope of a future remedy. But, said one to me, 'the people can never be roused again.' I know that, and it is therefore safe to refer them to a future day. The people would begin to look back when passion had subsided, and thus see the precipice on which they had been standing. Let the law go into operation, and they would not find it the evil they imagined it to be."

The above reasoning would not be likely to suggest itself to one brought up under a despotic government, where the sovereign is every thing and the people nothing; where obedience—mere obedience, is all that is required; and where the crouching slave must prostrate himself before the cap and plume of power. It is a kind of reasoning which, perhaps, savors of Machiavelism — yet there are but two ways of influencing the action of the people, moral suasion or brute force. The proud spirit of the freeman is not to be subdued by a frown or a blow; whenever this is the case, the vital spark of liberty is extinguished. The sovereign will of the majority must, notwithstanding, be respected, and the people made to yield to it as, in part, their own will; and, at the same time, care must be taken not to crush that sturdy spirit of resistance, without which free institutions will soon degenerate into despotism. Mr. Brackenridge, always a democrat, maintained that a free people should be induced by reason to be the conquerors over their own passions, and not humbled and broken by outward force. These were the sentiments which governed his course during the insurrection: the reverse of those which then prevailed in the Federal party, with its strong Hamiltonian government, its sedition laws and its standing army. In a government like ours, all the arts of persuasion and peace should be exhausted, before a resort to force; not so with despotisms and those who mimic them.

During the negotiations, a publication appeared in the Pittsburgh *Gazette*, which had an injurious effect, both as respects Mr. Brackenridge personally, and the object he was then laboring to effect with so much earnestness. It was a spurious attempt at wit in the form of a dialogue of Indian chiefs, either intended as a burlesque on the insurgents, or a satire on the excise law, it is difficult to say which. Persons of little discrimination attributed this production to Mr. Brackenridge, as is often the case, merely on the ground of his reputation for wit; for there is not the slightest resemblance in style, and besides, without any motive which could induce him to write such a thing. He promptly denied it, and the denial was corroborated by Mr. Scull, the printer. Moreover, it appeared afterward that the production was that of a decided friend of the excise law, who left his name with the printer for any one who might wish to know it. The puerile production was ascribed to Mr. Brackenridge by his enemies, and represented as intended to ridicule the government. Even after the lapse of half a century, his enemies persist in attributing it to him, and Mr. Wharton, in his voluminous compilation in the volume entitled "State Trials," says it was denied by Mr. Brackenridge at the time in a "lame sort of way." It was impossible for the denial to have been more explicit, and the fact placed beyond doubt by the editor of the paper.*

In these negotiations, it will be seen that Mr. Brackenridge occupied that position to which his superior talents and high character entitled him. The transactions were too much of a public and official character, to permit Findley, and others prejudiced against him, to cast him in the background by exalting Mr. Gallatin above him. Let justice be done; and there is nothing further from the desire of the author of this work than to detract from the merit of Mr. Gallatin; he freely acknowledges his eminent talents, and valuable services in putting a stop to the insurrection. He goes farther, and does not hesitate to defend him from those enemies of his, and of the rights of the people, who assailed him with the epithets of disorganizer and demagogue, and even traitor, on account of those resolutions, passed at public meetings two years before, against the excise law. The whole history of these transactions—the government documents and admissions—all prove that this was oppressive and unequal; that the people had reason and right to complain, even in language rude and "intemperate." If those complaints must only be uttered in humble and temperate language, who is to prescribe the terms of that language? The oppressor, of course, would not be the fit person to prescribe it! Surely the rights of the people stand upon higher ground than this! Yet, I admit, that the people should be solemnly impressed with the sentiment, that there is nothing more atrocious in a free government, than violent and forcible opposition to the laws, or re-

---

* "Understanding that a certain publication which appeared in our paper some time ago, containing speeches in imitation of an Indian treaty, and supposed to reflect on the militia of Jersey, &c. has been attributed abroad to Mr. Brackenridge, we are ready to declare that Mr. Brackenridge is not the author.

"The printer is sorry that the publication above alluded to has given offense. The author, who has always been an open and avowed advocate against the violent proceedings, had no other intention than to give the commissioners of the United States a representation of the different ideas of the people in this country at that time, without meaning a reflection on any man or set of men. It is expected that these facts will remove all prejudices that may have taken place."

sistance to their execution, which saps the foundation of all government and all security. While this truth was fully acknowledged by the conferees, it will be seen, by the correspondence, that they were most careful to preserve to the people the right to pursue all constitutional and lawful means of procuring a repeal of the excise laws, which they honestly regarded as unjust and oppressive.

The terms offered by the commissioners on the part of the President, cannot be too much praised. They bear that stamp of humanity and firmness combined, which distinguished the true greatness of Washington. It is a lamentable reflection, that they were not afterward adopted as frankly and as promptly, by the standing committee at Brownsville, and a large portion of the people, as they were by the committee of conference. If this had been the case, the country would have settled down in peace, and much misery, suffering and anxiety would have been spared. At this distance of time, it is difficult to account for the fact that terms so reasonable and moderate, presented in a way so little calculated to offend the feelings of the proudest freeman, were not at once, and unanimously, embraced by the people. Let us hope that since that day our countrymen have made some advance in virtue and intelligence.

Although a vantage ground had been obtained by the committee of conference, in the favorable terms obtained from the commissioners, still the battle was yet to be fought; and owing to the height of insane passion to which the people had been wrought, the issue was very doubtful, and full of danger to Messrs. Brackenridge and Gallatin, (and especially to the former,) who would be compelled to confront this mass of violence and ignorance—bold, noisy, and perhaps outnumbering the peaceful and well disposed, who would gladly hail the report of the conferees as the harbinger of peace.

Already the leaders in the committee of conference, and especially Mr. Brackenridge, began to feel the effects of vulgar detraction. A great outcry was made, and more particularly among those who had been most active in the late scenes of violence. It was asserted that he had been bribed; that it was known that lawyers would take fees; that the commissioners had brought gold with them; and that he had received enough to render it unnecessary for him to practice law during the remainder of his life! His moral courage was put to the test, while his personal safety was by no means certain. By voluntarily incurring the loss of his present popularity, he had abandoned all hope of being elected to Congress, for which he was then a candidate, and previous to this, with almost a certainty of being elected. As to Bradford, he very soon relapsed into

DISSATISFACTION OF THE PEOPLE.

his old ways—the moment he thought the popular tide was beginning to turn, he was swept along with it; and showed himself at the last to be the same weak, mischievous being that he had been from the first. Was he possessed of eloquence, the only quality on which his popularity could rest? No; but he could declaim, and thus supplied a voice to the rash and inconsiderate. There is also a reason which may be discovered, by looking a little deeper into human nature. The acts of violence committed in burning Neville's house, had formed a sort of conscious separation in society between those who had shared in it and those who had not—a separation of the bulls from the goats, which served to keep alive the ferocity which had been engendered by that act of outrage. Those who had openly approved of that and other similar acts, were placed in the same footing with the participators of them. It was guilt thirsting for the commission of new crimes, or companionship in its worse than misery.

Mr. Gallatin in his evidence on the trials, says: "I spoke but two words, 'amnesty and repeal.'" He spoke the word "repeal," but Mr. Brackenridge first spoke the word "amnesty"—and in addition, the word "submission." These two words were first spoken by him at the Mingo Creek meeting, where he so happily drew the line of distinction between those who were compromised in the late acts of violence, and those who were not. The idea of amnesty was never lost sight of by him, and events had verified what he then said of the mildness and clemency of Washington, and "his unwillingness to shed the blood of his countrymen, by whom he knew he was universally beloved." The evidence of Mr. Henry Purviance is conclusive on this head. It is alone sufficient to put to rest the slanders of a thousand Hildreths and Craigs—his words are, "The course pursued by Mr. Brackenridge, through the whole of the insurrection, had but two objects in view, to bring about submission, and at the same time procure an amnesty for the country." Mr. Purviance stood high as a lawyer, and at the time of making this statement, was the public prosecutor. What more meritorious motives could actuate any man than those just mentioned? He sacrificed a most brilliant political career in Congress, (afterward occupied by Mr. Gallatin,) to his love of country, and his devotion to virtuous principles. When we have the evidence of all his distinguished cotemporaries, without a single contradiction, is it not surprising that any one at this day should have the audacity to speak of him in the language of the two writers just named?*

* Hildreth and Craig.

NOTES TO CHAPTER VIII.

An Indian Treaty.

"Speeches intended to be spoken at a Treaty now holding with the Six United Nations of White Indians, settled at the town of Pittsburgh, on the 20th of August, 1794, by the Commissioners sent from Philadelphia for that purpose.

"Captain Blanket, an Indian chief, spoke as follows:

"'BROTHERS—We welcome you to the old council fire at this place—it is a lucky spot of ground for holding Indian treaties. No good has attended your treaties at Beaver Creek, Muskingum, &c. As the proffer of this treaty has originated with your great council at Philadelphia, we therefore expect you have good terms to offer. But you know, brothers, that it ever has been a custom to pay Indians well for coming to treaties; and you may be assured, that unless we are well paid, or *fully satisfied*, your *attempts of any kind* will not have the least effect. However, we do not doubt but the pay is provided; and that you have a sufficiency of blankets and breech-clouts, powder and lead; and that the wagons are close at hand. You know, brothers, that our neighbors, the British, over the lakes, pay their Indians well; that they have inexhaustible stores of blankets and ammunition, and that if they were offering us a treaty, they would not hesitate a moment to satisfy all our demands.'

"Captain Whiskey spoke next:—

"'BROTHERS — My friend, Captain Blanket, has indulged himself in a little drollery about blankets, &c. but I must speak to the point. I am told that the people of your great council call us a parcel of drunken ragamuffins, because we indulge ourselves with a little of our homespun whiskey; and that we ought to pay well for this extraordinary luxury. What would they think if the same was said of them, for drinking beer and cider? Surely the saying will apply with equal force in both cases. We say that our whiskey shall not be saddled with an unequal tax. You say, it shall; and to enforce the collection of three or four thousand dollars per annum of net proceeds, you will send an army of 12,950 men, or double that number if necessary. This is a new fashioned kind of economy, indeed. It is a pity that this army had not been employed long ago, in assisting your old warrior, General Wayne, or chastising the British about the lakes. However, I presume it is the present policy to guard against offending a nation with a king at their head. But remember, brothers, if we have not a king at our head, we have that powerful monarch, Captain Whiskey, to command us. By the power of his influence, and a love to *his person*, we are impelled to every great and heroic act. You know, brothers, that Captain Whiskey has been a great warrior in all nations, and in all armies. He is a descendant of that nation called Ireland; and to use his own phrase, he has peopled three-fourths of this western world with his own hand. We, the Six United Nations of White Indians, are principally his legitimate offspring; and those who are not, have all imbibed his principles and passions—that is, a love of whiskey; and will therefore fight for our bottle till the last gasp. Brothers, you must not think to frighten us with fine arranged lines of infantry, cavalry and artillery, composed of your watermelon armies from the Jersey shore; they would cut a much better figure warring with crabs and oysters, about the capes of the Delaware. It is a common thing for Indians to fight your best armies, in a proportion of one to five; therefore we would not hesitate a moment to attack this army at the rate of one to ten. Our nations can, upon an emergency, produce twenty thousand warriors; you may then calculate what your army ought to be. But I must not forget that I am making an Indian speech; I must therefore give you a smack of my national tongue—Tougash Getchie—Tougash Getchie; very strong man me, Captain Whiskey.'

"Captain Alliance next took the floor:

"'BROTHERS— My friend, Captain Whiskey, has made some fine flourishes about the power of his all-conquering monarch, Whiskey; and of the intrepidity of the sons of St. Patrick in defense of their beloved bottle. But we will suppose when matters are brought to the test, that if we should find ourselves unequal to the task of repelling this tremendous army, or that the great council will still persevere in their determination of imposing unequal and oppressive duties upon our whiskey, who knows but some *evil spirit* might prompt us to a separation from the Union, and call for the alliance of some more friendly nation. You know that the great nation of Kentucky have already suggested the idea to us. They are at present Mississippi mad, and we are whiskey mad; it is, therefore, hard to tell what may be the issue of such united madness. It appears as if the Kentuckians were disposed to bow the knee to the Spanish monarch, or kiss the Pope's a——e, and wear a crucifix, rather than be longer deprived of their darling Mississippi; and we might be desperate enough, rather than submit to an odious excise, or unequal taxes, to invite Prince William Henry, or some other royal pup, to take us by the hand, provided he would guarantee equal taxation, and exempt our whiskey. This would be a pleasing overture to the royal family of England; they would eagerly embrace the favorable moment, to add again to their curtailed dominions in America, to accommodate some of their numerous brood with kingdoms and principalities. We would soon find that great warrior of the lakes, Simcoe, flying to our relief, and employing those numerous legions of white and yellow savages for a very different purpose to what they have now in view. If the Kentuckians should also take it into their heads to withhold supplies from your good old warrior Wayne, who is often very near starving in the wilderness, his army must be immediately annihilated, and your great council might forever bid adieu to their territory west of the mountains. This may seem very improbable indeed; but as great wonders have happened in Europe within the course of three years past.'

"Captain Pacificus then rose, and concluded the business of the day:

"'BROTHERS—My friend Alliance has made some very alarming observations; and I confess they have considerable weight with me. A desperate people may be drove to desperate resources; but as I am of a peaceable disposition, I shall readily concur in every reasonable proposition which may have a tendency to restore tranquility, and secure our union upon the true principles of equality and justice. It is now time to know the true object of your mission; if you are messengers of peace, and come to offer us a treaty, why attempt to deliver it at the point of the bayonet. If you are only come to grant pardons for past offenses, you need not have fatigued yourselves with such extraordinary dispatch on the journey; we have not yet begged your pardon; we are not yet at the gallows or the guillotine, for you will have to catch us before you bring us there. But as I am rather more of a counselor than a warrior, I am more disposed to lay hold of the chain rather than the tomahawk. I shall therefore propose that a total suspension of all hostilities, and the *cause* thereof, shall immediately take place on both sides, until the next meeting of our great national council. If your powers are not competent to this agreement, we expect, as you are old counselors and peaceable men, that you will at least report and recommend it to our good old father who sits at the helm. We know it was his duty to make proclamation, &c. &c., but we expect every thing that can result from his prudence, humanity and benevolence, toward his fellow creatures.'

"A belt on which is inscribed 'Plenty of whiskey, without excise.'"

"A report of the proceedings of the committee appointed at the meeting at Parkinson's Ferry, on the 14th of August, 1794, to confer with the commissioners on the part of the Executive of the Union, and on the part of the Executive of Pennsylvania, on the subject of the late opposition to the laws of the Union, and violation of the peace of the State government.

On the part of the Executive of the Union.
William Bradford, Attorney General of the United States.
Joseph Yeates, Associate Judge of the Supreme Court of Pennsylvania.
Jasper Ross, Senator in the Congress of the United States.

On the part of the Executive of Pennsylvania.
Thomas M'Kean, Chief Justice of the State of Pennsylvania.

William Irvine, Representative in the Congress of the United States.

COMMITTEE OF CONFERENCE.

Westmoreland County.	Washington County.
John Kirkpatrick,	David Bradford,
George Smith,	John Marshall,
John Powers.	James Edgar.
Fayette County.	Allegheny County.
Edward Cook,	Thomas Morton,
Albert Gallatin,	John Lucas,
James Lang.	H. H. Brackenridge.

Ohio County (Virginia).
William M'Kinley, William Sutherland, John Stevenson.

"A committee having met on the 20th, proceeded to the election of a chairman, upon which Edward Cook was nominated and took his place.

"A question was made, whether the proposed conference with commissioners from the government should be private or public. It was determined that it should be private, as less liable to interruption, and as leading the commissioners from the government to give a more frank and full communication of their sentiments and intentions; and that after the preliminary arrangements, the correspondence as to what was material, would be in writing, which the committee were not at liberty to communicate to the public immediately, but to report to the committee of safety, which was to meet on the first Tuesday of September.

"It was moved and directed that two members be appointed to wait upon the commissioners on the part of the Union and of the State government, and to adjust with them the place and time of conference,

"Thomas Morton and James Edgar were appointed.

"Agreeable to arrangement, a conference took place at ten o'clock next day, and was opened by a communication on the part of the commissioners of the

Union, stating with all the solemnity due to the occasion, the extreme pain it had given to the Executive, to have heard from time to time of the deviations from the constitutional line of expressing a dislike of particular laws, to those means of violence and outrage which would lead to the having no laws at all; that in the case of the present infractions, they were solemnly called upon by the constitution to exert the force of the Union to suppress them; but that in the first instance all those lenient measures of accommodation were about to be tried, that the great reluctance of the Executive to have recourse to force, had induced it to use; that for this purpose they had been commissioned with certain powers from the Executive, in order that, if possible, short of bloodshed, submission to the laws might be obtained, and peace restored; that in the meantime the most effectual and decisive measures had been taken, that should a pacification be found impracticable, by an address to the patriotism and reason of the people, submission must be enforced, and however painful, the strength of the Union drawn out to effect it; that the militia were actually draughted, and their march delayed only until the first of September next; within which time, it behooved the people of this country to make up their minds and give answer, that the government might know what to expect.

"On the part of the commissioners from the Executive of Pennsylvania, it was stated, that it was in like manner with great pain that it had been heard by the State government, that a resistance to the laws of the Union, and violations of the public peace, had taken place within this particular jurisdiction; violations of so flagrant a nature as the invasion of personal security in a domestic habitation of an officer of government; the burning down his mansion house; reducing him to the necessity of relinquishing the country by a flight at an unreasonable hour, and by a circuitous route of many hundred miles through a wilderness; the attacking the Marshal; expelling an Associate Judge, the Prothonotary of the county, &c., and above all, invading the cabinet of government, in the intercepting of the public mail, and violating the right of the citizen by breaking the repository of his private thoughts, which ought to have been considered as sacred as in his scrutoire; that the laws of the Union were a part of the laws of Pennsylvania, and the State government, on principles of delicacy and honor, could not avoid taking a very sensible part in defending them, independent of that obligation under which it was by the constitution; but that these outrages were breaches of the municipal law, and as such the State government was under the indispensable necessity of taking notice of them, and by every necessary coercion repressing them; that for this purpose the Governor had determined to give the most prompt and decided assistance to the general government, in the requisition of militia, and had thought it proper to call the Assembly, in order to make provision for any further force that the exigency of repressing the insurrection might require; but that it must be peculiarly distressing to be under the necessity of arming against a country always heretofore respectable for its obedience to the laws; a country which had been peculiarly the object of attention with the present Executive; nevertheless, it was impossible to avoid it, unless order, by the voluntary act of the citizens, could be restored; that to effect this object the Governor had commissioned them to coöperate in their good offices with the commissioners on the part of the Union, and for this purpose, inasmuch as the consciousness of having violated the laws might lead to a further violation as a means of impunity, they were authorized, on an accommodation with commissioners of the United States, and an assurance of a disposition to preserve peace, to stipulate and engage a free and full indemnity for what was past, so far as regarded the commonwealth of Pennsylvania, and that it would give them, personally, great pleasure indeed, if by these means a return could be f .litated to this country to the bo: . of peace and happiness.

"On the part of the committee, a narrative was given of the grounds of that uneasiness and discontent which have existed in this country, and have grown up at length to that popular fury which has shown itself in the late transactions.

"To this the commissioners replied, and then proceeded to state more particularly the nature of their powers, and that certain assurances were necessary previous to their exercise, all which having been reduced to writing, the documents will speak for themselves. They also declared their expectations that the committee would declare their sense on this subject.

"It was answered by the committee, that it was their duty to hear, and report, for to this purpose were they appointed; but no power lay with them to stipulate for the people.

"It was stated on the part of the commissioners, that such was their situation, that they could not dispense with requiring from the committee, at least to recommend what opinion they themselves should form on the subject of the propositions made, as otherwise they could have no encouragement to go on, and wait the result of the opinion of the people of the country.

"This was thought reasonable, and it was agreed on the part of the committee that it should be so.

"It was then agreed that the propositions of the commissioners should be received in writing, and the conference was adjourned."

"The following letter was now received from the commissioners on the part of the Union:

"At a conference between Thomas M'Kean and William Irvine, commissioners appointed by the Governor of Pennsylvania, in behalf of said State, and Messieurs Kirkpatrick, Smith, Powers, Bradford, Marshall, Edgar, Cook, Gallatin, Lang, Brackenridge, Morton and Lucas, appointed at a meeting of committees from the several townships within the counties of Westmoreland, Washington, Fayette and Allegheny, for the purpose, in behalf of said counties, had at Pittsburgh, in the presence of three commissioners appointed by the President of the United States, August 20th, 1794:

"1st. It is insisted upon as a preliminary by the commissioners for the State, that the gentlemen conferees for the four counties, each for himself, shall sign an instrument in writing, expressing that they will at all times be obedient and submit to the laws of the State, and also of the United States of America; and that they will jointly and severally recommend the like obedience and submission to our fellow-citizens within the said counties, and moreover engage to use their utmost exertions and influence to insure the same.

"2d. It is proposed that the committee of sixty, denominated the committee of safety for the said counties, shall jointly and severally give satisfactory assurances to the commissioners of the State in an instrument in writing, signed by them, of the same import and effect with the preceding article, and that on or before the — day of August, inst.

"3d. In case the above articles are

bona fide complied with, and the people of said counties shall keep the peace, and be of good behavior until the first day of June next, the commissioners for the State, conformable to the power and authority delegated by his Excellency, Thomas Mifflin, Esq., Governor of the State of Pennsylvania, do promise an act of free and general pardon and oblivion of all treasons, insurrections, arsons, riots, and other offenses inferior to riots, committed, perpetrated, counseled, or suffered by any person or persons, complying as aforesaid, within the counties of Westmoreland, Washington, Fayette and Allegheny, since the fourteenth day of July last past, so far as the same concerns the State of Pennsylvania or the government thereof.

THOMAS M'KEAN,
WILLIAM IRVINE.
"Pittsburgh, Aug. 21, 1794."

"PITTSBURGH, Aug. 22, 1794.

"GENTLEMEN:—The committee of conference having made up their opinion and expressed it to the commissioners on the part of the Union, that it is the interest of this country that on the terms of accommodation proposed by them, there should be a submission to that law which has been the occasion of certain acts of opposition, lately said to be committed within the jurisdiction of Pennsylvania, it will of course be the opinion of this committee that acts of opposition shall cease, and they will be disposed to recommend this temper and principle to others. They will report it particularly to the committee of safety, to whom they are to make report; and they will state the reasons which have influenced themselves in being disposed to wish a general subordination to the laws of the Union. But the signing any instrument of writing will have the air of a recognizance, and of having broke the peace, or of being disposed to do it on their part, whereas in fact we expect to be considered as a body well affected to the peace of the country, and coming forward not only on behalf of those who may have violated the peace, but of the great body of the country who have organized themselves in committees in order to preserve it.

"As to what the committee of sixty may do, must remain with themselves. We shall make report to them of the proposition.

"We wish it to be understood that it will be one thing for us or them to declare our sentiments, and to support them by arguments, and another to subscribe our names to any writing in any other manner than as other public bodies by their official representative of chairman or president. We would request, therefore, that the proposition would be reconsidered, and that some other evidence of submission to the laws may be accepted from the people which may substantially have the same effect, without a form which may be misunderstood by them, and in which they may not so readily acquiesce.

"It is also our wish and expectation that the proposition of an amnesty may extend to the county of Bedford.

"It is our idea also, that it will have a good effect in reconciling the public mind to have the amnesty considered as absolute at this time, liable to be forfeited only as to its benefits, by the future violation of the laws by the individual.

By order of the committee.

EDWARD COOK, *Chairman.*

THOMAS M'KEAN and
WILLIAM IRVINE,
   Commissioners on the part of Pennsylvania."

"PITTSBURGH, Aug. 22, 1794.
"GENTLEMEN:—We have received your

answer, signed Edward Cook, chairman, of this day's date, and observe that you have in a degree confined yourselves to a subordination of the laws of the Union. These we consider as part of the laws of Pennsylvania—but independent of a breach of the laws of the United States, you cannot be insensible that the laws, the peace and dignity of the commonwealth of Pennsylvania have been more essentially violated in the county of Allegheny; and though from a knowledge of your characters and confidence in your dispositions, we rest assured of your cheerful obedience to the laws of the State, and that you will inculcate the like among our fellow-citizens, yet we would have been pleased had it been expressed.

"Your objections to signing your names respectively to your answer, we have considered, and, though the signing the name as chairman, speaker or president, in regular constituted bodies, implies the consent of the majority, which binds the whole, yet it means no more; and in the present body of twelve, one-half of the number present may not have acquiesced in the act, and yet it may be formally true. For this reason we wished for your respective signatures; or that it had been written, signed by the unanimous consent of the committee, or that you had otherwise ascertained the number.

"We have never before heard it suggested, that a person signing his name to any instrument, implying an engagement or promise to do a lawful act, had the air of a recognizance; nor did we ever mean that it could be supposed, that any gentleman of this committee was implicated in the late riots in these counties. We only wished to have the weight that your names and character would give to the effectual quieting the present uneasiness among the people.

"When we were* commissioned to the present pacific and humane service, it was not known to the Governor that any aggression of the nature you allude to had been committed in the county of Bedford, and of course our powers do not extend to them; but if no future violations of the peace shall happen on a similar occasion, it is no more than probable his Excellency will extend his pardon to what has passed since, and which may require an amnesty.

"We cannot grant a general pardon as yet, but when we shall receive reasonable assurances that the inhabitants of these counties have returned to their duty, to obedience to the laws, and that peace, order and tranquility have been restored, we shall rejoice in having the opportunity of granting it without a day's delay.

We are, gentlemen,
Your most obedient servants,
THOMAS M'KEAN,
WILLIAM IRVINE."

"PITTSBURGH, August 23, 1794.

"GENTLEMEN:—We are satisfied with the explanation given of what was intended by requiring our individual signatures to any assurance we should have given of our own disposition to preserve peace, or to conciliate that temper in others.

"We are certainly disposed to preserve peace and to recommend it to others, not only with regard to the laws of the Union, on the terms of accommodation settled with the commissioners from thence, but more especially with regard to the laws of our respective States, and Pennsylvania in particular; we are *unanimous* in declaring our resolutions to support the laws so that no impediment shall exist to the due and faithful administration of justice, and we can with the

* Printed *are* in the *Daily Advertiser.*

REPORT OF COMMITTEE OF CONFERENCE.

more confidence engage this on behalf of our fellow citizens, as at a general meeting of the representatives of townships, on the 14th of August, inst., a resolution to this effect was expressed by the unanimous voice of the meeting: and in fact we can assure you, though it may have been otherwise construed, that a great and leading object of that meeting was the establishment of peace amongst ourselves, and subordination to the State government.

By order of the committee.

EDWARD COOK, *Chairman.*
The Commissioners on behalf of the State."

"The committee deliberating on the above, the great and solemn question was considered whether we should accede or reject, in other words, whether we should have peace or a civil war.

"It was considered that a convulsion at this time might affect the great interests of the Union—that notwithstanding an unworthy debt was accumulated in the hands of moneyed men, by means of the funding system, yet the foreign debt was justly due, and also a considerable part of the domestic, for which actual service had been rendered, or value given—that it might affect the payment of these two species of debt, to countenance an opposition which might communicate itself to other branches of the revenue. That a convulsion of this nature becoming general might affect a nation of Europe struggling at this moment for life and liberty, by impeding the United States in making those remittances in payment of the debt due to them, which their situation essentially demanded; that a convulsion even in this country might affect the negotiations pending, in which our interests were essentially concerned—the free navigation of the Mississippi—the delivery of the western posts, and our protection from a frontier enemy. That it might give offense to our fellow citizens elsewhere, who might excuse a sudden outrage, but might resent a formed system undertaken without their consent; more especially as they might not yet know the local and peculiar grievances of this country, and be disposed to make a proper allowance for the consequences; that the constitutional means of remonstrance might not yet be altogether exhausted, and so it might become us still yet to persevere; that even a contest with the United States, should it be successful, must involve this country, for a time at least, in ruin.

"That for this reason, he ought to lay his hand on his heart and answer, whether he would think himself justifiable in countenancing the idea of the war; he ought to make up his mind, and be sure that on every principle he was justifiable, having a confidence not only of right, but of power also.

"For these and other reasons it was thought advisable to concede, as contained in the answer to the commissioners."
—*American Daily Advertiser*, Sept. 5, 1794.

CHAPTER IX.

REPORT OF THE COMMITTEE OF CONFERENCE LAID BEFORE THE STANDING COMMITTEE — DIFFICULTIES ENCOUNTERED — VOTE BY BALLOT — MAJORITY FOR PEACE, BUT NOT SATISFACTORY TO THE COMMISSIONERS.

THE report of the conferees, with the proposals of the commissioners, were intrusted, by common consent, to Mr. Brackenridge, to lay before the standing committee for its approbation, which was to be followed by a general amnesty. A very strong current of prejudice against him prevailed at this time among the people, on account of the part he had taken in the committee of conference. Five or six hundred copies of his report had been printed, for the purpose of being distributed. From the sudden outcry raised against the conferees as soon as it was known that they had agreed to submit, he was apprehensive of being stopped on the way and the papers taken from him; he succeeded, however, in reaching Brownsville in safety. Bradford had gone to Washington, and finding the current of obloquy very strong against the acceptance of the terms among his more violent partisans, denied having ever agreed to them, and threw the blame on Brackenridge and Gallatin. The former, who had hitherto enjoyed a solid popularity, found that popularity, for the present, greatly impaired. He was even apprehensive of personal danger; for by this time the revolutionary spirit had reached its height of effervescence; it was in fact boiling over, and the enragé thought more of giving than of receiving an amnesty. Yet, it was just at that crisis when a turn may take place equally sudden. They were exasperated at the thought of having been betrayed, as they believed, by their agents, the conferees; but they were also in that state when that feeling might re-act, if they could be convinced that the best that could have been expected had been done for their interests.

The committee met on the 28th of August, on the Monongahela, at Brownsville, then a very small village in Fayette county. Mr. Gallatin, although in his own neighborhood and less obnoxious than Mr. Brackenridge, was not free from apprehension of personal risk.

The first thing which occurred after the committee had convened, which was at an early hour, was the appearance of about seventy men, armed with rifles, who had marched from the upper part of Washington county, some twenty or thirty miles, but it is said, ignorant of the intended assemblage of the committee on that day. Their intention, it was said, was to burn the barn, mills and dwelling of Samuel Jackson, a Quaker, who had incurred odium by calling the committee a scrub congress! A circumstance curious to notice, as showing the light in which they regarded the authority established by themselves. They were dissuaded, with some difficulty, from effecting their purpose, but held the offender in custody, and now brought him before the committee for trial and sentence. The committee being organized, Col. Cook in the chair and Albert Gallatin secretary, the first business was the case of the unlucky Quaker, against whom the charge was proved by two witnesses; but there was a difficulty to know what to make of the case. In the Scripture language, it would be "speaking evil of dignities;" by the Scotch law, "leasing-making." It might be construed sedition at the common law, in the then critical state of the country, as tending to lessen the respect due to the *constituted authorities*, and evincing a bad disposition to the cause of the people.

Mr. Brackenridge, according to his usual manner in desperate cases, resorted to pleasantry, as more efficacious than any attempt to reason this armed mob out of their predisposition to lynch-law. "I recollect," said he, "to have read, that in the time of Oliver Cromwell, Lord Protector of England, when he was in the height of his glory, a person came to him and gave him information of words used by another, greatly contemptuous of his dignity, viz. 'He has said that your Highness may kiss ———.' 'You may tell him,' said Cromwell, 'that he may kiss mine!' This Quaker has called us a scrub congress; let our sentence be that he himself be called 'a scrub.'" The story of Cromwell produced a sudden, involuntary and loud laugh, and had thrown a light on the affair of the prisoner, introducing a proper sentiment with regard to him, viz. that there was more magnanimity in disregarding his expressions than in punishing them. The armed party which had arrested, took him off to give him the epithet; he got a bucket of whiskey and water to drink with them, and nothing more was heard of an affair which might have had a tragical end.*

---

* Dr. Carnahan, who was probably present, gives the following account of the affair: "Mr. Brackenridge very gravely proposed that he should be punished according to the Jewish law, 'an eye for an eye, a tooth for a tooth.' He eulogized this law as one of the most just and humane laws ever enacted; that it required injuries to be punished in kind, just in proportion to the offense—neither more nor

The report was read, and appeared not to be well received, either by the committee or the bystanders. At some sentences there was a murmur, as in a church at the response—not "Lord help us to keep this law," but "Good Lord deliver us." The people had expected a repeal of the excise law—at least a suspension of it—and were greatly disappointed. It was seen by the author of the report, that it would not do to urge its acceptance immediately. Notwithstanding his apparent acquiescence, Bradford urged the rejection of the terms without delay. He said the conditions were so degrading, that no one possessing the spirit of a freeman would hesitate a moment. It was important to give time to prepare the minds of the committee, and some of the outsiders. Findley, Gallatin, Smiley, and other persons capable of exerting an influence, were on the ground, and might go among the people. Edgar begged for a little time for considering, before they took a step that might involve their country in a civil war. In a strain of keen irony, which Bradford mistook for truth, he extolled the talents, learning, penetration and courage of the eloquent gentleman. He said that Mr. Bradford could see, by intuition, into the most difficult subjects, and when he saw the path of duty plain before him, he had the skill and courage adequate to every consequence. For his part, he was slow of apprehension; he could not, at once, like the gentleman who urged an immediate decision, know what might be said against the motion. He wanted a little time to think the subject over, and perhaps he might be brought to see his way clear to follow the gentleman, as his leader. There might be others in the same state of mind with himself, and he appealed to the gentleman's acknowledged candor and liberality, to give his weaker brethren a little time to think of

less. He also told an anecdote respecting the manner in which Oliver Cromwell punished a man who had used insulting language toward him; and although this was the most effective part of his speech, I shall not repeat it. 'My proposition,' continued Mr. Brackenridge, 'is, that we punish this man according to the Jewish law, and after the manner of that illustrious republican, Oliver Cromwell. And whereas it has been proved that Samuel Jackson has called us, the honorable the representatives of the four western counties of Pennsylvania, ' the scrub congress,' I move that we pay him in his own coin—that we call him ' a scrub,' and that he be known by the name of ' scrub Samuel,' as long as the world lasts, and then we shall be even with him.' This motion was carried by acclamation in the midst of a tremendous roar, in which the riflemen heartily joined. Jackson apologized, and ordered a couple of buckets of whiskey to be brought out, took a drink with the riflemen, and they parted good friends." The apearance of the riflemen, although not premeditated, had its effect on the committee, and was one cause of the fear, after this, over the members.

the subject; that unanimity in so important a crisis was greatly to be desired. It was moved to adjourn until the next morning. When this took place Bradford called out the Washington members, and they retired to consult apart.

Mr. Brackenridge had crossed the river to a farm-house to pass the night, and in order to be out of the way if any violence had been meditated, which he thought not improbable in the present excited state of the assemblage; that is, of the committee and outsiders. "For," says the author of the "Incidents," "what is popularity at such time? It is but the turning of the hand up or down, from the height of favor to the lowest point of obloquy and persecution. Was there any man in Pennsylvania more popular than Dickinson, at the commencement of the American Revolution? He was said to be opposed to a declaration of independence, and became obnoxious. James Wilson was at the height of his political power amongst the people; but he had disapproved of the form of constitution they had adopted in the commonwealth, and they were about to murder him in his own house. I possessed, up to this present time, the best kind of popularity—a popularity obtained after much obloquy, which had been suffered to correct itself through a series of years—a popularity obtained, doubtless, by sailing a little with the popular gale, at least not opposing it; but chiefly by a steady and upright demeanor in my profession. The popular mind, though passionate, is generous, and if it becomes sensible that it has wronged a man, it will repair the wrong. I knew that a breath on the subject of the excise law would put it to a temporary death. However, I had no thought of the loss of popularity, but so far as it would produce personal danger on the ground. Gallatin was in his own county, and yet was not without fear, and with reason."

The appearance of the seventy men armed, and with a lawless design, gave good reason for uneasiness; for no one could tell how far this spirit extended with others, or what direction it might take. There had been, during the evening, much warmth among the Bradford party, and even some talked of offering violence to the opposite leaders. Mr. Brackenridge crossed back early in the morning, and met Gallatin, James Lang and others of the committee of conference, who were much alarmed at the bad feeling which prevailed. Strong terms were applied to Mr. Brackenridge for having employed his talents as a lawyer to persuade the committee of twelve. Bribery was insinuated; in fact, such a disposition seemed to prevail, that he began to doubt the propriety of proceeding any farther in the business, as it was not understood that the conferees were to run the risk of their own lives in recommending to the people their interests. But, as Gallatin was disposed to try it, he determined to run the same risk. It now became a question who should lead off in the appeal to the exasperated people. Mr. Brackenridge proposed that James Edgar* should open the way; but he declined for some reason or other, and it was therefore assigned to Gallatin.

The meeting having convened, with a formidable number of outsiders —many of them from the Mingo Creek settlement, the hot-bed of the insurrection—Gallatin addressed the chair in a speech of several hours, and, contrary to expectation, was listened to with great attention, not the slightest interruption or disturbance occurring during its delivery; a circumstance which, perhaps, goes to show that there was more appearance of violence than reality. The speeches, of which we are about to give a mere naked outline, were no holiday declamations, but true eloquence brought forth by a real occasion, where the object was to sway the minds of a reluctant audience, and to prevail upon them to adopt the measures proposed by the speakers. It was unlike the case of those modern "stump speeches," as they are called, where the design is to amuse, or produce a general impression, and not to carry a distinct proposition by means of argument and persuasion. Such occasions rarely occur, unless it be on jury trials.

Gallatin began by tracing, in the clearest manner, the difference between the case of the people in the western counties and the cause of the American Revolution. In the present case, no principle had been violated; the West had been represented in making the law; it was their act by their own agents, and not the mandate of one assuming a false supremacy. He then entered into a minute examination of the law itself, and the alterations it had undergone from time to time, to accommodate it to the convenience of the people. The amount of tax had been reduced, and the mode of collecting it changed; and there was just reason to expect that the law would be repealed altogether. Every effort would be made to effect the repeal, and there was a well-founded hope of success.

---

* The following is the characteristic notice of this gentleman, by Mr. Brackenridge, in the "Incidents:" "He was an Associate Judge of Washington county and a leader in the Presbyterian Church of the western country; had been a Presbyter or Elder from his youth; had been a member of committees in the early period of the Revolution, and of legislative assemblies or deliberative committees, ever since. His head was prematurely gray; his face was thin and puritanic, like the figures of the old republicans of the Long Parliament. He was a man of sense, and not destitute of eloquence."

He explained the concessions of the United States commissioners, as set forth in the report of the conferees, in relation to relinquishment of arrearages, as comprehended under the words, "beneficial arrangements will be made."

He proceeded to discuss, very fully, the local and existing reasons of complaint against the government. He spoke of the prevailing Indian war, the obtaining the posts, and the navigation of the Mississippi, through the negotiations of the Federal government, and which it would be impossible for this small portion of the Union to accomplish, of itself.

He represented the mischiefs that had been done and were likely to follow, if the people persisted in their opposition. It would have the effect of weakening the spirit of liberty itself; for ultimately they would be compelled to yield. An example may be seen in the State of Massachusetts—formerly the most democratic, now the most aristocratic—since the insurrection in that State was put down by military force. Certain it is, that illegal opposition, when reduced, has a tendency to make the people abject and the government tyrannic. He then represented the injury done to the spirit of liberty throughout the Union, and the injury to the republican cause throughout the world.

He demonstrated the superiority of the structure of our republic over all that had been, and denounced the atrocity of shaking or undermining so fair a fabric. Then followed a clear and conspicuous view of the comparative strength of the Union in a contest with this country, and the folly of looking for aid from Spain or England, or any of the adjoining States. Next followed an estimate of what would be lost and what would be gained, even by success.

Finally, the complicated ignominy and ruin on all these principles which would attend the persisting in this course of opposition, when there was no longer the slightest reason for it.*

---

* Mr. Gallatin was a native of Geneva, in Switzerland. He was of a good family, received an excellent general education, and came, in early youth, to the United States; that is, during the Revolutionary War, in which he took some part. He excelled as a mathematician and financier, but was not bred to any particular profession. His talent for public speaking was developed by circumstances. Without being eloquent or animated, he commanded attention by his clear and forcible reasoning and extensive information. He was at first opposed to the Federal constitution, and it is believed that his mind was cramped by the narrow confederacy in which he was born, so as to disqualify him, in some measure, for conceiving the possibility of one adapted to the vast surface of the United States of America. In consequence of this, he was rather opposed to the extension of our territory. His brilliant political career belongs to our national history.

Mr. Brackenridge followed Mr. Gallatin, under the disadvantage of a subject on which the prominent topics had been elaborately and very ably discussed. Gallatin had been didactic and deliberate, though animated. Mr. Brackenridge entered more directly into the question to be determined, and was more vehement and impassioned, addressing himself chiefly to their consciences, their interests and their fears. It may be remarked, that the speakers all seemed to take it for granted that the question to be decided was one of peace or war, as it would be the necessary consequence of the acceptance or refusal of the terms offered by the commissioners.

He began by asking, what end did they propose to attain by refusing to accept the propositions held out by the commissioners? Do you not know that the consequences will be war? Are you prepared for war? Have you seriously considered the responsibility of such an act? Can you make war upon the Federal government, yet remain part of it? No; you must declare independence; and not only of the United States, but you must also separate from the State. Have you reflected upon this necessity? Where are your armies, your supplies of military stores, your treasury? You have none of these; and yet, you harbor the idea of going to war with fifteen States, possessing them all; and with experienced officers and Washington at their head!

Do you expect to obtain a repeal of the law by war, and such a war? The idea is madness. There can be but one alternative—we must overthrow the government, or it must overthrow us; and is there any man so visionary as to think that in the end you will not be compelled to yield, whatever small advantages you may obtain in the beginning? And even if success were possible, you cannot, as moral men, reconcile it to your consciences. You owe a part of the public debt contracted in the war of Independence; can you quit the confederacy without discharging your share of that debt? The state has public lands in the western countries, have we any right to deprive her of these? Have we any right to shake off the burdens of the present Indian war, in which the government is engaged for us? We can do none of these things without a disregard to common honesty as well as patriotism. Neither a citizen of any community, nor any portion of that community, can honestly abandon it, so long as there are obligations yet remaining to be fulfilled. He is a deserter who quits his country under such circumstances.

But where is the imagination so wild as to hope for success against such odds? It is not in your power to secede. The example of success would be fatal to the confederacy. It cannot be permitted. The whole force of the nation will be brought against you. Suppose that, by seizing the passes of the mountains, you give a check to the first fifteen thousand men, double the number will return. The passes of the mountains will be taken and fortified. You know the firmness of Washington; his duty will require him to call forth the whole energies and power of the nation, and it must subdue us in the end. What will be your condition then, and what your sufferings in the mean time? Your country laid waste, your towns in ashes, and your bones and those of your sons bleaching on many a field of battle! The Indians defeated Harmar, then St. Clair, and are now driven into the lake by Wayne! Can you maintain a war of years against numbers and the purse? Can you even count upon a perfect union and fidelity among yourselves? This country is new and thinly settled, and every part is not equally in concert in the cause. And you will blindly persevere in an opposition which can lead to nothing but war—civil war, the most horrible of all wars. You are even now standing on the brink of a precipice!

Let us suppose the attempt at separation successful, what can you gain? Its fruits would be poverty, dependence and degradation. You would be shut out from the sea on the east; the mouth of the Mississippi would still be closed to you; and on the north-west the British would still retain the posts, as a refuge for the Indians. If the whole force of the Union has not been able to accomplish the two last, how can you expect that it will be effected by a small, disjointed portion of that Union? Do you count upon the aid of England or Spain? This would be like leaning on a broken staff. You would be compelled to pay for such aid by servile dependence; and have you so soon forgotten the struggles you went through in the war of Independence? War is a dreadful state under any circumstances, but more especially civil war—brother against brother, father against son, and nearest neighbors either at daggers drawn or living in fear of each other. Do you think all are sincere who are clamoring for war? Some wish to be thought brave, some have no experience of the sufferings incident to a state of war, others join the cry from the mere force of example, and because they are wanting in the moral courage to think and act for themselves. Let the voice of the majority be for peace, and you will soon find all on that side. I have my eye on men in this very committee, and could name them, who have privately avowed themselves for peace, and yet affect to be for war from a fear of expressing their real sentiments. These very men are desirous of getting out of the present difficulties, almost on any terms; and after what has passed, almost any terms short of life should be accepted.

The outrages which have been committed have been wanton, grievous, useless. In construction of law, they amount to treason. And yet, through the benevolence of Washington, a way has been opened for reconciliation and for oblivion of the past, which you can accept without humiliation or dishonor. Those acts were committed, it is true, under the influence of passion, but they were wrong, they were criminal; and now that there has been a time for reflection, this senseless and aimless opposition should cease.

The committee of conference, in its negotiations with the commissioners, has been careful to stipulate, that in accepting the amnesty you surrender no legal and constitutional right to seek for a repeal of the excise law, by constitutional means.* When the hunter is on a wrong track, his course is to go back and take another start. The amnesty will leave you where you were before these unlawful acts were committed; you may then start fair again in efforts better directed and better deserving success.

We are destined to be a great, flourishing and powerful nation, if we are only true to ourselves. Nothing can prevent it but such dissensions and disorders as we have recently witnessed. The prospects of this confederacy are glorious, and if unfortunately we have done any thing to mar these prospects, let us hasten to repair the error. I have, I confess it candidly, felt myself, like others, at a loss what course to pursue, until the offer of amnesty was so generously tendered by the President. The way is now clear; nothing but obstinacy and slavery to unbridled passion can induce any man to hesitate. I own I have regarded the feelings of the country with partiality of heart, and would make every reasonable allowance for the prevailing dislike to the law, on account of its inequality and hardship. I have made excuses in my own mind for their breaking out in open acts of violence. I have attributed these to wrong judgment in not distinguishing between the right of opinion and the right to act. I was impressed with the reflection that the disapprobation of the law, having been general in the country and expressed by almost every one, no man could tell how far, by words, he might have contributed to that current of sentiment, which, swelling beyond the constitutional bounds of

---

* Mr. Gallatin said, in his evidence: "I spoke but two words—amnesty and repeal." The word amnesty was first spoken by Mr. Brackenridge. It is surprising to find, in one of the fine reasoning powers of Mr. Gallatin, the strange inconsistency of uniting the two words, *amnesty* and *repeal*. This would be, in fact, offering an amnesty to the government on the condition of repeal! It is strange that he did not see this, after the attempt to compel the repeal by force of arms; it was for the *government* to hold out *a pardon, on condition of submission.*

remonstrance, has at length broken out into open acts of insurrection. Every man should feel a disposition to repair the mischief that has been done, and use his endeavors to save those who have rashly been drawn into the commission of acts not previously contemplated—acts in violation of the peace and safety of society—acts destructive of his own happiness. It is but natural that my feelings should be enlisted for those among whom I have resided for so many years, and with whom I have been so often connected in business and social intercourse, or in professional relations. My attachments are all here; and I have no higher aim than to save my fellow-citizens by giving the best advice in my power. If I, who have not participated, directly or indirectly, in any of these acts which have brought our country to its present crisis, am willing to embrace the amnesty, surely those who have been actually implicated well may.

When I was the first to suggest an amnesty, and application to the clemency of the Executive, I had little thought it would have been tendered to us in the manner it has been. I have uniformly disapproved, whenever a suitable and proper opportunity presented itself, of those unfortunate doings which require the act of oblivion on the part of the government, and I disapprove of them now. No man who is not blinded by passion can approve them. This is my last effort, and my last advice to you is to accept of the proffered amnesty. Having done my duty as a citizen, I am determined to withdraw for the future from all intermingling in these affairs; conceiving myself discharged, in honor and conscience, from all farther participation in these negotiations.

The acceptance of the amnesty, cheerfully, and if possible unanimously, is the only course left to save the country, whose march of prosperity has already been much impeded by these events. Notwithstanding the causes of complaint, it was beginning to improve; farms were opened, buildings were erected, and lands were improving in value. We now see the reverse of this picture. A depression has followed upon this general state of insecurity. Instead of an accession of population, many are endeavoring to sell their lands for the purpose of going farther west—to some country where law and order still prevail. No country can flourish where person and property are insecure. Every man has felt the effect already in the depreciation of his farm or his house. I don't value what property I possess at more than half what it was worth before the late disturbances. I give it, then, as my last and most earnest advice, that you accept the act of oblivion, so generously tendered to you by the President of the United States, and presented, as it is, in a form so acceptable by the commissioners, with whom our committee was appointed to confer.

James Edgar followed in a speech of some length and solemnity of manner; his speech was replete with good sense, and well adapted to the persons to whom it was addressed. From the respectful attention given to these speeches for at least ten hours, great hopes were entertained that they had produced a favorable effect.

Bradford now rose to speak; he had been urged by his followers, who besought and threatened. What, said they, will you suffer Brackenridge and Gallatin to run us down? Thus urged on, and contrary to his engagements to the commissioners, he broke out in one of his most violent fits of declamation, and in the Sempronius style, declaring himself "still for war." In allusion to the concluding part of Mr. Brackenridge's speech, he said, "Dastardly to talk of property, when liberty is at stake; we will defeat the first army that attempts to cross the mountains; we will seize their arms and baggage, and then organize an army that will prevent any further attempt." "Not so easy, either," said one of the outsiders—a Col. Crawford, an old Indian fighter, who had some experience of war, which Bradford had not. Bradford continued, in a speech or declamation, in favor of war, and even used the word *independence*, in his boasting harangue, perhaps the only instance in which it was spoken by the enemies of peace during the insurrection, but which must be regarded as mere idle boasting. He sought to rekindle the flame of the violent, while the fears of many, and the conscious guilt of others, appeared to counterbalance the sound and wholesome advice they had just listened to from the other speakers.

Gallatin, after some remarks, now moved to take the vote on the propositions of the commissioners. Objections were made to taking any vote at all. The question was put, shall a vote be taken? It was determined in the negative, the committee of conference, only, rising. It was then moved to take a vote by ballot on the propositions, as it was presumed that there might be a reluctance among the members of the standing committee, to let their sentiments be known. It was moved, shall a vote by ballot be taken? But this was also negatived, the committee of conference alone voting.

Here was a moment of delicacy indeed. The refusal to take a vote was tantamount to a rejection of the propositions; and what would be the consequence? Measures must have been taken instantly to prepare for war. Bradford would have come forward with his specification of arms, ammunition and funds, in which he had been baffled at Parkinson's Ferry. Brackenridge and Gallatin would probably have been arrested on the spot. For the example of the French terrorists was then in the public mind, especially with Bradford, who had caught not a little of the revolutionary spirit of France.

Gallatin, at this critical juncture, proposed to take a vote by ballot, not to be made a part of the answer to the commissioners, but merely "to know our own minds." There was unwillingness at first to agree even to this, for every man was afraid that the handwriting of his ballot would be known, and it might transpire how he voted.

In this unpleasant dilemma, which so singularly displays the despotism of public opinion in a democratic community, a member of the committee of sixty (whose name has not been preserved,) rising, and having a scrap of paper in his fingers with the word *yea* written on one part and *nay* on the other, held it up, and proposed that sixty such scraps, with the words yea and nay, written in the same manner, should be prepared by *the secretary*, and a scrap given to each of the members; and let every one divide his scrap into two parts, with the yea on the one part and the nay on the other, and let him chew or tear the nay or the yea, as he might think proper, and put the other piece into the hat held by the *secretary*. When these were drawn out, it would be seen what the private sense of the committee was, without the possibility of knowing how another voted. This was thought safe, and adopted; thus virtually, and to all intents and purposes, taking a vote by ballot. Perhaps the curiosity to know where the majority existed, was the principal inducement to the adoption of this singular plan.

It was curious to observe the care with which every one divided his ticket so as to conceal his vote. All having now voted, and the tickets drawn out, there appeared thirty-four yeas and twenty-three nays.* Here was certainly a very respectable majority, and verified the declaration of Mr. Brackenridge, in his speech, that there were members who privately entertained a different opinion from that which they publicly avowed. And yet it is surprising, that after the masterly reasoning and powerful appeals of Brackenridge, Gallatin and Edgar, there should be so many votes in the negative. The vote was, notwithstanding, decisive, and suddenly changed the face of affairs. The supposed dreaded majority was now proved to be a minority, and the fearful influence of that supposed majority was gone. The mountain, if it may be so called, was enraged, but it was the rage of disappointment, despair and impotence. The friends of order were suddenly relieved from the reign of terror, and began to exhibit a bolder countenance. The clouds of insurrection were broken, and began

* Six afterward declared that they had voted *nay* by mistake; the vote then stood forty against seventeen.

to scatter; the mutterings of the thunder were still heard, but it was of the retiring, and not of the coming storm. Bradford stood appalled; his power and influence were at an end; he withdrew from the place almost immediately, and was not heard of again until some time after, when he was one of the first to hasten to seize the horns of the altar, or in other words, to take the benefit of the amnesty, in the midst of his deserted followers, who now cried out, "Dagon, how art thou fallen!" But being excepted, on account of his last act, and perhaps on account of his robbery of the mail, he took to the river and escaped, leaving a lesson to after-times of the folly of empty popularity.

After a short recess, the standing committee again met in the afternoon; in the meantime, the outsiders, who had manifested the most decided disapprobation of the vote, had, for the greater part, withdrawn, leaving the committee almost alone. The opposition had no leader in the committee. The resolution approving the report was adopted without objection, and even without a division, and was certified to the commissioners. It was now proposed to choose a new committee of conference, in order to see if some modifications of the terms, and prolongation of the time, might not be obtained; but nothing was hinted as to unwillingness to submit, or of opposing the excise law, after the passage of the resolution declaring it to be the interest of the people to adopt the report of the first conferees. These conferees could not, with propriety, oppose the new motion, and were no doubt pleased with this fair opportunity of withdrawing from their thankless office. Yet they were convinced that it was idle to hope for better terms than those which had been obtained, or even a desirable modification of them, as they had been assured by the commissioners that they had already gone to the full extent of their powers in favor of the people. They had at the same time privately intimated, that the alarming intelligence from the east of the mountains rendered any delay out of the question. It thus appears that the state of mind of the people in the eastern counties, whether exaggerated or not, had an unfortunate influence on the disposition of the commissioners toward those in the west; and it is very possible, that but for this, the severe terms afterward exacted would not have been imposed.

The friends of peace in the committee, who had been afraid of expressing their sentiments, were now emboldened in each neighborhood, and six of them, after the balloting, endeavored to exculpate themselves from the suspicion of having voted in the negative, by asserting that the *nay* had been given by mistake. The more timid, or those who had been most violent on former occasions, but had been convinced in the committee, were still afraid to avow themselves openly, through fear of their neighbors, or from unwillingness to incur the charge of inconsistency. Yet there was no instance of any insult or violence offered to any one for his vote. The feeling which showed itself in the committee after the removal of the restraint of fear, was now visible over the whole country. The violent were awed, and the lovers of peace and order ceased to be afraid to speak out; and this state of things continued rapidly to gain ground—public meetings were called every where in favor of submission, until the approach of the army, when all appearance of opposition had not only ceased, but was changed into general alarm for their own safety.

The standing committee adjourned without day, and the resolution, which was expected to be followed by a general amnesty, was certified to the commissioners, accompanied by a letter from the chairman, explaining the appointment of the new committee of conference.

"At a meeting of the standing committee of the western counties, held at Brownsville on the 28th and 29th of August, 1794,

"The report of the committee appointed to confer with the commissioners of government being taken into consideration, the following resolutions were adopted to wit:

"1. *Resolved*, That in the opinion of this committee, it is the interest of the people of the country to accede to the proposals made by the commissioners on the part of the United States.

"2. *Resolved*, That a copy of the foregoing resolution be transmitted to the commissioners.

(A true copy.)   EDWARD COOK, *Chairman.*
ALBERT GALLATIN, *Secretary."*

Letter of the Chairman.

"BROWNSVILLE, Aug. 29, 1794.

"GENTLEMEN:—Difficulties having arisen with us, we have thought it necessary to appoint a committee to confer with you, in order to procure, if possible, some further time, in order that the people may have leisure to reflect on their true situation.

I am, gentlemen, your obedient servant,   EDWARD COOK.

"P. S.—Inclosed, you have a copy of the resolutions on that subject.

"The Honorable the Commissioners of the United States."

The new committee of conference was composed of the following persons: John Probst, Robert Dickey, John Nesbit, David Phillips, John M'Clelland, George Wallace, Samuel Wilson and John Marshall.

It is much to be regretted that the measures so wisely devised by Washington were not accepted, at once and unanimously, without any further proceeding in the vain hope of improving the conditions, but which could have no other effect than to give the appearance of a reluctant assent, and make it the justification for imposing terms more severe. If this had been done, it is probable that there would have been a general amnesty according to the stipulation and agreement between the first conferees and the commissioners, and the army would have been disbanded. At least, this ought to have been the case, unless the administration, entertaining the views imputed to the Secretary of the Treasury by Findley, had determined that the army should march in any event.

The commissioners took a different view of the subject. In their opinion, the acceptance was imperfect and unsatisfactory in the committee, on account of the opposition there and the want of unanimity; that the reign of terror which deterred the peaceful citizens from accepting, still prevailed; that it prevailed to such a degree as to be incompatible with the free, full and liberal terms offered by the government. The author of this work cannot but regard that view of the subject as unfortunate, and with the highest respect for the eminent talents and unimpeachable intentions of the commissioners, erroneous. This has been attributed to the Secretary of the Treasury by Findley, whose leaning toward a strong government was well known; but that he ever entertained or expressed the sentiment imputed to him, that the new government could not be considered as permanently established until it made itself felt by physical force, the author is unwilling to believe, without more positive evidence than he has yet seen. He is rather disposed to attribute this determination on the part of the commissioners to the distance between the scene of action and the seat of government, and the great difficulty of knowing the true state of things on the east as well as on the south-west side of the mountains. It is impossible, at this day, to form any just idea of the state of communication at that period, between portions of country between which all barriers have been removed. The author firmly believes that if Washington could have been on the spot to judge with his own eyes, the insurrection might have ended differently. The great body of the western people were influenced by an honest belief that they had been treated unjustly, and were neither depraved nor disloyal. It could not in reason be expected, that after so much excitement, the terms of submission, however reasonable, would be at once accepted, and without some appearance of reluctance. The opposition could not be quelled instantaneously, without, at the same time, breaking down the spirit of a free people, and with it all the nobility and worth fitting them to be the citizens of a free country. The *substantial adoption* of the terms, the author cannot but think, was a sufficient fulfillment of the compact between the conferees and the commissioners. A bare majority ought to have sufficed, even if the commissioners had any right to go behind the resolution to inquire how it was passed. The opposition having been once defeated, we know that it is in the nature of things, in such assemblies, for the majority to grow stronger and the minority weaker. All that was asked was the further favor of a short delay, but not as a condition attached to the acceptance of the terms; and the only effect of the denial would be to leave the resolution in full force, as if nothing of the kind had accompanied it. This subject will be again adverted to.

On the 1st of September, a few days after the adjournment of the standing committee, the new committee appeared in Pittsburgh and addressed the following note to the commissioners on the part of the United States:

"PITTSBURGH, Sept. 1st, 1794.

"GENTLEMEN:—The committee appointed by the committee of safety at Redstone, the 28th of August last, to confer with the commissioners of the United States, and State of Pennsylvania, and agreeable to the resolutions of said committee, do request:

"1st. That the said commissioners give an assurance on the part of the general government, to an indemnity to all persons as to the arrearages of excise, that have not entered their stills to this date.

"2d. Will the commissioners aforesaid give to the 11th day of October next, to take the sense of the people at large, of the four counties west of Pennsylvania, and that part of Bedford west of the Allegheny mountains, and the Ohio county in Virginia, whether they will accede to the resolution of the said commissioners, as stated at large in the conference with the committee of conference met at Pittsburgh the 21st day of August last.

"By order of the committee.   JOHN M'CLELLAND.

"The Honorable the Commissioners on the part of the United States, and of the State of Pennsylvania."

To this ill-concocted letter, the commissioners returned the following reply:

"PITTSBURGH, Sept. 1st, 1794.

"GENTLEMEN:—We have received your letter of this date; and as time presses, have determined to give it an immediate answer, although we shall be prevented thereby from making so full and correct a reply as the importance of the subject requires.

"In our correspondence with the late committee of conference, we detailed those assurances of submission to the laws, which would have been deemed full and satisfactory, and which were necessary to the exercise of the powers vested in us. This detail was minutely settled in the conference, with a sub-committee of that body. From a desire on our part to accommodate, and to render the proposals as unexceptionable as possible, they were altered and modified at their request, till being superior to all exception, they received the unanimous approbation of those gentlemen.

"The detail thus settled, required from the standing committee assurances of their explicit determination to submit to the laws of the United States; that they would not directly or indirectly oppose the execution of the acts for raising a revenue upon distilled spirits and upon stills; and that they would support as far as the laws require, the civil authority in affording protection due to all officers and other citizens. These assurances have not been given. On the contrary, we learn with emotions, difficult to be repressed, that in the meeting of the committee, at Redstone, resistance to the laws and open rebellion *against the United States were publicly advocated, and that two-fifths of that body, representing twenty-three townships, totally disapprove the proposals, and preferred the convulsions of a civil contest to the indulgence offered them by their country.* Even the members composing the majority, although by a secret and undistinguishing vote they expressed an opinion that it was the interest of the people to accede to the proposals, did not themselves accede to them, nor give the assurances, nor make the recommendations explicitly required of them. They have adjourned without day, and the terms are broken on their part.

"Our expectations have been unfortunately disappointed; the terms required have not been acceded to. You have been sent hither to demand new terms; and it is now necessary for us to decide whether we will return home, or enter into other arrangements.

"Upon reflection, we are satisfied that the President of the United States, while he demands satisfactory proofs that there will be in future a perfect submission to the laws, does not wish the great body of the people should be finally concluded by the conduct or proceedings of that committee; and if the people themselves will make the declaration required of the standing committee, and give satisfactory proofs of a general and sincere determination to obey the laws, the benefits offered may still be obtained by those individuals who shall explicitly avow their submission as hereinafter mentioned.

"It is difficult to decide in what manner the said declarations and determinations of the people to submit peaceably, should be taken and ascertained. We have thought much on this subject, and are fully satisfied that a decision by ballot will be wholly unsatisfactory, and that it will be easy to produce by these means an apparent but delusive unanimity. It is, therefore, necessary that the determination of every individual be publicly announced. In a crisis, and on a question like this, it is dishonorable to temporize. Every man ought to declare himself openly, and give his assurances of submission in a manner that cannot be questioned hereafter. If a civil contest must finally take place, the government ought to know not only the numbers, but the names of the faithful citizens, who may otherwise be in danger of being confounded with the guilty. It therefore remains with you to say, whether you will recommend such a mode of procedure, and will immediately arrange with us the manner in which the sense of the people may be publicly taken, and written assurances of submission obtained, within the time already limited. We desire an explicit and speedy answer in writing.

"You request us to 'give assurances on the part of the United States, that an indemnity shall be granted, as to the arrears of excise to all persons that have not entered their stills to this date.' If it were proper to remit all arrears of duty, we cannot conceive why those who have entered their stills should not receive a similar indulgence with those who have refused to do so; nor why you demand peculiar favors for the opposers of the acts, while you abandon those who have complied to the strictness of the laws.

"We have gone on that subject as far as we think advisable. The clause was introduced at the request of the late committee of conference; and even the style of expressing it was settled with them. We, therefore, have nothing more to add to that subject.

"You require also that time be given until the 11th day of October, in order to ascertain the sense of the people. That is wholly inadmissible. On the day of the conference, the time allowed was deemed sufficiently long; and we are sorry to perceive that delay only tends to produce an indisposition to decide. There are strong reasons, obvious to a reflecting mind, against prolonging the time a single hour. Nothing is required but a declaration of that duty which every man owes to his country, and every man before this day must have made up his mind on the subject. Six weeks have already elapsed since the ordinary exercise of civil authority has been forcibly suppressed, the officers of government expelled, and the persons and property of well disposed citizens exposed to the outrages of popular violence. The protection which is due to peaceable citizens, the respect which every government owes to itself, and the great interests of the United States, demand that the authority of the laws be quickly restored. To this we may add that the militia (which, by late orders from the President, have been increased to 15,000 men, including 1,500 riflemen from Virginia, under the command of Major General Morgan,) have received orders to assemble; and we cannot undertake to promise that their march will be long suspended. All possible means to inform, to conciliate and to recall our fellow-citizens to their duty, have been used. That their infatuation still continues, we regret, but are persuaded that further moderation and forbearance will but increase it.

"If the whole country shall declare its determination peaceably to submit, the hopes of the Executive will be fulfilled; but if a part of the inhabitants of the survey shall persist in their unjustifiable resistance to the lawful authority of the United States, it is not the intention of the government to confound the innocent with the guilty; you may therefore assure the friends of order and the laws that they may rely upon promptly receiving all the protection the government can give; and that effectual measures will be taken to suppress and punish the violence of those individuals who may endeavor to obstruct the execution of the laws, and to involve their country in a scene of calamity, the extent and seriousness of which it is impossible to calculate.

"It is easy to perceive, from the whole scope of this letter, that no part of it is addressed to the gentlemen of Ohio county, Virginia.

JAMES ROSS,
JASPER YEATES,
WM. BRADFORD.

"Messrs. Dickey, Probst, Nesbit, Marshall, Phillips, M'Clelland, Wallace and Wilson."

The conferees replied as follows :

"PITTSBURGH, Sept. 2, 1794.

"GENTLEMEN:—We have received your letter of yesterday, and after having duly considered its contents, we are all of opinion that it is the interest and duty of the people of the western counties of Pennsylvania to submit to the execution of the laws of the United States, and of the State of Pennsylvania, upon the principles and terms stated by the commissioners; and we will heartily recommend this measure to them. We are also ready to enter into the detail with you of fixing and ascertaining the time, place and manner of collecting the sense of the people upon this very momentous subject.

"Signed by the unanimous order of the committee.

JOHN M'CLELLAND.

"To the Commissioners of the United States and of the State of Pennsylvania."

Thus it appears that the new committee, which does not seem remarkable for ability, instead of obtaining better, very gladly accepted worse terms than those presented by the report of the first committee of conference. It is proper to remark here, that they do not refer these terms to the standing committee, which had ceased to exist; all they had authority to do, was to request some favorable modification of the conditions proposed to the first committee. If they failed in this, the only question that arose would be as to the fact of rejection or acceptance of the propositions by the standing committee. On this question, we have taken issue with the commissioners. We contend that the vote was a sufficient acceptance—and there can be no question, but that the arrangement entered into with the new committee was totally unauthorized, and cannot be regarded in the light of a compact, as in the case with the first committee of conference. The following is the record of the new conference :

"At a conference between the commissioners from the United States and the State of Pennsylvania, on the one part, and Messrs. Probst, Dickey, Nesbit, Marshall, Phillips, M'Clelland, Wallace and Wilson, conferees, appointed by the standing committee at Brownsville, (Redstone Old Fort,) on the 28th and 29th days of August, 1794, it was agreed, that the assurances required from the citizens in the fourth survey of Pennsylvania, should be given in writing, and their sense ascertained in the following manner:

"That the citizens of the said survey, (Allegheny county excepted,) of the age of eighteen years and upward, be required to assemble on Thursday, the 11th instant, in their respective townships, at the usual place for holding township meetings; and that between the hours of twelve and seven, in the afternoon of the same day, any two or more of the members of the meeting who assembled at Parkinson's Ferry on the 14th ultimo, resident in the township, or a justice of the peace of said township, do openly propose to the people assembled, the following questions, 'Do you now engage to submit to the laws of the United States, and

TERMS OF SUBMISSION.

that you will not hereafter, directly or indirectly, oppose the execution of the acts for raising the revenue upon distilled spirits and stills? And do you also undertake to support, as far as the laws require, the civil authority in affording the protection due to all officers and other citizens? Yea, or nay?'

"That the said citizens, resident in Allegheny county, shall meet in their respective election districts on the said day, and proceed in the same manner as if they were assembled in townships.

"That a minute of the number of yeas and nays be made immediately after ascertaining the same.

"That a written or printed declaration of such engagement be signed by all those who vote in the affirmative, of the following tenor, to wit:

"'I do solemnly* promise henceforth to submit to the laws of the United States; that I will not, directly nor indirectly, oppose the execution of the acts for raising a revenue on distilled spirits and stills; and that I will support, as far as the law requires, the civil authority in affording the protection due to all officers and other citizens.'

"This shall be signed in the presence of the said members or justices of the peace, attested by him or them, and lodged in his or their hands.

"That the said persons, so proposing the questions stated as aforesaid, do assemble at the respective county court houses, on the 13th inst., and do ascertain and make report of the numbers of those who voted in the affirmative in the respective townships or districts, and of the number of those who voted in the negative; together with their opinion whether there be such a general submission of the people in their respective counties, that an office of inspection may be immediately and safely established therein.

"That the said report, opinion and written or printed declarations, be transmitted to the commissioners, or any one of them, at Uniontown, on or before the 16th instant.

"If the said assurances shall be *bona fide* given in the manner prescribed, the commissioners on the part of the United States do promise and engage in the manner following, to wit:

"1. No prosecution for any treason or other indictable offense against the United States, committed within the fourth survey of Pennsylvania, before the 22d day of August last, shall be commenced or prosecuted before the 10th day of July next, against any person who shall, within the time limited, subscribe such assurance and engagement as aforesaid, and perform the same.

"2. On the said 10th day of July next there shall be granted a general pardon and oblivion of all the said offenses, excluding therefrom, nevertheless, every person who shall refuse or neglect to subscribe such assurance and engagement in manner aforesaid, or shall, after such subscription, violate the same, or willfully obstruct or attempt to obstruct the execution of the said acts, or be aiding or abetting therein.

"3. Congress having, by an act passed on the 5th day of June last, authorized the State courts to take cognizance of offenses against the said acts for raising a

---

* This word, and "henceforth," being objected to, was omitted by consent of the commissioners.

revenue upon distilled spirits and stills, the President has determined that he will direct suits against such delinquents to be prosecuted therein, if, upon experiment, it be found that local prejudices or other causes do not obstruct the faithful administration of justice; but it is to be understood that of this he must be the judge, and that he does not mean by this determination to impair any power vested in the Executive of the United States.

"4. Certain beneficial arrangements for adjusting the delinquencies and prosecutions for penalties now depending, shall be made and communicated by the officers appointed to carry the said acts into execution.

JAMES ROSS,
J. YEATES,
WM. BRADFORD.

"Signed, in behalf of the committee * representing the fourth survey of Pennsylvania, unanimously by the members present—John Probst, Robert Dickey, John Nesbit, David Philips, John Marshall, Samuel Wilson, George Wallace, John M'Clelland. Pittsburgh, Sept. 2, 1794."

"We, the underwritten, do also promise, in behalf of the State of Pennsylvania, that in case the assurances now proposed shall be *bona fide* given and performed until the 10th day of July next, an act of free and general pardon and oblivion of all treasons, insurrections, arsons, riots, and other offenses inferior to riots, committed, counseled, or suffered by any person or persons within the four western counties of Pennsylvania, since the 14th day of July last past, so far as the same concerns the said State, or the government thereof, shall be then granted; excluding therefrom every person who shall refuse or neglect to subscribe such assurance, or who shall after such subscription willfully violate or obstruct the laws of the State or of the United States.

THOMAS M'KEAN,
WILLIAM IRVINE."

The proceedings in relation to the amnesty having been thus detailed, the measures which were adopted by the commissioners will be considered on the principles of justice and sound policy. There is no reason why these should not be the same as would govern other parties in their negotiations; when the government condescends to negotiate at all, this must be admitted. What was the question presented to the standing committee, as a recognized body? It was the adoption or rejection of the terms of amnesty which the committee of conference had agreed to recommend to the standing committee of sixty, and which they could not do unless they were first approved by the conferees; this must be implied without any express declaration on their part to the commissioners. The conferees, it cannot be denied, fully complied with their engagements, by urging the acceptance of the terms by every means in their power. These

---

* In behalf of a committee which had not authorized them, and which at the time of signing had ceased to exist.

terms formed a part of their report, in language that could not be mistaken, and the acceptance was certified by the chairman and secretary. The mere phraseology, whether it be expressed in the simple words, "we accept the terms proposed," or, "we consider it *the interest* of the country to accept them," can make no difference—the meaning is the same.

On what grounds was the acceptance rejected by the commissioners? First, that the resolution was not adopted by a sufficient majority, or by *unanimity*, being only three-fifths in its favor; and second, that the vote was not open, or *viva voce*, but secret, by ballot; and for that reason, not a fair expression of the will of the voters. The answer to the first is, that to expect absolute unanimity, as in the case of a Polish diet, was unreasonable, and contrary to all our republican ideas. Among freemen, where diversity of opinion will prevail, it is next to impossible to obtain a unanimous vote on any proposition which has been the subject of free discussion. And as to the vote by ballot, surely no one will contend that it is not the most reliable mode of obtaining an expression of the unbiassed will of the voter. No matter how the vote was taken, provided it was free, and, in point of fact, was taken. There was no mode prescribed. The commissioners, as one party, had nothing to do with the mode, but only with the result. The mode was for the standing committee, and the commissioners had no right to know what passed in it, what angry debates took place, or what arguments were used, or who opposed, or who sustained the resolution. There was no agreement that the vote should be taken *viva voce*, or be unanimous. There was none that the acceptance should be in any set form of words, or in exact terms prescribed by the commissioners. The recommendation to the people was the proper mode, because the standing committee was only acting on delegated power from the congress of delegates, who had the power to give the final decision, although practically the vote of the standing committee would be regarded as conclusive. That congress did actually assemble in two weeks after, and *unanimously* ratified the resolution, and *accepted the terms in the very words and in the manner required by the commissioners!*

As to the violent debates in the committee, it could not be expected that nothing but passive submission would be witnessed there; and with respect to the treasonable expressions said to have been uttered, this was only imputable to one man; and the Christian religion might as well be rejected, because there happened to be a Judas among the Apostles. During nearly ten hours the committee and outsiders listened to the speeches of those who supported the government and urged submission, and this without impatience or interruption, which surely ought to counterbalance the intemperate language of a few speakers on the side of the opposition. No one, except Bradford, rose to reply to Messrs. Brackenridge, Gallatin and Edgar. But the sudden and great revulsion which took place the moment the vote was announced, not only with the committee and *circumstante corona*, but throughout the country, ought to have been known and weighed by the commissioners. From that moment, it was evident to all that the insurrection was broken down; and it became certain that the beautiful spectacle was about to be exhibited, of an insurrection against the laws subdued by the moral power of the people themselves, without the necessity of calling out the military force—a spectacle a thousand times more interesting to humanity than the experiment whether there was sufficient energy in the government to subdue them by the bayonet! The additional reason given by the commissioners, that there was danger of the rising of the people on the other side of the mountains and in Maryland, (no doubt much exaggerated,) only goes to prove that they themselves were not in a situation to judge coolly and impartially. At this distance we can view all the circumstances with a degree of coolness which no one was capable of at the time. Even the two cotemporary writers, Mr. Brackenridge and William Findley, are disposed to cast the censure on the standing committee rather than on the commissioners; perhaps influenced by chagrin, or mortification at the unreasonable difficulties made by the standing committee.

If the rejection of the vote of the standing committee by the commissioners, does not meet the approbation of the author of this work, still less, on fair and just principles, can he approve of the substitute, requiring *individual* assurance, instead of the general one, by the whole country in its *collective* or representative capacity. That substitute confounded the innocent with the guilty—it was revolting to a man who was conscious of having done his duty as a citizen, and on no occasion having opposed the execution of the laws, to be required to make a declaration which he felt as degrading, as publicly expressing repentance for a crime which he never committed, and making a promise to refrain for the future from the commission of acts which he never contemplated. It was like the passing *subjugum*, or under the yoke, of the inhabitants of conquered cities in ancient times. Besides, practically considered, it was impossible for the whole population, in one day, even in separate districts, over an extent half as large as the whole State, without allowance for sickness or other causes which might prevent attendance, to comply with the terms imposed. At least a week should have been allowed for signing. The mode agreed upon on the part of the conference would have answered

INJUSTICE TO THE WESTERN PEOPLE. 241

every purpose—the plan of general submission, instead of the one requiring each individual to come in person to affix his name to a paper. There was nothing to prevent the commissioners from presenting the question to the congress of delegates, which could have been assembled in a week.

Again, there is a serious question to be answered—by what authority was the arrangement made with the new committee? The standing committee, after adopting the report of the first conferees, appointed the new committee for a specific purpose, and then adjourned without day, neither requiring them to report to themselves nor to the congress at Parkinson's Ferry. The duty of the new committee was to obtain, if possible, a prolongation of time, to allow the people to become more fully impressed with the necessity of submission, and to declare it through their delegates. This was perfectly compatible with the resolution declaring it to be the interest of the people to accept the terms offered them by the commissioners; and if that request were refused, then the resolution still remained in force, notwithstanding the appointment of the new committee. The new agreement, accepting new and less favorable terms, was a nullity; they had no authority to set aside a benevolent stipulation, and accept in its stead one of the most unjust and unreasonable.

In concluding this chapter, one observation ought to be made in justice to the people of the western counties, then new and little better than a wilderness frontier, now populous enough to form a kingdom; it is this: with the exception of the riot at Neville's house, and some half dozen other minor acts of violence over the whole extent of Western Pennsylvania during four months, no serious outrages were committed on the property or person of any individual. How different from the ruffianly acts of other countries in such a state of anarchy! The people, although legally wrong, honestly believed they were morally right. The excise law was universally odious; the Legislature of the State had instructed their Senators to exert themselves for its repeal, and the State Executive had protested against it in strong language. It was acknowledged by the Federal government that it required amendments to satisfy well grounded causes of complaint, and some additional modifications were stipulated by the commissioners, as far as they had authority to do so. The western people were, without mitigation, stigmatized as insurgents, and their acts associated, in the minds of many, (and continue to be at this day,) with those of thieves, incendiaries and outlaws—not *murderers*, for not a drop of blood was shed by them during the whole period, although the lives of some of them were sacrificed. Without attempting to justify their unlawful acts, still, in order to do justice to them, their motives, as well as their general conduct, should be taken into consideration. But whatever may be said, by way of apology or palliation, it was not the less obligatory to maintain the supremacy of the law, and crush all opposition to the lawful authority. It was the duty of the good citizen to submit to the evils of the law until, in the proper way and at the proper time, they could be removed, there being no evil greater than anarchy and insubordination.

Hitherto but one side, and that the unfavorable side, as respects the insurgents, has been given by historians and public functionaries There is another side, and it is that of the conduct of the government agents to the western people, in the pretended suppression, by military force, of an insurrection already suppressed by themselves. In doing this, there was a hundred times more gross violation of law—more cruel injustice—more wanton, ruffianly acts, than were committed by the insurgents, and this without provocation. These outrages have hitherto been passed over almost in silence; but, if it be a duty to record and pronounce sentence of condemnation on the opposition to law and order, as a warning in future, it is not less so to hold up to just reprobation the cruel, wanton and oppressive of those government subordinates.* All this would have been avoided by a simple proclamation of amnesty to the whole country, as at first proposed, by the commissioners, under the instructions of Washington, agreed to by the first committee of conference, and, as we contend, sufficiently ratified by the standing committee. Reason, gratitude, interest—every consideration in this case, would have shed their benign influence over a well-meaning, but erring people. The march of an army of fifteen thousand men, at a greater expense than the whole whiskey tax ever yielded—a tax which, after the trial of a few years, was repealed—would not have taken place, to subdue a portion of our own fellow-citizens; and the historian would not have had to record this unfortunate episode in our national history.

*Macaulay, in his recent volumes of the History of England, has been justly censured for his leniency to William, on the subject of the massacre of Glencoe. The difference in that case and the present, is, that William did not forbid the act, while, in the case of the arrests of the "dreadful night," they were in plain disregard of the orders of Washington. The perpetrators were not called to account, because the victims were outlawed in public opinion by having the epithet of *insurgents* applied to them. For that reason it becomes the more urgent duty of the historian to do them justice.

NOTES TO CHAPTER IX.

Extract from the Report of the United States Commissioners to the Executive.

"The hopes exerted by the favorable issue of this conference, [*the first conference,*] were not realized by a correspondent conduct in the citizens who composed what was called the 'standing committee.' They assembled at Brownsville, (Redstone Old Fort,) on the 28th of August, and broke up on the 29th, and on the following day a letter was received from Edward Cook, their chairman, announcing that difficulties had arisen, and that a new committee of conference was appointed; and although *the resolve which is hereto annexed was passed*, it did not appear that the assurances of submission which had been demanded had been given.

"The underwritten were informed by several of the members of that meeting, as well as other citizens who were present at it, that the report of the committee of conference,* and the proposals of the commissioners were unfavorably received; *that rebellion and hostile resistance to the United States* were publicly recommended by some of the members, [*by Bradford only,*] and that so excessive a spirit prevailed that it was not thought proper or safe to urge a compliance with the terms and preliminaries prescribed by the underwritten, or the commissioners from the government of Pennsylvania. [*This was done by Gallatin, Brackenridge and Edgar.*] All that could be obtained, was the resolve already mentioned, the question upon it being decided by *ballot;* by which means *each mem-*

* That is, they met with *opposition!* Nothing is said of the *earnest support* they received, or the addresses of Messrs. Gallatin, Brackenridge and Edgar. Is this fair?

ber had an opportunity of concealing his opinion, and of sheltering himself from the resentment of those from whom violence was apprehended. [*A very strange objection!*] But notwithstanding this caution, the opinion was far from being *unanimous,* [*was this reasonable?*] that out of fifty-seven votes there were twenty-three nays, leaving a majority of only eleven; and the commissioners have been repeatedly assured by different members of that meeting, that if the question had been publicly put, it would have been carried in the negative by a considerable majority.*

"With a view of counteracting the acts and influence of the violent, the underwritten on the 27th of August addressed a letter to the late conferees, authorizing them to assure the friends of order, who might be disposed to exert themselves to restore the authority of the laws, that they might rely upon the protection of government, *and that measures would be taken to suppress and punish the violence of those individuals who might dissent from the general sentiments.* [*Where was the protection of government at that moment? And what would be the effect of such a threat? This is most astonishing!*] This letter was delivered to one of the conferees going to Brownsville; but he afterward informed the underwritten, that the gentleman to

* How does it appear that the "resolve" was not passed by an unanimous vote? The fact is not expressly communicated by the chairman—it must have reached the commissioners from other sources—but there is reason to believe that the "resolve" was not passed on the *ballot* vote alone, but afterward ratified in the afternoon, when that for the appointment of a new committee was passed, and which takes it for granted that submission was agreed to.

whom it was addressed, did not 'think it prudent to make use of it,' as the temper which prevailed was such that it would probably have done more harm than good. [*Most certainly—where would have been the freedom of deliberation, with such a threat suspended over them? Any man of spirit would have regarded it as a gross insult.*]

"The conduct of the meeting at Brownsville, notwithstanding the *thin veil* thrown over it, by the resolve already mentioned, was said to be considered by many, and especially by the violent party, as a rejection of the terms. [*This is strangely incorrect. The propriety, the necessity of submission, the great question to be decided, was never called in question after that resolve. Every subsequent act of the people took this question as settled.*] It was certainly a *partial* rejection of those proposed by the commissioners, who had acquired assurances *from the members of that meeting only*, and not from the people themselves. [*And was not this assurance given by the members of the meeting, by the acceptance of the report, in the most comprehensive terms, and without attaching any condition? It is true, they asked for some modification of the terms after accepting them, but this was a matter of favor, which, if not granted, left the matter where it was at the adoption of the resolve. The subsequent acts of the people, in their delegations as well as mass meetings, prove their determination to submit, although many of them objected to the mode of exacting that submission, which no reasonable man at this day can defend.*]

"Having, therefore, no longer any hope of an universal or even general submission, it was deemed necessary by a solemn appeal to the people to ascertain as nearly as possible the determination of every individual; [*this unwise determination, and unjust, more than unwise, has been already discussed;*] to encourage and *oblige* the friends of order to declare themselves; to recall as many as possible of the disaffected to their duty, by assurances of pardon, *dependent on their individual conduct;* and to learn with certainty *what opposition* the government might expect, if military coercion should be unavoidable. [*The best course would have been, immediately after the Brownsville meeting, to have recommended a general and universal amnesty. It would have had the effect of magic, and all opposition would have ended—every one would have vied in the emulation to display their loyalty—the standing committee having voted to submit, no opposition could have been expected.*]

"To secure these advantages, the underwritten were of opinion that the assurances of submission required of the people, should not only be publicly given, but ought also to be reduced to writing; and that the state of each county should be certified by those who were to superintend the meetings at which the disposition of the people was to be ascertained.

"On the 1st instant, nine of the gentlemen [*new committee of conference,*] appointed by the meeting at Brownsville, assembled at Pittsburgh, and in the afternoon required a conference with the commissioners, which was agreed to. They produced the resolves by wh they were appointed, and entered in some explanation of the nature of their visit; but being desired to communicate in writing, they withdrew, and soon after sent a letter addressed to the commissioners of the United States and of the State of Pennsylvania, to which an answer was immediately written.

"As no part of their letter, although addressed to the commissioners of Pennsylvania, related to the preliminaries presented by them, they made no answer in writing; but in a conference held the next morning with those nine gentlemen, *they verbally declared to them their entire concurrence in the sentiments contained in the letter from the underwritten;* and they expressed at some length their surprise and regret at the meeting at Brownsville. The conference declared themselves satisfied with the answer they had received; avowed an entire conviction of the necessity and propriety of an early submission in the manner proposed; and offered immediately to enter into the detail for settling the time, place and manner of taking the sense of the people."

The whole of the letter of the commissioners, or rather report, will be given in the appendix to this work,* and will afford a practical commentary on the working of the plan devised by them. It will prove that the plan was in fault, and not the disposition of the people to submit. This second committee not only went farther than the first in willingness to submit, *but were willing to accept any terms offered by the commissioners.* Can it be inferred from the appointment of such a committee, that the standing committee were less disposed to submit after, than before the passage of their resolution? If it proves any thing, it proves that somehow or other, *a very great change had taken place both in the standing committee and among the people,* for we say again, the only question now was as to the *time and mode* of submission; and we think it will be seen, that with some few exceptions of no importance, this was the only difficulty. We repeat, that a general proclamation of amnesty, as agreed on with the first conferees, would have produced an *universal acquiescence,* according to the wish of the commissioners. The majority of the people would have echoed the majority of the committee, (as in fact it did,) and that majority would have gone on increasing, until all appearance of opposition would have ceased. That there should have been, at first, some partial display of opposition after the resolve, was to be expected; it was not in human nature for perfect quiet to be instantly restored among a free people; the dead calm of despotism ought not to have been required, instead of the gradual subsiding of the billows after the storm. The writer feels great reluctance in expressing these sentiments, but the justice and truth of history demand a fearless and unbiassed judgment, without regard to the authority of great names — and that judgment supported only by the weight of reason. To this decision we refer the reader, without arrogance on the one hand, or affected humility on the other.

* Omitted.

CHAPTER X.

RELUCTANCE OF THE PEOPLE TO SIGN THE SUBMISSION — MEETING OF THE CONGRESS OF DELEGATES, AND A GENERAL SUBMISSION.

As had been foreseen, the plan of submission proposed by the commissioners would be very reluctantly acceded to by the people. The objections suggested, not only as to the manner, but the time allowed, were fully sustained by the event. The 5th of September was the day appointed for the whole extent of the four western counties, including Bedford, lying partly within the mountains, the whole equal in extent to three or four of the New England States. Although the two cotemporary historians pass no censure on the motives of the commissioners, in thus unintentionally defeating the benevolent design of Washington, yet they unqualifiedly disapproved of their plan. They supposed, however, that they could not act otherwise, in the circumstances in which they were placed, and they conceived themselves to be acting in conformity to the spirit and letter of their instructions. Findley is of opinion, that as their own powers terminated the day after that appointed for the submission, they could not afford longer time to the people; but it does not seem that this would have been any very great stretch of authority. There was certainly too much haste in a matter of such importance. The report of the commissioners to the Executive was evidently written in the midst of much excitement, occasioned by the prevailing temper of the people; nor could they foresee the change which a few weeks, or even days, would produce in their minds. Findley is more full on these topics than Brackenridge, having written a year afterward, with the advantage of facts subsequently brought to light, and at the same time of more mature deliberation. The views presented by the commissioners, given in this hurried manner, are therefore to be received with caution, as well as allowance.

The test to be subscribed, by each individual, in the presence of two members of the standing committee, or a justice of the peace, was as follows:

"I do solemnly promise, hereafter to submit to the laws of the United States, and that I will not, directly or indirectly, oppose the execution of the act for raising revenue on distilled spirits and stills; and that I will support, as far as the law requires, the civil authority in affording the protection to all officers and other citizens."

The test, which was regarded as a nauseous dose as soon as made public, was not printed until the 4th of September — having been agreed to by the new conferees two days before—and was not generally circulated until after the 4th, when the conferees left Pittsburgh. But six days were therefore allowed for the distribution of the papers over the extensive region before mentioned, containing a very scattered people, and possessing imperfect means of intercommunication. It was soon discovered that the word *solemnly* was objected to by religious people, as equivalent to an oath; and the commissioners, in consequence, gave notice in the Pittsburgh *Gazette*, the only paper then printed in the western counties, that it might be omitted; but this reached few of the districts in time. With the peculiar views of the rigid Presbyterians, much importance would be attached to the use of such words. It was also thought by other conscientious persons, that the word *henceforth* implied that *heretofore* they had committed acts in violation of law and hostile to the government, and which they denied to be the fact. Many of those who had taken the extreme caution to remain quietly at their homes, and had abstained from attendance at any of the meetings, of whatever description, were unwilling to attend those appointed by the commissioners, and there was not time to enlighten them on the subject. Some, in remote districts, received no notice at all; but the greater number of those who would not attend, were influenced by a mistaken but honest opinion, that the signing the submission would carry with it the acknowledgment that they had committed some act which required this evidence of repentance; and being conscious of having done nothing in violation of the laws, they thought they could not, on principle, make such an unjust, self-accusing confession. These were honest scruples, and entitled to respect, but unforeseen by the commissioners, and ultimately proved the whole plan to be radically defective. In fact, the people generally, in the rural districts, when they attended, had no opportunity of reading and examining the test (or whatever it might be called,) until the moment of their coming together; there was, of course, but little opportunity amid the confusion for the more intelligent to make the necessary explanation. Some had objected to the words *directly or indirectly*, which they construed to extend even to the right of petition for repeal; others, on being better informed of the nature of the test, became solicitous the next day to sign, and even followed those who had the papers, in order to obtain permission to write down their names. All these things serve to prove the necessity of a longer time; and to this cause may be attributed the want of a more general acquiescence, rather than to the fear of the violent, which operated to a much less extent than was represented at the time. It was not reasonable to expect that an uninformed people, unless slavishly indifferent to their rights, or basely submissive, could, in so short a time, make up their minds to subscribe a new test of allegiance, mixed up with what appeared to be confessions of guilt, when they were conscious of innocence.

On the other hand, there were, in many districts, persons who hang loosely on society, and who take advantage of such occasions to show their power over the more respectable people by exciting terror and alarm. It is a fact, that on the withdrawal of the army after the insurrection, it was chiefly among persons of that class that enlistments were made of the standing force, kept up for some time, to overawe the insurrectionary propensity which might still exist, and for which these very people had been most conspicuous. The distrust which had been engendered, especially by the anonymous threats of "Tom the Tinker," and the shortness of time, prevented the well disposed from coming to proper understanding with each other. The lawless conduct alluded to, occurred in some small districts where no excesses had been previously committed. In two or three instances the papers were seized and torn up, and in one place the papers were saved by concealing the genuine document and giving up a copy. Although such ruffians formed but a small proportion of those assembled, yet, says Findley, "desperation and threats of burning supplied the place of numbers, and it was not thought prudent on that day to put the law in execution, as the country districts did not know the situation and feelings of the county towns, or whether the attempt to arrest and take to prison might not lead to further riots." It is to be feared that there is no state of society in which characters of this description will not be found; and who, during this partial condition of anarchy, will not be drawn forth by the spirit of mischief to take revenge for their insignificance in a settled state of things, and where they are made to feel that contempt which their worthlessness entails. "The result," says Findley, "was, that out of about forty different places of meeting, at only two of them were the papers destroyed by a desperate banditti. One of these was at a place where the people who needed the amnesty were numerous; the other was that in which I reside, where very few had been guilty of any excesses. At one place in Allegheny county, the signing was prevented by violence, or terror, where it was the interest of many to subscribe; at a few other places the subscribing was accomplished with difficulty. Nevertheless, those who had been deeply engaged in the excesses, signed, with the exception of a few of the most ignorant and obstinate. There were some, indeed, who had dared to engage in the greatest outrages, who had not courage to subscribe from fear of their own safety, lest they should be considered as deserters." Thus it would appear, that the fear of public opinion among themselves was even greater than that of the threatened march of an army.

In some of the townships on the frontier, even those who attended refused to sign, because there were none among them who had given offense or were opposed to the excise law. They probably had no stills; it was only in the older and more wealthy settlements that the business of distilling was connected with farming. These poor, out of the way settlers, more hunters than agriculturists, took offense at the very idea of being called upon to sign a paper of submission. Some districts in the upper part of Washington county were not even notified. In fact, the people around the whole frontier were very little implicated in the disturbances, and scarcely knew of them until called upon to send delegates to Parkinson's Ferry for the purpose of restoring order; and they contributed every thing in their power to that desirable end, until called upon to sign the submission, when their answer was, "Let those sign in the places where they have been involved; we have had nothing to do with it." They had not only behaved well, but from some places, had actually tendered their services to General Wilkins to assist in quelling the insurgents.

But the county of Fayette furnished the most remarkable illustration. Not more than fifteen persons of the county were at Braddock's Field, and those from patriotic motives; not one had been in any of the riots; and having made no opposition to the service of process, but on the contrary, having employed counsel to defend the suits — their delegates having exerted themselves to restore order — they could not comprehend the necessity of the form of individual submission, which to them appeared to confound the innocent with the guilty. The whole county, therefore, rejected the terms of submission; but in order to show that this was not done through any hostile feeling to the government, they pursued a course of their own, and at a meeting of delegates from the different townships, those delegates unanimously agreed to submit to the laws of the United States, and of Pennsylvania, and not to oppose, directly or indirectly, the laws for raising revenue on distilled spirits and stills. They further called on the people in their election districts to declare their submission to the laws. Many declined to attend, especially in those districts which were remote from the scene of the disturbances. Our later experience proves how small a proportion usually attend these special or irregular meetings, for vague purposes; but of those who did attend, five hundred and eighty voted for submission, and two hundred and eighty against, and most of these, in all probability, from misapprehension. When the army, and the United States Judge, afterward came to the county, but one arrest was made, and that of an innocent man, who had been out of the State during the disturbance. Can there be a greater proof than this, that the course adopted by the commissioners, to say the least, was ill-advised? And were they not in error in representing the whole of the western counties in a state of open opposition to the government, which nothing but an army could put down? In Westmoreland county not a single arrest was made. The whole opposition was confined to parts of Allegheny and Washington counties, and in only two townships were the people forcibly prevented from signing. But it must be admitted, that this state of things could not have been so well known to the commissioners at the time they left the county, and there can be no doubt that they were under a mistaken impression as to the extent and depth of the opposition to the laws when they prepared their report. And yet it is highly probable that in the excited state of the people against the excise law, if some act of more than ordinary atrocity, such as the burning the town of Pittsburgh, had been perpetrated, and no check given to the insurrectionary spirit by the delegation at Parkinson's Ferry and the committee at Brownsville, after the conference with the United States commissioners, followed by the offer of amnesty, the whole of the western counties would have been ultimately involved, as in the late Revolutionary war. Bradford had been twice thwarted in his attempt to raise the standard of rebellion, and who can tell what would have been the consequence if he had not been defeated? If Pittsburgh had been burned and plundered, and the war measures of Bradford had been carried at the Parkinson's Ferry meeting, there is reason to believe that the flame would have spread every where, and the peaceful and well-disposed either drawn into the vortex, or compelled to fly the country. These reflections will enable us to appreciate the merit of the suggestion of the amnesty, the dextrous management of the delegates, and the powerful efforts of Messrs. Brackenridge and Gallatin at the Brownsville meeting of the standing committee. Blessed are the peace-makers, and happy is the people which possesses within itself the moral energy to restrain its own destructive passions!

If there was a portion of the ignorant and reckless among the western people, perhaps some of the dregs of the Revolutionary war, there was a

THE RESTORATION OF ORDER. 251

much larger one composed of the intelligent and patriotic. The county towns contained men of distinguished abilities and patriotism, and there were many officers and soldiers who had secured homes for themselves, as cultivators of the soil, in the beautiful region round the sources of the Ohio. In the narrative of the events of the insurrection, although on a scale comparatively limited, we have all these classes of people exhibited before us on a moving panorama. The transactions of men furnish the great lessons of history, whether they relate to the events of mighty empires or small communities, although from habit we regard the latter of less importance. There is the peculiarity of the people of whom we have been speaking, which may be characterized as American, and having its origin in the spirit of freedom; and it is this, their conduct, in the absence of all restraints or coercion, but only that of their own sense of right and wrong, is strikingly contrasted with that of the ruffian, ferocious mobs of enslaved countries. We might enlarge upon this subject, but we leave it to the reflections of the unprejudiced reader—we say unprejudiced, because there is even at this day an astonishing amount of prejudice against the *villainous insurgents*.

The restoration of order among the great body of the people, commenced with the known result of the conference with the commissioners, although the reign of terror, if the term in a comparative sense be applied, did not cease at once. The courts were opened by Judge Addison, the district judge, and not the slightest resistance was shown to the civil authority. Bills of indictment were found against those who had insulted the commissioners, by riotously and *routously* raising a liberty pole in front of their lodgings in Pittsburgh, and for breaking some of the windows of their hotel in Greensburg, acts highly disapproved by public opinion. Any offender could at this time have been arrested and brought before a justice of the peace. This even before the decisive vote in the standing committee at Brownsville—but after that time, when a majority of more than two-thirds were in favor of submission, and after the second committee had accepted worse terms than those granted to the first, the opposition had died away to nothing, or was confined to a few of that lowest class of desperate characters, who were afraid that their conduct had been too bad to be covered by any act of oblivion. The opposition among all other classes subsided so rapidly and completely, that Sheriff Hamilton, of Washington county, and a part of whose regiment, without his consent, had been engaged in burning Neville's house, offered with twenty men to arrest any man, or set of men, in the western counties, on legal process. Great praise is due to those individuals who exerted themselves to induce the people to sign the submission. In this work the clergy were conspicuous, and they are never more in the line of their duty than when counseling obedience to the laws and government. The Rev. John M'Millan, of Washington county, and the Rev. Mr. Porter, of Westmoreland county, very influential clergymen, exerted themselves with their congregations, and elsewhere, with much effect. General Wilkins, at the time of the insurrection the most popular man west of the mountains, organized an association for the purpose of enlightening and persuading the people with respect to their interests, and their duty on the occasion. Many other patriotic individuals rode from district to district for this laudable purpose. Mr. Brackenridge attended four districts during the day, and did not reach home until after midnight. He consequently had no opportunity of signing until next morning. His enemies afterward attempted to deprive him of the benefit of the amnesty, at least so far as to subject him to arrest, because while engaged in persuading others to sign, his own name was not affixed until a few hours after the expiration of the time. The discovery was made after the arrival of the army, by some good natured friends, who wished to curry favor with those who ruled the hour, and would have shamefully abused their power if they had had their will.

Even the violence displayed in a few districts contributed to the reaction which had commenced throughout the country. This is evident from the numerous facts related by the author of the "Incidents," who entertained, however, a more favorable opinion of the disposition to submit than did Findley, although equally confident that nothing but time was wanting, at most a short delay, to bring about universal acquiescence. This difference in opinion, I attribute to the fact of the former residing nearer, or rather in the midst of the scenes described by him. The courts had been held by Judge Addison, at Pittsburgh, Greensburg and Washington, where he delivered charges on the subject of the recent violations of law, which would not have been attempted only two weeks before. Warrants had been issued against Miller and others, who had been engaged in the riots but who had already fled the country. Mr. Brackenridge is of opinion that no more effectual method could have been taken to satisfy the government of the return to order, than the arrest at this time of some notorious offender, and sending him to Philadelphia. At Washington, there was a meeting on the 17th of September, of township delegates, for the purpose of expressing their willingness to submit. Mr. Brackenridge, who happened to be there, proposed calling a meeting of the original delegates to Parkinson's Ferry, which was agreed to, and he was requested to insert a notification to that effect in the Pittsburgh *Gazette*, which he did.* A number of persons who had not signed after the day, consulted him on the subject, and were advised to continue to sign, as in his opinion the case would be liberally considered by the President, where there had been no opportunity to sign, or forcible interference had prevented. In the public notice all magistrates were requested to bring in papers of submission, that they might be forwarded to the Executive.†

The delegates of townships met on the 2d of October, the day appointed, and without opposition passed the following resolutions:

"1. *Resolved*, unanimously, That it is the opinion of this meeting that if the signature to the submission be not universal, it is not so much owing to any existing disposition to oppose the laws, as to a want of time and information to operate a correspondent sentiment; and with respect to the greatest number, a prevailing consciousness of their having had no concern in any outrage, and an idea that their signature would imply a sense of guilt."

2. The second resolution was an assurance of submission in the very words required by the commissioners of the conferees.

* "At a meeting of a considerable number of the inhabitants of Washington and other counties, on the west of the mountains, the present state of the country, with respect to the late disturbances, was taken into consideration; and from comparing information it appeared to them that the country was progressing, if not in fact wholly arrived at a state of general submission to the laws; so as to render it unnecessary for any advance of force, on the part of the government, for the purpose of assisting the civil authority in suppressing the insurrection and preserving the peace; and that measures ought to be taken, as speedily as may be, to communicate information of this favorable state of things to the government.

"*Resolved*, That a meeting of the delegates of townships of the 14th of August, at Parkinson's Ferry, be called to convene at the same place, on Thursday next, the 2d of October, to take the above into consideration. And as it is of great moment, the delegates are requested to be punctual in their attendance, and at an early hour that day.

"And it is recommended that all justices of the peace, and members of the committee, obtain and bring forward all signatures of the declaration of submission that may be taken, in order to lay them before the meeting, and forward to the government, with such address or such commissioners, on the part of the country, as may be thought advisable."

† Dr. Carnahan states, (141) "All the commissioners had returned to Philadelphia, except James Ross, who remained to carry the signatures to the government. Two scoundrels, who, armed with rifles, had prevented their neighbors from signing, followed Mr. Ross a day's journey, giving out when they left home, that they were going to take the papers from him; but when they overtook him, they begged him to carry their names to the President as submissive citizens. Bradford and Marshall signed on the day appointed. Bradford made a long speech, and exhorted the people to submit, putting his own submission on the ground that he was deserted by others."

3. The third resolution was to appoint William Findley and David Reddick, on the part of the meeting, as commissioners to the President, and to give this assurance of submission, and to explain circumstantially the state of the country, in order to enable him to judge whether an armed force would be necessary to support the civil authority in the western counties.

Bradford and Marshall had attended the meeting—but how changed from what they were in the same body less than one month before! The former, particularly, was much crestfallen, and had become the most humble in suing for peace. He denied that he had deserted the cause—it was the people who had deserted him!

If the assurances required of the standing committee were considered sufficient by the commissioners to found the general amnesty, much more the unanimous declaration of the whole body, of which that committee was a part! Here was the unanimity which was required of the committee; here was a *viva voce* confession of that unanimity, and without any opposition! Why, then, was not this deemed sufficient to arrest the march of the army? Without adopting the harsh opinions of Findley, with respect to the supposed policy of the Secretary of the Treasury, or attributing too much to the misconceptions occasioned by the erroneous representations of the banished persons, we may be allowed to say, that if these assurances would have sufficed before the army was ordered to march—these, with the actual fact of the complete submission of the whole country, ought to have arrested the march afterward. While the government agents carefully collect and magnify every act of irregularity before and after the last meeting of the representatives of the people, these great and prominent evidences are carefully passed over in silence! Nothing is ever said in those histories which condemn the insurgents, respecting the unanimous vote of the congress of the 2d of October! The conclusion is irresistible, that the march of the army was not to put down an insurrection which no longer existed—or military *combinations*, as it was expressed, which did not exist at that time, and what is more, never had existed. Was it for the sake of vengeance for the past, or for the purpose of displaying the power of the new government to put down insurrection in future? Is not such action more in accordance with despotic power than with republican institutions? The whole truth has not been told so as to do justice to the western people. A single regiment—a mere escort of cavalry, would have been as effectual as the march of fifteen thousand men, which might indeed have been mustered and held in readiness, but only moved when strong necessity called for it?

Mr. Brackenridge, and his colleague General Wilkins, at first entertained some fears that the assurances, although representing the true state of the country, were, perhaps, too strongly expressed, and therefore might possibly deceive the government; but in a very short time their fears were removed. Judge Addison, who acted as secretary, declared himself perfectly satisfied as to the three counties in which he had lately held his courts, Westmoreland, Fayette and Washington, and the Allegheny county delegates vouched for the good disposition of that county; the others were willing to place confidence in the representation which the persons chosen as delegates might make to the President. This was the last time that Mr. Brackenridge took part in the transactions growing out of the insurrection, excepting in his own immediate neighborhood.* It was not long before he was subjected to persecutions, as the only reward of his important services, his enemies having succeeded in establishing the most unjust impressions in the minds of the government agents, which like other prejudices, when once fairly rooted, can never be entirely eradicated. This will appear in the further progress of this history, and may well excite the surprise of the reader.

Previous to the second assemblage of the congress of delegates at Parkinson's Ferry, the following resolutions were passed at a town meeting in Pittsburgh, for the purpose of considering the proscription of certain citizens, during the late disturbances, in which necessity and policy led to a temporary acquiescence on the part of the town, it was unanimously resolved, "that the said citizens were unjustly expelled, and the said proscriptions are no longer regarded by the inhabitants of the town of Pittsburgh, and that this resolution be published for the purpose of communicating these sentiments to those who were the subjects of the said proscriptions."

With the last meeting of delegates, the flame of insurrection was entirely extinguished, and not a spark remained. Individuals who had been the most violent, became the most submissive. There were, doubtless, many on whom fear operated more than patriotism, but the result was the same, or even more complete. It is very possible that the effect

* "Bradford nominated John Cannon to the chair; who took it. It struck Judge Addison and others as improper, Col. Cannon having been the chairman of a former obnoxious committee at Pittsburgh, and also deeply involved in the late outrages; and it would be no good symptom to the President, that we had made him chairman on the occasion. This was hinted to Col. Cannon himself, and pressed with all possible delicacy; but Bradford insisted on his keeping his chair, and Cannon himself was tenacious of it. However, in making out our report, we kept his name out of view, and made no mention of a chairman at all."—Incidents, vol. ii. 32.

of calling out the military, and the preparations of the government, lent their aid; but the submission of the people began before the army was embodied, and influenced by motives which would have rendered any further resort to it unnecessary. It was the majority declaring itself at Brownsville, on the 2d of September, which settled the question, and not the fear of military coercion! The war fever was then at its crisis, and the prevailing temper was to set the army at defiance, and in all probability it would have been done, if the all-important discovery had not been made, that the warlike portion was in a decided minority. The minority found itself without support from the people, and their cause hopeless. The magic of majorities is well known to our republican experience, and is familiar to every American. In this country the majority, in other words, public opinion, is the ruling power; and it is as difficult to contend against it, as against royalty, and military force under despotisms. It is one of the imperfections of human contrivances, that this power, so favorable to liberty, may also be brought to bear in a despotic manner, on the rights and privileges of individuals.

In a publication called "Olden Time," by Neville B. Craig, the author of "The History of Pittsburgh," we find a letter from his father, Major Craig, to Neville, dated Pittsburgh, 26th September, 1794:

"The leaders of the insurrection are now endeavoring by a new finesse to lull government by a representation that the country is in a state of peace and submission to the laws, and that the interference of an armed force is altogether an unnecessary expense, and therefore they request that the army may not proceed any farther. I hope this representation may be treated with that degree of *contempt it so justly merits;* for notwithstanding a few have taken the benefit of the amnesty offered by the commissioners, yet several of them immediately after openly declared that no excise man shall exist in this country. This you may be assured is the general disposition of the people; indeed it is evident from what we daily hear and see, that the weight of the Executive *armament must be sensibly felt in this country* before any law of the United States can be enforced."

The foregoing is a sample of those misrepresentations, chiefly traceable to the "Neville connection," by which the government was deceived. The reader who has followed our narrative, can scarcely suppose it possible that there could be such a perversion of the truth; but it will not so much surprise him, when he considers that it proceeds from the same person who represented the citizens of Pittsburgh as *all insurgents*, excepting a certain Thomas Baird, a blacksmith in the employment of the

Quarter-Master, and James Robinson.* It is only a bolder flight of fancy to embrace the whole western country, and all its most patriotic citizens, in one compendious libel. There is scarcely a word of truth in the letter; and yet it, no doubt, had a pernicious influence, when backed by the other members of the Neville connection, on the spot. Who were those leaders of the insurrection "endeavoring by a new finesse to lull the government?" The insurrection at that time had no leaders, and there was nobody to be led. A more false and unprincipled misrepresentation can with difficulty be found in the history of any community, and especially in the atrocious design to induce the government to send a force to *dragoon the people into submission*, when there was not a show of resistance any where; and when every patriotic citizen—every good man in the country, was endeavoring to prevent this calamity! It would not be stretching presumption too far to ascribe the most malignant motives to such acts—the desire of revenge on the community which held the writer in little respect, and of malice toward individuals against whom he entertained a personal enmity, or who refused allegiance to the Neville connection, which to the narrow mind of the writer was almost as great a crime as that of treason to the government! It is scarcely possible to speak too severely of one who could write such a letter. The Major was not a bad man in private life, but ignorant and circumscribed in his views, and capable of doing much more mischief than persons of higher intellect. The "leaders of the insurrection," in his mind, were not Bradford and Marshall, but Gallatin, Findley and Brackenridge, especially the latter, whom he believed to be the chief mover, and constantly engaged in dangerous plots against the government and the "connection," at the very moment he was doing everything in his power to arrest the progress of the insurrection by other means than military force. He was unceasingly endeavoring to fix on Mr. Brackenridge the imputation of being the principal leader of the insurgents; and no doubt did much to mislead the other members of the connection, as well as the government, by his secret correspondence. Brackenridge had laughed at him—had made him the butt of ridicule. The Major could not afford it!

The election for Congress took place on the 14th of October, ten or

---

* James Robinson was not properly a resident of Pittsburgh; he owned and kept the ferry on the other side of the Allegheny river, where he was one of the earliest settlers. Here the Franklin road, the great thoroughfare to the lakes, commenced. His land afterward formed a part of the city of Allegheny. The elegant mansion of his son, Gen. William Robinson, now occupies the site (or near it) of the primitive log cabin in which the General was born.

fifteen days after the meeting of the delegates at Parkinson's Ferry. The vote, as might be expected, was unusually small; there were four or five candidates, (such as we call at this day volunteers,) each relying on his personal popularity. They had all taken part against the excise law. Mr. Brackenridge had been the most popular, and there was no one doubted of his election until his speech at the Mingo Creek meeting, where he denounced the burning of Neville's house as treason, and defeated the vote to approve the conduct of those who had been engaged in it, and who were chiefly from that neighborhood. His negotiations with the commissioners, and his effort in favor of submission at Brownsville, it was thought, had left him no ground of popularity to stand upon. It was reported that he had withdrawn his name from the contest, and this report was industriously circulated by some of the candidates. Although entertaining no hope of success, he considered it due to truth and to himself to contradict this report,* but this being published only a few days before the election took place, was known only in his own neighborhood. It bears the stamp of an honest mind. It appeared in the sequel that if this had been done earlier, he would have been elected, notwithstanding his distrust of the sentiments of the voters, showing that many expressed in public, opinions different from those entertained in private. Mr. Gallatin was taken up on a short notice, and was elected. Mr. Brackenridge stood next to him in number of votes, and what was not a little significant, he received the lowest in the neighborhood which had been most active in the riot at Neville's, while the favorite candidate of that injured "connection" received the *highest vote there!* Mr. Brackenridge states that Major Craig was particularly active, and freely used the public horses in bringing up votes to be cast against him. The vote of that hot-bed of the insurrection, the Mingo Creek district, does not prove that they had been secretly and diabolically instigated by Mr. Brackenridge to burn Neville's house, as was preposterously alleged by some of that family!

* "*Citizens of the District of Washington and Allegheny:*—
"Previous to the late disturbances, it was proposed to me to give my name as a candidate for the Congress of the United States; I accepted the compliment. It is now circulated that I have declined it. No—considering the delicacy of the times, I might wish I had not thought of it; but, as it is, it would imply fear of submitting my conduct to investigation, to withhold my name from the public. I have therefore not done so. I may at present have less popularity than I had; but the time will come when I shall be considered as having deserved well of the country, in all the delicate conjunctures in which I have been placed.
H. H. BRACKENRIDGE."

THE ELECTION TO CONGRESS. 259

"I had no thought of popularity now," touchingly observes Mr. Brackenridge. His mind was bent on more important considerations. Yet the sagacity or candor of Hildreth, in his pretended account of the insurrection, could discover no motive for the course pursued by Mr. Brackenridge, but an insane desire to be elected to Congress, as if this was any extraordinary stretch of ambition in a man of his standing and talents. If such was his object, he took the course to defeat it by sacrificing his popularity for the good of the people. Mr. Purviance—who was on the spot, and better able to judge than Hildreth, who wrote fifty years after— assigns a very different motive, and the unprejudiced reader may decide between them: "to arrest the progress of the present violence, and obtain an amnesty for that already committed." Mr. Brackenridge, no doubt, had ambition, but it was not for office or place, but for the estimation of this fellow-citizens for those high qualities of integrity, talents, and patriotic services, to which he aspired. No man was more sensitive to detraction, or more alive to commendation. He regarded a stain on his reputation as a wound, and even carried this to a degree of morbid sensibility. Hildreth, not satisfied with this, elsewhere asserts that Mr. Brackenridge had betrayed the people for a bribe from the United States commissioners; and again, that he was only suffered to escape by turning State's evidence against his accomplices! It was a very convenient thing for Neville Craig to find such a coadjutor in his imputations, so inconsistent, contradictory and absurd! Dante, in his "Inferno," has provided a particularly hot place for those who slander by insinuation or inuendo. Hildreth could see no merit in any one but Bradford; and yet condemns Brackenridge, Gallatin and Findley, as insurgents. To be consistent, he ought to have justified the outrages of the insurrection, which he charges as crimes on innocent persons. Bradford had succeeded, at this time, in enlisting the Neville interest in his favor, but even their efforts could not save him. Their object, no doubt, was to induce him to be a State's evidence against Mr. Brackenridge, but it so happened that, as in the case of the knife-grinder, he had no story to tell, with the exception of some contemptuous expressions about Major Craig! But Bradford took to flight before the approach of the army.* Hildreth is much puzzled to

---

* On the advance of the army, a number who had been involved, or were not within the amnesty, had absconded. These, as far as could be ascertained, were denounced in a proclamation by General Lee of the 29th of November, 1794. Among them was Bradford, who escaped by the Ohio with considerable difficulty. A small Kentucky boat had been prepared, which was to have received him at Grave Creek; but being pursued by a man from whom he had liberated a negro,

account for the fact, that Mr. Brackenridge did not take to flight also, as well as Bradford; it never seemed to enter his mind, that conscious merit as well as conscious innocence, gave him courage to stand his ground and encounter the powerful assaults of his enemies.

Dr. Ferguson, of Edinburgh, in his "Treatise on Moral Science," after speaking of the conclusion of the "Incidents," as possessing singular beauty in point of language, disapproves of the incentives to action which influenced the writer, and holds that men should look only to the approval of the divine law for their guide, without thinking of any worldly consideration. This is certainly true from the pulpit, and the only doctrine proper to be inculcated thence. But with men of the world there may be other incentives not incompatible with religion, and not to be condemned; such as the love of honorable fame, and the esteem of our fellow-citizens, which exert so powerful an influence over the warrior, the statesman and the patriot. The keen sense of shame and disgrace, and the abhorrence of any base or mean act, have a powerful effect on such minds. The saint may be above such considerations, and the villain indifferent to them. We should have much less veneration, even for a saint, who was indifferent to the good opinion of his fellow-men, although this sensibility may exist in a morbid degree. We shall here insert the passage from Mr. Brackenridge's "Incidents"—a work which has been, for the purpose of disparagement, called an apology, although the word does not mean, in its proper sense, an excuse for an acknowledged fault, but rather a defense or vindication, as in the case of "Barkly's Apology for Quakerism," and others of the same kind:

"I have now finished the detail I had in view. That my information under the abolition law of Pennsylvania, he was obliged to leave his horse and take a canoe. Descending in this, and passing Gallipolis, he was pursued by a party of five men, despatched from Gallipolis by D'Abecourt, the commandant of the militia at that place. He had lain all night in his canoe at Sandy Creek, and had got into a coal boat, in the service of the contractor, cold and hungry, about two hours before the party in pursuit of him came up. They entered the boat, demanded Bradford, and took hold of his arm to drag him away; he made no resistance, but a lad from Washington county seized a rifle and singly defended him, obliging the party to relinquish their design and withdraw. This youth had himself absconded, under apprehensions from having painted the device of a liberty pole. Bradford continued his course, pursued by Capt. Jolly as far as Red Bank, which he passed two days before. He succeeded in gaining the Spanish dominions, where he was well received by the authorities; had lands granted him—became a planter, and left considerable to his family. And this man is the subject of Hildreth's eulogy!

may not have been correct in all cases; that my memory may have led me into error; that my imagination may have colored facts, is possible; but that I have deviated from the strictness of truth knowingly, is what I will not admit. That I have been under the painful necessity of giving touches which may affect the feeling of some persons, is evident. But it has been with all the delicacy in my power, consistent with doing justice to myself. If I have done them injustice, they have the same means with me in their power—an appeal to the public. This is the great and respectable tribunal at which I stand. For, though I have not been arraigned at the bar of a court of justice, yet, from the first moment of obloquy against me, I have considered myself an arrested man, and put upon my country. From that day the morning sun shone upon me less bright; the light of night has been more obscure; the human countenance presented nothing but suspicion. The voice of man hurt me; I almost hated life itself. For who can say that I have pursued riches? Who can say that I have been a devotee of pleasure? Who can say I do not love honorable fame? What then have I, if I lose the hope of estimation? Was I traitor to my country? Was I traitor to that class of men with whom I am in grade of education? Would I disgrace the praise of science, the advantage of an enlightened reading?—who are taught to know that virtue is glory, and benevolence and truth, that alone which can assimilate with the Divine nature. And what greater deviation than to disturb the settled order of government, while that government remains republican? and any man who touches it with any other views than to contribute to its support and preservation, deserves the anathema of the people."

NOTES TO CHAPTER X.

FINDLEY gives the following compendious view of the rise and fall of the Insurrection, page 136:

"Though it may be admitted that there was a latent predisposition to violence among a few individuals, who had been formerly attached to the Inspector, (Neville,) and encouraged by him to oppose excise officers under the State, and though this was known to himself, and he was prepared for defense, yet no such thing was generally known in the country, and its breaking out at the time was owing to accident, and circumstances of a local nature. Inconsistent and useless resistance, by shedding blood too abundantly, which the Inspector was more successful in doing, by being prepared in a manner of which the assailants were not aware, exciting a more formidable attack, and drew many into the vortex of riot, who would have been far from engaging in it, if they had had time to deliberate on the consequences. Numbers thus involved in crimes, became desperate, and endeavored, by drawing others into the same situation, to make a common cause, and being unfortunately aided in these mistaken views by Marshall and Bradford and others, who attempted to give a more violent complexion, and greater magnitude to the mischief by drawing the whole western country into a combination against the excise laws, and for this purpose, contriving the rendezvous at Braddock's Field, and using every means to influence the minds of the citizens, and to overawe with terror those who might oppose their designs, and for this purpose magnifying the numbers at Braddock's Field, and advertising that thousands had been on their march to join them, from places where there was not a person who knew of the rendezvous. I say, by these mad exertions, the insurrection progressed for a few days, like the paroxysm of an inflammatory fever, spent its force in frequent and irregular convulsions, and finally subsided as suddenly, and to many, as unexpectedly as it commenced; the most alarming symptoms were discovered at Braddock's Field, and the last struggle was a feeble attempt to raise a party a few miles south of Greensburg."

CHAPTER XI.

CALLING OUT THE MILITARY TO SUPPRESS THE INSURRECTION — THE DELEGATION TO THE PRESIDENT FROM THE WEST.

WE have already related the measures taken by the Executive of the United States, as soon as information was received of the resistance to the Marshal, the destruction of the office of the Inspector, and the assemblage at Braddock's Field. A report was made by the Secretary of the Treasury, who, not confining himself to the occurrences of recent date, enumerated all the acts of opposition to the excise laws, both of the State and general government, not as exceptional cases, but as evidence of the prevailing temper throughout the whole country. The resolutions passed by the primary meetings were also enumerated as being among the causes of the insurrection, the expression "intemperate" being applied to them—and which, if justifiably applied, might in practice impair the right to obtain a repeal of an obnoxious law, even by constitutional means.* These resolutions, as already observed, were passed two years before the late outrages; the excise laws had been amended, so as to render them less objectionable, with the exception of the ruinous practice of taking persons across the mountains for trial, and even this had been provided against by law, but of which the people were not fully informed, and the writs issued under the old, although the report of the Secretary leaves the impression that they were issued under the new. The growing disposition to submit to the law, the peaceful service of all the writs except the last, in the immediate neighborhood of the Inspector, and the sudden outbreak which followed, which had all the characteristics of a common riot, without preconcerted design to resist, much less to overturn the government—were passed over by the Secretary. On this report, and on no other evidence, except public rumor, (at least none other was

---

* The rights of citizens as to meetings and petitions, were not fully appreciated by all in the first days of this government. On a petition from Northumberland county, Pennsylvania, December 30th, 1791, Mr. Gerry said, "He thought the petition improper, as it prays for a repeal of the (excise) law." Gales & Seaton, 2d Cong., p. 299.

given to the public,) Judge Wilson, a United States Judge, gave his certificate, making a case under the constitution and the laws to authorize the Executive to call out the military force.* That such had occurred in point of fact, there can be no doubt, but the Judge has been censured by Findley for being too hasty in granting the certificate without sufficient evidence, or without a careful investigation deliberately made. Whether a case had or had not occurred, the certificate was granted in an irregular manner, which ought not to be regarded as a precedent in other cases. There was some opposition in the cabinet to the immediate resort to force; Randolph, Secretary of State, on one side, and Hamilton and Bradford (Attorney General) on the other. The Governor of Pennsylvania coincided with the Secretary of State; in consequence of this, and in conformity to the benign policy of Washington, the suggestion (attributed to Chief Justice M'Kean,) was adopted of sending commissioners from the Executive of the Union and of the State, to make an effort to bring the people to submit by peaceable and friendly means. These were appointed, as we have seen; the issuing of the President's proclamation, and the partial failure of the friendly mission have been related, ascribed to the too great haste in requiring the submission. The blame of this failure has been cast by some on the Secretary of the Treasury, who is supposed to have controlled the operations connected with the insurrection, and by others attributed to the lateness of the season, and the lawless spirit manifested in some of the counties east of the mountains, and in Maryland, doubtless much exaggerated. It must be confessed, that at such times it is extremely difficult to judge correctly of the extent of disaffection from the universal distrust which always prevails in a state of society bordering on anarchy or revolution. Let this serve as a warning to the well meaning, how they give encouragement to such a state of things, by word or deed! I maintain the right of the people to remonstrate, in the strongest language, against what they may feel as oppressive; yet, for the sake of a good cause, and to avoid the exciting immoderate passion among those who do not reason with sufficient clearness,

---

* "PHILADELPHIA, Aug. 4th, 1794.

"SIR:—From the evidence which has been laid before me, I hereby notify to you that in the counties of Washington and Allegheny, in Pennsylvania, laws of the United States are opposed, and the execution thereof obstructed by combinations too powerful to be suppressed by the ordinary course of judicial proceedings, or by the powers vested in the Marshal of that district.

"I have the honor to be, with the highest consideration and respect,
       Your most obedient and humble servant,   JAMES WILSON.
"The President of the United States."

these remonstrances should be guided by prudence and moderation. It is a great mistake to suppose that they will be less effective on that account. The condescension of the Executive was unexpected to Mr. Brackenridge, who first suggested the idea of an amnesty in the West; his idea was to send a deputation to solicit one from the government. His suggestion, however, had the effect of drawing the line of distinction between those who had committed acts of violence and those who had stopped short of that length, and was undoubtedly the first check to the insurrection, or rather of preventing an outrageous riot from running into that state.

In the meantime, in order to be prepared for the worst, the President, as soon as he received information of the riot at Neville's house, and the subsequent assemblage at Braddock's Field, and after the report of the Secretary of the Treasury and the certificate of the Judge, issued his proclamation of the 17th of August. On the same day he made a requisition on the Governors of Pennsylvania, New Jersey, Maryland and Virginia, for twelve thousand (afterward increased to fifteen thousand) men, to be immediately organized and held in readiness to march at a moment's warning.

By the constitution of the United States, it is the duty of the President "to see that the laws be faithfully executed," and the same duty is imposed on the Governor of the State of Pennsylvania. By the act of Congress for calling out the militia, "to execute the laws of the United States, to suppress insurrections, and repel invasions, &c.," it is enacted, "that whenever the laws of the United States shall be opposed, or the execution thereof obstructed, in any State, by combinations too powerful to be suppressed by the ordinary course of judicial proceedings, or by the powers vested in the Marshals by that act, the same being notified to the President of the United States, by an associate justice or the district judge, it shall be lawful for the President of the United States to call forth the militia of such States to suppress such combinations, and cause the laws to be duly executed." It is also provided by the same act, that when the militia of the State where the combinations exist shall refuse or be insufficient for the purpose, the President may then call on the militia of the adjoining States. It thus appears that the first steps must be taken by or with the concurrence of the Executive of the State. In the present instance, in a conference between the President and Governor Mifflin, in order to avoid any collision of authority, the course adopted was settled between them. The requisitions on the other States met with no obstacles; but the case was different in Pennsylvania. The orders to the brigade inspectors were generally disregarded; the people declaring that although willing to march against a foreign enemy, they would not do so against their own fellow-citizens of the West. The Governor, in order to bring the militia to a proper sense of their duty, made a tour through the most populous of the eastern counties, and addressed the people at public meetings, a course which evidently produced a good effect; at the same time, a special meeting of the Legislature was convened, to authorize the calling out of the militia out of their classes—to procure substitutes and volunteers, and to propose bounties to others who would engage in the service. These measures had the desired effect, at least in procuring the requisite number.

The day after the report of the commissioners, the President issued his proclamation of the 25th of September, declaring the western counties in a state of insurrection, and calling on the militia force to march for its suppression.

We cannot refrain from contrasting the efforts made on the part of the Executive, on the east side of the mountains, to march an army to put down, by force, a resistance to the laws, with similar efforts made on the western side, at the very same time, by the well disposed among the people, to bring about a voluntary submission. The committee of twelve from the Parkinson meeting had unanimously accepted the terms of the commissioners; the committee at Brownsville had accepted them by a vote of two-thirds; and this was so rapidly followed by the subsiding of the opposition, that only two weeks afterward the original congress of delegates met at Parkinson's Ferry and unanimously resolved to accept the terms! The entire and complete cessation of all opposition to the government, which has been related, forms a very singular contrast with the mighty preparations going on at the very same moment to subdue a people, whose only passion now was fear and alarm at the threatened vengeance of the government, on account of the past! Here is a most striking proof of the want of information of the country west of the mountains; for certainly the government could not have been correctly informed, when it continued to speak of "lawless combinations," and of the "disposition of the insurgents," as if they were permanently embodied and arrayed in arms against the government; instead of which, at this time, a single unarmed individual might have traversed any portion of the western counties, and with a slip of paper have arrested "Tom the Tinker" himself, if to be found, without meeting the slightest resistance! The circumstance affords, at least, a very strong reason in favor of turnpikes, rail roads and telegraphs, and other rapid means of communication.

The troops from Pennsylvania and New Jersey were ordered to march to Carlisle previous to proceeding to Bedford; and those from Maryland and Virginia were to rendezvous at Cumberland, on the Potomac. The command of the whole was given to General Lee, then Governor of Virginia. These different corps, drawn freshly from the people, were composed of very different materials; the greater part without discipline, and, of course, under very imperfect subordination. A large portion of those from Philadelphia and the adjacent county were hired substitutes, the very worst kind of military mercenaries, actuated by no higher motive than the expectation of plunder, and the bounty and pay held out as inducements. The militia generally, who served in their classes, were actuated by better feelings, and restrained by worthy motives. The Jersey volunteers and militia are spoken of more favorably; they were under the command of Governor Howell, while the Pennsylvania troops were commanded by Generals Irvine and Chambers. Those of Maryland were er General Smith, and the Virginia troops under General Morgan.

The Pennsylvania and Jersey troops, notwithstanding the better disposition of the latter, soon manifested the most violent feelings of hatred to the insurgents, and talked familiarly of killing and hanging them, as if they were all pirates and cut-throats. They seemed to think that they were called out to take a signal vengeance on all such monsters in human shape, and were against every man, woman and child west of the mountains! The inflamed state of their minds had, in part, been produced by the exaggerated representations of the recruiting service, as well as by the activity of some of the exiles, who had personal resentments to gratify. "One individual," says Findley, "who had distinguished himself by his industry and address, was to be skewered, shot, or hanged on the first tree." The individual here referred to was Mr. Brackenridge, who was industriously represented as at the bottom of the insurrection, and the prime mover of it. The Jersey men, especially, were offended at some touches of ridicule in the absurd production attributed to him, which has been already noticed.* This exasperation was not only di-

* Findley says: "The publication already mentioned, and by one who was a friend of the government, wrote in the character and manner of an insurgent, on purpose to excite the militia of New Jersey and the lower counties of Pennsylvania, had an incredible effect in inflaming the citizens of these States, and others; particularly the following words in it: 'Brothers, you must not think to frighten us with fine arranged bits of infantry, cavalry and artillery, composed of your watermelon armies, taken from the Jersey shores. They would cut a much better figure in warring with crabs and oysters about the banks of the Delaware. It is a common thing for Indians to fight your best armies, in the proportion of one to five;

rected against the western people, but even against those among themselves who contended that the military should be subordinate to the civil authority, or hinted that those who killed citizens in cold blood, would be answerable for murder! In short, the temper and composition of this body of men, without the discipline of regular troops, or the proper sense of duty as citizens, were badly suited to aid the civil magistrate in the execution of the laws. A very large proportion of the recruits, especially the hired substitutes, were greater ruffians than the worst of those who had taken part in the insurrection. Two men were assassinated by them; one on the road near Lebanon, and the other near Carlisle. The first by the New Jersey troops, on some slight provocation; the other by a light-horseman of Philadelphia, who went into the country to seize some persons suspected of assisting to raise a liberty pole! The latter was a sick boy, who was flying from the guardians of the law, and shot, as it is said, accidentally! Here was an earnest of what might be expected in the West, when such acts were committed where there was no insurrection, and the laws were in force. The presence of Washington was never more necessary; he soon after arrived, when he took decided measures to prevent such acts in future, at the same time establishing subordination among the troops. No complaints were made after this, until he left them at Bedford.

Before the march to Bedford, the delegates, Findley and Reddick, had arrived, and obtained an interview with the President at Carlisle, then the head-quarters. They found the army violently hostile to them, as the supposed messengers of peace, insomuch as even to give rise to personal apprehension. They even dared to speak disparagingly of the President himself, for showing civility to rascally insurgents or rebels, instead of hanging without ceremony or shooting them as the only favor they deserved. They were, notwithstanding, kindly received by him. The President listened respectfully to their representations. They informed him that since the report of the commissioners all opposition or appearance of opposition had ceased; and, moreover, that the original delegates at Parkinson's Ferry (in which opposition had existed on the first arrival of the commissioners,) had recently re-assembled, and had unanimously adopted resolutions, as the representatives of the whole

therefore, we would not hesitate a moment to attack this army at the rate of one to ten.' This dialogue having been ascribed to Mr. Brackenridge on account of a faint imitation of his style, together with his letter to Tench Cox, written at a time when there was danger of letters being intercepted, occasioned a very high degree of resentment.''

population of the western counties, going even farther than those submitted to the standing committee at Brownsville. That the delegates had been appointed to lay these before the President. They further assured him that the sentiments of the people were entirely in accordance with those of the late meeting; that the riotous indications had subsided as rapidly as they had arisen; that the courts of justice were in full operation, and that not a single individual could be found in opposition to the execution of the laws. They, therefore, besought him to countermand the march of the army—or if it should march, that he would accompany it in person, as the people were now alarmed at the excesses it might commit, especially as they had heard unfavorable reports of its disposition toward them, no doubt exaggerated—as the accounts from the West had been at the East. They also stated that they had learned with surprise, that many of the most meritorious citizens who had exerted themselves to restore order and to quell the disturbances, had been denounced as the principal movers of the insurrection.*

The President, in answer, expatiated at length on the evils occasioned by the insurrection, and the injury done to the cause of liberty and free government throughout the world. The outrages committed against the

---

* It will appear, from the following extract from the "Incidents," that the remark of the commissioners to the President, at least of Mr. Reddick, had a particular reference to Mr. Brackenridge:

"I had more reason to be apprehensive than I was aware. A few days after the return of the commissioners from the President, Mr. Reddick called upon me, and with great appearance of solicitude, gave me to understand the unfavorable point of view in which I stood with the army, and of the great personal danger I had to apprehend, from the threats against me. That having occasionally mentioned my name to the President, as not being concerned in the insurrection, he was silent. But those about him appeared to have strong prejudices. This brought to my mind an expression I had seen in the address of the President at Carlisle, exhorting, among other things, 'to detect intriguers.' Thought I, that savors a little of chevalier Neville; he knows that I cannot be charged with any overt act, and may have insinuated there, as he has done here, that I have intrigued against the government. The fact is, the intriguers here were all on the side of the government; there was nothing but open force against it."

There can be no doubt that the cruel and ungenerous prejudice was created by the exiles, and especially by the Nevilles, toward Mr. Brackenridge, against whom the elder Neville, Kirkpatrick and Craig entertained a personal enmity. The only intrigues were those employed by the friends of the government, to persuade the people to cease their open violence and submit to the laws, in the hope of obtaining an amnesty for the acts rashly committed. If there be guilt in such intrigues, we must strike out from the Good Book the words, "Blessed are the peace-makers."

government, had agitated the United States from one side to the other like an electric shock, and disposed them very generally to turn out in support of the violated laws. He spoke in high terms of the army, then at the place of rendezvous or on their march, and of the alacrity with which they had turned out; he said, that it had even been found necessary to send expresses to prevent too great a number from marching, especially from New Jersey. He lamented the sacrifices that the farmer and merchant were under the necessity of making, and the great expense that would be incurred by the government by the expedition. He expressed his astonishment that the people were so blind to their own interests, as not to have prevented the necessity of it by giving to the commissioners such assurances of their submission to the laws as would have sheltered them from punishment, and secured the restoration of order, and that we and other well disposed citizens had not been more successful in persuading them to take that salutary course. He concluded his observations on this subject by giving his opinion, that the resolutions which they presented were not sufficiently unequivocal to justify him in dismissing the army, now when they were rendezvoused, and the greatest proportion of the expenses incurred, and the sacrifices of the farmer and merchant already made by engaging in the expedition. He did not mention, however, in what respect the assurances were insufficient or equivocal. He further observed, that the objects to be attained by the expedition, were the unequivocal assurances of submission to the laws, and protection to the officers of the revenue for the future; and the good disposition of the government, expressed by the commissioners, being rejected, rendering the march of the troops necessary, some "atonements" would be required for the infractions of the laws.* Observing that the resolutions referred to the delegates for further information, he invited them to proceed to give him that information.

* This expression, "some atonements," is remarkable, coming from Washington! (See Findley's account of the conference, in his History, p. 170.) What atonement could there be, except the legal punishment of the guilty? The great question was, whether this could be effected without marching an army of fifteen thousand men? Was this atonement to be exacted of the whole country, in its aggregate character, the innocent included with the guilty? "Atonement!" It is an ill-omened expression, reminding one of Asiatic notions of justice, of visiting on the innocent the sins of the guilty—a life for a life, instead of the more enlightened practice which repudiates retaliatory, or vicarious suffering, and makes each one answerable only for his own acts, not as compensation, but punishment. This does not seem to accord with modern enlightened notions of justice. It is painful to find such sentiments attributed to Washington; they look more like the policy of

The delegates stated in reply, that the resolutions of which they were the bearers, were in the exact terms required by the commissioners, that they were adopted without a dissenting voice; that they went even beyond what had been required, in the submission to the laws, and that they were now universally approved by the people. All that had been wanting, was a little longer time to give the proper information to the people, scattered over so large a space; it was impossible, on account of the brief period allowed, that they could become fully acquainted with the nature of the submission. In a few districts, the signing had been prevented by some violent men; and others who had refused, did so from conscientious, or mistaken notions, but when better informed, had requested permission to do so, almost with tears. The allowance of but one day, throughout the whole of a country of such great extent, was entirely too short a time for the purpose. The delegates then proceeded to give a brief outline of the beginning and progress of the insurrection, observing that great allowance should be made for exaggeration by the time the accounts of it had crossed the mountains; just as at this moment, the hostile temper and violence of the army were exaggerated at the West.

The insurrection, (they proceeded to say,) as it has been called, but in reality only a riot, it is true, of an aggravated nature, was a sudden, unpremeditated act, confined to a small district, in the immediate neighborhood of the Inspector, at a period of the year, the harvest time, when the people of the country were more easily assembled, and more excitable than usual. Perhaps not a tenth part of the population had any knowledge of the unlawful acts, until after they were committed; and of course

Hamilton, whose party views, bordering a little on monarchy, were then prominent. The great dread of Hamilton as to the permanence of the new government established by the constitution, was from anarchy; hence he conceived the necessity of proving to the world, that it had sufficient innate moral and physical power to sustain itself, independently of the support of the people. If the government could thus sustain itself even in the gristle, it could certainly do so when time had given it firmness and consistency. It is difficult to shake off the veneration for great names, and the sentiments emanating from them; but it is the duty of the historian to do so, in weighing their just claims to respect. The truth is, it was difficult, if not impossible, to prevent the army from marching, being once under way; and this disposition was far from being diminished by the belief that they were not likely to meet with opportunities to signalize their valor! If the passes of the mountains had been seized by a few thousand riflemen, this valor might not have been so conspicuous. On the approach of the army to Bedford, all those who had not signed the submission fled the country. It is said by Mr. Brackenridge, that more than two thousand riflemen of the western counties left their homes; some retired to the wilderness, others descended the river.

could have had no previous concert with the rioters, nor was it in their power to take any measures to compel them. Even among those who were at the destruction of Neville's house, there was a large proportion of patriotic citizens, who attended with a view of restraining the multitude, as far as possible, and many were compelled, by threats, to accompany them. With respect to the assemblage at Braddock's Field, although in appearance alarming, yet when its character is considered, it should rather be viewed, as far as relates to the people, as a mere freak of folly and ignorance, with no common design, or fixed determination against the government. They had been called out by some presumptuous and shortsighted individuals, by issuing a circular, as if for a regular review of the militia, at their usual place of rendezvous. The greater part did not know for what purpose they were assembled, further than it was something connected with the excise laws, which were, and still are, generally unpopular; but not a single act, or a single expression, showed any hostility to the government. Many of the militia officers accompanied their commands, as also many patriotic individuals and civil magistrates, with the sole view of preventing mischief, and prevailing on them to disperse, which they did, after an idle display during only one day. The riots at the house of Wells, and that at Webster's, were also the acts of a small portion of the worst of the population, most of them having little stake or interest, and in proportion the most violent and clamorous. With very few exceptions, these acts were all disapproved by the more orderly and respectable part of the community, who have been active from the commencement of these unfortunate acts, in resorting to every means in their power to restore order, and bring the people to a proper sense of their duty to the government and themselves.

The meeting at Parkinson's Ferry, it was hoped by those who proposed it, would be the means of restoring order; but unfortunately it was found that in the election of delegates, too large a number of the ill-disposed had been sent; yet, in spite of this, the resolutions passed by them, and the appointment of a sub-committee to meet at Brownsville, and a committee of conference, showed a disposition to submit on reasonable terms. In the appointment of a committee of conference, that committee, without hesitation, acceded to the terms of the commissioners on the part of the government, and afterward, with the exception of one individual, made every effort to prevail on the sub-committee at Brownsville to submit. The delegates here assured the President that they sincerely regretted that the acceptance had not been unanimous, and in this feeling, almost every man in the West of respectability, property or intelligence, fully participated. They regretted still more the reluctance shown by the people, in signing the submission; yet, without the explanation which they proposed to give, it was natural to ascribe this conduct to other than the real motives.

In some of the township meetings, a few lawless persons, by threats and violence, prevented the well-meaning from signing the paper. But this was confined to the most obstinate and ignorant class—a class to be found in all countries. These persons took advantage of the present state of disorder to gratify their envy and hatred, but on the first return of society to a settled condition they would fall back into their primitive insignificance. Their threats of burning property, of acts of personal violence, although alarming, were not carried into execution on that occasion. These were not the people to give trouble in settled times. They assured the President, that except in the neighborhoods of the riots, very few of those who opposed the signing had been guilty of any other acts of outrage. In other places, those who declined signing, did so from conscientious objections, where they were able to attend the places of meeting, which many, from various causes, could not on the same day, as they could have done, if several days in succession had been appointed. Many believed that in signing they would agree to renounce their right to make a legal opposition to a law universally unpopular. Many, feeling themselves entirely innocent of any act, or even intention to violate the laws, refused to sign from the most honorable, though mistaken motives; but when afterward better informed on the subject by the suggestions of the intelligent, and by their own reflections, would willingly have signed if an opportunity had been presented. On this principle the whole county of Fayette had declined signing the submission; but by a general vote, had, by a large majority, declared themselves in favor of it. In that county no acts of opposition to the laws had occurred: the same remark would apply to a considerable part of Westmoreland, and the remote districts of the frontier, which had taken no part, and in fact were little acquainted with the occurrences. But since the day appointed for the signing, in no county was there a more rapid change in the sentiments of people. The most prominent movers, or leaders, had signed the submission, and left those who were still inclined to violence, to shift for themselves. Others of the more conspicuous would avail themselves of the first opportunity, on the approach of the army, to make their escape from the country. From this circumstance, if the President meant by his expressions that an atonement must be made to the government, by the bringing to punishment the leaders of the riots by arrest, and judicial trial, then they would be already beyond its reach. The conduct of these leaders had opened the eyes of the common people, who now found themselves deceived, and now willingly listened to the representations of their more honest and intelligent friends. The feeling of submission had become universal, of which no stronger proof could be given than the result of the meeting of the original delegates at Parkinson's Ferry, who had now sent them on their friendly errand to the President. They, at the same time, took occasion to express their sense of the enlightened and humane course pursued by him, and the kind and indulgent manner in which their representations had been received on this occasion.

The President, in reply, assured the delegates that it would have been his wish to have authorized the commissioners to have given the people sufficient time for the agitation to subside, and be informed of the terms, and to deliberate on them, without ordering the militia to be in readiness for marching, if time and other circumstances would have permitted; but that the time the insurrection commenced was not of his choosing, and was too near the winter to enable him to afford the time he wished to have given; and that the flame having caught in Maryland, and symptoms of it having been discovered in some other places in Pennsylvania, rendered it improper to delay the expedition till the spring, lest the flame should spread farther. He said there were some disorderly corps in the army—that some disorders had been committed on the march to Carlisle—that two men had been actually killed; he described, circumstantially, the manner in which they were killed, and said, that though from the information he had received neither case appeared to have been murder, yet he had given up the authors of both these offenses to the laws of our own State, and would do so in every instance where the laws required that this should be done; and he assured the delegates that he would provide, by dispersing the disorderly corps among better troops, or otherwise, that they should be kept in strict subordination; that in every instance where infractions were made on the laws by any of the army, they should be subjected to punishment. He further gave assurances that the army should not consider themselves as judges, or executioners of the laws; but as employed to support the proper authorities in the execution of them. That he had been obliged to leave Virginia, before he had transacted some necessary business, to come in haste to Philadelphia on account of the insurrection, and that he had left Philadelphia, where he knew his presence was necessary to prepare for the meeting of Congress, in order to come to the army; that he mixed and conversed daily with the officers, and that his great object in all this was to impress the army with a proper sense of the importance of submitting to the laws; and that unless they did so, the last resort of a republican government would be defeated. He added, that he would go to the Maryland brigade, then rendezvoused at Williamsport, and from thence to the Virginia troops, at Fort Cumberland, and return by Bedford, where the troops now on their march from Carlisle would encamp for some time; and that his great object would be to impress on the army in those different places, a sense of the necessity of its subordination to the laws.

With respect to the expense, &c., of the expedition, he said there might some good grow out of it to console, if not compensate the West. That though we had made a republican form of government and enacted laws under it, yet we have given no testimony to the world of being able or willing to support our government and laws; that this being the first instance of the kind since the commencement of the government, he thought it his duty to bring such force as would not only be sufficient to subdue the insurgents, if they made resistance, but to crush to atoms any opposition that might arise in any other corner; that this would operate in favor of humanity, by effectually discouraging any that might be otherwise so disposed, from provoking bloodshed; and that in the result it might teach the citizens to be more cautious of writing or speaking in such a manner of the measures of government as might have a tendency to inflame the citizens; and would also convince other nations that we could defend ourselves. He said that the questions asked by the delegates with respect to further assurances, would require some time for consideration; and appointed five o'clock in the evening for further conference.

Although there is much to admire, and little to complain of by the most fastidious, in these observations of Washington, yet we cannot but regret the expression of a sentiment in the last sentence, which seems to narrow the freedom of speaking and writing of public measures. The progress of public opinion since that day has placed this matter on a different footing; and in this instance, even the wisdom and magnanimity of Washington erred, according to the settled judgment of the present day. Great allowance is to be made for Washington, considering the yet unsettled state of the new government, while the purity of his intentions cannot be questioned. It could not be expected that he could at once rise so far in political foresight above such intellects as that of General Hamilton, and those of his administration who constituted the dominant political party. With these, it is clear that the freedom of speaking and writing disrespectfully of government measures had much greater weight in the scale; and the "intemperate resolutions," although violating no law, were regarded as a more serious crime than the senseless and brutal riots which had broken into flames, and then exhausted themselves. The intelligent and philosophic reader will here find the clew to the erroneous and mistaken policy under which the formidable army was marched into the West, in order to put down an insurrection which, as we repeat, had ceased to exist, and ostensibly to sustain the laws when they needed no extraneous support. How much more noble a spectacle would have been exhibited—how much more powerful in its moral influence—in the appearance of a disturbed community returning to order, of its own accord, and through the force of its own sense of propriety! Surely such a spectacle would afford a thousand times better assurance of security and permanence, than that to be ascribed to the application of external force! The individual who struggles with, and controls and subdues his own evil passions, exhibits, certainly, a more striking and impressive example than the case of the criminal who is restrained by chains and dungeons.

In the evening the conference was resumed, by the President declining to transmit, by the delegates, orders for the arrest of any particular offenders, which they had proposed as a test of the efficiency of the laws; observing that the people of the West ought to know among themselves who were the offenders, and take the proper steps. He, however, encouraged them to obtain more unequivocal assurances from the people, but gave no promises of amnesty on account of these assurances, although saying, repeatedly, that they might do good. He particularly impressed on the delegates the utmost care, that not a gun should be fired against the army, as in that case he would not be responsible for the consequences. They assured him, in turn, that no resistance would be made; but on this caution being repeated, observed, that if some fool, or desperate man, should fire, it would be hard to hold the well-meaning and innocent accountable. He answered, that he did not intend that they should; but it was impossible to foresee what would be the consequence of such an act. He told them that he did not command the army in person, but had appointed Governor Lee commander-in-chief; at the same time mentioning the names of those who commanded the forces of the different States; causing, also, to be read, the orders he had prepared for the government of their conduct, and which were admirably designed to establish the subordination of the military to the civil authority.

The delegates conversed freely upon every topic upon which they thought proper to touch, and were listened to with the composure and dignity which might have been expected from the character of Washington. Secretary Hamilton, who was present, inquired what were the grounds of the confidence of the delegates, in the submission to the laws and the protection to the officers, in different parts of the country. In answer to this, they gave the particular instances of the recent enforcement of the laws to prove the ability to do so, and the disposition of the people to submit. They spoke also of the activity of the clergy, who had required submission as a ground of communion in their churches, and who had greatly contributed to bring their people to a sense of their duty, after the effervescence had passed off. They further stated, that the judges of the courts, in the different counties, without exception, the justices of the peace, and all who had ever been, or were then, members of the Assembly, with few exceptions, were, and always had been, well disposed, and the friends of order; that these were generally men of understanding, to whom their neighbors had been in the habit of looking for advice, excepting during the late brief period of popular frenzy. That during that period many erroneous views had been propagated among the people, both as respects the Federal and State governments; but, that being now completely undeceived, there was no probability of their being again led away in a similar manner; that in fact a most extraordinary reaction had taken place, scarcely credible to those who had not witnessed it, and entirely at variance with the exaggerated accounts which were still believed east of the mountains.

On being asked by the Secretary what ground of confidence there was with respect to the country adjacent to the Monongahela, they answered, that not having been present at the late meeting at Parkinson's Ferry, they could not speak from personal knowledge; but that Alexander Addison, president of the State courts in that district, who had been secretary of the meeting referred to, had informed them by letter, that he had conversed with the principal distillers, who resided there, and that they had assured him they would submit to the laws. They added, that Mr. Andrew M'Farlane, who resided in the settlement where the opposition had been the most violent, and who had himself been obnoxious to the rioters, had traveled down the road with them, and assured them that he would be responsible with all his estate, which was considerable, for submission to the law, and protection to the officers in that settlement.

The delegates admitted that a number had been unwilling to believe that the militia would march against them, but this was occasioned by the reports they heard every day of liberty poles being erected in the old counties; of the militia refusing to turn out, or determining to join the insurgents when they did come; that hearing of the threats of violence which had been uttered by some in the army, greatly magnified by report, packhorsemen and other travelers were afraid to tell the truth, unless they were certain of the company they happened to be in. But this kind of deception and distrust now no longer existed, and had prevailed only among the most ignorant, always the most difficult to govern, because of their inability to comprehend the reasons and representations of the better informed. Among the latter, the anxiety of mind, false alarms and suspicions by which they had been perplexed for some time past, had rendered them and the citizens generally, extremely desirous for the restoration of order; that before it had been so far accomplished, every man of influence, property or understanding was fully convinced that it was for our interests that the laws should be supported, and the public officers protected in the discharge of their duty. The State and county officers also had found that in suppressing excisemen, insulting judges and other legal agents, they were destroying their own authority, and rendering their functions useless; from which circumstances they were particularly active in bringing about submission. The delegates said, in conclusion, that this very anxiety and apprehension would operate more powerfully in support of government than any express declaration in any set form of words. They suggested that any declarations made through fear, on the approach of the army, for the purpose of making examples, would not be so sincere, and might possibly, in case of any acts of severity, rather increase the discontent and give a new direction from public outrages to private revenge, which would be more demoralizing, as well as difficult to guard against. The march of a conquering army over a prostrate people, would also have a tendency to break down that spirit which forms the best support of our republican institutions. They expressed the opinion that it would exhibit a much more pleasing spectacle to see the people return to their subjection to the laws and proper authorities of their own accord; and of this the delegates did not entertain a doubt, for it was already done, and the unnecessary march of the army would only leave unfavorable impressions toward the government and its institutions.

The President informed the delegates that it was the opinion of a number of the most respectable of their fellow citizens, that the march of the army would be necessary, not only for the restoring submission to the revenue laws, but for the protection of well disposed persons! This information the delegates had already contradicted in their previous statements. It may be readily traced to the exiles, especially the Nevilles, and no small portion of this unfriendly advice may be ascribed to feelings of revenge against the people of the western counties and particular individuals. Events proved this conjecture to be true. The delegates admitted that appearances about the time the government commissioners left the country seemed to justify such opinions; but since then, things had undergone an entire change—a change so sudden that it was impossible for them to have foreseen it; that they entertained no doubt that some of the best informed of those, who had but a few weeks before given that opinion, had now been convinced to the contrary. That since then, the courts having been held throughout the whole of the counties, the citizens vying with each other in their support, no one who had remained in the country, and witnessed the progress of public sentiment, could be mistaken. They asserted positively, that not one of these could be found who would now advise the march of the army.

They inquired whether advantage would be taken of want of form in signing the declaration of submission? The President answered, that he could not inform them without knowing the circumstances. They explained, that they meant only such want of form as did not arise from any fault in the person claiming the amnesty, but from the conduct of others; as from the papers being torn after being signed. He replied, that no advantage would be taken of such want of form. The same reasoning would have covered the ground of persons prevented from other unavoidable causes, such as inability to attend, or being absent on the precise day, or while occupied in prevailing on persons in other places to sign.

The delegates finally undertook to procure more positive assurances, and transmit them to the army, which they were assured would halt some time at Bedford before proceeding across the mountains. They then withdrew, intending to return homeward next day, but the President sent his private secretary, early next morning, to their lodgings, to request them to wait on him again before they left town; when they called he had gone out to the army, but as he returned from seeing the last division on its march, he stopped his horse before the door of their lodging and called them to him—conversed with them some time in the street, and invited them to see him again in the evening, which they spent in conversation similar to that which had before taken place. The delegates say: "We were dismissed as politely as we had been received, and in all the opportunities we had of conversing with the President, were treated with that candor and politeness which have at all times distinguished his character." It is pleasing to read these noble traits, although there could be no reason to expect anything different from Washington.

At parting, at this and the former interviews, the delegates expressed their earnest desire that the President would accompany the army to its farthest destination; yet, they admitted that he had given every assurance that it should be kept in subordination, short of what his own presence and authority would exercise. He replied that if, at Bedford, he discovered that his presence would be necessary to insure subordination, and he could be spared from the seat of government, he possibly would stay with the army if it advanced into the western country. He was anxious to prevent bloodshed, and at the same time anxious to enforce the laws with as little annoyance as possible, and by encouraging them to obtain additional assurances, he was accomplishing a principal object of his expedition. In fact, it will be seen that while the army was still at Bedford these assurances were obtained, which ought to have sufficed, if that army had not been determined to march, under any and every condition of things, for their own gratification, rather than for the purpose for which it was drawn out. The President, according to Findley, (from whom the account of these conferences is chiefly taken,) was fully sensible of the inflammable and ungovernable disposition of some of the troops, which had discovered itself before his arrival at Carlisle; and he had not only labored incessantly to repress that spirit and prevent its effects, but also to remove the fears of the delegates. As often as they suggested their fears, he gave assurances that discipline and subordination to the laws would be enforced; and also that the disorderly corps would be dispersed among those better disposed; or if this could not be done, they would be dismissed, with disgrace. Orders were given to this effect, and in some instances punctually executed; in others, the fears of the delegates were but too well founded. The bad temper manifested by a large portion of the troops has been already adverted to; the respect due to Washington could not restrain some of the more outrageous from indulging in insolent vituperation against him for lending a respectful ear to the representations of the d—d insurgents, through their delegates. They breathed nothing but vengeance, and appeared to think that there was nothing to be done but to shoot, burn, plunder and destroy. Some of them gave out threats and used language suitable only to outrageous banditti; there were, however, some honorable exceptions, especially in the troops from New Jersey and Maryland, and in one company, that of Captain Dunlop, from Philadelphia. The substitutes, who took the place of the non-combatants, were decidedly the worst and most unscrupulous. We extract the following from Findley's history:

"The President's attention to promote subordination to the laws, and curb the disposition to licentiousness, which was too evident, and to give us sufficient confidence to encourage the people in the western counties, was sound policy; for though nothing could be conceived more distressing to us than the very thoughts of hostile opposition to the government of the United States, yet if the army had marched to the western country under the prevailing influence of that inflammatory and licentious spirit which discovered itself amongst part of them at Carlisle, we must have thought it our duty to have returned with all haste and told the people what they had a right to expect; and in that case desperation must have supplied the want of resources, the innocent being compelled to make common cause with the guilty. For there is no law, human or divine, which obliges people tamely to submit to be skewered, shot or hanged in cold blood, and this was the declared object for some time, of those who made the most noise. It was a singular circumstance, that such citizens of the western country as had made the greatest exertions in preventing the spread of the disorders and restoring submission to the laws, were destined to be the first victims of their lawless rage."

Messrs. Findley and Reddick hastened home in order to obtain the additional assurances they had undertaken to procure. This was done by again calling together the original delegates at Parkinson's Ferry, for which purpose Mr. Reddick proceeded to Pittsburgh to have the notices struck off; whence they were distributed in all directions with as little loss of time as possible. About the same period a good opportunity was presented by the fall muster of the militia, which was not neglected. All whose names were on the rolls and could attend, were called upon to sign a paper of submission, which they did without hesitation, at the instance of the brigade inspectors and commanding officers.*

The meeting was convened on the 24th of October, under very different circumstances from the first assemblage. They were unanimous in favor of peace and submission to the laws. The number exceeded a thousand, and none acted as delegates, and no credentials were produced. It was more properly a mass meeting, representing the whole population of the western counties. Bradford, Fulton, Parkinson, Marshall, and others who had been conspicuous in opposition to the laws, had either embraced the amnesty or fled the country. On this occasion the assemblage did not think proper to organize themselves as a deputation, but as

---

* The inhabitants of Greensburg and Hempfield township, Westmoreland county, David Marchand presiding, met on Wednesday, 22d October, 1794, adopted resolutions of full and unequivocal assurance, and to the number of four hundred and twenty signed a certificate thereof.

a meeting of the people in their primary capacity, and it was the largest of the kind that had ever been held in the West. James Edgar was called to the chair, and Albert Gallatin appointed secretary. When it was opened, Messrs. Reddick and Findley gave a narrative of their mission; of their reception by the President; and then stated the propriety of giving more unequivocal assurances of the determination on the part of the people to support the laws and to protect the officers of the government, and as nearly as possible in the words suggested by the President. They also cautioned those whom they addressed to use every possible vigilance to prevent any foolish person from doing anything which might provoke the army, in case it should march into the country; either by firing a gun, or any other act which might be regarded as an offense, and afford them a pretext to break through military discipline. In order to increase this caution, they were informed that the same inflammatory temper which had recently prevailed in the West, and now happily at an end, had taken possession of a part of the army, who would be with difficulty restrained. They repeated the assurances of the President, that all who behaved with propriety, and who had taken the benefit of the amnesty, should be protected, no matter what their crimes might have been before that act. In all these observations there was a perfect acquiescence, and the following resolutions were adopted without a dissenting voice:

"1st. *Resolved*, That in our opinion, the civil authority is now fully competent to enforce the laws, and punish both past and future offenses, inasmuch as the people at large are determined to support every description of civil officers in the legal discharge of their duty.

"2d. *Resolved*, That in our opinion, all persons who may be charged, or suspected of having committed any offense against the United States, or the State, during the late disturbances, and who have not entitled themselves to the benefits of the act of oblivion, ought immediately to surrender themselves to the civil authority, in order to stand their trial; that if there be any such persons among us, they are ready to surrender themselves to the civil authority accordingly, and that we will unite in giving our assistance to bring to justice such offenders as shall not surrender.

"3d. *Resolved*, That in our opinion, offices of inspection may be immediately opened in the respective counties of this survey, without any danger of violence being offered to any of the officers, and that the distillers are willing and ready to enter their stills.

"4th. *Resolved*, That William Findley, David Reddick, Ephraim Douglass and Thomas Morton, do wait on the President with the foregoing resolutions."

Armed with these resolutions, and it is impossible to conceive of any assurances more complete, the delegates proceeded to Bedford. Unfortunately Washington had been compelled to return to Philadelphia, leaving the command to General Lee. The Secretary of the Treasury remained some time with the army, and it would seem, represented the President, but with a degree of power not possessed even by him. Their reception, according to Findley, was very different from that which they had met with from Washington; and finding their mission useless, they returned home, trusting to the general orders, admirably drawn up by the President, although signed by Lee, but unfortunately too little regarded in practice. It will become our painful duty to examine this subject with rigor, and pronounce the sentence required by the truth and justice of the case.

NOTES TO CHAPTER XI.

Instructions to Governor Lee.

"BEDFORD, 20th October, 1794.

"SIR:—I have it in special instruction from the President of the United States, now at this place, to convey to you, on his behalf, the following instructions, for the general direction of your conduct, in command of the militia army, with which you are charged.

"The objects for which the militia have been called forth, are,

"1. To suppress the combinations which exist in some of the western counties of Pennsylvania, in opposition to the laws laying duties upon spirits distilled within the United States, and upon stills.

"2. To cause the laws to be executed.

"These objects are to be effected in two ways:

"1. By military force.

"2. By judiciary process, and other civil proceedings.

"The objects of the military force are two-fold:

"1. To overcome any armed opposition which may exist.

"2. To countenance and support the civil officers in the means of executing the laws.

"With a view to the first of these two objects, you may proceed as speedily as may be with the army under your command, into the insurgent counties, to attack, and as far as shall be in your power, subdue all persons whom you may find in arms, in opposition to the laws above mentioned. You will march your army in two columns, from the places where they are now assembled, by the most convenient routes, having regard to the nature of the roads, the convenience of supply, and the facility of coöperation and union, and bearing in mind that you ought to act until the contrary shall be fully developed, on the general principle of having to contend with the whole force of the counties of Fayette, Westmoreland, Washington and Allegheny, and of that part of Bedford which lies westward of the town of Bedford; and that you are to put as little as possible to hazard. The approximation, therefore, of your columns, is to be sought; and the subdivision of them, so as to place the parts out of mutual supporting distance, to be avoided, as far as local circumstances will permit. Parkinson's Ferry appears to be a proper point toward which to direct the march of the columns for the purpose of ulterior measures.

"When arrived within the insurgent country, if an armed opposition appear, it may be proper to publish a proclamation inviting all good citizens, friends to the constitution and laws, to join the standard of the United States. If no armed opposition exist, it may still be proper to publish a proclamation, exhorting to a peaceful and dutiful demeanor, and giving assurances of performing, with good faith and liberality, whatsoever may have been promised by the commissioners, to those who have complied with the conditions prescribed by them, and who have not forfeited their title by subsequent misdemeanor.

"Of these persons in arms, if any, whom you may make prisoners; leaders, including all persons in command, are to be delivered to the civil magistrates; the rest to be disarmed, admonished, and sent home, (except such as may have been particularly violent, and also influential,) causing their own recognizances for their good behavior to be taken, in the cases which it may be deemed expedient.

"With a view to the second point, namely, the countenance and support of the civil officers in the means of executing their laws: you will make such dispensations as shall appear proper, to countenance and protect, and if necessary, and required by them, to support and aid the civil officers in the execution of their respective duties; for bringing offenders and delinquents to justice; for seizing the stills of delinquent distillers, as far as the same shall be deemed eligible by the supervisor of the revenue, or chief officer of inspection; and also for conveying to places of safe custody such persons as may be apprehended and not admitted to bail.

"The objects of judiciary process and other civil proceedings shall be:

"1. To bring offenders to justice.

"2. To enforce penalties on delinquent distillers by suit.

"3. To enforce the penalties of forfeiture on the same persons by the seizure of their stills and spirits.

"The better to effect these purposes, the Judge of the district, Richard Peters, Esq., and the Attorney of the district, William Rawl, Esq., accompany the army.

"You are aware that the Judge cannot be controlled in his functions. But I count on his disposition to coöperate in such a general plan, as shall appear to you consistent with the policy of the case. But your method of giving direction to proceedings, according to your general plan, will be by instructions to the district attorney.

"He ought particularly to be instructed (with due regard to time and circumstances,) 1st, To procure to be arrested all influential actors in riots and unlawful assemblies, relating to the insurrection and combination to resist the laws; or having for object to abet that insurrection and these combinations; and who shall not have complied with the terms offered by the commissioners, or manifested their repentance in some other way, which you may deem satisfactory. 2d. To cause process to issue, for enforcing penalties on delinquent distillers. 3d. To cause offenders who may be arrested, to be conveyed to jails where there will be no danger of rescue—those for misdemeanors to the jails of York and Lancaster—those for capital offenses to the jail of Philadelphia, as more secure than the others. 4th. Prosecute indictable offenses in the court of the United States; those for penalties, or delinquents, under the laws before mentioned, in the courts of Pennsylvania.

"As a guide in the case, the District Attorney has with him a list of the persons who have availed themselves of the offers of the commissioners on the day appointed.

"The seizure of stills is of the province of the supervisor, and other officers of inspection. It is difficult to chalk out a precise line concerning it. There are opposite considerations which will require to be nicely balanced, and which must be judged of by those officers on the spot. It may be useful to confine the seizure of stills to the most leading and refractory distillers. It may be advisable to extend them far into the most refractory county.

"When the insurrection is subdued, and the requisite means have been put in execution to secure obedience to the laws, so as to render it proper for the army to retire, (an event which you will accelerate as much as shall be consistent with the object,) you will endeavor to make an arrangement for attaching such a force as you may deem adequate, to be stationed within the disaffected counties, in such a manner as best to afford protection to well disposed citizens, and the officers of the revenue; and to suppress by their presence the spirit of riot and opposition to the laws.

"But, before you withdraw the army, you shall promise, on behalf of the President, a general pardon to all such as shall not have been arrested, with such exceptions as you shall deem proper. The promise must be so guarded, as not to affect pecuniary claims under the revenue law. In this measure it is advisable there should be a coöperation with the Governor of Pennsylvania.

"On the return of the army, you will adopt some convenient and certain arrangements for restoring to the public magazines, the arms, accoutrements, military stores, tents, and other articles of camp equipage and entrenching tools which have been furnished, and shall not have been consumed or lost.

"You are to exert yourself by all possible means to preserve discipline amongst the troops, particularly a scrupulous regard to the rights of persons and property, and a respect for the authority of the civil magistrates; taking especial care to inculcate, and cause to be observed this principle—that the duties of the army are confined to attacking and subduing of armed opponents of the laws, and to the supporting and aiding of the civil officers in the execution of their functions.

"It has been settled that the Governor of Pennsylvania will be second, the Governor of New Jersey third in command; and that the troops of the several States in line, on the march, and upon detachment, are to be posted according to the rule which prevailed in the army during the late war, namely, in moving toward the seaboard, the most southern troops will take the right—in moving toward the north, the most northern troops will take the right.

"These general instructions, however, are to be considered as liable to such alterations and deviations in the detail, as from local and other causes may be found necessary, the better to effect the main object upon the general principles which have been indicated.

"With great respect, I have the honor to be, Sir,

Your obedient servant,
ALEXANDER HAMILTON.
"Truly copied from the original.
B. DANDRIDGE,
Secretary to President of the U. S."

"Messrs. Findley, Reddick, Douglass and Morton, inform the inhabitants of the counties of Westmoreland, Washington, Fayette and Allegheny, that in consequence of their appointment to wait on the President of the United States, they proceeded on that duty, but on their way to Bedford, where it was expected the President might probably be seen, they learned that he had left the army for the seat of government; they, therefore, on consideration, took the right wing of the army, commanded by the Governor of the State of Pennsylvania, in their way, where they conversed with the Governor as well as with the Secretary of the Treasury on the subject of their mission, and proceeded to the other wing, to Governor Lee, of Virginia, (the commander-in-chief,) who, after receiving the various papers and faithful information which they could give, presented them with the following letter, which they now lay before the people for their serious consideration :

"'Henry Lee, to Messrs. Findley, Reddick, Morton and Douglass, deputies from the people of the counties of Fayette, Washington, Allegheny and Westmoreland.

"'GENTLEMEN:—The resolutions entered into at the late meeting of the people at Parkinson's Ferry, with the various papers declaratory of the determination of the numerous subscribers to maintain the civil authority, manifest strongly a change of sentiment in the inhabitants of this district. To what cause may truly be ascribed this favorable turn in the public mind, it is of my province to determine.

"'Yourselves, in the conversation last evening, imputed it to the universal panic which the approach of the army of the United States had excited in the lower order of the people.

"'If this be the ground of the late change, (and my respect for your opinions will not permit me to doubt it,) the moment the cause is removed the reign of violence and anarchy will return. Whatever, therefore, may be the sentiments of the people respecting the present competency of the civil authority to enforce the laws, I feel myself obligated by the trust reposed in me by the President of the United States, to hold the army in this country until daily practice shall convince all that the sovereignty of the constitution and laws is unalterably established. In executing this resolution, I do not only consult the dignity and interest of the United States, which will always command my decided respect and preferential attention, but I also promote the good of this particular district.

"'I shall, therefore, as soon as the troops are refreshed, proceed to some central and convenient station, where I shall patiently wait until the competency of the civil authority is experimentally and unequivocally proved. No individual can be more solicitous than I am for this happy event, and you may assure the good people whom you represent, that every aid will be cheerfully contributed by me to hasten the delightful epoch.

"'On the part of all good citizens I confidently expect the most active and faithful coöperation, which, in my judgment, cannot be more effectually given than by circulating in the most public manner the truth among the people, and by inducing the various clubs which have so successfully poisoned the minds of the inhabitants, to continue their usual meetings for the pious purpose of contradicting, with their customary formalities, their past pernicious doctrines. A conduct so candid should partially atone for the injuries, which in a great degree may be attributed to their instrumentality, and must have a propitious influence in administering a radical cure to the existing disorders.

"'On my part, and on the part of the patriotic army I have the honor to command, assure your fellow citizens that we come to protect and not to destroy, and that our respect for our common government, and respect to our own honor, are ample pledges for the propriety of our demeanor.

"'Quiet, therefore, the apprehensions of all on this score, and recommend universally to the people to prepare, for the use of the army, whatever they can spare from their farms necessary to its subsistence, for which they shall be paid, in cash, at the present market price; discourage exaction of every sort, not only because it would testify a disposition very unfriendly, but because it would probably produce very disagreeable scenes.

"'It is my duty to take care that the troops are comfortably subsisted, and I cannot but obey it with the highest pleasure, because I intimately know their worth and excellence.

"'I have the honor to be, gentlemen, your most obedient servant, with due consideration, HENRY LEE.

"'Head Quarters, Uniontown, November 1, 1794.'"

About this time a committee from Washington county waited on General Lee, with an address, to which he made a reply.

CHAPTER XII.

THE ARMY ENTERS THE WEST—ITS FEROCIOUS TEMPER—THE ATTEMPT TO ASSASSINATE MR. BRACKENRIDGE—THE MILITARY INQUESTS—THE EXAMINATION OF MR. BRACKENRIDGE, AND ACQUITTAL.

THE army, leaving Bedford, entered the western counties about the 1st of November, 1794, and encamped near the Monongahela, so as to be within striking distance of any of the four counties. And now the question naturally suggests itself, what was there for it to do? There was certainly no fighting to be done; and among those of that army who most aspired to military glory, this was a subject of intense regret, as they were obliged to expend their rage merely in words of contempt and indignation against the cowardly insurgents. Instead of finding parties of these arrayed for war, and regularly embodied, not a hand, or even a voice, was raised to oppose them, or resist the government. The rural population remained distressingly quiet in their sylvan homes, widely scattered over the extensive forest region, the prevailing feeling being that of alarm, on account of the reported threats and ferocity of the army. The more zealous among the officers, perhaps not the most patriotic, were continually crying out that "atonements" must be made, insurgents must be seized, examples must be exhibited pendent from the limbs of trees, to prove that their march had not been in vain. It mattered not whether people were guilty or innocent, for it was held that it was the duty of the latter to restrain the former, whether they had required the amnesty or not, or whether they had exerted themselves on the side of the government, and aided in the execution of the laws. They were all insurgents, and but for the restraints of discipline imposed by such officers as General Irvine, Governor Howell, General Chambers, and some others, the western country might have been a scene of murder and conflagration. Some of the most patriotic western men began now to think that it would have been better for them, with arms in their hands, to have met them as invaders.

It is not difficult to see what would have been the proper course to pursue with this formidable army. After having entered the country, and discovering that not the slightest resistance was to be expected, that there were neither "combinations," nor any of those fearful clubs referred to in the letter of General Lee—it should, as soon as was convenient, have commenced its retreat, leaving only a sufficient force, say one or two regiments of the most orderly and best disciplined, to sustain the civil authority, in case they should possibly be needed. To aid the civil authority was now the only legitimate use that could have been made of them, as there was no longer any military opposition to put down. Instead of this, the business of the army was now supposed to be, not to prevent the commission of offenses, but to punish those that had been committed, which was the duty of the civil magistrate, and not of the army, until expressly called upon to lend its assistance; such was clearly the idea of the President, in his orders addressed to General Lee. These punishments should have been inflicted by course of law, and not by the bayonet, and for the same reason arrests should have been made by civil officers, on process issued by the civil magistrate. The courts, the marshals, or sheriffs, should have been the agents—at least these should have been first tried, before calling on the soldiery. But the worst was the sending the arrested to Philadelphia for trial, which was more dreaded than the arrest itself, and as we have seen, was the immediate cause of the disturbances which have been related. Why could not a court have been organized for the trials in the county itself? There was an act of Congress in force, authorizing this course. But atonements were wanted, and captives to grace the triumphal entry of the victors! A district judge of the United States, Judge Peters, a marshal, and a district attorney accompanied the army; but these, in the investigation of supposed offenses, acted a subordinate part to the Secretary of the Treasury, (who had no judicial authority,) and even to the military officers; thus practically confounding the judicial, military and Executive powers. The greater is the necessity for placing in the strongest light the glaring infringements on the rights and privileges of the citizens!

Against those persons who had been most active and successful in bringing about a peaceable submission on the part of the people, the demonstrations of the soldiery was most violent, and especially against Mr. Brackenridge and Mr. Gallatin. The recent election of the latter to Congress, was some protection, but the absence of any peculiar enmity toward him, on the part of the Neville connection, was a surer ground of safety, while its violence increased the danger of Mr. Brackenridge. Nothing but putting to death in any way, was spoken of as the fate of the latter. General Neville was with the army, together with some others of the exiles, as they were called; and these were never wearied of their denunciations of him. The common language of the old General was that Brackenridge was "the greatest scoundrel on God Almighty's earth;" that Bradford and others were merely his tools, while he was the instigator of all the mischief. The Secretary of the Treasury seems to have caught this language, as appears by the letter written by him from Bedford, published in his posthumous works, in which he uses the General's phrase, "it is now discovered that Brackenridge is the greatest of all scoundrels." Nine days afterward, when he had an opportunity of examining and judging for himself, he retracted this hasty opinion, founded on such information as could be furnished through the medium of Major Craig.*

While the army was at Bedford, by way of showing what it could do, it had arrested four persons, who were sent to Philadelphia. The account of the affair is derived from Findley:

"Four prisoners were sent from Bedford, as the army advanced; one of them, Herman Husbands, was extensively known on account of some singularities of character. After suffering four months in prison, and such prisons as are happily unknown at the present day, there appearing nothing against him, [not even his interpretation of the visions of Ezekiel,] he was discharged, with a crowd of others, by the court; but his constitution had received such a shock that he died before he could leave the city, and return to his home in the mountains. Another of the name of Filson, who kept a large store in the village of Berlin in the same county, after being taken to Philadelphia, was refused to be admitted to bail, although this favor was warmly solicited by respectable merchants in the city. The prosecution was conducted against him with unusual rigor; being first acquitted on a charge of treason, he was tried for a misdemeanor, in which the verdict was also not guilty. Of the two others, one was an old inoffensive German, named Weisgarver; after being imprisoned four months, he was admitted to bail, and no bill was found against him at court. The last, whose name is Lucas, was a sergeant in the army during the war, and was well known at the time of the revolt of the Pennsylvania line, and though he was one of the leaders of that revolt, in that situation he rendered such essential service to the public as to have a premium assigned him. A general officer who had been well acquainted with his services, now obtained his release after four months of imprisonment. On his trial nothing was found against

* It is to be regretted, for the fame of General Hamilton, that the editor of his posthumous works had not rejected this letter; there can be no doubt that if living, he would have done so himself. The editor was probably not aware of the subsequent examination of Mr. Brackenridge by Hamilton in person.

him. He was poor, and had a large family of small children." Can anything more strongly exemplify the impropriety of such illegal arrests, and dragging men beyond their vicinage? If the cases just related had been submitted to a grand jury in their county, this suffering and injustice would not have occurred. But these are of a trifling nature, compared to the wholesale arrests and harassing inquests subsequently practiced by the *military* guardians of the laws in the western country.

Mr. Brackenridge had received intimations of the threats against his life, and had at first thought of quitting the country; but conscious of innocence, and feeling indignant at the ingratitude manifested for his important services, and after a night passed in anxious meditation, resolved, if doomed to perish, to die on his own hearth. After drawing up an account of the transactions in which he had been concerned, addressed to James Ross, with a request that he would do justice to his memory, he determined to face the danger which threatened him, whatever it might be. In this, his enemies were, no doubt, disappointed; as in all probability they would rather hear of his flight from the country. A detachment of troops under General Morgan entered the town, escorting Col. Neville and some others of the exiles in a sort of triumph or ovation. The same night a party of Morgan's corps proceeded about eleven o'clock to the house of Mr. Brackenridge, with the intent of putting their murderous designs into execution; but information having been communicated to the General and Col. Neville, they ran out without taking time to put on their hats, and interposing themselves, declared that the ruffians must pass over their bodies before they could perpetrate the deed. A regard for their own characters called for this energetic interference, for if the murder had been perpetrated by those under their control, the world would have held them responsible. Mr. Brackenridge, therefore, gave them no thanks, and considered himself bound to them by no feeling of gratitude; and it is highly probable that the habitually intemperate mode of speaking of him by the Neville connection, may have induced some of their hot-headed followers to believe that they would be doing them a service by ridding them of a hated enemy.*

* The houses of Col. Neville and Mr. Brackenridge were little more than a hundred yards apart. He says: "The troops had advanced within twenty yards of my house, when an officer who had been apprised of their intention, and in vain labored to disperse them, having run to General Morgan, who was in the house of Neville the younger, and not yet gone to bed, gave him information. The General and the Colonel ran out without their hats, and the General opposing himself to the fury of the troops, said, that it must be through him they would reach me;

In the course pursued by Mr. Brackenridge, he had given evidence of a true courage, according to the definition of Abbé Barthelme in Anacharsis: "He knew his danger, feared it, yet met it." The narrative will be followed up in his own words:

"The right wing of the army had crossed the mountains and were in the western country. It was like the approach of the tempest to me; I could hear the thunder at a distance; and every day new accounts reached me of butchery denounced against me, without judge or jury. I began to hear General Neville raise his voice, 'The d——st scoundrel that ever was on God Almighty's earth.' The left wing had already crossed the mountains, at the distance of thirty miles to the westward. I could hear of Colonel Neville at the table of General Lee, and publicly elsewhere, throughout that camp, denounce vengeance against 'the d——d rascal,' meaning me.*

"I began to think it would be unsafe to stand it; that I could not have sufficient confidence in the good disposition of the commanding officers, much less in their power to restrain their troops; and that it might be advisable to be out of the way until I could see whether subordination to the civil authority was practicable or not. I had the wilderness behind me; and as before I had meditated to escape from 'Tom the Tinker,' so now I meditated an escape from an equally outrageous banditti, as I began to think them, by going to the West. My sensations were violent at the time; but I ought to be excused, as I must have thought it very extraordinary in people to have come to support the laws, and to be talking of violating them. I communicated to General Wilkins my resolution of going neither to the Spaniards nor to the British, but of taking my chance among the Indians for a month or two, until I could have a proper assurance of protection in surrendering myself to the judicial authority. I had thought of a hunter whom I could employ to go to the woods with me.

"General Wilkins could not but acknowledge the expediency of going, from all that he had heard or seen, and proposed a hunter whom he knew, and thought more expert than the one I had named, and engaged to speak to him to go with me. He was to send him to me next morning.

that I had stood my ground, and would be cognizable to the judiciary; and let the law take its course." The above fact shows the imperfect state of discipline in the new levied army. If the deed had been perpetrated, there would have been such historians as Hildreth and Craig to excuse it; and the *good name of the victim* might have continued forever blasted by the same party rancor which has so long continued to villify the whole population of Western Pennsylvania.

* This was before the attempted assassination.

"I lay upon a couch and thought of it till midnight. I reflected that people would always talk more than they would do; and that putting me to death would be more in the language than in the intention of the mass. It was the fashionable speech of the camp, and every one adopted it without meaning to carry it into effect; but I reflected, also, that the very strain of talking, though not originating from the intention to act, yet might lead some unprincipled and inconsiderate man to perpetrate what had been spoken of; more especially as I had heard of the violence of the Nevilles, and had suspected that the horrid resentment which they appeared to entertain against me might prompt them to encourage assassination.

"However, after deep thought of many hours, I sprang from my couch-bed, and expressed my determination, that if I was to be assassinated, it should be in my own house. It never should be said that I would move a foot from the ground. Having now determined to wait my fate, I employed a day or two in putting my papers in order, and making a short sketch of the outline of my conduct during the insurrection, and directing it to be delivered to James Ross, who knew the greater part of his own knowledge, with a request that he would give it to the public, and do my memory justice. I knew the rage against me was founded on the misconception of the multitude and the malice of individuals. It had been the case with La Rochefaucault, Clement de Tennere and others, at an early period of the French revolution."

The discovery had been made, that Mr. Brackenridge had not signed the amnesty until the day after the time; and it was thought that means would be found to destroy him, by way of prosecution. "I was diverted," says he, "by a speech of General Neville reported to me, when some people, alarmed for their situation, had gone to solicit his favor. 'Children,' said he, 'it is not you that we want; it is some of the big fish—Brackenridge, Gallatin and Findley, that we want.' Thought I, it is bad enough to find myself in the same school of fish with Gallatin and Findley, when I have had political difference with Findley, which has produced a coolness that still exists; and as to Gallatin, I never spoke to him in my life, until I met him at Parkinson's Ferry. But there was ingenuity on the part of the old general. Knowing the hostility between these men and Secretary Hamilton, he wished to couple me with the same party." The enmity between the Secretary and the persons just named, judging from repeated statements by Findley in his book, was very bitter. They had assailed his favorite financial system in the Legislature, as well as at public meeetings; at the same time there was a strong personal antipathy on his part toward these men, and which was reciprocated by them. The strong language of Mr. Brackenridge in his letter to Mr. Cox, in speaking of the funding system, must also have given offense, as Hamilton was very sensitive to any objections to his financial plans. It is, however, natural, and therefore probable, that when the Secretary came on the spot, and found that the powerful Neville connection were attempting to use him for the purpose of gratifying their private enmity, his pride was offended at the idea. It was not long before he would begin to suspect that the connection, now strengthened by the accession of General Morgan, were disposed to exert their influence against an individual who had not even the good will of the populace in his favor, having given them offense by his efforts to induce them to submit to the government, and by his public denunciation of their conduct. It would not be strange if Neville's violence should offend the self-esteem of Hamilton, at this attempt to gratify personal revenge at the expense of his character for justice and magnanimity.

We have stated, (and it cannot be too often repeated,) that instead of proceeding against supposed offenses in the recent riots, and bringing the accused, who were not entitled to the amnesty, before the judges by civil process; or impanneling a grand inquest, to call witnesses before it previous to accusation and arrest by civil officers—a nondescript commission of inquiry was instituted—the district judge taking an inferior part in it, and the arrests made at the point of the bayonet! A proceeding so strange requires to be minutely related, in order that it may stand as a beacon to avoid a similar anomaly in future.* The Inspector, as already stated, was regarded as the party aggrieved, or the general plaintiff; the Secretary of the Treasury assumed the authority of supreme director over the whole proceedings, civil and military. Some resemblance to this may perhaps be found in European despotisms, or where English liberty was not so well defined; but in a country where the safeguards of the common law exist, it is almost incredible. As a sample, we will extract the following from Findley:

"During the time that Sheriff Hamilton was waiting to have his case examined, and before he was put into close confinement, a certain John Baldwin was under examination. He was interrogated, alternately, by Secretary Hamilton, Judge Peters, the District Attorney, the Inspector, and a Mr.

---

* It may be said, that so many were implicated that it was difficult to procure juries. But this was not the fact—at all events the experiment was not made, and the instructions to Gen. Lee implied that the civil authority could act where properly supported.

Vaughan, a light-horseman from Philadelphia. The two last (the Inspector and the light-horseman,) treated him with the greatest indecorum. In the course of the examination, every means were used to induce him to testify against the sheriff. Baldwin had candidly informed them of himself being one of the committee at the burning of Neville's house, and of the persons concerned in that riot; and assured them that the sheriff was not concerned in it. He was then urged to testify that the sheriff had notified his regiment to assist at that riot, and when he refused to give testimony to that purpose, because it was not true, he was insulted, and told that he equivocated, and evaded swearing the truth; and was assured, that by his conduct he had forfeited the benefit of the amnesty, to which he was otherwise entitled; and that his life and property were endangered by not testifying to what they demanded of him, and which was not true; he was told that he could only save himself by giving such testimony."

If this stood as a solitary instance, one might be strongly inclined to doubt it; but it sinks to nothing compared with the numerous other cases which will be related. The Spanish inquisitorial mode of seeking evidence and forcing it by threats, (short only of the boot and the rack,) and the most revolting appeals, seems to have been the ordinary mode of proceeding. Why was not Sheriff Hamilton confronted with the witnesses? Why not permitted to ask questions as well as the impertinent light-horse examiner? The cases of Sheriff Hamilton and Major Powers, although less striking than the wholesale outrages of law and right which followed, are so characteristic, that we will relate them separately, on the cotemporary authority of Findley; and no one was bold enough ever to question the truth of the account at that day.

"Major Powers had not only behaved well through the whole of the troubles, but had been zealously employed in endeavoring to restore order, from an early period until it was finally established. He had been a member of several meetings for that purpose, and was one of the committee of twelve who had settled the terms of the amnesty with the commissioners at Pittsburgh. After the judiciary and part of the army had gone to the town of Washington, Major Powers was invited, by a polite letter, to wait on the Secretary at that place, which was about thirty miles distant. When he arrived, the Secretary examined him about the conduct of certain characters, with some of whom he was not even acquainted; but particularly about the conduct of Mr. Gallatin at Parkinson's Ferry. On Major Powers not answering to his satisfaction, he complained of the difficulty of obtaining information, and advised Major

Powers to retire an hour or two to refresh his memory in order to be reexamined; and spoke to an officer present, to conduct him into another chamber. In all this the Secretary appeared to treat him politely, but he was not a little surprised when he found himself thrust into a room among the other prisoners, and there confined under the point of the bayonet. At the time appointed, he was taken again into the presence of the Secretary, who asked him if he had recollected himself so far as to give more satisfactory information; on being answered that he had nothing further to recollect, having already related all he knew, the Secretary then suddenly assuming all his terrors, told Major Powers that he was surprised at him; that having the character of an honest man, he would not tell the truth; asserting that he had already proof sufficient of what he knew he could testify, if he would. After some further insulting language and threats, Major Powers was committed a close prisoner under a military guard; and though the most unexceptionable bail was offered for permission to go to his family, it was refused; and he was marched under a military guard to Pittsburgh, and there detained until the eighth day after he was taken into custody.* The Secretary being gone, the judge sent for Major Powers, and when he was brought into his presence, invited him politely to sit down, assuring him that he had no charge at all against him."

There is no reason to doubt the statement of Findley; it was never questioned, as we have already stated, and appears to have been received from Major Powers himself; but the affair was public and notorious. It exhibits the Secretary in a light which is painful to contemplate—in the assumption of power—in the attempt to influence the witness in the most reprehensible manner, in order to extort unfair testimony—and added to this, in the use of the bayonet in what ought to have been a mere judicial proceeding! It shows, also, the subserviency of the district judge, who condescended to act a secondary or inferior part in the ministrations of his office, to one who had no judicial authority whatever.

"It will appear in various other instances," says Findley, "that it was usual with the Secretary to assert to those whom he was examining, that he was possessed of sufficient proofs already of the facts to which he endeavored to extort testimony. The spring following, Major Powers was much inclined to institute an action against the Secretary; but finding that he would be obliged to go to New York, on the advice of his friends he relinquished the design."

* By what authority did the Secretary act in this individual capacity? By what law was the military guard employed?

The case of Sheriff Hamilton, one of the most estimable men in the western counties, was much more aggravated. It is unpleasant to be obliged to record such incidents, but having no reason to doubt their truth, the historian does not consider himself at liberty to reject them; and they are too important to be passed over in silence. The Secretary of the Treasury was unquestionably a great man, and rendered great services to his country—but of strong passions, and possessed of some peculiar ideas on the subject of energetic government. Nothing in the whole course of our history as a people has appeared to me so revolting, as the *exparte* military and fiscal inquests for the purpose of discovering subjects to make "atonements," to use the unhappy phrase on which I have already remarked. The case of Sheriff Hamilton is thus related by Findley:

"John Hamilton, of Washington, is high sheriff of that county, and colonel of a regiment of militia in the Mingo Creek settlement; though a number of this regiment were known to have had an active hand in the attack on Neville's house, and were in fact considered the greatest promoters of the insurrection, yet he not only kept himself free from these outrages, but endeavored, as soon as he heard of the design, to prevent the rendezvous at Braddock's Field. It was he who informed Bradford that the arms and ammunition in the garrison at Pittsburgh were designed for General Scott's expedition against the Indians; and with the assistance of some others, persuaded him to countermand the orders, and procured his promise to prevent the march. When he could not prevent this, he put himself at the head of his regiment, and was very instrumental in preventing further outrages from being committed. At the court that was held for the county of Washington, a short time after the commissioners left the country, he proposed to take any twenty of those alleged to be insurgents, and lodge them in the county jail, if writs were issued for the purpose; but it was not thought advisable to issue the writs, until it should be known what measures the commissioners would recommend to the President, and until the inflammatory spirit should be more effectually cooled down. To show, however, that he could have accomplished what he proposed, he served several writs of capias, which he had in his hands, without difficulty. He attended all the meetings for restoring order, with a view to prevent outrages; and living where he did, he merited higher approbation than if he had resided in Boston.

"Colonel Hamilton was informed by a friend of the designs against him, time enough to make his escape; but conscious of his innocence, he preferred traveling above thirty miles to where the judiciary then was, and presenting himself to Judge Peters, informed him that he had heard there was a charge against him, and requested to have it examined. The judge said that he was then too much engaged, but would call on him presently; that day, however, passed till evening, when Major Lennox, the Marshal, in the most delicate manner he could, told him he must put him under guard; but afterward dispensed with arresting him, and only took his promise that he would not depart until the judge had an opportunity of conversing with him; but the next day the Marshal informed him that he had special orders to put him under guard, which he did accordingly, though with evident regret. The sheriff here remarked, that Major Lennox treated him with as much friendship and politeness as the nature of the case would possibly admit; and let me add, that that officer's politeness is generally well spoken of.

"On the third day after he had demanded an examination, and the second after he had been put under guard, he was sent back to Washington town, from whence he had come, in custody of a small troop of horse. The judge having arrived at Washington, the sheriff applied again to him to have his case examined, who told him he would in half an hour; but on the ninth day after he had first applied to the judge, he was sent a close prisoner to Pittsburgh, and thence to Philadelphia, where he was paraded through the streets (with others,) with an ignominious badge on his hat, and thrown into the cells without his case having ever been examined! After an imprisonment of near two months and a half, he was brought before the Supreme Court on a writ of habeas corpus; and on examination, there not appearing the slightest evidence against him, he was admitted to bail. At the Circuit Court held in Philadelphia the June following, a bill for misprision of treason was sent to the grand jury against him, but every witness that was sworn testified in his favor. There was not even a suspicious circumstance against him, and consequently no bill was found."

It cannot but excite the liveliest indignation to read the details of this case; and the natural inquiry is, to whom should the blame attach? To all concerned in these extraordinary military perquisitions; the Nevilles—the Secretary of the Treasury—the District Judge—the General of the army. Findley remarks on this case as follows: "Thus a man who was at the time sheriff of the county, and a colonel of the militia, and who in a part of the country and in circumstances where temporizing might have been excusable, was not only clear of any charge, but had merit—was selected by the Secretary as a victim, illegally taken from the exercise of an office at that time of importance to the peace of the county; and without examination, or being confronted with his accuser, perhaps a secret enemy, dragged down to Philadelphia in the winter by a military guard—paraded in a barbarous manner through the streets, thrown for some time into the cells, compelled to wear the word insurgent in his hat, and then cast into prison; and after a long confinement, admitted to bail! After this he was again required to cross the mountains to meet his trial, at which nothing was alleged against him! It is not easy to assign the motive for selecting these two men, Powers and Hamilton, as objects of vengeance. They had both been friends of order during the disturbances; naturally quiet, they had never distinguished themselves in political contests, or taken any part in the discussion of public measures. Perhaps the motive for treating Major Powers with such unjustifiable severity, was to extort testimony from him, and to teach others what they might expect if they did not give such testimony against certain characters as the Secretary required. As Col. Hamilton was the sheriff of the county, and colonel of the battalion where the insurrection originated, his rank and the relation in which he stood to the county, were probably the reasons of his being selected."

These illegal military inquests, and unauthorized examinations, were carried on extensively; many hands being employed in the work. The most guilty had either fled or taken the benefit of the amnesty, to which some respect was paid at first. Great numbers were dismissed, both of the innocent and guilty, the latter generally being the most favored; probably protected by their own insignificance. The Inspector, who acted as the prosecuting or injured party, had acquired, from the fortuitous circumstances in which he was placed, an immense power over his fellow-citizens, which, without extravagance, might be compared to the revolutionary tribunals of France, under the control of Couthon and St. Just, differing only in degree of atrocity. It is terrible to reflect on the possession of such power in any man; especially if he be naturally vindictive, and has antipathies to gratify. Having made some extracts from Findley, some will also be given from the other cotemporary writer, Mr. Brackenridge, bearing on this subject.

"It may seem to reflect on the judiciary, to have it supposed that they would give so facile an ear to General Neville as may seem to be insinuated. Let it be considered, that they would find, in the course of their examination, that even at the burning of the house of the Inspector there were persons who had been under the impulse of fear for themselves, and were carried there by constraint. But more especially at Braddock's Field, many were present under compulsion; and through the scene in general, many were obliged to appear what they were not. The *quo animo*, therefore, was to be determined, a good deal, from what had been known to be their sentiments and conduct heretofore. To whom could this be referred better than to the Inspector of the revenue, who knew the people? And this gave him unlimited influence in his representations. I have no disposition to be dissatisfied with the use the Inspector made of this advantage, in saving individuals. I wish I could equally excuse the use he made of it in punishing others! I can only soften my censure by acknowledging, that so far as I have heard, he exercised favor in more instances than prejudice. But in both instances he must be considered as having misled the judiciary. It would have been better to have declined his attendance on the examinations—to have been escorted home to his house, and have remained there; leaving the judicial investigation to an operation unbiassed by him, so as not only to avoid the influence of opinion, but the suspicion of it.* But this is a delicacy the noble mind has from nature, or which a refined education gives."

The contrast between the manner in which the two cotemporary authors speak of the same transaction, is that of a refined mind and of a coarse and harsh nature; the one cuts like a sharp instrument, the other like a butcher's cleaver. The very apology for the Inspector, made by Mr. Brackenridge, is ten times more severe than the downright assault of Findley. Taken together, they represent a state of things which can scarcely ever occur again in this republic, and which the present exposition may possibly contribute to prevent. Mr. Brackenridge speaks of the judiciary in these curious examinations, when, in fact, the judiciary had very little to do with them; or, at least, as only subordinate to the Secretary of the Treasury, and his inferior officer, the Inspector. In the case of Mr. Brackenridge, as related by himself, this is fully displayed.

After Mr. Brackenridge had escaped assassination, the cry among the arriving troops was, "Hang him, hang him." The quarter-master had selected his house, being a large and commodious one, for the accommodation of General Lee; but the unexpected meeting was an awkward one, on both sides. Being a younger graduate, Lee had been under the tuition of the former at Princeton College. The General soon procured other quarters, as it was a matter of delicacy, both for himself and a host who was denounced as the chief insurgent, and whom the army was eager to hang. Through Mr. Ross, he represented to Judge Peters his readiness

---

* This is certainly a very mild view of the case of General Neville.

to attend, at any moment when called upon, in order to avoid the mortification of an arrest; and the gentleman just named pledged himself to that effect. As arrests were usually made in the night, he lay on his couch, dressed and ready for the event. Anxiety of mind from this state of suspense, and a bitter sense of the injustice to which he was subjected by the malignity of his enemies, brought on a return of a nervous affection which he had experienced in early life from severe application to study. "I had at first," says he, "feared assassination; now I began to apprehend danger from a judiciary process. I looked forward to a trial before a jury in Philadelphia, heated with prejudice against me. Besides, the part I had been drawn in to act was so various, and of such a nature, that it would take a multitude of witnesses to explain the *quo animo;* and the mere expense of a trial would ruin me. But what alarmed me still more, from a stroke that I received twenty years before, from leading a sedentary life—I am subject to a delinquency of nerves, especially when any thing strongly affects my mind; and I was afraid my feelings would kill me, under a sense of the arts that were practicing against me. I bore it with apparent fortitude, but my sensibility was greatly affected. Not that I was uncommonly afraid of death, but I regarded my memory for the sake of my family; and was apprehensive that I might sink under it, and that it would be resolved into a consciousness of guilt, and not the pain which the ingenuous mind feels when it is wronged by the world.

"I had heard all that I apprehended confirmed; that there was the strongest disposition with the judiciary, and through all the branches of the assistant examiners, to find ground for arresting me. This was so strikingly observed by the country, that it quite restored me in their good opinion; and if the election had been to take place then, there would have been no question of my obtaining their suffrages. They were satisfied they had wronged me, in supposing that I had stipulated an indemnity for myself particularly; or had made fair weather with the government by deserting them. I had nothing to fear from the body of the people; they would rather lean in my favor; but there were still enough of unprincipled persons that might be brought forward, or who would offer themselves in order to obtain favor. It was amusing to me to see the numbers of those passing themselves for friends of government, whom, during the insurrection, I had a great deal of trouble to keep down. They took their revenge now, and joined in the cry against Brackenridge. Some poor fellows did this to save themselves; I had given them leave to do it. They came to me with tears in their eyes, to consult whether they should go off or not, or stand a trial. The army had then crossed the mountains. I directed them to contrive to let my 'brother of the bar'* hear them curse me, and say they had voted against me at the election; this would be carried to the ears of my adversaries, and they would be represented as friends of the government. They did so, and it had the effect.

"I will not say that the Nevilles were usually capable of deliberately contemplating the putting me to death. The father is outrageously passionate, but not vindictive or cruel; the son is a man of good temper and humanity; but they labored under irremovable misconceptions, owing to a variety of circumstances; and their pride had also been wounded by acts of mine, which, at the time, I thought virtuous, and think so still. I know well that the misconception of the Nevilles had been in a great measure established by 'my brother of the bar,' and that their rage had been fanned by his information. He was now busy at the camp with General Neville. The General, who had been the subject of the outrages, was there in the light of a private prosecutor; and in aid of the judiciary, was assisting in bringing forward and interrogating witnesses. 'My brother of the bar' was busy in sounding and marshaling them; and if on examination any thing was omitted, he took the General aside and gave him a hint of it; the General would then return to the charge with fresh questions. This is the account I have from witnesses, and gentlemen occasionally present.

"When the matter was thought to be pretty well fixed against me in the *exparte* inquisition, the great and concluding stroke was to be given. A treasonable letter of mine, addressed to a certain Bradford, had fallen into the hands of my adversaries. It was dark and mysterious, and respected certain papers, a duplicate of which I wished him to send me,

---

* The "brother of the bar" here alluded to, was General John Woods, between whom and Mr. Brackenridge there existed a mortal feud, growing out of professional and political rivalry, such as often exists in this republic between men equally honorable and high-minded. He is not named, from delicacy to his brother-in-law, Mr. Ross, who was a friend of Mr. Brackenridge. Gen. Woods was the professional adviser of the Nevilles, and was thought by Mr. Brackenridge to have mingled personal enmity with the service of his client, the Inspector; and to have employed his talents, which were of a high order, ungenerously against him. He speaks of him with much more asperity than of the Nevilles; perhaps from the circumstance just mentioned, and regarding him as a "foeman more worthy of his steel." Gen. Woods was absent during the disturbances, and returned in company with Neville; that absence he regarded as an additional reason why Gen. Woods should take no part against him. In fact, although the Nevilles were the principals in the designs against him, they stood only second in his resentment.

having mislaid the first copy; that these were so essential I could not go on with the business without them. This letter was now produced. 'What do you make of this?' said Secretary Hamilton to James Ross, who was present; 'you have averred, as your opinion, that Brackenridge has had no correspondence with Bradford; look at that—is it not the handwriting of Brackenridge?' 'It is the handwriting,' said Ross, pausing a moment, 'and there is only this small matter observable, that it is addressed to William Bradford, Attorney General of the United States.'*

"When a blast transverse takes a shallop on the river and throws her on her beam ends, with all her sail set; or, when a scud of wind takes the standing corn of the farmer, and on the field bows the stalk to the earth, so languished 'my brother of the bar.' The old General stood motionless and speechless, and to this hour had been standing, had not Secretary Hamilton broke silence. 'Gentlemen,' said he, 'you are too fast; this will not do.'

"The late circumstance had weakened the credit of the prosecution; and all things considered, especially when James Ross was examined, it began to be doubted whether it would be for the honor of the government to prosecute me. However, the case remained open for further testimony.

"Charles Smith, son-in-law to commissioner Yeates, one of the assistant examiners, with the judges, had come to town and said to a person, who communicated it to me, that my arrest was certain; that he was astonished that I was still in Pittsburgh! Had I no regard for my life? That others also, who had no apprehension, were in a like predicament; and that thirty-six hours would make a great difference in Pittsburgh. Thought I, my adversaries have been more successful in marshaling the presumption of guilt in my case than I had conceived. I take it for granted that I shall be arrested beyond question, now. However, I had composed my mind a good deal by this time, and thought I had fortitude to bear all they could accomplish; and if there was any chance of justice at all, I would finally triumph over them.

"Notwithstanding it was known that I remained in Pittsburgh, yet it might be supposed that, as danger approached I might become more alarmed, and abscond, if direction was given to take me in the day-time; and for that reason, and because it would gratify my enemies to accumulate humiliations upon me, I counted upon being arrested in the night. I therefore lay on a couch, without undressing, ready at a moment to obey the mandate and

* It had been picked up by the same busy-body who made the discovery that he had not signed the amnesty on the day—a fact which had already been communicated by letter to Hamilton, at Bedford. See the posthumous letter referred to.

go with the guard that should call for me. I lay two nights in this manner, not sleeping much, but consoling myself with reading some of the lives of Plutarch. Reading that of Solon, I meditated upon his laws, making it death for a citizen, in a civil tumult, not to take part; for by taking part on the one side or the other, the moderate citizens will be divided, and mixing with the violent, will correct the fury on both sides until an accommodation can be brought about.* It was on that principle I had aided in the insurrection, and by seeming to be of the insurgents, had contributed to soften all their measures, and finally prevent a civil war. But I saw that the law of Solon would apply only to a small republic where the moderate men were known to each other, and could explain themselves in the course of the negotiation. I had been treading upon the edge of a precipice, making an experiment extremely dangerous to myself. My intentions were laudable, but my conduct hazardous. It is true, I had embarked in the business, in the first instance, at the request

* N. B. Craig assumes the office, without the qualifications of the literary critic, on this passage, and accuses Mr. Brackenridge of misquoting the law of Solon! The learned Theban mistakes the gloss, or commentary of Plutarch, for the law of Solon, or rather confounds them together. The words of Solon are, *that in case of civil dissension, he shall be regarded as infamous who shall remain neutral.* These words are correctly given by Mr. Brackenridge, but with his own commentary, which corresponds with that of Aulus Gellius and other writers: "that the wise and just, as well as the envious and wicked, being obliged to take some side, matters were more easily accommodated." The gloss of Plutarch which has been mistaken for the law, is, that in thus taking sides, *the right may prevail.* Now, it is not always the strongest party that is in the right, but it is usually *that party* which prevails. Solon gives no reason for his law, but we find the true one in Dante:

<blockquote>
Aquel cativo coro
Degli angeli, che non furon rebelli
Ni fur fideli a dio, ma por se furon.
</blockquote>

<blockquote>
That caitiff crowd
Of the angels, who neither rebelled,
Nor faithful stood—from love of self alone.
</blockquote>

The law of Solon was directed against the *selfish neutral;* against him who stood by and saw his country rent by civil war, watching the opportunity to benefit by the misfortunes of both parties, while by his interference he might have made peace. This is Mr. Brackenridge's application of the law of Solon. He had acted upon it, and only involved himself in serious difficulties in consequence, and gaining the enmity of both parties. For that reason, he declared that if the same were to be acted over again, he would not follow the law of Solon, but leave the parties to settle their own differences. But this was the language of chagrin— he had acted according to the generous impulse of his nature, and in all probability, under similar circumstances, he would act so again.

of a public officer; and through the whole scene was in confidence with men who would not only be unsuspected, but had the confidence of the government. But I was at a great distance from the seat of government, and not in direct communication with those at the head of it; so that I was at the mercy of others. Now, if I should be placed again in similar circumstances, I will not act on the principle of Solon's law. Let people that are to be expelled by revolutionary violence get out of the country the best way they can, or run the risk of being put to death; and let the executive and insurgents settle their own negotiations; I will have nothing to do with them."

These reflections of Mr. Brackenridge were the result of chagrin and a sense of injustice. He had rendered the most important services; saved the town from destruction, and at the same time the whole western counties from the horrors of civil war; perhaps the confederacy itself from a fatal wound. To meet the reward of a criminal for all this, was, no doubt, most trying; but following the impulse of a generous nature, the presumption is, that if the same thing were to occur again, he would meet the same risk in the cause of humanity and patriotism.

The expected arrest came at length in the form of a subpœna to testify before Judge Peters! He accordingly attended, and was referred by him to Secretary Hamilton. The account of this examination will be given in the words of Mr. Brackenridge, being more fresh and graphic than any in which it could be conveyed by another.

It is, moreover, important, as it relates to one who was stigmatized as the chief actor in the so-called insurrection, but whose efforts had been directed to arrest it in its very commencement, and by whose talents and address it was finally suppressed. Conscious not only of innocence, but of his important services, it was most painful to be thus, even for a time, placed on the rack by false and groundless suspicions.

"I was received by Mr. Hamilton with that countenance which a man will have when he sees a person with regard to whom his humanity and his sense of justice struggle; he would have him saved, but is afraid he must be hanged; was willing to treat me with civility, but was embarrassed with a sense that in a short time I must probably stand in the predicament of a culprit, and be put in irons. He began by asking some general questions with regard to any system or plan, within my knowledge, of overthrowing the government. I had known nothing of the kind. After a number of general questions, to which I had to answer in the negative, I proposed to put an end to that, by giving a narrative of everything I did know. It was agreed, and he began to write. I gave him the outlines of the narrative I have given in this publication, until I came to that particular where, after the burning of Neville's house, I represented the people as calling on Bradford and Marshall to come forward and support what had been done, under the pain of being treated as Neville himself had been. At this the Secretary laid down his pen and addressed himself to me: 'Mr. Brackenridge,' said he, 'I observe one leading trait in your account; a disposition to excuse the principal actors; and before we go farther, I must be candid, and inform you of the delicate situation in which you stand; you are not within the amnesty; you have not signed upon the day, a thing we did not know until we came upon the ground, I mean into the western country; and though the government may not be disposed to proceed rigorously, yet it has you in its power, and it will depend upon the candor of your account what your fate will be.' My answer was, I am not within the amnesty, and am sensible of the extent of the power of the government; but were the narrative to begin again, I would not change a single word." It is difficult to find language to express the sense of surprise, in all men of right feeling at such an appeal! The practice of such methods, in this instance, (and in the others on the authority of Findley,) cannot be read without indignation at the present day. Testimony obtained in such a manner would be scouted with abhorrence by a court of justice, under the free common law adapted to a republican government. The reply of Mr. Brackenridge must, in every rightly constituted mind, place him infinitely above the examiner in point of dignity and elevation of character. What was it on the part of the Secretary, but holding out the inducement to commit perjury, as the means of saving the witness' life? It must be admitted, however, that with this exception, the conduct of the Secretary, on this particular occasion, was highly honorable to him, and such as might have been expected from a man of his great talents and high functions.

"Having passed through the circumstances of the Marshal and Neville being privy to my giving my opinion to Black and Hamilton on the effect of the writ of subpœna to delinquent distillers, and Neville requesting me to go to the Mingo meeting, my examination was adjourned, Mr. Hamilton being called upon to dinner; and I was desired to attend in the afternoon. At three o'clock I returned to my examination; Mr. Hamilton entering the room where I waited for him, appeared to have been reflecting, and said, 'Mr. Brackenridge, your conduct has been horribly misrepresented.' I saw that he never before heard the least of my being solicited by Neville the younger to go to the meeting at Mingo Creek, but having just dined in company with him at the house of Major Craig, where I was then examined, he had asked Neville, and he acknowledged it. This last is conjecture."

There can be no doubt of the fact, since it was not denied by Neville at the time of the publication of the "Incidents." Neville would not deny the fact of Mr. Brackenridge attending the meeting at his instance, when the question was directly put; but where was his pledge to Mr. Brackenridge, to make known the motive for his going there? He must have known that the going to the meeting was used as one of the most serious circumstances against Mr. Brackenridge, by his father and Major Craig. The Secretary must have been struck with this want of good faith, even as respected himself, and the indiscreet zeal of the connection must have deeply affected him; his pride was wounded at the idea of being made the mere instrument to gratify the hatred of these persons. The continued round of dinners, and the incessant abuse of the connection against particular individuals, must have become nauseating to such a man as Hamilton, hence his exclamation, "Mr. Brackenridge, your conduct has been horribly misrepresented." And by whom? Of course by the Neville connection.

"I went on to give an account of the Mingo Creek meeting. The Secretary appeared not satisfied. 'Mr. Brackenridge,' said he, 'you must know we have testimony extremely unfavorable to you, of speeches made at that meeting; in particular your ridiculing the Executive.' I saw that some fool had misunderstood, and had been giving an account of what I had deduced from the lenity of the President in the case of the Presq' Isle establishment, and my introducing General Knox and Cornplanter making speeches. I was extremely hurt to think, that after I had been called upon, in the manner I was, to go forward on that occasion, (the Mingo meeting,) I should be at the mercy of the accounts of persons who did not understand me, and obliged to answer for the pleasantry I had found necessary to use to secure attention to what I had further to say. My answer was—Five persons were chosen to go with me to that meeting, for the express purpose of bearing testimony of what I should say; let these be called. It was the express condition with Col. Neville, that I consented to go at all. Is it reasonable that I should be at the mercy or prejudice of ignorant individuals, or their voluntary misrepresentations? He was silent. I went on to give an account of the town meeting at Pittsburgh. I stated it, as moved by me, that we should march and pretend to join the people at Braddock's Field. I saw the Secretary pause at this, and sink into deep reflection. It staggered him. Was it any more, said I, than what Richard the Second did, when a mob of one hundred thousand men were assembled at Blackheath? The young prince addressed them, put himself at their head, and said, 'What do you want, gentlemen? I will lead you on.'

"My narrative now continued. After some time the Secretary observed, 'My breast begins to ache—we will stop to-night; we will resume to-morrow at nine o'clock.' I was at a loss to know whether his breast ached for my sake, or from the writing; but disposed to construe every thing unfavorably, I supposed it was for my sake, and that he saw I must be arrested.

"Waiting on the Secretary at nine o'clock, my examination was resumed. In the course of the narrative, his countenance began to brighten, and having finished the history, there was an end. 'Mr. Brackenridge,' said he, 'in the course of yesterday I had uneasy feelings, I was concerned for you as a man of talents; my impressions were unfavorable; you may have observed it. I now think it my duty to inform you, that not a single one remains. Had we listened to some people, I know not what we might have done. There is a side to your account; your conduct has been horribly misrepresented, owing to misconception. I will announce you in this point of view to Governor Lee, who represents the Executive. You are in no personal danger, you will not be troubled even with a simple inquisition by the judge; what may be due to yourself with the public, is another question.'

"In so delicate a case, where life had been sought by insidious men; and when, what I felt with more sensibility, my hopes of estimation in the world were likely to be blasted, at least for a time, it may easily be supposed that not a word escaped me, or will ever be forgotten.

"My sensibility had been greatly wounded when I waited on Judge Peters with the narrative to sign, as directed by Mr. Hamilton; it was with difficulty I could write my name five times to the five different sheets of paper, of which my narrative consisted. I returned to my house with different feelings from those I had for a long time before."

The author cannot refrain from noticing in this place a singular proof of the coarseness of the descendant, in his allusion to the circumstance of Mr. Brackenridge having been required to sign each of the five separate sheets, as an evidence that he was "*such a rogue*," that he could not be trusted with one signature to the whole! Is this the ignorance of the descendant, or is it a vulgar appeal to the ignorance of others? In his allusion to the infirmity of the signer, whose hand trembled—the effect of a nervous disease, increased on the present occasion by intense anxiety of mind—there is a want of delicacy of feeling which might be expected of a New Zealand savage, but is indeed astonishing in our state of civilization.

As soon as the acquittal of Mr. Brackenridge became known, it gave great satisfaction to the public. His popularity with them was entirely restored. His persecution by the connection had convinced the people of the injustice they had done him in supposing he had been bribed by the government. They now saw his conduct in its true light, as stated by Mr. Purviance, that it is, "to induce the people to submit to the laws, and the government to grant an amnesty for the past." The old General (Neville) was enraged. "Brackenridge," said he, "is the most artful fellow on God Almighty's earth. He put his finger in Yeates' eye—in Ross' eye—and now in Hamilton's eye. He is the most artful fellow on God Almighty's earth."

The following is the notice of this acquittal, by Findley: "Mr. Brackenridge had conducted with such address, in a situation which rendered it necessary for him to temporize, that he knew he was in no danger from the usual mode of process; but he also knew that the power of the government conveyed another idea.* He had observed the innocent and the guilty, indiscriminately, in many instances in the West, subjected to unusual sufferings and insults, by the power of government. If such powerful addresses were made to the hopes and fears of Mr. Brackenridge, who from his profession was able to judge of his situation, what may we not expect was done with such ignorant people as did not know what part of their conduct or expressions might be deemed criminal. It is observable, that though the subpœna for Mr. Brackenridge came from Judge Peters, yet the examinations were conducted, and the terrors, &c. dispensed, by the Secretary!"

Mr. Brackenridge, at least, had no reason to complain of Hamilton, and although differing from him in politics, always spoke of him personally with respect. He had done him justice, which he did not expect, considering the prepossession and the influences brought to bear against him. To obtain bare justice, or rather to escape injustice, was something to be grateful for in such times; but that gratitude is not required by any generosity of sentiment to be carried beyond himself. This was a different case from his escape from assassination; he felt no gratitude, nor was there any due to those who saved him, as it were, from their own servants, for whose acts they would be responsible.

Mr. Craig affects to entertain some doubts as to the details of the ex-

* Findley had not sufficient magnanimity, or justice, to ascribe this acquittal to innocence, but regarded it as the result of *management on the part of an astute lawyer!*

amination of Mr. Brackenridge; on what ground? On the technical ground of *exparte* evidence; there was no one present but Hamilton and himself! He appears not to know the difference between historical evidence and the narrow rules of courts under the common law, intended to shut out falsehoods, but which more frequently shut out truth. He says it is *exparte* evidence. But this does not mean evidence of the party, which is often received in courts of justice; but where confined exclusively to the breast of the witness, and there exists no possibility of contradiction, and given without notice to enable others to contradict him. Here there was ample notice—the appeal was to the bar of public opinion; the facts published in the presence of the parties interested to controvert; the person named with whom the transaction took place. There was also a formal challenge to deny the facts of the "Incidents," generally. How easy would it have been to have addressed a letter to Hamilton, calling on him to contradict the statements, if not true? The Nevilles were implicated in what was said by Hamilton—to them alone could he have referred, when he said, "had we listened to some people," &c. They were silent. Can we admit the wretched excuse of the descendant, that Col. Neville was too indolent, and the others of the connection not competent? No attempt was made to deny the fact of the acquittal, and it was a subject of common conversation at the time, and the whole probably repeated before the publication a year afterward in a book. Hamilton was still living; why, I repeat, was there no appeal taken? The subject will not bear a moment's consideration.

Craig again asks, why was not the document alluded to (his examination,) produced by Mr. Brackenridge? This is an unfortunate question, for Craig. No copy was retained, as is evident from the circumstances; the five sheets, or twenty-five pages, having been immediately delivered to Judge Peters, and therefore in the hands of the government. But the question may be turned against him. Why was it never brought forth by the friends of the government? A very plausible reason for this may be given. It contained a statement of the leading facts of the insurrection, so entirely convincing to Hamilton, that it produced an entire change in his mind; but it exhibited a view of the whole affair entirely different from that which the government agents had presented to the public, and if it convinced Hamilton, it might have convinced others; and here was a reason for its suppression, which was not in the power of Mr. Brackenridge to do, as he did not retain the document.

If Judge Wilkinson is good authority in favor of the Nevilles, his evidence is not to be rejected when he speaks of the conduct of the government agents who came to suppress the insurrection. He speaks of the "star chamber" proceedings in the "inquisitorial court," opened by General Hamilton, and of "informers influenced by prejudice or malice." He relates that "a lieutenant of the army, while it was halting at Pittsburgh, visited his uncle in the vicinity, and accompanied him to a husking party, where, on using the term rebel as applicable to the citizens generally, he was rebuked by a respectable old man of the party. The officer replied insolently, upon which a young man (for young men in that day always felt bound to protect the aged,) interposed, and would have beaten him with deserved severity, had not my father begged him off. The officer returned to Pittsburgh, and the next day both of those who had offended him at the husking were arrested. The young man found friends who procured his liberation, but the old man, notwithstanding efforts were made for his release, *was carried to Philadelphia and imprisoned for more than six months, without trial.*" There is no reason to question this fact, and others of frequent occurrence; but Judge Wilkinson, the eulogist of the Neville connection, does not appear to be aware of the quarter on which his censure would fall—not merely on General Hamilton, but also on the "general plaintiff" in the outrages committed.

CHAPTER XIII.

THE MILITARY ARRESTS, AND ATROCIOUS TREATMENT OF THE PEOPLE—THE DREADFUL NIGHT—WITHDRAWAL OF THE ARMY—THE END OF THE INSURRECTION.

THE army of the western expedition, as it was called, had been about ten days encamped in two or three divisions in the West, while no symptom of disaffection was discernible, much less any embodied force; on the contrary, every disposition was manifested by the magistrates and the people to comply with the wishes of the military, as well as of the accompanying United States civil authorities. The judges of Westmoreland county, General Jack and others, waited on them, and offered their service to issue process and arrest any persons that might be designated. Their services were not accepted; and they were dismissed in a way which indicated that other and more summary modes of proceeding were in contemplation. Of this, the details of the last chapter will have given some idea. The military and civil inquests being completed, it was now determined, once for all, to strike a blow that would be felt through the whole of society in these counties, and be long remembered, like the military chastenings of Claverhouse, in crushing the unruly spirit of the Highland Scotch.

It will appear by the letter of instruction to General Lee, that the military force was to act "*where it met with combinations or individuals in arms against the government,* or when called to assist the civil authority." These orders were utterly disregarded. There was no resistance, either to the military or civil authority; it was the duty of the army, therefore, to remain passive, and confine its operations to its camps. The words of the order are so distinct and clear, that it is impossible to mistake them. "The objects of the military force are two-fold; to overawe any *armed opposition* that may exist, and to countenance and support the civil officers in the means of executing their offices." And again, "You are to preserve discipline amongst the troops; particularly a scrupulous regard to the rights of persons and property, and a respect for the authority of the civil magistrate; taking especial care to inculcate and cause to be observed this principle: that the duties of the army are confined to attacking and subduing of *armed opponents to the laws,* and to supporting and aiding of the civil officers in the execution of their functions." It is not pretended that a single man was found in arms in opposition to the government; where, then, was the justification of the military arrests and military agency in the prosecution of those alleged to be amenable to the law for offenses committed during the disturbances or riots which had occurred?

We shall here present the orders of General Lee, addressed to General Irvine, under which the arrests were made; and he that reads an account of them for the first time, cannot do so without astonishment and indignation. Never since there was a government in these States, was there anything witnessed so disgraceful as the proceedings under these orders which we are about to relate. Such orders are a stain on the history of our own country. Although General Lee is admitted to have acted, so far as he was personally concerned in the particular cases, in an unexceptionable manner, and General Irvine, to whom the orders were directed, in a manner worthy of praise; yet the execution of the orders from their nature would necessarily be intrusted to inferior and subaltern officers, and to expect them to be executed without abuse, was against all probability. The responsibility of issuing them, must, therefore, rest on their author, whoever he may be.

"HEAD-QUARTERS, NEAR PARKINSON'S FERRY,
November 9th, 1794.

"SIR:—From the delays and danger of escapes which attend the present situation of judiciary investigations to establish preliminary processes against offenders, it is deemed advisable to proceed in a summary manner, in the most disaffected scenes, against those who have notoriously committed treasonable acts; that is, to employ the military for the purpose of apprehending and bringing such persons before the Judge of the district, to be by him examined and dealt with according to law.

"To you is committed the execution of this object within that part of Allegheny county to which you are advancing.

"As a guide to you, you have herewith a list of persons (No. 1,) who have complied with the terms offered by the Commissioners of the United States, are entitled to an exemption from arrest and punishment, and who are therefore not to be meddled with. You have also a list, (No. 2,) who, it is understood on good grounds, have committed acts of treason; and who may therefore be safely apprehended.

"Besides these you may, in the course of your operations, receive satisfactory information of others who have committed like acts, and whom, in that case, you will also cause to be apprehended. The acts alluded to are the following: 1st. The firing upon, imprisoning, or interrupting in the course of his duty, the Marshal of the District. 2d. The two attacks on the house of John Neville, Esq., Inspector of the Revenue. 3d. The assembling, or aiding the assembling, of an army at Braddock's Field, in the county of Allegheny, on the 1st of August last. 4th. The assembling and acting as delegates at the meeting at Parkinson's Ferry, which began on the 14th of the same month. 5th. The meeting at Mingo Creek meeting-house, termed a society—sometimes a congress. 6th. The destruction of property and the expulsion of persons, at and from the town of Pittsburgh. 7th. The interruption and plundering of the public mail; and the injuries to the houses and violence to the persons of Benjamin Wells, John Webster and Philip Regan, officers of the revenue. 8th. The planting of May poles, impudently called liberty poles, with the intention to countenance and coöperate in the insurrection. You will carefully direct your inquiries toward civil and military officers, who have been extensively concerned in the enormities committed; it being their special duty to have prohibited, by their exertions, every species of enormity. But in the apprehension of persons not named in the list, (No. 2,) you will use great circumspection to embrace none but real offenders; nor will you be too promiscuous or too general. The persons apprehended ought to be leading or influential characters, or particularly violent. You will find a list, (No. 3;) this paper comprehends witnesses. The individuals are to be brought forward and treated as such.

"Direct all who may be apprehended by you to be conveyed to your camp, until further orders. Send off your parties of horse, with good guides, and at such a period as to make the surprises, however distant, or near, at the same moment, or intelligence will precede them, and some of the culprits will escape. I presume the proper hour will be at daybreak on Thursday morning, and have therefore desired the operation to be then performed, in every quarter.

"I have the honor to be, sir, with great respect, your most obedient servant,
(Signed) HENRY LEE.

"List No. 1, mentioned in this letter, is in the possession of Governor Howell, and will be sent to you, if required. Wait not for it.

"List No. 3 is not to be expected, as no witnesses are to be summoned for the district for which you act."

It appears that No. 1, containing the names of those who were entitled to the benefit of the amnesty, was never delivered. This was also the case with No. 3, containing the names of those who were to be arrested as witnesses, but many of these were embraced in No. 2, so that no difference was made in their favor. The order was directed to General Irvine, who of course re-issued the same orders in circulars to the inferior officers, who were to execute them. The conduct of the General was perhaps military, and all agree that wherever he had any personal agency he acted with humanity, but he would have been entitled to still higher praise if he had taken the responsibility of disobeying such an extraordinary and illegal order.

It was thus left to the discretion of some subaltern or inferior officer, ignorant, and of brutal passions, as the case might be, to commit the grossest violations of the rights of the citizen. At his pleasure, the domestic sanctuary was to be violated in the dead hour of the night, without any other warrant but the sword; men were to be torn from their beds and distracted families for suspected offenses; some of these offenses being merely political, or no offenses at all, and many of them merely as witnesses! Every man's house, in contemplation of law, is his castle, and when thus invaded he has as much a right to defend it against lawless bands of soldiers, as against the ferocious savages. He would have been as justifiable in shooting the assailants, and it is a wonderful proof to what degree the people were crushed by submission, that no instance of the kind occurred. The only excuse for this proceeding was, that the supposed culprits might otherwise escape! But what is this compared to the ten-fold outrage committed against men presumed in law to be innocent, and many of them beyond question were so, or had signed the amnesty. The wretched excuse is an insult to the understanding of those to whom it is addressed. It is scarcely equaled by those acts in other parts of the world, which are held up by all modern historians for the execration of the just and wise.

The special directions from No. 1 to No. 8, instead of limiting this revolting discretionary power, confided to dragoons over the liberties, lives and domiciles of the western people, tends to enlarge and aggravate it. One or two of those special cases deserve particular notice. Those who attended the Parkinson meeting are mentioned as proper subjects of arrest. Now this meeting of the citizens had for its object, with those who originated and controlled it, to bring about a peaceable submission to the laws. Where was the offense in this unarmed assembly? It was even recognized by the President, in his instructions to the commissioners, who were directed to open a communication with it. If its members were to be all treated alike, then the committee of conference which negotiated with the commissioners and exerted itself to bring about a submission, was in the same manner liable, especially as it was composed of members of the Parkinson's Ferry meeting. The harmless assembly at Braddock's Field is also to be regarded as treasonable, although no act of treason was committed, unless that the mere assemblage, without inquiring into the *quo animo* of the mass or of individuals, is to be regarded as treason. The planting liberty poles is also to be regarded as treasonable, and the dragoon is to be the judge in the first instance! But the most singular of these instructions is the direction to seize on all civil and military officers whose duty it was to prevent the commission of these acts of outrage, because they failed to do so, no matter whether it was in their power or not. If we reflect on the distance from the scenes where these acts were committed, to other parts of the country, and the fact that they were not even heard of by the greater part of the inhabitants until afterward, the duty required of the civil and military officers is a very severe one, indeed. What would we think of applying this doctrine to the riots which have been committed since that day in the narrow limits of many of our towns and cities, and hold the magistrates and peaceful citizens responsible for them? Why were not the officers and the whole army held responsible for the two murders committed while it was encamped at Carlisle? We are reminded of the Chinese idea of justice, where the culprit is ordered to be put to a horrid death, with ten of his nearest relations, the village in which they live to be burned to ashes, and the inhabitants driven out to starve! Is it not astonishing to find such perversion of reason in our enlightened country? To pursue the subject further would be a prostitution of the reasoning faculty.

From this brief review of the principles of action, we will proceed to the relation of the outrages committed in pursuance of them. The principles are bad enough, but their practical operation too atrocious for words to characterize with sufficient force; in fact, the simple narrative goes far beyond any language of reprobation. He is a false historian, who would skulk from the relation of such acts of iniquity, or attempt to gloss them over by frothy excuses or equivocations. The following is the general account given by Mr. Brackenridge:

"The 13th of November was a 'DREADFUL NIGHT' through the western country. Hundreds were arrested; offenders and witnesses together. Though directions were given to discriminate in their treatment, it could not always be done in the first instance. Men were thrown into jail, kept in cold barns or out-houses, or tied back to back in cellars. The officers, in some instances, behaved with mildness; in others, with wanton and unnecessary severity. A Captain Dunlap, of Philadelphia, is said to have conducted a number of prisoners from Washington to Pittsburgh with humanity. A Capt. ——— is said, on the other hand, to have driven a number under his custody like cattle before him, at a trot, in muddy roads, through the Chartiers creek to the middle; then impounded them in a wet stable, and insulted them, by ordering to be thrown into the manger dough and raw flesh to eat! Passing to Washington some time afterward, I examined the stables and collected these facts."

The foregoing was derived from information; the cases which came under his own observation were even more atrocious:

"Of list No. 2, were personally known to me, Andrew Watson, Norris

Morrison, Samuel M'Cord, John Hannah, William Amberson, William H. Beaumont, Alexander M'Nickle, Mordecai M'Donald, Martin Cooper and George Robinson. Of these, all had signed the amnesty except George Robinson and Mordecai M'Donald.* And with regard to Robinson, I never heard a syllable alleged, but on the contrary, he was a most worthy, peaceable man, the chief burgess of Pittsburgh. His not signing the paper of submission was owing to a mistake of pride, which had existed with many, thinking that it would be a virtual acknowledgment of having done something wrong in violation of the laws.† Nevertheless, these were arrested on the night of the 13th of November, all except M'Nickle and Amberson; the last of whom had received some hint of it, and surrendered himself to the judiciary then sitting in his house. M'Nickle found favor, and by some direction of General Irvine, was passed over; Martin Cooper, (a lame man,) was also passed over, and never knew that he was on the list of the proscribed until I showed him the list some time afterward.‡ Nothing could be a greater proof to me of favoritism and prejudice, than the forming this list, and the management respecting it. Jeremiah Sturgeon had been arrested as the person intended under the name of Alexander Sturgeon. I will now assume four of these, Andrew Watson, William H. Beaumont, Jeremiah Sturgeon and George Robinson—than whom, I will pledge myself, there are not four less suspected persons, much less offending men, in the whole town of Pittsburgh. With regard to the others, there had been allegations with respect to raising a liberty pole; but as to the greater part of them, found afterward to be groundless. Andrew Watson was my neighbor, one of the most worthy men on earth, and a person who had suffered as much uneasiness from the disturbance as any man could do; he had demeaned himself in the most unexceptionable manner. Of Jeremiah Sturgeon, one of our most unoffending men, and George Robinson, I have already spoken. They were little known out of the town of Pittsburgh; and it must have

* Besides these, there were in the list for Pittsburgh, Alexander Sturgeon, James Hunter and Henry Parker.
† He had accompanied Mr. Brackenridge to the Mingo Creek meeting, at the special request of Neville. It seems by the order already cited under the fifth head, that this was an offense, if it does not relate to the members of the club or society, which met at that place, which seems probable. A curious cause for either a military or civil arrest!
‡ It was asked, with a show of indignation, how did Mr. Brackenridge obtain the lists? It matters not, their genuineness was not questioned. Its publication was said to have displeased General Irvine—others had better ground to be displeased.

been from thence that any information against them could have come.* They were dragged out of their beds at two o'clock in the morning, but partly dressed; obliged to march, some of them without putting on their shoes, thus dragged away amid the cries of children and the tears of mothers; treated with language of the most insulting opprobium, by those apprehending them; driven before a troop of horse at a trot, through muddy roads; seven miles from Pittsburgh, impounded in a pen on the wet soil. The guard baying them, and asking them how they would like to be hanged; some offering a dollar to have the privilege of shooting at them; carried thence four miles toward the town; obliged to lie all night on the wet earth, without covering, under a season of rains, sleet and snows; driven from the fire with bayonets, when some of them, perishing, had crawled, endeavoring to be unseen, toward it; next day impounded in a waste house, and detained there five days, then removed to a newly built and damp room, without fire, in the garrison at Pittsburgh; at the end of ten days brought before the judiciary, and nothing appearing against them—discharged!"

It is painful to contemplate such acts under any form of government, and especially under free institutions. It appears that some of the citizens who had most exerted themselves in support of the laws, and had made great efforts to bring the people to submission by persuasion, were the victims of this dragoonade. As there was no force at the time to put down the disorderly, no standing armies as in despotic countries, if good citizens were thus rewarded, who will, hereafter, exert themselves on such occasions? The effect must be most pernicious. According to Dr. Moor, in the despotic aristocracy of Venice it was a crime for the citizen to intermeddle with, or even to speak of the affairs of the republic, whether in praise or dispraise. All he had to do was to submit and obey. Such appears to be the ideas of some of those who came to put down the Western Insurrection, and who acted in a way so directly at variance with all preconceived notions of what is due to the citizen, and so inconsistently with the express orders of Washington.

The foregoing is related by Mr. Brackenridge as within his own knowledge; the further facts on a more extended scale, which he relates, were matters of public notoriety. "About three hundred arrests were made by the different military parties in the same night, chiefly in Washington and Allegheny counties. With few exceptions these arrests were made

* That information was of course given *in secret*—and shows the bad influence then at work behind the curtain—with this detestable military inquisition. Heaven defend us from military government, or military police!

with a total disregard of the amnesty, an instance of bad faith most disgraceful to those concerned, and contrary to the express command of Washington in the general orders signed by Hamilton."

Findley, who wrote a year afterward, gives other instances and somewhat more in detail, from documents collected by him. No one at the time doubted the truth of the statements; the author, although then but a boy, remembers well to have heard the horror of the "DREADFUL NIGHT" related by many of the sufferers themselves, and as a subject of common conversation among the people. Although in his "Incidents," Mr. Brackenridge relates with proper indignation the occurrences we have just recorded, yet at the same time there is an evident disposition to reconcile the people to the government, and even to palliate and apologize, rather than encourage disaffection. We now make the following extract from Findley:

"The agonizing distress of those citizens and their families, who were made the victims of perhaps *private resentments* on this occasion, can be more easily conceived than expressed. The consternation of others, when they observed the innocent, those who had signed the amnesty, witnesses and criminals, treated with such undistinguishing severity, was inexpressible. They justly apprehended that no man was safe, let his conduct have been ever so innocent, or his assurance of protection from government ever so great, if those who influenced the judiciary had enmity against him.

"I have already stated that many of them had signed the amnesty; others had refused to sign from the pride of ignorance, or an acknowledgment of guilt. A number of them were men of unimpeachable behavior throughout the whole of the insurrection. Though there had been a good deal of heat and irritation among the most ignorant class of the people at Pittsburgh, yet there was no higher crime committed, even by them, than erecting a liberty pole; but a proportion of the prisoners were not of that class; one of them was a respectable and well behaved magistrate of the town.

"A captain with a detachment of the army who took a number of prisoners in the southern parts of Washington county, is asserted to have driven the prisoners like cattle at a trot, through creeks up to their middle in water, and to have impounded them in a wet stable at night, and otherwise to have maltreated and insulted them; though this fact has been confidently asserted and never contradicted, yet not having the vouchers for it before me, I shall pass it over without being more particular.

"The greatest outrage, however, against humanity and decency, was committed by General White in the Mingo Creek settlement. It is said that he had been solicitous to have command of the New Jersey militia on the western expedition, but from an apprehension of the peculiarity of his temper, rendering him unfit for such a trust, arrangements were made that prevented him from attaining that rank; but being determined to be employed in the expedition, and holding the rank of Brigadier General in the militia, he marched to Carlisle with the light-horse volunteers; and after a part of them were incorporated with the legion, he continued to command the Jersey light-horse until the return of the army. When Governor Howell took the horse, all but a small corps which he left with General White, he gladly accepted the charge of taking down the prisoners, after that trust had been declined by others. Governor Howell returned with the horse by way of Northumberland, and behaved in such a manner as to do honor to himself and the corps he commanded both in the western country and on the return. Though there seemed to be a general conviction that General White was not possessed of sufficient discretion to be intrusted with the delicate charge of arresting prisoners, yet by some means I never could learn of any officer of whom I had an opportunity of inquiring, how he was intrusted to superintend the taking of prisoners in Mingo Creek settlement on the 13th of November, before mentioned, which from his conduct more than that of any other officer in that country, was known by the name of the 'dreadful night.' I shall state his conduct on that occasion, nearly in the words by which it is expressed in the voucher now before me.

"On Thursday, the 13th of November, there were about forty persons brought to Parkinson's house by order of General White, and he directed to put the d——d rascals in the cellar; to tie them back to back; to make a fire for the guard, but to put the prisoners back to the farther end of the cellar, and to give them neither victuals nor drink. The cellar was wet and muddy, and the night cold; the cellar extended the whole length under a new log house, which was neither floored nor the openings between the logs daubed. They were kept there until Saturday morning, and then marched to the town of Washington. On the march, one of the prisoners who was subject to convulsions, fell into a fit; but when some of the troop told General White of his situation, he ordered them to tie the d——d rascal to a horse's tail and drag him along with them, for he had only feigned having fits. Some of his fellow prisoners, however, who had a horse, dismounted and let the poor man ride. He had another fit before he reached Washington. This march was about twelve miles. The poor man who had the fits had been in the American service during almost the whole of the war with Great Britain.

"Having heard much of this inhuman business, and having occasion last summer to go to Washington, I traveled that road for the first time that I had ever been in the settlement, and lodged a night at the place. The plantation is the property of Benjamin Parkinson, but rented by him to a Mr. Stockdale, who keeps tavern at it, and who seems to be a decent man, and against whom there was no charge. He not only confirmed what I have stated above, but added a variety of other particulars equally shocking. Stockdale was forbid on the peril of his life to administer any comfort to his neighbors, though they were perishing with cold and famishing with hunger. The General treated the prisoners as they arrived with the most insulting and abusive language, causing them all to be tied back to back, except one man who held a respectable rank, and who, however, was said to be one of the most guilty in his custody. One of the nearest neighbors, who had a child at the point of dying, and observing that they were bringing in the whole neighborhood prisoners, without regard to guilt or innocence, went and gave himself up to General White, expecting that as they were conscious there was no charge against him, he would be permitted to return to his family on giving bail; but he also was inhumanly thrown into the cellar, tied with the rest, and refused the privilege of seeing his dying child; nor was he permitted to attend its funeral, until, after many entreaties, he obtained that liberty, accompanied with the most horrid oaths and imprecations.

"The most of these prisoners were found to be innocent men, and liberated. There were but three sent to Philadelphia for trial; one of them after having been dismissed at Pittsburgh, and perhaps taken a hearty grog through joy at regaining his liberty, expressed himself unbecomingly to some of the light-horsemen; he was afterward pursued near thirty miles and taken to Philadelphia, but there was no cause of action found against him at the court. He had served with approbation during the war; his name was Samuel Noy. Captain Dunlap had a discrimination made in his orders between witnesses and supposed criminals, and treated them all with humanity; had them comfortably lodged, and provided with victuals and drink, previous to taking any refreshments himself. By the orders delivered to General Irvine, he was obliged to take and treat all as criminals, but he did not insult any of them himself, nor permit them to be insulted by others in his hearing; and he provided for them as well as the camp would admit, and that being a very uncomfortable situation, he had them removed from it as soon as he could. That they were ignorant persons, who had sheltered themselves under the faith of the government, or were only called as witnesses, was not known to the General till it was discovered in the result; but General White was himself the leading, or perhaps the only man of his corps, who insulted the prisoners with the most opprobrious language, and punished them in the most shocking manner short of inflicting death. Of all that were taken on that 'dreadful night,' only eighteen were sent to Philadelphia, and none of these convicted on trial."

Two or three might have been convicted and punished for misdemeanors, but they were tried for treason. One of the three, Captain Porter, the father of Mr. Porter of Tarentum, and grandfather of the present representative, J. H. Porter, when put on his trial it appeared that he had been taken by mistake for another of that name, as in the case of Sturgeon! These men remained five or six months in prison, and not in such prisons as are kept at the present day. The writer has had access to the journal of Captain Porter, which is well written, and forms a most interesting narrative. He was one of the eighteen innocent men paraded through the streets of Philadelphia, their hats labeled with the word "INSURGENT," in large letters!

"As the army returned through Westmoreland, two arrests were made in the southern extremity of that county, and one in the neighboring parts of Fayette. They were taken to Philadelphia; the last had been in Kentucky during the insurrection, and did not return until the riots had ceased. Isaac Meason, a judge of Fayette county, followed Judge Peters near forty miles into Bedford county, and offered himself and Judge Wells of that county, both of them acknowledged friends of the government, as bail for the prisoners, but was absolutely refused. As Meason knew that the prisoner was guilty of no crime, which evidently appeared to be the case, by no bill being found against him, he and Mr. Wells complained of the judge for not admitting him to bail on their application. Judge Peters being well known to be a man of feeling and humanity, his conduct in this and several other instances can only be accounted for from some overshadowing influence, and his apprehension that it was necessary that a considerable number of prisoners should be brought down, in order to prevent the inflammatory part of the army from committing outrages at leaving the country. His mind was tortured at being obliged to send down so many prisoners, and his peace was disturbed by being teased for dismissing such numbers of them.* One of the two prisoners from Westmoreland was found guilty of setting fire to the house of Wells, the collector, and condemned to be hanged; but was afterward reprieved and then pardoned by the President. He was a very ignorant

---

* This singular apology for the judge, presents the conduct of the army in a worse light than the direct accusation.

man, said to be of an outrageous temper, and subject to occasional fits of insanity."

A certain John Mitchell, who, with the assistance of another person, had robbed the Pittsburgh mail, gave himself up to General Morgan, who, instead of confining him, gave him a pass to go to Philadelphia, thereby putting it in his power to escape; but he went there, and being found guilty on his trial, was condemned to be hanged. The result was inevitable on the fact being established; but the President first reprieved for a time, and then pardoned him.

The Rev. Dr. Carnahan, President of Princeton College, in his account of the insurrection, fully corroborates the statement made by the previous writers on the subject of the arrests. Although at the cost of some repetition, the paragraphs relating thereto are given entire.

"Companies of horsemen were scattered in different directions over the country, and as there was no opposition, it was thought the army was about to return. On the night of the 13th of November, a frosty night, about one o'clock, the horse was sallied forth, and before daylight arrested in their beds about two hundred men. A company of Virginia horse were stationed for several days near Canonsburg, and I give the manner of their proceedings as a sample of what probably occurred in other places. About two o'clock in the morning they surrounded the house where I lodged, and some came in and ordered my landlord, an old man, to rise and guide them to a neighborhood about eight miles distant, where he was well acquainted. He had no horse. They inquired where a horse could be found. He named two or three places. They wanted a guide to the stables. The old man had no servant in the house. Two boys belonging to the academy lodged in an upper chamber. The older one, of an impetuous temper, had talked big in favor of the insurgents, and he believed the horsemen had come to arrest him, and he lay trembling in bed. The younger, more considerate, had always condemned the insurgents. Conscious of innocence, he jumped up and ran down stairs half dressed, to see what was going on. The horsemen slapped him with their scabbards and ordered him to show them the stables. He had to go, and run about a quarter of a mile without shoes, frosty as it was. No horse was to be found at the first stable, and then he had to run as far in a different direction, and happily found a horse. The epithet 'young insurgent,' with additional hard words, were liberally applied with an occasional slap, to quicken his steps. This lad was afterward the Rev. Dr. O. Jennings, of Nashville, Tennessee.

"My own lodgings were in a back room below stairs, in company with a student of the academy, several years older than I was. He was a sober, pious young man, who had been compelled to go to the burning of Neville's house, and also to Braddock's Field. On hearing the noise, I made an attempt to rise, but my friend, believing the men with swords were in search of him, begged me to lie still. There he lay, with head covered, trembling and panting, until the horsemen had departed. In justice to the Virginia, Maryland and Philadelphia horsemen, it must be said they made arrests and treated their prisoners with as much gentleness and humanity as practicable. Yet we can easily imagine what terror seized mothers, and sisters, and wives, when their sons, and brothers, and husbands were taken out of bed and carried off, they knew not whither. That night was afterward called the 'dreadful night.'

"To the New Jersey horsemen was assigned the duty of arresting those who resided in the Mingo Creek settlement, the region where the insurrection commenced, and where the most disgraceful acts of violence had been committed. Whether this region was assigned by accident to the New Jersey horsemen, or that they might have an opportunity of taking revenge for the insults Tom the Tinker had offered, calling the New Jersey militia the water melon army, &c., we know not. But the universal testimony is, that arrests were made in that region accompanied with circumstances of barbarity and terror seldom equaled. Men were dragged out of their beds, loaded with curses, threatened with hanging and death in the presence of their wives and children, and not permitted to collect clothes necessary to protect them from the inclemency of the season, and driven off on foot when they had horses in their stables. About forty of these men were brought to a house near Parkinson's Ferry, and thrust into a wet and muddy cellar, tied two and two back to back, and kept there twenty-four hours without food or drink. A fire was kindled for the guard, but the prisoners were not suffered to come near it, nor was the owner of the house permitted to do anything to relieve the sufferings of his neighbors. The following day they were driven twelve miles on foot, through mud and water, to Washington. During this march, instances of cruelty are told too bad to be repeated. This treatment was attributed to the commanding officer, (Brigadier General White,) rather than to the men. Indeed, the men, when they saw their prisoners exhausted and ready to faint, alighted from their horses, placed their prisoners on their saddles, and waded themselves through mud nearly knee-deep. A large number of prisoners from Washington county were collected together in the county town, and taken thence to Pittsburgh under guard. The object in taking them to Pittsburgh was that they might be examined by the district judge, so as to ascertain which of them ought to be taken to Philadelphia for trial. I saw them when on their way, as they entered Canonsburg, and were placed in a large upper room in the academy, to lodge for the night. They were conducted by the Philadelphia and New Jersey cavalry. The contrast between the Philadelphia horsemen and the prisoners was the most striking that can be imagined. The Philadelphians were some of the most wealthy and respectable men of that city. Their uniform was blue, of the finest broadcloth. Their horses were large and beautiful, all of a bay color, so nearly alike that it seemed any two of them would have made a good span of coach horses. Their trappings were superb. Their bridles, stirrups and martingales glittered with silver. Their swords, which were drawn and held elevated in the right hand, gleamed in the rays of the setting sun. The prisoners were also mounted on horses, of all shapes, sizes, and colors; some large, some small, some long tails, some short, some white, some black, some fat, some lean, some of every color and form that can be named. Some had saddles, some blankets, some bridles, some halters, some with stirrups, some with none. The riders also were various and grotesque in their appearance. Some were old, some young, some hale, respectable looking men; others were pale, meagre, and shabbily dressed. Some had great coats, others had blankets on their shoulders. The countenance of some was downcast, melancholy, dejected; that of others, stern, indignant, manifesting that they thought themselves undeserving such treatment. Two Philadelphia horsemen rode in front, and then two prisoners, and so two horsemen and two prisoners, alternately, throughout a line extending perhaps half a mile. I have more than once seen gangs of fifty or sixty negroes tied to a long rope, two and two opposite to each other, and marched to a distant slave market, but their anguish and indignation was not to be compared to that manifested by these western men. If these men had been the ones chiefly guilty of the disturbance, it would have been no more than they deserved. But the guilty had signed the amnesty, or had left the country before the army approached. It has been estimated that between one and two thousand men with rifles in their hands, had withdrawn and remained absent until the army left the country. The district judge and prosecuting attorney had a most arduous and delicate task, to discriminate between those who were guilty and those who were innocent; and the great number arrested made it impossible for a single judge to examine, within any reasonable time, the case of each individual. There were several persons not clothed with judicial authority, who assisted in making preliminary examinations. Among these,

Alexander Hamilton, Secretary of the Treasury, took an active and distinguished part."

Mr. Brackenridge went to Philadelphia under recognizance to testify, but was called on but once as to some general matters. In fact, the government had discovered that the prosecutions were not worth pursuing. Mr. Brackenridge had prepared himself to appear in the defense, but he soon found that prejudice ran so strongly against him, that he would, on that account, rather prejudice than benefit the case of his clients. As the trials went on, however, that prejudice was gradually removed, and he had the satisfaction to find, in a very short time, his popularity restored both at home and in the city. The notes of his intended argument are published in the "Incidents," and form a good outline of a treatise on the law of constructive treason. The same doctrine was afterward recognized by Chief Justice Marshall on the trial of Aaron Burr. It is now well understood that no treason had been committed—and considered merely as riots, they sink into trifles compared to some which have since occurred in Boston, New York, or Philadelphia.

The victory of Wayne over the Indians, which occurred during these troubles, completely changed the face of things in the West. It threw open the navigation of the Ohio and Mississippi, enabling the western people to find a market for their produce; it caused the surrender of the western forts, and gave security from a savage enemy. The army expenses had given a circulating medium, and the farmers having now the means to pay their tax, made no further complaints of the excise law. It is said that about two thousand of the best riflemen of the western counties had left the country before the approach of the army, but their places were soon supplied by others, and from this time the western counties advanced rapidly in population and wealth. After the lapse of half a century, (so short lived is mere tradition,) there are but few who have any knowledge of the Western Insurrection, although their fathers and grandfathers were involved in its difficulties and sufferings. The writer, at this day, meets with few persons who can converse with him on the subject of the Western Insurrection, having scarcely heard of these important occurrences in the history of their own immediate country.

Such was the termination of the Insurrection, which, for so long a time after it was over, served as a by-word and a stigma on the people of Western Pennsylvania, and some of its most eminent and deserving men. Its origin and character may be given in a few words. It originated in the opposition of the people to an unequal, oppressive and unjust law, and which was impliedly admitted to be such by the repeated amendments and concessions, yielded to their petitions, remonstrances and resolutions passed at public meetings—resolutions stigmatized as "intemperate" and as the cause of the subsequent outbreak, although it was the right of freemen to express their disapprobation of the oppressive law in any language they pleased. Two years afterward, when they became partially reconciled to the law, the Marshal was sent to serve process on delinquent distillers, to compel them to appear in Philadelphia to answer, at an expense sufficient to sink almost each man's plantation or homestead. In serving the last process out of about forty, in the harvest time, a sudden passion seized the farmers of the neighborhood, who pursued the officer and fired on him. The same passion continued; a party repaired to the house of the Inspector the day following to demand his commission, and prevent the return of the writs, which they believed would involve them and their families in ruin. They were fired upon, and blood was spilled; they retired, and the excitement spreading, they returned with a larger force—they were again fired on, and more blood was spilled. The house of the Inspector was burned; but not a drop of blood was shed by the rioters on this occasion, nor on any other during the whole of the disturbances! Two small inspection offices were destroyed in other parts, remote from each other; but these outrages having nothing in their character beyond simple riots against an odious law and unpopular individuals—the intelligent and patriotic portion of the community, the men of talents and intelligence, now came forward to exert themselves to arrest the progress of the popular violence. They called meetings of delegates, and after consultation, and by judicious management, succeeded in composing the disturbance and bringing their fellow citizens to a sense of their duty to themselves and to the laws. And now let us look at the other side. An army is marched into the country, and military law is executed, not proclaimed, over an unresisting people; hundreds of innocent persons, in violation of every legal right established for their safety, are dragged from their houses in the dead hour of the night, and treated in the most cruel manner; some of them meritorious men, who had entitled themselves to the gratitude of their country for their efforts to restore its peace, are insulted, persecuted and slandered! It will be asked, is this the history of our own country, or of some of those hideous tyrannies of past ages in other lands? And yet there are persons at this day who still raise the cry of rascally whiskey boys and insurgents!

Why did not the atrocities just related ring through the country, when told by two cotemporary historians? Because the interests, the pride, and the passions of party, would not permit the truth to be told. It would reflect too seriously on the existing administration. Its defense was *silence;* and it was the only way in which it could be met, except by gross and unmeasured contumely cast on the western people, and the supposed leaders of the acts of violence, whose character lay between riot and insurrection—for it never approached rebellion. How hard to turn the current of obloquy when it has once received a wrong direction? How hard to turn back the tide of calumny, of prejudice and settled conviction, however unjust or unfounded! Many attempts of this kind have been made of late years, and some of them with success. But where error of judgment becomes a second nature from habit, pride and bigotry, to overturn it is like the attempt to remove a mighty rock from its place—it cannot be done at once; it must be left to the slow operation of the current of time and truth.

NOTES TO CHAPTER XIII.

TARENTUM, 20th July, 1859.

J. M. PORTER, Esq.

Dear Sir—You were so good as to promise me a few extracts from your grandfather's Journal during his imprisonment, at the time of the Whiskey Insurrection. As I am now about closing the publication of my history, I beg leave to trouble you for them. The whole history of that insurrection is so full of romance, that I have no doubt the day will come when it will be the theme of many a story requiring no invention of facts. Perhaps the publication of your grandfather's manuscript might bring others to light preserved in families. No part of our national history has been so grossly and scandalously falsified as that of the Western Insurrection! I have tried to set it right, and that on evidence which no mere epithets of abuse, no mere assertion, no falsehoods can overturn.   Yours, sincerely,

H. M. BRACKENRIDGE.

Extracts from Captain Porter's Narrative.

HON. H. M. BRACKENRIDGE:

Dear Sir—In compliance with your request, I send you, briefly, the substance of such portions of the manuscript touching the Whiskey Insurrection as may perhaps interest you.

The manuscript was written by my grandfather, and is a faithful narrative of many of the facts and incidents connected with the Whiskey Insurrection, but more particularly relating to the arrest of sundry persons, charged with being insurgents—of their treatment during the time of their removal to Philadelphia and up to their discharge.

My grandfather (Captain Robert Porter,) had been an officer during the war of Independence, and afterward commanded a company in defense of the frontiers against the depredations of the Indians. He still held command of this company when the disturbance of the Whiskey Insurrection broke out, and although he never was an actor or participator in the foolish method by which the people of the western counties attempted to redress their grievances, yet the fact of his being the commander of a company of men in the immediate scene of the insurrection, was sufficient to awaken the suspicion of government.

Having from the first refused to take part in anything like an armed resistance to the execution of the excise law, nor in any way violated, as he conceived, his duty as a citizen, he refused, or neglected to sign the amnesty, from the fact of not being conscious of any act on his part which would make him liable to government.

Having afterward understood that one Pollock was making himself busy charging him (the captain) with being an insurgent, &c., he "determined to deliver himself up, and demand that the matter should be examined into, that he might refute the charge." Accordingly on November 13th, 1794, he went to the mouth of Mingo creek, to General Matthew's encampment, and delivered himself up to Colonel Campbell, and asked an examination of his conduct. Pollock being sent for to confront him, "came so drunk as to be scarcely able to walk, bringing with him his son, (a child not more than eleven years of age,) to prove his charges against the captain. Upon examination, Colonel Campbell was convinced that Pollock was ignorant of any facts to support his charges, and that his motives were from spite, he therefore ordered Pollock out of the camp for a drunken vagabond."

Captain P., however, was not released, but Colonel Campbell politely told him "he would be compelled to hold him in custody, as something might turn up yet to implicate him in the insurrection." They then sent a guard to search his house for papers, particularly the muster roll, to see if any of the men upon it were known to be active in the insurrection; but the whole company "were found to be men of peaceful habits, and were at their daily labor." But still the captain was not released, as they said they had two men, named Hampton and Southard, who would give evidence against him at Pittsburgh; but this was a subterfuge, as these men never appeared against him, either at Pittsburgh or Philadelphia.

On the night of the 13th November, 1794, James Stewart, Joseph Chambers, Jacob Forwood, Joel Ferree, George Swasick, Sr., George Swasick, Jr., James Swasick, George Sickman and James M'Bride were brought into camp, handcuffed, and delivered over to the provost guard. On the 14th, Colonel Lane's regiment, with the prisoners, marched down the river to Benjamin Bentley's, the balance of the army with the baggage marching by Esq. Barclay's, "the army constantly swearing and heaping imprecations against the rebels that occasioned them coming so far over hills and mountains, without the satisfaction of a man to oppose them, or a gun fired upon them." At Bentley's "the prisoners were confined in a log cabin over night, without fire, though it was a cold, snowy, stormy night, and neither chunking nor daubing in the cabin."

On the 15th they were ordered down to the Governor's (Lee's) body-guard, and by them delivered over to Captain George Denial, and were marched the same day through the snow storm toward Pittsburgh, where they arrived on the 16th. On the 17th they were conducted to the garrison (Fort Fayette) and delivered to the care of Colonel Butler.

On the 25th the prisoners were called out of the garrison, and surrounded by forty of the garrison soldiers, under the command of Ensign M'Cleary, and paraded before a detachment of Major James Durham's troop of cavalry, to whose charge they were to be delivered at Greensburg. The following is a list of the prisoners:

Rev. John Corbly, Washington county.
Colonel John Hamilton, "
Colonel Wm. Crawford, "
John Black, "
David Bolton, "
James Kerr, "
Thomas Sedgwick, "
John Burnett, "
Captain Robert Porter, "
Joseph Scott, Allegheny county.
Marmaduke Curtiss, "
James Stewart, "
Thomas Miller, "
Thomas Burney, "
Isaac Walker, "
John Laughery, Ohio county, Va.
Caleb Mounts, Fayette county.

At Greensburg "they found Samuel Nye, (who had been placed there for some rash expression against officers and government, made when in a drunken frolic,) Philip Wylie and Joseph Parey, which augmented their number to twenty."

On the 25th, about 10 o'clock, "being formed rank and file, and placed in the centre of the aforesaid forty soldiers, commanded by M'Cleary, they started for Greensburg." On the 27th they arrived at Greensburg and were lodged in jail. On the 29th they were drawn out and paraded in the street, and compelled to stand mid-leg deep in mud and snow, and were formally delivered over to the charge of Major Durham. They then proceeded on their weary march to Philadelphia.

The order of marching was "each prisoner marching on foot between two of the troop or guard, who were on horseback, and who were ordered by Blackbeard (Gen. Anth. M. White) to keep their swords always drawn, and that if any attempt should be made to rescue, that the heads of the prisoners should be cut off and brought to Philadelphia." At night they "were placed in cellars, barns and such other places as suited the disposition or fancy of our guard."

Such was the order of their weary and dismal march to Philadelphia, for thirty days, through snow and mud, in the most inclement time of the year.

"On the 25th December (I quote from the MS.) paraded at half past eleven before the Blackhorse tavern. The prisoners drawn up rank and file, were presented with slips of white paper by the Major as cockades, to be put in our hats to distinguish us as insurgents from the rest of the crowd that we were to march through, or as trophies of victory. This was done by the express command of General White, alias Blackbeard, though the Major remonstrated with White, but to no purpose. My fleur-de-luce I kept in my hand until in view of the spectators on the other side, when I took the opportunity of tearing it to pieces, and threw it on the bridge. We were marched through 20,000 spectators by a circuitous route through the city to the new jail, where we were placed in cells and kept all night without food or light, which depressed our spirits to the lowest degree.

"Upon our arrival here we found Mr. Herman Husbands, Bedford Co.
Robert Philson, "
George Lucas, "
George Wisegarver, "
William Bonham, Northumberland Co.
John Criswell, Cumberland Co.
confined here as insurgents.

"On the 13th January, James Kerr admitted to bail. On 3d February, petitioned court to be tried in the counties where the offense was alleged to have been committed, as we would be better able to obtain testimony to refute the charges. The court refused.

"20th, Colonel Hamilton admitted to bail; 23d, Wisegarver was admitted to bail; 28th, Thomas Sedgwick, Samuel Nye and George Lucas admitted to bail.

March 2d.—John Criswell, by direction of Judge Titus, removed to Chester jail, as there was difficulty of bailing him, being committed by Judge Yeates.

March 4*th*.—Rev. Corbly admitted to bail.

March 23*d*.—David Bolton admitted to bail.

May 7*th*.—"My bill (quote from the MS.) having been before the grand jury since Monday, and having by solemn vote yesterday passed, to be returned ignoramus, was this day returned a true bill, on Mr. Baldwin testifying that he knew no other than that every officer commanded their own men at the destruction of General Neville's, the 17th July, 1794, as the committee (he being a member,) resolved that every officer should command his own men, and I being a captain in the district he lived, and being at Couch's Fort, he knew of nothing to the contrary. Upon this small testimony they found a bill, after having previously examined thirty-five witnesses to no purpose."

9*th*.—Messrs. Black, Scott and Pasey acquitted by the grand jury.

11*th*.—"Thomas Burney acquitted by the grand jury. When the evidence was called and sworn against him, they all swore they knew nothing about him in the matter, which made Rawle cry out, 'Good God, can I get nobody to swear against this man.'"

Thursday, 12*th*. — Messrs. Bonham, Black, Mounts, Husbands, Pasey, Walker, Burney and Scott, discharged and taken out of jail.

On the 18th May, Captain Porter was tried. Wm. Rawle and Wm. Bradford were the attorneys for the United States, and Wm. Lewis and Joseph Thomas for Captain Porter.

After hearing the witnesses on the part of the United States, the captain's attorneys thought it unnecessary to examine a single witness for the defense, so entirely groundless was the prosecution.

By mutual consent of the attorneys, Mr. Rawle addressed the court.

"May it please your Honors, I have examined twelve of the most substantial witnesses against the prisoner at the bar, the rest are only circumstantial. The attorneys on behalf of the prisoner and us have agreed to leave it to your Honors to give charge to the jury." On which Judge Patterson rose and said,

"Gentlemen of the Jury, you have heard the charge read against the prisoner, Robert Porter; you find it has not been supported by one single evidence. The Court is of the opinion that he is not guilty. You will, therefore, show mercy on the favorable side; and if you think he is not guilty, you will bring in your verdict of the prisoner, not guilty." To which charge the jury made a bow, and in one or two minutes, without leaving their box, agreed upon their verdict of not guilty. The captive was then discharged, being in all six months and six days a prisoner.

So ended the trial, and for the honor of the judiciary of our country, I trust there may never be a similar one. The case may be summed up in a few words. A drunken fellow makes charge before the military officers against him. The captain voluntarily appears and demands an investigation promptly, that he may refute the charges. Instead of an investigation being granted, he is held a close prisoner—torn away from his family—dragged to Philadelphia—bail refused him—kept six months in close confinement, and yet after all, from beginning to end, not one single evidence to convict him of being guilty of one unlawful act. The only circumstance against him was the fact that he was the commander of a company of men. If the matter had not been attended with such serious results, it might have been regarded as a farce. So with most, if not all the other prisoners—most of them admitted to bail, with no intention of ever bringing them to trial, others acquitted by the grand jury, notwithstanding Rawle's anxiety to have a victim.

Some of the charges alleged against the prisoners were of the most ridiculous character, such as would excite a smile of derision at the present day. For instance, such as * " erecting large poles, with or without seditious inscriptions, understood and declared to be intended to indicate their treasonable intentions, thereby adding to the enemies of the United States, giving them aid and comfort." This was the sin of poor Caleb Mounts. But it was a little too ridiculous to risk a trial upon, even at that time. I might extract perhaps much more, but as I have already occupied more space than I intended, I will not trespass upon your patience further.

Yours, truly,
J. M. PORTER.

Note on the above.—This is the place to quote, for the second or third time, the passage in Craig's history, relating to the cruel exile of Colonel Neville. Craig complained, in our controversy, of my repeating certain passages oftener than was agreeable to him; but in my opinion truth cannot be too often contrasted with falsehood.

"In recently looking over some old letters, [from Colonel Neville,] *written while he was in exile*, and while the ashes of

* Taken from a list of charges against the prisoners, furnished by Rawle to them.

his father's mansion, and barn, and negro huts *were yet warm*, I was struck with the following kindhearted expression :

" 'The prisoners arrived yesterday, and were, by the ostentation of General White, paraded through the different parts of the city, (Philadelphia.) They had large pieces of paper in their hats to distinguish them, *and wore the appearance of wretchedness*. I could not help being sorry for them, *although so well acquainted with their conduct.*' "

It was *not true* that Colonel Neville was *yet in exile* when he wrote the above letter. He had been restored to his home in triumph by General Morgan's division of the army, and it was after this that the arrest of the prisoners was made. Neville, at the time of writing the letter, was in Philadelphia as a member of the Assembly, and as a witness against these very prisoners. He never had been exiled, for he was met on his way after leaving Pittsburgh the first time, by a summons to attend a *special session* of the Legislature. Now, as to his knowledge of the conduct of the unfortunate prisoners, why did he not testify when called upon ? Because he knew nothing about it ! Such is history, and especially Craig's history of Pittsburgh. Let the reader peruse the statements of Captain Porter, and then say whether the sympathy of the public was due to them, or to Colonel Neville.

I do not expect to silence Neville Craig, but I think I have furnished ample materials to enable the country to judge between us, and to its judgment I leave the case, I trust forever.

Letter of Major Craig to David Bradford.

"MR. SCULL—Your inserting the following letter and the answer thereto, will oblige your humble servant.

ISAAC CRAIG.

Pittsburgh, 9th October, 1794."

MAJOR CRAIG'S LETTER.

"PITTSBURGH, October 1st, 1497.

"SIR—When the commissioners of the United States were at this place, they were told by H. H. Brackenridge, Esq., in my presence, that had it not been for his interposition, I would have been proscribed at the time the people were at Braddock's Field. It is said the circumstance which induced this, was facts stated by you; viz., that I had said I would suffer my own house to be made an excise office of, &c. This, if true, was what any citizen was justifiable in doing, but not so with respect to me. I consider the lie to have been designed for my destruction, and now call on you for your authority. I could not have addressed you on this subject, had I not supposed that you were deceived in your information, and could point out the *scoundrel* [the habitual phrase of the Neville's] with whom it originated, and from whom I might seek redress for the injuries intended and *suffered*.

I am, Sir, your obedient servant,
ISAAC CRAIG.
David Bradford, Esq."

Note on the above.—The real object of the letter of Craig is too plain to deceive any one. It was to open a correspondence with Bradford to give him an opportunity of implicating Mr. Brackenridge, and enable the Neville connection to interest themselves in his favor. The pretext is truly frivolous; but there is no conceivable cause which would have justified Craig in addressing such a man at such a time. It seemed he *suffered;* what did he suffer? At the instance of Mr. Brackenridge, the motion of banishment by Bradford was superseded by one to *petition the President for his removal!* and his case passed over in the committee of officers at Braddock's Field.

The following is Bradford's reply:

"WASHINGTON, October 5th, 1859.

"SIR—I received yours of the first of this current month, in which you have said, that Mr. Brackenridge asserted in the presence of the commissioners of the United States, that had it not been for his interposition on your behalf at Braddock's Field, that you would have been banished.

"I must inform you that Mr. Brackenridge has either a very treacherous memory or a strong disposition to assert falsehoods, if he asserted as you state. The truth of the case was, that he evidences to me the strongest desire to have you banished. I shall state to you his expressions, or at least some of them. You may then judge for yourself.

"The first day at Braddock's Field, Mr. Brackenridge told me the people of Pittsburgh were well pleased, that the country were about to banish the persons whose names had been mentioned; he added that they ought to go further; that little Craig ought to be banished, for he was one of the same d——d junts. I replied there appeared to be no ground to proceed against you, that there was no letter of yours intercepted, mistaking facts or the conduct of individuals to the government. Further conversation took place, which had manifestly for its object to irritate me against you.

"The next day when the commissioners [committee of officers] sat, Mr. Brackenringe took me aside, and mentioned to me your conduct of burning Neville's house; that you assumed high airs in contempt of everything that had been done by the people, that you had declared in the most positive manner, that you would keep up the letters designating the office of inspector at every risk; and though the people of Pittsburgh requested you to take them down

23

you would not. In short, that you were determined to keep the office in contempt of the then ruling opinion.

"He told further that he put in operation a stratagem to see whether you had firmness enough to support all the vaunts and blasts you had made. He said he went out in the street and asked the first person he met if he had heard there were five hundred of the Washington county people coming down armed to burn Pittsburgh, because the inspection office was kept open; the answer was, no. He asked the next he met the same question, the same answer was received; by this means the news was spread over the town in a few minutes, that five hundred men were approaching the place to burn it, &c. The letters were immediately torn down; in short, he told me you were one of the warmest sticklers for the revenue law, and that you had been as odious to the citizens of Pittsburgh, and the neighborhood, as the excise officer himself had been.

"I then mentioned to Mr. Brackenridge that he had better state to the commissioners [committee of officers,] the circumstances he had just related to me; he said it was disagreeable to him, as he lived in the same place; I replied that I could open the way, and immediately stated to the committee a report which I had heard respecting your conduct after the burning of Neville's house, and stated precisely what Mr. Brackenridge had stated one minute before, not mentioning from whom I had the report. I observed, as it was only a report, it would be improper to take it up as true, till it could be discovered whether true or false. I then called upon the gentlemen from Pittsburgh to give information, if they knew anything of the subject. Mr. Wilkins observed that he did not not know anything against you. Mr. M'Masters to the like effect, and Mr. Brackenridge also concurred. He declined to give the narrative which he had done to me just before, although I opened the way, on what principle I know not.

"I shall here mention another circumstance, *though it does not concern you*, it may, perhaps, obviate false insinuations which he may be disposed to make. On the morning of the second day's meeting of the committee at Parkinson's Ferry, Mr. Brackenridge told me there was a young man in Brison's office, attending the committee for the purpose of presenting a petition for the return of Brison. He wished me to oppose it, suggesting reasons that he had always been a pest to them at Pittsburgh; that he was a great friend to the excise, alluding to a certain period when a number of suits were brought, or indictments preferred to the grand jury; that Brison was known to be at the bottom of that business; that he was a d——d scoundrel, and conceited coxcomb—that nothing could ever turn out about Pittsburgh but he must be writing to the Governor—a puppy, added he, what had he to do with the Governor? It was his place to have sat in his office, and issue writs when called upon. I observed to him if he had any reasons to offer to the committee why Brison should not be suffered to return, he had better offer them himself; no petition was presented. These are facts which I have related; and I leave you at full liberty to make any use of them you may think proper. I would have answered your letter before, but I have been much indisposed.

I am, Sir, your humble servant,
                    DAVID BRADFORD.
Major Isaac Craig."

The strongest argument in favor of the truth of Bradford's letter is, that its contents are too frivolous to be worth the trouble of inventing them. But they are untrue—that is, they contain about one grain of truth to a pound of falsehood. Mr. Brackenridge had no such private conversation with him, as he alleges, nor any private conversation at all with him. It is at variance with what Bradford himself admits was said in public. But let us see what was the testimony of others, whose testimony cannot be questioned.

Extract from Justice Meetkirk's Affidavit.
—"Mr. Bradford then spoke concerning the expulsion of Major Craig, for he said that Major Craig should have said immediately after the burning of General Neville's house, that he would let the d—d rascals see that the excise law should be enforced, for that he would open an office of inspection in his own house. Mr. Bradford was then requested to give his authority; he replied that he could not recollect, but that he heard it mentioned among the people. It was then referred to the gentlemen in the committee, who represented the people of Pittsburgh, Wilkins, M'Masters and Brackenridge; and it appeared that neither of them could give any information on the subject."

Statement of James Ross.—"One of the committee then denounced Major Craig for having said he would keep an inspection office in his own house, rather than the excise law should be defeated. A good deal was said on this subject; his expulsion was prevented by a proposal of yours,* that a petition should be sent to General Knox for his removal, it being very questionable whether Major Butler would not protect him in the fort, as belonging to the army; and at all events the public business would suffer for the want of a public officer to take care of the military stores. This was agreed to."

* Brackenridge.

From the Statements of General Wilkins.
—"David Bradford moved in addition to these two, that Major Craig should be expelled, saying it was reported that he had offered his house for an office of inspection, should another not be found. Bradford called on the Pittsburgh members to know if this was true. You [H. H. Brackenridge] answered, *it was not true;* and stated some circumstances tending to show the falsehood of the report. But, notwithstanding, Bradford and others pressed for his banishment; in order to obviate, you mentioned it would be an injury to the expedition then carrying on against the Indians, as he had charge of the stores for the use of the troops; and proposed that the commitee should address the Secretary of War to remove him; *which I considered as management on your part to save Major Craig.*"

The above will suffice, although a number of other similar extracts might be made from the documents published in this work.

Findley's History.

By an oversight, the following extract from Findley's history was not inserted in the right place, that is in the account of the meeting at the Mingo meetinghouse, and Mr. Brackenridge's speech there.

"Brackenridge, in a speech of considerable length, drew their attention by amusing them, *and seeming to countenance their conduct;* but before he concluded he ventured to suggest, that though what had been done might be morally right, yet that was legally wrong, and suggested the propriety of their consulting their fellow citizens, in other parts of the survey, and in the meantime, of their sending commissioners to the President. He endeavored to convince them of the *bad policy* of having those who had not been engaged in the attack on the Inspector involved, because in that case they could not act as mediators for those who were obnoxious. The meeting *was divided in opinion about the sentiments he expressed; some thought he was warm in the cause, but the more violent were offended;* it was pleasing, however, to those who like himself were not yet involved. He had been sent for by some of the leaders, but declined coming until he was advised by Col. Neville, who assisted in procuring others to accompany, to be witnesses of his conduct. He retired before the meeting resolved on any measures."

It is difficult to conceive a more gross perversion of the truth, than this paragraph of Findley's. He was not present, gives no proof, but evidently derives his knowledge from Mr. Brackenridge's account in the "Incidents," which he thus falsifies, as the reader may see by turning to the chapter of this history containing that account. Fortunately, he will also find there the statements of the persons who accompanied Mr. Brackenridge, and which give Findley's the lie. The perversion of fact, and mean detraction of Mr. Brackenridge, on the part of Findley, has been shown in various parts of this work. Although not in general regardless of truth, yet when his personal enmity is concerned, he had not the magnanimity of the noble mind to do justice to his enemy. He was not a Sallust, either in his style or in his ethics.

Where is his authority for saying, "and seeming to *countenance their conduct?*" There is nothing of the kind in the statement of Mr. Brackenridge, or of his witnesses. In answer to Parkinson, who put the distinct question—"I wish to know whether we are right or wrong, in what we have done." Mr. Brackenridge replied, it *may be morally* right, but it is legally wrong—it is TREASON—any other language would have been a direct insult to Parkinson. But this was not the theme of his speech; it was his opposition to the motion of Bradford to "sustain the brave fellows who were engaged in burning Neville's house." This was defeated by him, and caused the meeting to break up without doing anything but adopt his suggestion of calling a larger meeting, before anything was done, or resolved. Thus the ball of insurrection was stopped before it was set in motion.

The most curious part of this willful perversion of the truth, is the following confused sentence: "Some thought he was *warm* in the cause, but the more violent were offended; it was pleasing, however, to those who like himself were not involved." The violent of course were offended, and those not involved were pleased; but what was that third portion who considered him *warm* in the cause, which he pronounced *treason?* Findley endeavors to convey the idea, that Mr. Brackenridge's speech was equivocal; instead of this, the blunderer has only succeeded in writing nonsense!

Findley's account, however, admits the following: 1. The speech had the effect of preventing a vote to support those who had burnt Neville's house. 2. The calling a larger meeting commensurate with the four counties, before any action should be taken. 3. The separation of those involved in the treasonable acts, from those not involved. 4. The application for an amnesty for the past.

INDEX

ADAMS, George 89 John 27 146
ADDISON, A 183 Alexander 68 93 178 277 Judge 92 117 127 129 142 172 177 178 251 252 255 Mr 172
AMBERSON, William 317
AMHERST, 137
AUDRAIN, Mr 62 Peter 58 68 89 119 135
BAIRD, James 119 Mr 87 Thomas 256
BAKER, Hilary 56
BALDWIN, 92 John 79 Mr 331
BARCLAY, Esq 329
BARNEY, 32
BEAUMONT, H 137 William 73 167 William H 58 143 317
BEDFORD, Dr 56
BEER, 27
BENTLEY, Benjamin 329
BIDDLE, Nicholas 32
BLACK, 306 John 51-54 56 330 Mr 331
BLACKBEARD, General 330
BLAKENEY, Col 91 97 110 113 Mr 87
BOLTON, David 330 331
BONHAM, Mr 331 William 330
BOQUET, Col 16
BRACKENRIDGE, 33 79 80 95 119 189 228 246 301 303 H H 76 87 89 90 93 95 96 107 119 147 169 212 258 333 335 H M 328 Hugh H 123 145 174 Hugh Henry 68 180 John 44 Mr 20 25 26 29 43-47 50 52 53 55-58 60-62 64-76 83 91 92 95-97 99 108-110 112-116 120 121 124-126 128 129 131-137 139 141-144 146 152-162 164-172 176 178-182 186-188 191-196

BRACKENRIDGE (continued) 204-209 214 218-222 224 226 229 240 243 250 252 254 255 257 258 259 260 265 267-269 271 289-294 300 302 304-310 316-319 326 334-336
BRADDOCK, 31 100 60 61 65 66 69 79-82 84 85 87 92 100 101 103 105 107 108 111 112 133 134 152 153 155 156 158 160 161 163 164 170 171 173 186-189 191 194 205 208 218 221 228 230 240 243 250 253-255 257 259 260 262 281 297 302 306
BRADFORD, Attorney General 264 Col 113 D 83 David 36 59 72 84 93 94 101 122 169 212 332-335 General 114 Mr 69 120 123 124 162 177 190 192 204 214 220 William 80 212 303 Wm 201 203-205 235 238 331
BRADLY, Nathaniel 36
BRADY, 47
BRISON, 88 90 91 108 112 115 132 334 James 87 93 96 175 Mr 97 122 124
BROADHEAD, 32
BRON, George 122 Mr 121
BURNETT, John 330
BURNEY, Mr 331 Thomas 330 331
BURR, Aaron 40 326
BUTLER, 47 Col 175 329 Major 86 87 97 102 107 109 113 118 335 Thomas 175
CALHOUN, 47
CAMPBELL, Col 329
CANNON, John 255
CANON, J 83 95 John 82
CARNAHAN, D 38 Dr 219 253

CARNAHAN (continued)
  Rev Dr 323
CARROLL, 34
CHAMBERS, General 267 288
  Joseph 329
CHASE, Samuel 76
CLARK, Mr 47
CLOW, James 89 141
COCHRAN, William 28
COOK, Col 22 58 85 113 115 116
  186 219 Edward 36 37 59 60
  107 156 169 202 203 212 215-
  217 231 243 Mr 155 196 204
  214
COOPER, Martin 317
CORBLY, John 330 Rev 331
COUTHON, 299
COX, Brinton 146 Mr 142 294
  Tench 137 143-146 182 268
CRAIG, 34 75 107 110 119 173
  269 310 Isaac 31 32 332-334
  Major 32 36 54 55 62 65 75 86
  108 109 113 115 118-122 125
  131 175 179 192 256 259 290
  306 307 332 335 Mr 34 133 309
  N B 31 32 62 119 172 179 304
  Neville 332 Neville B 27 33
  114 118 256
CRAWFORD, 47 Col 228 Wm 330
CRISWELL, John 330 331
CROMWELL, 39 Oliver 219 220
CURTISS, Marmaduke 330
DALLAS, 190
DANDRIDGE, B 285
DAY, 88 90 115 Edward 87 93 96
  97 108 132 175 Mr 97 122 124
DENIAL, George 329
DETENNERE, Clement 293
DEVERGENNES, Count 146
DICKEY, Mr 235 236 Robert 231
  238
DOUGLASS, Ephraim 282 Mr 285
  286
DUNLAP, Capt 316 321
DUNLOP, Capt 280
DURHAM, Major 330
EARL, William 89
EDGAR, 220 James 166 169 212
  222 228 282 Mr 153 204 214
  229 240 243
ERNEST, Matthew 87 89 96 119
  121

EVANS, David 89
EVE, (free colored woman) 179
FAULKNER, Capt 28
FERREE, Jacob 142 Joel 329
FILSON, 290
FINDLEY, 20 22 24 26-28 33 50
  77 80 81 85 94 95 127 134 153
  157 159 161 168 187 188 207
  220 232 246 248 252 257 259
  268 293 295 296 300 306 309
  319 336 Mr 281 282 285 286
  William 95 167 240 254 282
FORWOOD, Jacob 329
FRENEAU, Philip 76
FRIGGLEY, Jacob 72 73
FULTON, 95 281 A 83
GALBRAITH, Robert 132
GALLATIN, 77 80 95 107 Albert
  22 156 169 186 212 219 231
  282 Mr 23 24 153-155 157
  159-162 164 165 167-169 171
  181 182 187-189 196 204 205
  207-209 214 218 220-224 226
  228 229 240 243 250 257-259
  289 293 295 Secretary 158
GERRY, Mr 263
GIBSON, 110 111 115 132 173
  General 56 87 91 96 97 108 120
  122 124 125 135 136 141 142
  175 George 91 John 175 Judge
  91 Major General 44
GORMLY, William 89
GRAHAM, 19 35
GREGG, Isaac 69
HAMILTON, 47 92 95 100 106 140
  149 190 264 271 294 306 309
  310 319 Alexander 18 51 285
  326 Col 297 299 331 Daniel
  106 David 49 51-57 67 79 80
  92 93 General 275 290 311
  John 85 106 297 330 Mr 306
  308 Secratary 67 Secretary 23
  25 27 37 38 67 178 276 294 303
  305 Sheriff 251 294 295 297
HAMPDEN, 39 157
HAMPTON, 329
HANCOCK, 34
HANNAH, John 317
HARMAR, 225
HENRY VIII, king of England 94
HOGE, John 117 176 177 Mr 172
  Senator 172

HOLCROFT, 41 53
HOOD, Zachariah 29
HOPKINS, Commodore 32
HOWELL, Governor 267 288 320
HUNTER, 19 James 317
HUSBANDS, Herman 162 188 290 330 Mr 331
INDIAN, Captain Alliance 211 Captain Blanket 210 Captain Pacificus 211 Captain Whiskey 210 211 Corn Planter 64 74 307
IRISH, Nathaniel 89
IRVINE, 190 Col 119 General 191 267 288 313 314 317 321 Mr 199 William 212 214-216 238
IRWIN, John 89
JACK, General 312
JACKSON, Samuel 219
JAY, 95 Mr 150
JEFFERSON, 77 180
JENNINGS, O 323
JOHNSTON, Robert 28 53
JOLLY, Capt 260
JONES, Paul 32
KERR, 27 James 330
KIDDO, James 28
KIRKPATRICK, 60 61 88 90 102 106 112 115 116 119 131 132 136 160 192 269 Abraham 32 34 93 96 144 173 175 John 169 212 Major 36 48-50 55 66 97 122 179 Mr 204 214
KNOX, General 97 109 118 175 307 335
LAFAYETTE, 31
LANE, Col 329
LANG, James 212 221 Mr 54 204 214
LANGE, James 169
LAROCHEFAUCAULT, 293
LAUGHERY, John 330
LEE, General 267 283 287 289 294 300 312 313 Governor 276 283 286 308 329 Henry 286 287 314
LENNOX, David 184 Major 298
LENOX, Major 40 144 Marshall 45 55 70
LEWIS, Wm 331
LOCKNY, L 83
LONG, Capt 108

LUCAS, 290 George 330 331 John 212 John B 183 John B C 169 Judge 143 172 178 180 Mr 204 214
LYNN, John 28 38
M'ALISTER, James 47
M'BRIDE, James 329
M'CLEARY, 330 Ensign 329
M'CLELLAND, John 231 233 236 238 Mr 235
M'CONNEL, Alexander 142
M'CORD, Samuel 317
M'DONALD, John 70 140 Mordecai 317
M'FARLAND, 49
M'FARLANE, 47 53 88 99 116 186 Andrew 101 277 James 48 49 102 John 56 Maj 115
M'INTYRE, Andrew 89
M'KEAN, 77 Chief Justice 190 264 Mr 199 Thomas 212 214-216 238
M'KINLEY, William 169 212
M'MASTERS, 335 John 89 107 Mr 120 334
M'MILLAN, 176 John 75 252
M'NICKLE, Alexander 89 317
MADISON, 77 Mr 76
MANSFIELD, Lord 43
MARCHAND, David 281
MARSHALL, 22 60 61 69 79 80 84 87 92 116 134 152 153 155-157 159 169 170 188 205 253 254 257 262 281 306 Chief Justice 40 326 Col 72 94 187 J 83 James 36 59 85 104 115 155 169 John 212 231 238 Mr 204 214 235 236
MARTIN, Luther 76 Mr 204
MATTHEW, General 329
MEASON, Isaac 322
MEETKIRK, Justice 335 Mr 87 William 56 97 120 141
MIFFLIN, 190 Governor 21 27 97 265 Thomas 215
MILLER, 35 40-42 68 Thos 330
MITCHEL, John 80 93
MITCHELL, John 323
MOOR, Dr 318
MOORE, Dr 59
MORGAN, General 31 34 87 97 267 291 294 323 332

MORGAN (continued)
  Major General 235
MORRISON, Norris 127 316 317
MORTON, Mr 214 285 286
  Thomas 36 212 282 Thos 169
MOUNTS, Caleb 330 332 Mr 331
MURRAY, Capt 110 111
NESBIT, John 231 238 Mr 235 236
NEVILL, John 29
NEVILLE, 41 44 46 48 52 54 62
  66 68 70 74 75 79 82 88 93 95
  106 110 111 115 119 127 129
  132 136 138 142 159 173 192
  209 251 256-259 265 269 272
  294 295 297 298 306 311 317
  333 334 Col 23 33 36 37 44 45
  51 55-58 60 67-69 72 75 86 87
  91 97 120-122 124 125 131 133
  135 137 141 175 176 192 291
  292 307 310 332 336 General
  21 31 33 35 36 40 42 50 56
  68-70 72 94 95 119 125 140
  141 144 174 179 180 197 289
  292 293 299 300 302 309 331
  335 Inspector 23 55 261 John
  31 34 183 313 P 69 Presley
  31-33 36 43 44 51 68 70 72 75
  97 124 the younger 107
NOY, Samuel 321
NYE, Samuel 330 331
O'HARA, Col 116
OLDHAM, 34
OLIPHANT, John 36
ORMSBY, 45
PAREY, Joseph 330
PARKER, Henry 317
PARKINSON, 62 63 65 72 76 113
  281 336 B 83 Benjamin 48 60
  61 72 80 94 99 102 112 138 321
PASEY, Mr 331
PATTERSON, Judge 331
PENN, 16 18
PETERS, Judge 289 294 298 300
  305 308-310 322
PHILLIPS, David 36 47 231 238
  Mr 235 236
PHILSON, Robert 330
PLUMER, William 36
POLLOCK, 329
PORTER, Capt 322 328 331 332 J
  H 322 J M 328 332 Mr 322 Rev
  Mr 252 Robert 328 330 331

POWERS, John 169 212 Major
  295 296 299 Mr 204 214
PROBST, John 231 238 Mr 235
  236
PURVIANCE, H 178 Henry 84 90
  122 123 126 133 209 Mr 75 87
  91 98 172 259 309
PYM, 39
RANDOLPH, E 190 Edm 185 186
  Edmond 137 Edmund 151 201
  Peyton 31 Secretary of State
  264
RAWL, William 284
RAWLE, 332 Wm 331
REDDICK, 268 David 84 254 282
  Mr 98 269 281 282 285 286
REGAN, Philip 29 314
RIDDLE, Capt 115
RITCHIE, Craig 58-60
ROBINSON, George 58 68 70 89
  120 317 James 119 257 William 257 William Jr 119
ROSS, 309 Commissioner 168
  James 69 76 84 98 103 106 109
  112 117 118 125 134 161 167
  173 176 201 203-205 235 238
  253 291 303 335 Jasper 212 Mr
  169 172 188-190 194 300 302
ROWAN, John 75 176
SAINT CLAIR, 105 225
SAINT JUST, 299
SAMPLE, William 71
SCOTT, General 297 Joseph 330
  Mr 172 331 Thomas 84
SCULL, John 89 142 Mr 206 332
SEDGWICK, Thomas 330 331
SEMPLE, William 58 73
SICKMAN, George 329
SMILEY, 20 22 77 153 220
SMITH, Charles 303 General 267
  George 212 Judge 179 Mr 204
  214
SNETH, John 169
SOUTHARD, 329
SOUTHERLAND, William 169
SPARK, 31
SPEARS, T 83
SPEER, Mr 82
SPRING, Samuel 76
STEVENSON, John 212 Robert
  169
STEWART, James 329 330

STOCKDALE, Mr 321
STOKELY, Col 85 Nehemiah 36 Thomas 84
STURGEON, Alexander 317 Jeremiah 317
SULLIVAN, Gen 32
SUTHERLAND, William 212
SWASICK, George Jr 329 George Sr 329 James 329
TANNEHILL, Adamson 68 95 119 Josiah 58 68 69 72 89
TAYLOR, George 186
THOMAS, Joseph 331
TITUS, Judge 331
VAUGHAN, Mr 294 295
WADSINS, Mr 117
WALKER, Isaac 330 Mr 331
WALLACE, Geo 100 George 87 89 93 96 119 135 231 238 Judge 97 Mr 235 236
WASHINGTON, 15 64 92 208 209 225 226 231 232 242 246 268 270 275 279 280 283 287 Geo 186 George 31 185
WATSON, Andrew 89 316 317
WAYNE, 211 225 326 General 116 210
WEBSTER, 129 272 John 314
WEISGARVER, 290
WELLS, 28 29 272 Benjamin 314 Judge 322

WHITE, Anth M 330 Brigadier General 324 General 319-321 330 332
WILKINS, General 44 87 89 92 97 99 101 104 107 115 118 119 122 134 142 162 178 249 252 254 292 335 John 89 92 123 132 141 John Jr 93 96 John Sr 135 Justice 135 Mr 120 172 334 William 89
WILKINSON, Judge 27 31 34 35 310 311
WILLIAM HENRY, Prince 211
WILLIAMSON, David 84
WILSON, 28 James 184 221 264 Judge 148 190 201 264 Mr 235 236 Samuel 231 238
WISEGARVER, 331 George 330
WOODS, General 176 John 36 302
WRIGHT, Zedick 102
WYLIE, Philip 330
YATES, Judge 179
YEATES, 309 Commissioner 303 J 201 203-205 238 Jasper 235 Joseph 212 Judge 192 331 Mr 190
YOUNG, John 36

www.ingramcontent.com/pod-product-compliance
Lightning Source LLC
Chambersburg PA
CBHW070934230426
43666CB00011B/2439